THE
REVOLT
OF
THE
MIND

THE
REVOLT
OF
THE
MIND

A Case History
of Intellectual Resistance
Behind the Iron Curtain

by Tamas Aczel and Tibor Meray

GREENWOOD PRESS, PUBLISHERS
WESTPORT, CONNECTICUT

Library of Congress Cataloging in Publication Data

Aczél, Tamás.
    The revolt of the mind.

    Reprint of the ed. published by Praeger, New York,
which was issued as no. 73 of Praeger publications in
Russian history and world communism.
    1. Hungary--Intellectual life. 2. Hungary--
Politics and government--1945-   I. Méray, Tibor,
1924-   joint author. II. Title.
DB956.A59 1974   322.4'4   74-20275
ISBN 0-8371-7851-7

*In the interest of historical accuracy, those
footnotes appearing in this book which describe
the individual experiences or observations of
one or the other of the co-authors are so initialed.*

**This book is Number 73 in the series
of *Praeger Publications in Russian History and World Communism***

Originally published in 1959 by Frederick A. Praeger,
Publishers, New York

Reprinted with the permission of Praeger Publishers, Inc.

Reprinted in 1974 by Greenwood Press,
a division of Williamhouse-Regency Inc.

Library of Congress Catalog Card Number 74-20275

ISBN 0-8371-7851-7

Printed in the United States of America

To The Memory of

IMRE NAGY
MIKLOS GIMES
GEZA LOSONCZY
PAL MALETER
JOZSEF SZILAGYI

Literature must become Party literature.... Down with non-partisan litterateurs! Down with superman literature! Literature must become a part of the general cause of the proletariat, "a small cog and a small screw" in the social democratic mechanism, one and indivisible—a mechanism set in motion by the entire conscious vanguard of the whole working class. Literature must become an integral part of the organized, methodical, and unified labors of the Social Democratic Party.

—Lenin
Novaia Jizn,
November, 1905

Foreword

Stalin died on March 5, 1953. The exact time of his death was 9:50 p.m. According to the official medical reports, the direct cause of death was cerebral hemorrhage.

In Moscow, the Central Committee of the Communist Party of the Soviet Union, the Council of Ministers, and the Presidium of the Supreme Council addressed a letter to every member of the Party and to every Soviet working man and woman: "The heart of Joseph Vissarionovich Stalin, Lenin's brother-in-arms, brilliant upholder of his cause, and wise leader and teacher of the Communist Party and of the Soviet people, has beat for the last time. . . . The immortal name of Stalin will live forever in the hearts of the Soviet people and of all progressive humanity. . . ."

A committee was formed to organize a funeral worthy of Stalin. The chairman of this committee was none other than Nikita Sergeyevich Khrushchev.

At the same time, in order to ensure the undisturbed continuity of Soviet life, the state and Party leaders took several steps. Georgi Maksimilianovich Malenkov was appointed Chairman of the Soviet Council of Ministers. Lavrenti Pavlovich Beria, Vyacheslav Mikhailovich Molotov, Nikolai Aleksandrovich Bulganin, and Lazar Moisseyevich Kaganovich became his First Deputies. Among other things, these men declared it imperative that Nikita Sergeyevich Khrushchev should work exclusively in the Central Committee of the Communist Party of the Soviet Union.

An editorial in *Pravda,* entitled "Powerful Concord and Unity," stated: "It is our task to protect the unity of the Party in the same manner that we protect our own eyesight. . . . Comrade Stalin's loyal disciples and brothers-in-arms, whom he himself trained, will resolutely guarantee the consistent realization of the domestic and foreign policy worked out by the Party. . . . The lifetime work of Lenin and of Stalin lies in reliable hands. . . ."

A huge mass meeting was assembled in Red Square to mourn Stalin. The meeting was opened by Khrushchev. Following him, as the first speaker, came Malenkov. The second speaker was Beria; the third, Molotov.

"The enemies of the Soviet state," said Beria, among other things, "hope and expect that the terrible loss we have suffered will lead to conflict and panic in our ranks. But their hopes are in vain, and they are in for cruel disappointment. Anyone who is not blind can see in these sorrowful days that our Party is closing its ranks and that its unity is unshakable."

The meeting was also attended by delegations from the "fraternal parties" of the satellite countries. Of these, the Hungarian delegation was led by Matyas Rakosi, Chairman of the Hungarian Council of Ministers and Secretary-General of the Hungarian Workers' Party.

In Stalin Square in Budapest, too, at the foot of a giant statue of the dead Premier, the Hungarian people were expressing their sorrow. Here, tens of thousands of Hungarians assembled, and the speaker on that occasion was Erno Gero, Deputy Chairman of the Hungarian Council of Ministers. Said Gero: "You have come to the statue of the great and immortal Stalin in order to pay tribute to the memory of the man who has done more than anyone else to free the peoples of the world and to establish universal peace and human progress. . . ."

In Budapest also, the Hungarian Parliament convened to pay

tribute to the memory of Joseph Vissarionovich Stalin. At this
session, a unanimous resolution was passed to revere the memory
of the great leader. Imre Nagy, Deputy Chairman of the Council of Ministers, submitted the motion to Parliament. Said Nagy:
"My heart is heavy as I mount this speaker's platform in order
to face our deeply mourning people. . . . To express their deep
love for our greatest friend and liberator and teacher, the Hungarian people are rallying around the Party, the Government,
and our beloved Comrade Rakosi, and they are devoting all
their energies toward carrying Stalin's great cause to triumph
in our country."

At a solemn meeting of the Hungarian Writers' Association,
the chairman, Jozsef Darvas, declared: "We Hungarian writers
pledge that we shall be worthy of him who has shown us the
way to all knowledge." On the pages of the official literary
monthly, *Irodalmi Ujsag,* and on those of the Party's official
daily newspaper, *Szabad Nep,* a long list of poets and writers
bade moving farewells to the departed one. Not much later, a
red, leather-bound book was published in Budapest. The volume
contained a collection of these and of earlier writings glorifying
Stalin, including, among many others, poems and prose by Tibor
Dery, Peter Veres, Gyula Illyes, Laszlo Benjamin, Zoltan Zelk,
Gyula Hay, Tibor Tardos, Peter Kuczka, Lajos Konya, Gyorgy
Hamos—and Tamas Aczel and Tibor Meray, the authors of
the present volume.

Six years have passed since that day.

And in those six years Nikita Khrushchev has, with the help
of authentic documents, proved that Joseph Stalin was one of
the greatest criminals in the history of the world.

During those six years, Lavrenti Beria has been shot down
like a dog, and Georgi Malenkov, Vyacheslav Molotov, Nikolai
Bulganin, and Lazar Kaganovich have disappeared through the
Soviet trap door.

In those six years, too, Matyas Rakosi and Erno Gero have
fled from Hungary, and the giant statue of Stalin has been
overthrown by an insurgent people.

In those six years, Imre Nagy became the leader of the first revolt against Stalinism—and now he has become its victim and its martyr.

In those six years, the Hungarian Writers' Association has been dissolved. Today, the majority of those writers who contributed to the leather-bound Stalin anthology are either in prison or living as "exiles" at home or abroad.

This book deals with these Hungarian writers and with the movement they initiated. How did they become contributors to the Stalin anthology? How did they become the vanguard of the Hungarian Revolution? In setting forth this story, one cannot avoid also setting forth the story of the country of Hungary, of the life of its people, of the Soviet colonization of that country, of the methods of the Communist Party, and of the inevitable crisis those methods produced.

The authors of this book were worse than Communists. They were Stalinists. They not only believed in the system, but they also fanatically supported it. And the system treated them generously. Both were awarded the Kossuth Prize; and one of them received the highest honor one can achieve in Soviet literature, the Stalin Prize, while the other, covering the Korean War as a correspondent, received the highest decoration conferred upon civilians by the North Korean Government. Their eyes were not yet opened even in the summer of 1953, when Imre Nagy announced his program to their country. It took another year— and the revelation of the unprecedented crimes committed in the Rajk affair—to make them at last realize the kind of system they were supporting.

The experiences described in this book were the personal experiences of its authors as well as of those about whom they have written. The servitude and shame of the Hungarian writers was the authors' servitude and shame. If there is any comfort for them (and, perhaps, a little pride), it is to be found in the fact that they, too, finally participated in their fellow writers' struggle for liberation.

It must be mentioned here that when, in the following pages, the authors refer to "writers," they almost always mean the young Communist writers. Naturally, they do not mean to infer that only such writers lived and struggled in Hungary. (On the contrary, the majority of significant personalities to be found in Hungarian literature were not Communists.) But it is the purpose of this book to describe the struggles of the Communist writers—of those who participated in the great literary movement preceding the Revolution—and, though these were certainly not the only, nor even the most important, writers of Hungary, their movement was surely the soul and the body of the revolt.

It is quite possible that the reader of this book will think the authors overestimate the importance of the movement they describe—that they see it too subjectively and are prejudiced in its favor. The authors concede in advance that the reader may be right. Their only excuse is that they are both under forty and that this movement was—and will forever remain—the greatest experience of their lives. They loved that battle. They loved its participants, its ups and its downs, its dangers and its risks. They believe that it embodied not only the greatest experience but also the greatest aspiration of their lives.

Valmondois
July 25, 1959

Tamas Aczel
Tibor Meray

CONTENTS

PRELUDE

Cogs and Screws

The supreme strength and the supreme pride of the Communist Party lie in its unity. The classic works of Communist ideology stress the importance of the unity of thought and of action, and this unity is the thing all Party leaders are under oath to respect.* Even the enemies of the Communist Party frequently admire and envy it for this virtue. Yet, in practice, this unity is both a reality and an illusion. It is a reality in that the leading clique of every Communist Party which is functioning reasonably well imposes its will on the thousands or hundreds of thousands of Party members—either by persuasion or by administrative methods, or, at times, by both—and acts always in its members' names and as their representative without calling for loud protests from this membership. At times, the leading clique even succeeds in mobilizing the membership toward the accomplishment of difficult tasks.

But the unity of the Communist Party is an illusion in that, behind the apparent unity of action and the uniformity of speech-making, there lies an endless variety of opinions and desires, and ideas. This is true not only of the membership, but also of the

* Stalin's famous oath following Lenin's funeral: "In leaving us, Comrade Lenin ordered us to conserve the unity of our Party as the apple of our eye. We swear to thee, Comrade Lenin, to honor thy command."

leaders, and it would be a miracle if it were not so. For, after all, even the leaders come from widely different backgrounds, belong to different age groups, pursue different professions, and have absorbed a different sum of knowledge and experience. It is obvious, therefore, that, however saturated the leaders and the members may become with Party ideology, they will react differently to different situations, will hold different ideas about the solutions of various problems and will never judge the victories or the defeats of their cause in quite the same way. If there were no other evidence to prove this fact, it would be sufficient to point out that few political parties in history have in so short a time witnessed so many inner conflicts—nor have they unmasked and liquidated so many "diversional" or "fractional" elements, nor so many "anti-Party groups," as, with a notorious cruelty and in the name of unity, have the Communist parties of the world.

And if this be true in the case of the ordinary members and the disciplined leaders of the Party (and it *is* true), how much more true is it in the case of writers and artists? Every writer, if he is a writer, is a freedom-loving individual. He has a mind and a heart of his own. When he joins the Communist Party, he does something that perhaps no other writer before him, at any time in any organization, has done. He submits of his own free will to a superior will that may often be imposed on his own. He submits to a homogeneous, carefully integrated ideology that will not tolerate individual thought. And, as a matter of fact, he even submits to a systematization of his emotions, for it is the Party that dictates at whom he must smile and at whom he must frown, and it is, in fact, the Party that dictates his loves and his hates.

"Communist writer"! This is his title. It is also the title of his fellow writer sitting next to him at the meetings of the Writers' Association *—a Communist with whom he will raise his hand

---

* The Hungarian Writers' Association, which shall be explained in detail later, was formed in 1945 at the initiative of the Communists and for the purpose of uniting all Hungarian writers. Membership was not

in unison when it comes to voting and with whom he will march in step at the May Day demonstration, bearing before him a large poster portrait of Marx or of Voroshilov.

Yet he is only thirty, and his neighbor is sixty. His education has been German-inspired, while that of his neighbor tends toward the Latin. He loves blank verse, but his neighbor swears by rhymes. He is a Catholic; his neighbor is a Jew. He considers Mayakovsky a great poet, but his neighbor despises Mayakovsky. Clearly, even in this brief example, something has gone a little awry with the unity of Communist thought. Luckily, however, it is in this instance to the disadvantage of our young writer's neighbor and not to his—because Mayakovsky (Stalin himself said so) is a great poet. Yet his neighbor argues that Lenin shared *his* view of the futurist Russian. Again, however, his neighbor can cite no evidence in defense for his own dislike of *The Siberian Rhapsody,* Stalin's favorite film, because, since it was produced twenty-five years after his death, Lenin was in no position to form an opinion about it.

These distinctions may sound like a joke. But they are not a joke. We have set forth this example to show that, regardless of the sublimity of the unity of thought, there is every reason for dividing Communist writers into several groups. At the same time, we must admit that our division is necessarily inexact. It is simultaneously too narrow and too broad. After all, there were not only two individuals attending the meetings of the

---

obligatory, but it was advisable to join. For a young writer, it was a great honor to be admitted. The admission of known writers, passed on by a committee, met with no difficulty. On the other hand, the Association would not admit writers wth a fascist past, and it rejected the application of several significant writers suspected of fascist sympathies, of a rightist attitude in the past, or of being "reactionary." All the Communist writers were, of course, members, and these formed a Party cell of their own within the Association. Until 1956, there was hardly any organizational life in the Association. From 1945 to 1951, the Chairman of the Hungarian Writers' Association was the "Muscovite" Sandor Gergely. From 1951 to 1954, the chairman was Jozsef Darvas, Minister of Public Education, and from 1954 to 1957, it was the peasant writer Peter Veres. The journalists had an association of their own. It was called the National Federation of Hungarian Journalists.

Communist writers. There were three hundred—and at least 180 of these marched in the May Day demonstrations. (Of these, forty or fifty sat on the sidelines watching the others march, and seventy or eighty were ill, or pretending to be ill, or were absent from the capital, or pretending to be absent.)

Three hundred men! There are a thousand little differences which divide that number of men, even though everyone of them may submit to the discipline of a single Party, accept a single political program, and be bound by the regulations of a single organization. This division is true, even if one admits the perfection of that Party's political program and organization.

There are a thousand little differences because they are writers. They are creators. They are individuals. The division must, therefore, remain superficial and, to a certain extent, even disproportionate. Yet it is a necessary division. It would be impossible to paint three hundred portraits of three hundred writers. To paint the portraits of three groups of writers seems easier— on both the author and the reader. The first of these three groups was the "Muscovites":

The Muscovites

The number and literary importance of this first group was far smaller than the place they occupied in Hungarian literary life in the period following 1945. In this period, they numbered no more than six,* but, as soon as they reappeared in their fatherland, they were immediately placed in key positions. One of them became Chairman of the newborn Hungarian Writers' Association. This was not because he was a good writer, for, in fact, he was much below the average. It was, instead, because he was a Muscovite. The second was appointed editor-in-chief of the weekly magazine of the Writers' Association. The third became Secretary-General of the Hungarian-Soviet Society.

The Muscovites created the impression of a united and closely knit group. But it was not true that they actually formed such a group. There were deep ideological differences among them— differences that would come to the surface only years later. And, as far as their personal relations were concerned, the only feeling they had for one another was hatred. Though they repeated

---

* The six were: Sandor Gergely, Bela Illes, Andor Gabor, Emil Madar- asz, Gyula Hay, and Gyorgy Lukacs. We must exclude two of these men from any generalization. These two were: Gyorgy Lukacs, the foremost Marxist philosopher-aesthete of our days, who was Minister of Culture during the Hungarian Revolution; and Gyula Hay, an outstanding play- wright, who was one of the leading figures of the Hungarian writers' movement. We shall deal with them later in this book.

the same slogans in their public life, the chasm between them in
their private lives was unbridgeable. Their hatred dated back to
the days of emigration; each knew something to the detriment
of the other. The fact that one prevented the other's play from
being performed in the Soviet Union was not even worth mentioning. There had been more severe sins in their history: there
had been love affairs, denunciations, temporary expulsions from
the Party, and reports to the GPU: there had also been all the
jealousies, the intrigues, and the treacheries of a bitter exile.

All this, however, was unknown to those at home in 1945.
The eyes of those at home shone with happiness. The comrades
from the Soviet Union had finally arrived, and here, at last,
were the first representatives in Hungary of the new socialist type
of manhood.

Of course, not all Muscovites were writers. Their number was
larger in the army, in the police force, and in the key industrial
posts. And it was the largest—we could even say disproportionately the largest—among Party and national leaders. The four
foremost leaders, who were known as the famous "Foursome,"
were the omnipotent Party Secretary and Prime Minister Matyas Rakosi, his Minister of Commerce, Erno Gero, his Minister
of Defense, Mihaly Farkas, and his Minister of Culture, Jozsef
Revai. All these were Muscovites from first to last, and it may
not be a waste of time to acquaint ourselves with these Muscovites—even though only a few of them were writers.

There have been political refugees in the history of every nation, and many have, after shorter or longer periods abroad,
returned to their native country. In this fact, the Muscovite
emigration had not differed from other emigrations. And yet, this
had been the only similarity, for these Muscovite men had spent
the last ten to thirty years of their lives in the Soviet Union—
and these years had left an indelible imprint on all their thoughts
and actions.

Thus, the chief characteristic of the Muscovite emigrants was
their sense of mission, for they did not simply return to their

native country at the end of the war. Instead, they were sent back with a specific task to fulfill. Naturally, this did not necessarily mean that they had returned to their fatherland as the paid agents or spies of a foreign power—i.e., of the Soviet Union. If, as in many instances, this was the case, the situation was then clear and obvious and simple. But with men who were inspired by a sense of duty on the one hand and by a sort of "calling" on the other, the situation was much more complicated. The important and confidential tasks which were entrusted to the Muscovites in Moscow before their return home had required absolute reliability, and these men were generally reliable. Now, their basic attitude had become unconditional loyalty to the Soviet Union—an unwavering fidelity to the country that had given them shelter for many years. And, to a certain extent, this attitude was understandable and acceptable. On the other hand, however, it was unacceptable that a Muscovite should unhesitatingly subordinate any interest (including, as he would do, national interest) to the interests of the Soviet Union.*

The true aim of the Muscovite mission was this, upon their return to Hungary: they were the outposts and the representatives of a foreign power's interests in their own fatherland. The returning Muscovites were nothing but good so-called "agitator-propagandist" who repeated in their own mother tongue the things that they had learned in a foreign tongue. Though this fact did not remotely mean that they had learned Russian well (it was, indeed, interesting to note that the returning Muscovites, except for the younger ones who were born in Russia, spoke the language very inexpertly and with a strong Hungarian accent), it nevertheless did not prevent them from fulfilling their master's

---

* This attitude had an ideological basis. When arguing with others or even trying to stifle his own doubts, the Muscovite referred to a Leninist dogma according to which the nationalist movement was part of the socialist movement of the whole world. If the part came into conflict with the whole, the whole had necessarily to come first. Thus, if the Hungarian (or Czech, or Rumanian, or Polish, etc.) interests clashed with those of the Soviet Union, the Soviet interests took precedence.

orders of introducing Russian methods into Hungary and, in a certain sense, the Russian language, too.*

In their jobs, these men became the first and most enthusiastic advocates of "Soviet methods." As a matter of fact, they knew no other methods but those learned in the Soviet Union. It was characteristic of their attitude that they tried zealously to implant Soviet methods and forms in an alien soil under fundamentally different conditions—and that thus each one of them (and each in his own field) soon came into conflict with the existing situation after beginning his work. In this conflict, there was no way out. According to the Muscovites, the Soviet methods were always right, and the cause of their inapplicability was always to be found in the social and human backwardness of the native country. The Soviet methods were not only correct ("This," they said, "is how we always did it in the Soviet Union"), but they were also the only expedient—in fact, the only enlightening—ones. Anybody who desired or even suggested alternative methods (after analyzing the conditions and the circumstances) had to do so with malice aforethought, because the comparison was not between method and method, but between Soviet method and non-Soviet method.

Such an attitude came to achieve twofold results. On the one hand, all those who preferred something other than the rules which the Muscovites had learned in the Soviet Union became suspect (their preferences being labeled petty-bourgeois ideas, or bourgeois remnants, or American methods). On the other hand, this dense atmosphere of suspicion and prejudice soon smothered all creative and independent and useful thought, since nobody would risk going to jail just because his opinions differed from Soviet methods. The result: since everybody knew that the Muscovites were, through common struggles and old friendships, in close contact with the supreme leaders of the Party and of the

---

*After the war, due to Muscovite penetration, innumerable ideas, words, and even phrases appeared in the Hungarian language which constituted an exact translation of the Russian original. This "Comintern language," or "functionary Hungarian" later became one of the most passionately hated targets of literary attacks.

Government (both of which were themselves dominated by Muscovites), everybody became increasingly silent.

It was a silence which the Muscovite never realized meant that trouble was brewing. Instead, he always attributed this silence to the successes he had achieved with the Soviet methods, for, in the course of a past spent as a Party or state functionary, he had always been isolated from public opinion and its real nature, and so the silence did not get on his nerves, but, on the contrary, filled him with deep satisfaction.

This satisfaction permeated not only his work, but also his life. The evolution of a lively, intelligent exchange of ideas is hardly imaginable in a mental atmosphere in which suspicion is bred. Those who insisted on independent thinking were designated enemies of the people. Those who disliked the regime were watched vigilantly. The Muscovite needed no such interchange. He was always definite, always sure of himself, always optimistic. He thought in slogans and he had an immediate solution for any problem, saying: "There is nothing new under the sun. We have seen these things *at home* in the Soviet Union. All we have to do now is to apply the methods which have always led to the desired results there."

Yes, the Muscovite was right. He had seen everything, and everything had happened to him. And there was also the inverse of it all, and it was this inverse which had molded one of the basic traits of his attitude. The Muscovite knew that no such thing as permanent truth existed—because no such thing ever existed in the Soviet Union. He knew that truth has many faces, and the only thing that concerned him was which face was on top just then. He was fully aware that, at all times, truth was what the Secretary-General or the supreme body of the Party held to be the truth, and, therefore, it did not particularly bother him that yesterday's truth had changed, by today, into a lie. This explanation he not only accepted, but he could also explain to others. His explanation was always pat and scientific, always supported by quotations from the Marxist classics, always seasoned with a few well-applied examples from the experiences of the Soviet Union. Since these explanations were rarely questioned, he was convinced that his "agitation-propaganda" assignment was highly successful and had served just causes. This philosophy he called "dialectics." "To the Communists" and this was one of his favorite slogans—"difficulties serve only to be overcome." Thus, day by day, he did nothing but overcome difficulties in order to be able to write reports to Party headquarters about exactly this overcoming of difficulties.

The Muscovite knew that these reports were the most important factors in his life. Whether he was a minor Muscovite or one in as high a position as Matyas Rakosi, he was aware that everything depended upon the reports. This he had learned in the Soviet Union. The reports became the center of his whole life. And he had also learned that a report could never be one-sided. If a report exaggerated the difficulties, or was gloomy, or threw no light upon the signs of progress (i.e., if it did not mention "our achievements"), it was a bad report, for, in this case, his superiors would consider him a pessimist who had lost faith in socialism. If, on the other hand, the report was too rosy, it was again a bad report, for "the comrades in the Party" might find that its author had lost his vigilance and had thereby failed to notice the enemy lurking in every corner. A Communist without vigilance was no Communist at all!

The report had, therefore, to be constructed with great care and with particular attention to proportions, regardless of what the truth was. There would be 70 per cent of achievement contained in it and 30 per cent of difficulty. This, as taught by his experiences in the Soviet Union, was more or less the correct proportion. Then, when the report was finished, he signed it with a flourish, snapped it into his large pigskin attaché case, climbed into the powerful car waiting at the door, and returned tiredly to his villa—a villa perhaps inherited from a deported, once very rich family of merchants, or, to be more exact, a villa allotted to him by the Party.

This was the point at which the Muscovite's public life ended

and at which his private life began. But, public or private, his
life was by no means enviable. Its leitmotiv was fear. A Muscovite's life was never safe, wherever he went—and least of all
in the Soviet Union. He knew that neither his age nor his long
Party membership would protect him. He knew that he did not
even have to commit a mistake in order to be relieved of his
job, or to be arrested and tried. To him, nothing was impossible.
After all, he had seen it all in the Soviet Union. His smile, his
loyalty, and his zeal served but one purpose: to survive. This
he understood. Though he did not like to talk about this fact
(and though he never did), it came out eight or ten years after
his return from the Soviet Union that practically all of the
best-known Muscovites had spent longer or shorter terms in
Soviet jails, for the whirlwind of the Trotsky-Bukharin trials had
not bypassed the ranks of the Hungarian emigration. Even Bela
Kun, who was Secretary of the Hungarian Party and who, in
1919, headed the Hungarian dictatorship of the proletariat, was
liquidated by Stalin as a Trotskyite agent. And Kun was not
the only one. Several other Hungarian Communists had perished
in jail, or in concentration camps, or on the gallows.

Yes, these Muscovites had seen everything.

But they said nothing. They knew that garrulity led to jail
and, subsequently, to death. Nor could anything ever surprise
them. They knew that everything was true, and that the opposite
was also true—and it was on this knowledge that they built their
lives.

Thus was engendered the most complete moral failure and the
most boundless cynicism—the dominant traits of every Muscovite's mental make-up. In what did they believe? In whom did
they believe? In nothing and in nobody. Their only desire was
that they should remain untouched by the storms that had almost destroyed them in the Soviet Union. They worked to give
full satisfaction to the Party. They had no independent will, nor
any independent opinion, and if they did manage to retain these,
they kept the fact a secret even from their wives. If it had been

possible, they would have kept it a secret even from themselves, too, for they were disenchanted with everything. When they had returned home after the war, they had still hoped that there would be no repetition of the years of horror. But when the arrests had begun, when one show trial after another had been arranged, they had understood that the days of silence and of unconditional surrender had returned.

They had understood there, too, that the accusations were false and that the victims were innocent. They understood that they themselves were repeating lies. They knew that their collaborators were lying to them and were hiding their real thoughts. And they knew that their own reports to the Party were false. Yet, they did not care. There was only one single thing the Muscovites cared about: that they should, after long years of fear and danger, be left in peace. They cared about their beautiful homes (of a type they had never had in Moscow or Novosibirsk), about nice furniture, and about "protocol" boxes at the opera house. The passionate search for truth and justice, the flaming desire to right social injustices, the emotions that had once made them join the Party and face the dangers of illegality and/or of the Spanish Civil War—all these had long been extinct in their souls. There was nothing left in those souls except the dream of a life of success without financial worries. They felt they deserved success and peace, for they had suffered enough *out there*. The people's cause was nothing but a slogan to them, used irresponsibly and thoughtlessly, out of habit. Sometimes, now, they woke in the night and listened in the great silence. But they no longer heard the voices of their consciences. Life in the Soviet Union had killed that which had been their greatest virtue at the time of their emigration: their faith. Now, when they remained alone, the obligatory smiles faded from their faces and the flowery slogans died on their lips. They had become bitter, old, lifeless. If there were anything left that they believed in, it was luck—that this time they would be lucky enough to escape disfavor. They hated everything they were doing, and yet they could not stop doing it. There were moments when they believed what they said, but, when they thought it over, they shrugged disgustedly.

Yet, who cared? They did not mind lying because they did not believe that truth could ever be spoken in this life. In fact, they had forgotten what truth was. They did not care if they were compelled to recant in self-criticism what they had said the previous day. Self-criticism was one of the basic elements of their life. They knew that if they wanted to survive, this was the only safe path. They shrugged, and they practiced self-criticism. They declared that, on the previous day, they had committed an error, and they promised the Party that they would watch with Communist vigilance even over themselves, and that they would eliminate the smallest mistake, unmask the enemy, and build up socialism. They knew that their Party did not care a fig for their souls, and that it was interested only in the spoken or the written word, even though everybody knew that the speakers and the writers were lying. Their cynicism was merely self-defense, not so much against the Party as against their former egos. How else could they have borne that terrible tragedy of those thirty years—a tragedy which was the violation of all their youthful dreams? What they most hated in themselves was that which they had had to bury deepest: their sincere emotions and their murdered faith. They were dead souls.

One of the prominent figures of the Muscovite emigration was the writer Bela Illes, who, at the end of the war, returned to Hungary after thirty years in the Soviet Union as a colonel in the Soviet Army. In his youth, he had been a very promising writer. Even Romain Rolland had praised one of his short stories. When Illes returned to Hungary, he became the most loyal, the most devoted, and the most unquestioning propagator of the Party's official cultural policy. A tall, handsome, gay fellow, full of *joie de vivre* and an inexhaustible fund of good stories, he was known not so much for his works as for his legendary fibs and his passion for boasting. He, if anyone, knew his Soviet Union. It was not without reason that, at the end of the thirties, he—a former secretary to Bela Kun—had taken a job as a waiter somewhere in Asia to escape arrest.*

Illes had been spared arrest, but not expulsion from the Party. When he was rehabilitated during the war, he again became the man Hungary came to know as "a devoted soldier of the Party" (as he, too, liked to call himself). After his return to Hungary, he fought "on the literary front" with a zeal worthy of better causes. But this genial, always gay, and voracious man—he once ate an entire goose at one meal—this man struggling against an ever-present fear of death, never for a moment forgot whence he came. When he wrote, he watched not himself but Matyas Rakosi, wondering what that great man would say to this or to that sentence. He hated Rakosi because he knew that the Party leader considered him a mediocre writer. But, since Rakosi was absolute master in the country, he knew better than to argue with a dictator. He had had enough of that. As editor-in-chief of the Writers' Association's weekly magazine, *Irodalmi Ujsag,* he trembled after each issue, awaiting Rakosi's telephone call and knowing only too well that the "leader and wise father" of Hungary would never call him just to praise him. Muscovite writers were not often praised in those days. Words of praise were reserved for the non-Communist writers—or for those who were no longer Communist—because these were considered potential allies of the Party. They were potential allies to be won over to the cause at any cost. Since Illes had long ago been won over, he was nothing but a servant who carried out orders without thought, and thus praise was not for him.

Illes was far too clever not to be fully aware of this unwritten

---

* Whether true or not, Illes' own story of how he escaped arrest is highly characteristic of the atmosphere of the times: "When Bela Kun 'disappeared,' I, too, was summoned. 'Do you know Bela Kun?' they asked me. 'Of course, I know him,' I replied. 'After all, I was his secretary.' My sincerity surprised the Soviet comrades no end. They had interviewed most of Kun's best friends, but, without exception, these had repudiated him, declaring that they had not seen him for years, that they had always known him to be an enemy, etc. My open and above-board answer surprised them so much that they thought I was crazy and let me go. . . ."

law. Though he often complained about it among friends, he was also far too experienced to discuss it openly when the opportunity arose. He put up with it, grumbling a little when it was not dangerous to do so. But his anger, mixed with envy against the non-Party writers and against those who pretended sometimes for purely practical reasons to lean toward the opposition, grew as the days passed. Whatever he felt, he resigned himself to his fate, and, though he was kind and understanding and tolerant and admiring to the non-Party writers to their faces, he accused them of the most impossible crimes behind their backs. This was not because he envied them their successes (for he did pretty well with his own books), but because of their privileged position, which he himself could never again achieve. It was difficult for him to bear the intimacy with which Peter Veres and Rakosi called each other by their first names, while all he got was a "You, Illes . . ." followed usually by "You have acted like an idiot again!" At such times, "Illes" replied with a forced smile, though bitter fury tore his heart. He constantly promised himself to be more careful, to be a better tactician the next time. Thus, tactics became the central element of his life. In fact, he reached the point at which, like so many other Party functionaries, he could no longer distinguish his real feelings from his tactical feelings; and thus falsehood became a basic trait of his character. The mendacious quality of his anecdotes was notorious, but he was so good a storyteller that the falsity of his stories was easily forgiven. He presented his lies in a highly literary form. They were well-rounded and always had a point. But the basic falsity of his whole attitude was not so easily acceptable. In vain did he chew to fragments every sentence he wrote. He could never calculate the mood of one or another Party leader, and he never knew whether the line which he considered right would not prove wrong in the evanescent political situation. He was not protected by the armor of nonmembership. It would not be he who would receive a severe, yet forgiving, reprimand for a political mistake. He would be the one who was rudely abused and mercilessly punished. After all, he, being an old Communist, "should have known better." The only trouble was that one could never know in advance what it was that one should have "known better."

Illes had sufficient humility to serve. But he did not possess enough of this quality to resign himself to his fate. His career was like a mad race after the laurels of success. He did not care how many copies of his books sold (although he often spoke of such sales). All he cared about was that Rakosi should call him up and give him at least one word of praise for his writings. But Rakosi, an excellent psychologist and an even better tactician, knew better than to calm the storms raging in Bela Illes' heart. And he also knew that his servant should, after all the abuse, be sometimes treated to a sweet word of praise. Thus, Rakosi would pick up the receiver and say: "I read your article, Illes. I won't say that it couldn't have been written better, but it was not bad. Not bad at all. It was useful. We'll talk about it some time." Then, replacing the receiver, Rakosi knew that at the other end of the wire there would stand a radiant Illes who not only understood but also knew what such praise meant.

To be useful! This was the most a Communist writer could expect, and Bela Illes knew that, to Rakosi, usefulness was more important than beauty, not to speak of truth. His usefulness strengthened his position—not merely in his job, but in his standing, in his place in the hierarchy. At such moments, he would open up like a flower in the sun, strutting happily up and down his office and awarding bonuses to the messenger boy, to the stenographer, and to his secretary, who listened solemnly to his account of the great moment when, over the wire, he had heard the voice of Comrade Rakosi. He was not stingy. He would have trays upon trays of pastry brought up from the pastry shop. Sometimes he even ordered champagne. Unfortunately for him, however, these moments were rare.

Usually, when the well-known voice, marked by a slight provincial accent, spoke to him with unnatural calm from the other end of the wire, it heaped abuse after abuse on poor Illes' head without allowing him time for a single argument in his own

defense. Sometimes Illes tried vainly to interrupt the flow of
words, but he would finally resign himself to listening. Rakosi
could be neither interrupted nor diverted from saying what he
wanted to say. And he was not at all interested in a reply. He
made his pronouncement, then put down the receiver, leaving
the person with whom he had been talking alone with his own
fears and doubts. At such times, Illes would be completely
broken up. He would not be able to stop sighing then, and he
would usually depart from the capital to some rest home in the
country in order to work on his latest novel, or, as he called it,
"the *chef-d'oeuvre*" of his life.

It was well known that one of his habits was to leave the
capital whenever trouble was brewing. This, too, was something
he had learned in the Soviet Union. It was always best to be
as far as possible from the center of the storm. If he were away,
he would not have to make declarations or take sides; and this
was always best, because nobody knew how the official opinion
would change in a day, or in two days, and then he, the old and
experienced Communist who "should have known better," would
certainly be hauled over the coals.

Illes, knowing all the secrets that he did, always behaved
mysteriously. His unfinished sentences and his little veiled insinu-
ations gave the impression that he knew a great deal, but that
he was not allowed to speak. Yet, he had not pledged secrecy to
anybody. His tongue was tied, instead, by his fear for his skin.
When the whole country—and particularly the literary circles—
was resounding with passionate arguments, Illes watched and
listened, mute with amazement. He dared not believe his ears.
His Soviet experiences warned him of danger. So he would
pack his bags and be off. But, before leaving, he would once
more call in his young and inexperienced colleagues. Naturally,
he would call them in one by one, in order that there should be
no witnesses to the conversation, for he had a holy terror of
witnesses. "Don't mention our talk to anyone," he would always
warn each of these. "But if you do, you had better be prepared
that I shall deny every word of it."

These conversations were highly characteristic of his fear and, to a certain extent, of his benevolence. For minutes on end, he would pace back and forth in the room, sucking his cold pipe and besprinkling everything about him—his jacket, the table, chair, and carpet—with ashes. Then he would stop. "Listen," he would say to his young friend, a Communist writer. "You know you can tell me everything that troubles you. But why talk in public? Must you bang your head against the wall? Do you think we haven't been through the same thing *out there?* Go on, tell me everything. Your doubts. Your worries. Do you think I don't know what is going on? But, for heaven's sake, be more careful! This will lead to terrible trouble, let me tell you. Terrible trouble!"

These and similar warnings were soon, however, no longer to any avail. Events were coming to a boiling point, and Illes found himself standing helpless and frightened in the maelstrom. In the summer of 1956, his patron and tormentor, Matyas Rakosi, suddenly disappeared from the scene. Illes was somewhere in the country, but he hurried to Budapest. He made an unexpected appearance in the editorial offices of *Irodalmi Ujsag,* although he had, for years, neglected that publication. He was pale. The purple rings around his eyes were darker than usual. He walked up and down in the badly furnished room. It seemed as though the people with whom he had always agreed at the bottom of his heart, but against whom he had passionately (or at least with a semblance of passion) fought for years, had, after all, been right. They had been convulsively and irrevocably right. He stopped at the desk and collapsed into the armchair. Tears poured down his old, withered face.

"You don't know, boys," he sobbed. "You can't know how much we trembled, how much we lied *out there* for thirty years!"

The "Old Fighters" . . .

Between the two World Wars, the word "Communist" took on an entirely different connotation in Hungary from that which it earned after 1945. In the Horthy era, it was easy to win this not exactly complimentary designation, since nearly everybody who did not see eye to eye with the regime was called a "Communist." In the official press and the parliamentary interpellations, the word "Communist" variously came to mean a bourgeois radical, a Social Democratic journalist, an anti-German liberal, or a Zionist university student. The worker who had never read a word of Marx or of Lenin, but who had the temerity to ask for a wage increase, was immediately branded a "stinking Communist," and so was the fifteen-year-old peasant lad who failed to exhibit enough discipline in the compulsory paramilitary youth organization. Yet, of real Communist Party members, there were no more than 2,000 or 3,000. The Party itself functioned illegally: its members, when arrested, were court-martialed; a few were even executed. The 1919 dictatorship of the proletariat had lost the Party its prestige. Thus, it no longer had any attraction for the masses.

Yet, things would have been the same even if the politics of the illegal Party had been less sectarian. For, the title of

"Communist" was justified in no more than 1 or 2 per cent of the cases, and the proportion was no different among the writers.

In 1919, the overwhelming majority of the writers acclaimed the dictatorship of the proletariat, some with a romantic enthusiasm, others indifferently, some with real faith, and others because it was a suitable subject for an article or a poem. This the Horthy regime had never fully forgiven, even in those who later publicly repudiated this "youthful mistake." Among the writers who were constantly considered "somewhat suspect" was the greatest prose writer of the age, Zsigmond Moricz. So was the liberal Catholic poet Mihaly Babits considered suspect, and so (for his poems in praise of the workers) was the gentle, God-fearing Gyula Jyhasz, not to speak of Gyula Illyes who, in addition to having lived in Moscow and Paris, wrote books on the poverty of the sons of the *puszta* and on the life of the rebellious poet Sandor Petofi.

Still, there were very few writers who had openly confessed themselves Communists, or who had joined the illegal Party, or who had even maintained contact with it. Some of these had emigrated to the Soviet Union or to the West. The others, who remained in Hungary, unmindful of the anxieties and the slights and the danger involved, had numbered not more than ten. Yet, contrary to the Muscovites the weight and prestige of these writers was not negligible, even though their numbers were. To this group belonged the greatest poet of the era, Attila Jozsef. To it also belonged the master of short-story writing, Lajos Nagy, and one of the foremost of novelists, Tibor Dery. Most of them had joined the Party in their early youth, and, for them, the Party was not merely the expression of their political opinion but also the first witness of their youthful dreams, their rebellion, and their passion.

What drove these writers into the Communist Party or, at least, into its sphere of influence? The answer: their opposition to social injustice. In those days, Hungary gave abundant cause for such a step. For thirty years the people and the nation were to struggle in a maze of unsolvable problems. This kingdom with-

out a king, governed by an admiral without a sea, was among
the first—or perhaps *the* first—to march toward fascism by
introducing a bloody and murderous "white terror." This National Christian trend was unable—and, in fact, it had no real
desire—to solve any of the problems at hand, for even the slightest change would have shaken the foundations of its very regime
—a regime bound by unbreakable ties to a feudalistic-capitalistic
system which had been improved, at best, by only a few unavoidable modernizations. Therefore, though the regime raised various
problems, it offered no radical solution. Thus, it passed no land
reform. For the sake of appearances, it parceled out the land
in certain areas and permitted the peasants to buy it; yet the
peasantry, which constituted the overwhelming majority of the
population, remained landless and were either forced into servitude or else forsook the land altogether and swelled the number
of the urban proletariat. The poverty of the peasants in those
days was legendary, but, at the same time, there were medieval
estates of a size unknown for centuries in the West. There were
estates spreading over tens or even hundreds of thousands of
Hungarian "holds," * like those of the Esterhazys or of the
Roman Catholic Church. And these estates were not considered
unusual.

The regime officially permitted the workers to organize, but
it prevented by police measures their doing so; it preached social
progress, but it practiced racial discrimination; it introduced
social insurance, but it tolerated unlimited exploitation; and,
taking advantage of the undeniable injustices of the Versailles
and Trianon Treaties, it incited the population by nationalist
propaganda against neighboring peoples in order to divert attention from domestic difficulties. It was not without reason that,
in the early thirties, Hungary was called "the land of three million beggars." The economic crisis that shook the world in the
thirties increased the internal difficulties and the social tensions,
and the ruling class, which was composed of the barons of

---

* A Hungarian acre.

finance and the aristocracy, attempted to avert trouble not only by means of increasing the terror at home but also by means of a German Nazi and an Italian Fascist orientation in foreign politics.

In Hungary, which had no democratic traditions or institutions to speak of, fascism could easily have won ground, particularly among the masses whose basic social problems had never been solved, because fascist demagogy promised over-all solutions. The majority of the population—and, particularly, the peasantry—watched the growing dominance of the radical fascistic trends with indifference and resignation. Finally, with its chauvinism, its revisionism, and its racist policy, with its anti-Jewish laws and its adherence to the Berlin-Rome axis, the official political line bound itself, almost unconditionally, to Hitlerite Germany. The democratic forces in the country were weak, and they lacked the means to make their influence felt.

The truly shocking social inequalities, the growing fury of fascism, the horror of racist and nationalist excesses drove many a significant writer to that Party which, as he believed, was fighting for the material and intellectual freedom of humanity. The struggle often seemed discouraging, and the outcome uncertain; yet these writers did not waver.

Their careers, however, and the artistic and political aspects of those careers, were entirely different from those of the Muscovites. While the Muscovites, being all too soon deprived of their ideals, lost faith and thereby lost themselves, the Hungarian Communist writers kept their ideals at least until 1949. Their faith was not a tactical lie based on fear; it was, instead, a passion fired by unforgettable experiences. Another fundamental difference from the Muscovites lay in this other group's attitude toward reality. While the Muscovites lived in a sham world, created not by life but by the Agitation-Propaganda Department of the Moscow Communist Party, the Communist writers who had remained in Hungary lived in the midst of reality. It was this reality that, in obedience to their calling, they wanted to mold into an artistic form, and their adherence to reality

Yet, the Party was never inclined to permit such criticism. He who dared to disobey one or another of the Comintern's commands offended against the Party, although during that illegal period the Party was but an intangible illusion, or a Fata Morgana, or an invisible body that passed resolutions and yet lacked the strength to enforce them. To be more exact, the Party lacked the strength to struggle against the existing social order, but had sufficient strength to wage bloody internal wars and to calumniate the Party members who provoked its disfavor. The critic was soon faced with the consequences of his temerity: Party penalty, expulsion, or, not infrequently, denunciation to the authorities.

One of the most hair-raising examples of this situation was that of Attila Jozsef, the shining star of Hungarian letters and one of the greatest poets of the twentieth century. Attila Jozsef was a proletarian poet in the purest sense of the word. He was a proletarian poet because he came from the ranks of the proletariat. His father, a soapmaker, had emigrated and left his wife (a washwoman) to live the rest of her life in dire misery. And Jozsef expressed the thoughts, the emotions, and the moods of the Hungarian working people on the highest literary level. He was a proletarian poet in the most severe Marxist-Leninist sense, in that he professed himself openly to be the revolutionary poet of the working class and sincerely tried to attain in his poems a synthesis of the intellectual and the emotional world of the working class and of the Communist Party. He joined the illegal Party, held Marxist seminars for the ordinary Party members, shared in the most trivial (but nonetheless highly dangerous Party activities), and willingly wrote such propaganda poems as those which, for instance, encouraged people to make contributions to the so-called "Red Aid," an organization formed to help jailed Communists. As a result of the intrigues and the machinations of petty politicians, of the intrigues of sham writers, and of the intrigues of ordinary rhyme-makers, Attila Jozsef was expelled from the Communist Party. The documents relating to the expulsion "disappeared" and were never again found, but it is known that the principal cause was a study written by the poet in which he attempted to reconcile the teachings of Freud and Marx. The petty bourgeois who had him expelled called him (though he was the only real worker from the working class among them) a "petty bourgeois." But the Muscovites went even further: in their periodical, they called him a "Fascist." Not much later, at the age of thirty-two, Attila Jozsef committed suicide. His schizophrenia, rapidly worsening as a result of the poverty in which the system maintained him, became fatal because of the reaction of his comrades in the Communist Party to his enthusiasm, his devotion, and his poetry.

In the period between the two World Wars, the relationship between the Communist writers and their Party had its almost regularly recurring ups and downs. According to the Party, these were caused by the vacillations of the writers of petty-bourgeois background, but in reality they were caused rather by the vacillations of the Party line.

Yet, when 1945 came, bringing with it a now-legal Communist Party, these writers joined that Party without exception. The war, plus the great and positive part the Soviet Union played in it, made them forgive and forget many an offense. Events, intrigues, and quarrels which had once seemed important now lost their significance. And, remembering the political and moral problems encountered in the past, the writers were suddenly assailed by doubt. Had they, after all, been wrong? Had not the course of events justified the others? True, they were not pleased with the Trotsky-Bukharin trials, nor with the Molotov-Ribbentrop Pact; nor did they relish the almost religious cult of Stalin's personality. And yet, they had no answer for the greatest question of all: Had not all this been necessary in order to make the Soviet Union strong enough to play such a decisive part in the defeat of German fascism? The blood shed by the Soviet soldiers had washed away many a blemish; the brilliance of Stalingrad had illuminated many a dark stain. The writers, who were among the first to ask for admittance to the new Party, being proud of their old membership cards and of their records in illegality, were no innocent children. There was much they could not believe in the official Party history, and they could not dispel all their doubts. But they believed that a new period was beginning and that the time had come for forgetting the past or, at least, for forgetting that which they had not liked in the past.

It must, of course, be mentioned immediately that the Party was far less generous than were the writers. True, in 1945, it admitted all these writers into its ranks and, for a while, even patronized them. But this honeymoon lasted only until the Party had firmly established its power and had become omnipotent in the world of literature. As soon as this was accomplished, it suddenly unearthed all the files which, in 1945, it had had every opportunity to discuss, but which, by 1948-1949, had become obsolete. In the meantime, many of these writers had enjoyed the highest official recognition, and not only the country but the entire "peace camp" had resounded with their names. Yet, this fact did not matter. The Party pretends at times to forget, but it never forgets those who have, at one time or another, turned against it. When the time is ripe, it sends its accounting.

One of the outstanding prose writers of this period was Lajos Nagy. He had spent a lifetime attacking the capitalist system in bitter and ruthless short stories and novels. He had suffered and starved for twenty-five years, but he had never given up. When censorship had been at its most severe in the Horthy regime, he had glorified the Soviet Union in a symbolical story. When everybody had spoken of the 1919 dictatorship of the proletariat as a "treacherous Bolshevik reign of terror," he—although he was not a Party member—had written a story glorifying the "Communists." After 1945, the Party could not do enough for him. He was allotted a beautiful villa and was among the first to be awarded the highest distinction, the gold medal of the Kossuth Prize. His books were published, one after another, in large editions, and every Sunday he had a short story in *Szabad Nep*. Then, in 1949, all this came to an end. His short stories no longer appeared in print. His most recent novel remained unpublished, and soon Jozsef Darvas, then Chairman of the Writers' Association, publicly declared that "Lajos Nagy is a coffee-house writer who sees life only through the windows of the coffeehouse."

There was just one grain of truth in this: Lajos Nagy did, indeed, adore the atmosphere of the coffeehouse. Between the two World Wars, the Hungarian writers had spent a great part of their lives around the marble-topped tables of the various coffeehouses, which were warm and brightly lit, and in which, for the price of a small black coffee, they could sit for hours, chatting, arguing, and writing. They could, when short of money, draw credit from the literature-loving headwaiters. It had been here that the most prodigious short-story subjects were born; it had been here that the best periodicals were edited; and it had been here that the most bloody battles in chess and in cards had been waged. Yes, Lajos Nagy was indeed a "coffee-house writer"; all his life he had liked sitting at a small coffee-house table and scribbling away in letters so minuscule (prob-ably in an effort to save paper) that they were hardly legible to the bare eye; and the hubbub about him, the air reeking with cigarette smoke, never disturbed him in the least. On the con-trary, this atmosphere was for him a veritable source of inspira-tion and a *sine qua non* of creation, just as the rotten apple had been to Schiller. After he was installed in his beautiful villa, he often complained to his friends that work was almost impossible in such "ideal surroundings" as lovely gardens and absolute quiet, and he frequently escaped to a smoky, noisy cafe to finish a short story. He was, indeed, a "coffeehouse writer," but, from behind the large glass panes of the coffeehouse, he created stor-ies vying with Gorki's and with Maupassant's masterpieces—stories that inspired, that incited against fascism and even against capitalism. It was at a coffeehouse table that he wrote his socio-logical novel entitled *Kiskunhalom*, the first real, almost scientific presentation of life in the Hungarian peasantry. This was long before sociological novels had, in the mid-thirties, came into fashion—a fashion created by a small group of writers to which Jozsef Darvas, Nagy's presently severest critic, also belonged.

Why was it necessary suddenly to accuse this old Communist of having been a "coffeehouse writer"? Nobody was ever able to answer that question. Yet, from that day on, he lived like a hunted animal. No, the villa was not taken from him, and he was even granted a monthly stipend, or advance, on his works by the Literary Fund; and thus he was able to live far better than he could have lived in the Horthy era. But the newspaper editors became a little formal and standoffish, returning his new manuscripts with awkward, ill-explained excuses. The publishers of the second half of his autobiography (the first part had appeared previously) suddenly produced all sorts of petty and negligible objections to the forthcoming work: the book would have to be most carefully revised; or the paper shortage hindered publication; or the leading role of the Party had not been sufficiently stressed. And from his home, always hospitably open night and day for friends who dropped in for a chat, and from his table, always loaded with wonderful homemade pastries and exotic delicacies, more and more of the old—but particularly the new—friends stayed away, deciding that, as things now stood, it was perhaps better not to be seen there too frequently.

The initiated were fully aware of the reason for this sudden change, and the author himself must have guessed it. Lajos Nagy had often, when among friends, let fall little remarks about aspects of everyday life in the Party that displeased him.* Particularly, he decried the increasing adulation of the Party's First Secretary, Matyas Rakosi. A poem that one of the most gifted and most faithful young Hungarian poets had written to Rakosi was published in those days. Lajos Nagy raged and ranted,

---

* When, after an absence of fourteen months in North Korea, I returned to Hungary, Lajos Nagy was one of the first people I went to see, because I liked and admired him. The old man received me with great warmth. I think he liked me, too. He questioned me at length about my experiences, then, smiling charmingly and innocently, he said: "I read your reports . . . and there is but one aspect I didn't quite understand. . . . How it is that all your North Koreans are heroes and great people, while the South Koreans are, without exception, cowards and scoundrels?" I explained, argued, and elaborated, but he simply nodded and smiled.— T.M.

partly because he had a high esteem for the young man's talent. "I can forgive him for saying that Rakosi created the world, for he is then only comparing Rakosi to God. . . . But how can a poet bring himself to write that, among poets, Rakosi is a greater poet than Shakespeare or Petofi?"

Naturally, this was not the only remark of this type that Nagy made. Usually, his comments were neither too sharp nor too offensive; they were rather mild, with a hardly noticeable edge of sarcasm. But his extraordinarily discerning eye frequently glimpsed absurdities that might have seemed natural to others, and he was soon denounced to Rakosi. It is more than probable that the denouncer was one of the Muscovite writers who visited him under the guise of friendship and who regularly reported his conversations to the Party. However, the information could not be used: not even among themselves would the Party bosses accuse anyone of "having made derogatory remarks about Comrade Rakosi." This would have impaired the dictator's prestige— and so the time had come to take recourse to the old files.

In 1934, Lajos Nagy, accompanied by a fellow writer, Gyula Illyes, had attended the First Congress of Soviet Writers in Moscow as a guest. Since not everything he had seen there had met with his approval, he had published a series of articles which were rather critical of the Soviet Union. These articles may have also been intended to allay the suspicion of Horthy's police, who were more suspicious than ever of Nagy after his Russian trip. Now, at the same time that the sneer of "coffeehouse writer" was being passed from mouth to mouth, a more secretive whispering campaign making use of this old misdemeanor was started against Nagy by the Party-directed literati. Rumors spread: "Lajos Nagy has always been anti-Soviet. . . . He has behaved very badly in the past. . . . It would, perhaps, be better not to be too intimate with him. . . ." Some might argue that this was not new, that everybody had known of it in 1945, and that he had still been admitted to the Party. But the rumors were compounded: "Certainly! But at that time that was the correct thing to do—for tactical reasons. . . . With the class struggle becoming fiercer, one has to be vigilant. The roots of his disloyalty are deep. . . . If he writes something good, it should be published, naturally. . . . But his work should be used in moderation. . . . There is no point in giving him too much publicity."

The old author—he was nearing seventy—suddenly noticed that he no longer received invitations to gala performances at the opera house, nor to the conferences of the Party's activist "writers," nor to receptions in the Parliament building or at the various embassies. He was taken off the protocol list. He had fallen into disfavor. He was old and tired, and he was suffering from neurasthenia. His powerful body—he had once been an amateur boxer—was wasted and bent. He wanted least of all to provoke the Party or Rakosi. All he wanted was to live and to work in peace. That ill-advised series of articles could not be unwritten, but at least he tried to come to terms with the dictator. He wrote a couple of short stories of which, indirectly, he made Rakosi the hero. In them, one or another of his characters mentioned how much Rakosi's coming to power had improved his life. Today, this may seem despicable and cowardly, but in those years Rakosi (not to speak of Stalin) was the subject of an entire literature in Hungary: on his sixtieth birthday, a whole volume was published containing the writings of the foremost Hungarian authors. Of these, of course, Rakosi was the hero.

Lajos Nagy's stories were rather bad. Perhaps he wrote them without conviction, or perhaps he detested himself for writing them. Either reason could explain why the Hungarian dictator never forgave him his past. The old man lived in utter solitude, neglected and forgotten. But, from then on, he kept his thoughts to himself, though his keen mind recorded everything that was untrue, or mere propaganda, or empty, or false, or oversimplified.*

---

* Not even the dead are always forgiven by the Party. Attila Jozsef, for example, was not that fortunate. True, in 1945, eight years after his death, the Hungarian Party "rehabilitated" him, admitting at the same time,

Lajos Nagy died in November, 1954. The Hungarian Government and the Communist Party buried him in great style. It was decreed that all his books be published in a commemorative edition. No pomp was spared at the funeral. His body lay in State in the building of the Hungarian Writers' Association, and the funeral procession marched across half the town. The man who eulogized him at the ceremony was Jozsef Darvas,† who was then Minister of Culture, and who was the very man who, a few years earlier, had excluded Lajos Nagy from official Hungarian literature by branding him a "coffeehouse writer." At Nagy's grave, Darvas spoke in moving terms of the "great Communist writer, Lajos Nagy."

---

however, that his expulsion had been a "mistake" committed not by the Party itself but by a few sectarian comrades. This "rehabilitation" was unavoidable since, in the meantime, the poet had grown into a classic example in the consciousness of the Hungarian people. Thus, Budapest forgave. But Moscow remained firm. In *The Great Soviet Encyclopedia,* one can still read that Attila Jozsef had failed to discern the world leadership of the Soviet Union and had thus been disloyal to the cause of the working class.

† Jozsef Darvas, Chairman of the Hungarian Writers' Association between 1951 and 1954, was, until 1953, Minister of Public Education in the Rakosi Government, and then, from 1953 to the Revolution, also Minister of Culture in the Imre Nagy and Hegedus Governments. He took over the latter function from Jozsef Revai, who had been Minister of Culture from 1950 to 1953. The schools, universities, scientific institutes, etc., were under the jurisdiction of the Ministry of Education. Literature, the arts, amateur mass cultural activities, and the press—with the exception of the Party publishing house and the Party press—were under the jurisdiction of the Ministry of Culture. The Party publications were handled directly by the Party headquarters staff.

. . . And the New Generation

If, after 1945, the Party meant bread and butter, or even cake, to the Muscovite writers, and if it meant, regardless of all former internal conflicts, justification, to the old Communist writers, it meant something far more to the largest group of writers in Hungary. These were the young writers—and to them the Party was the *answer*.

They came from many backgrounds, these young writers. There were among them those who had sympathized with, or even joined the Social Democratic Party before or during the war. There were apolitical *beaux esprits*. There were university students of Western culture who came from artistic families; and there were petty-bourgeois Jewish youths; and there were young provincials who had not been left untouched by fascist ideology. The majority of them had grown up on the works of the writers of peasant origin who, ever since the thirties, had "discovered" and described with growing passion and broadening perspectives the bitter fate of the peasants on the mammoth estates, and who had "studied" with semi-scientific ruthlessness the problems and contradictions of peasant life.

Yet, though their beginnings or their family backgrounds or their first influences may have differed, this generation—among which the writers of this book count themselves—had a great and overwhelmingly strong experience in common. This experience was the war. It was during the war that they realized for the first time the catastrophic consequences of the politics of the Hungarian ruling classes; and, almost without exception, they themselves were victims of those consequences. After the chauvinistic education they had received in school, it took some time before they could find their bearings, and it soon became clear to them that fascism was not the solution for the great problems of the nation. At the outset of the war, there were those who cherished illusions of victory, and these illusions were strengthened by the restitution to Hungary of part of the Uplands and of part of Transylvania, the former having been attached to Czechoslovakia since Trianon, and the latter to Rumania. But when, on January 16, 1943, the Russians broke through the front at Voronezh, routing the entire Hungarian army, and after the defeat of the German army at Stalingrad, Hungarian public opinion—with the exception of an insignificant little group of fanatical fascists—ceased to delude itself as to the outcome of the war. The nation lacked the strength to organize a strong resistance movement against the Germans. The German army of occupation was too strong and so was the fascist and semi-fascist indoctrination of the last twenty-five years. The bloody Hitlerite and Hungarian fascist terrors of the last war year, the destruction of the country, the deportation and gassing of the Hungarian Jews served only to horrify the more sensitive strata of the population, but not to fire them to active resistance.

It was during this chaotic, stormy, and terror-ridden period that the young generation consciously began to think. Driven by the desire to save the country and humanity, the younger generation tried to find its bearings and to establish a base from which to begin its search for a clear understanding of the involved, contradictory, and forbidding phenomena of the world. It was natural that it should throw itself—passionately and with a tormenting curiosity—into a study of the ideological currents which had prevailed during the war.

Young Hungary tried everything: it sampled the most varied

philosophical trends and the most varied psychological theories, from German positivism to the Diltheyan comparative study of the history of ideas, from Giono's peasant romanticism to Freud. There were months when Hungarian youth swore by Schopenhauer. Later, they considered Husserl's and Meinong's idealistic school the only salvation. They adopted Kretschmer's typology and they quoted, by heart, paragraphs from the *Jenseits von Gut und Boese* and the *Parerga and Paralipomena*. There were times when mysticism was popular, and then the youth proudly proclaimed its conscious schizophrenia. They considered Hieronymus Bosch the only great painter and Hoelderlin the only great poet. First the young people believed in God; then they rejected God. They dismissed St. Augustine's *Confessions* as a mediocre scribble and declared that Plotinus and neo-Platonism were again coming into their own. They learned the interpretation of dreams from Freud, sexual pathology from Stekel. The mind of this generation was at least as chaotic as the world-at-large, but, to make things worse, this chaos was topped with youth's eternal endeavor to create a synthesis out of its contradictory ideas. New universes and new ideological systems were born during endless walks along the boulevards and the banks of the Danube, until the youth found out that, though they had read everything that was available, they understood nothing of the world. And then they were drafted into the army.

The old soldiers and sergeants proved better teachers than Freud, Plotinus, Rabelais, and St. Augustine put together. Philosophy was child's play compared to what these sergeants were trying to do: to impose humility and obedience upon the champions of free-soaring thought. The young people brought up on Freud soon came into conflict with the fascist sergeants who translated the theory of liberated instinct into practice. In the brief but tormenting months of training, they discovered all that they had failed to learn in the little bistros and in the coffeehouses: that, if they wanted a world without sadistic monsters, they had, first of all, to create a situation in which such monsters could not be born. This almost-Marxist thought was their first—

but obviously most decisive—step toward Communism, because when they at last put their hands on a Marxist book containing simple and self-evident explanations for all the phenomena of the world, they exclaimed almost in chorus: "This is exactly what we need." They were intellectuals, and their store of information harmonized with their mental condition: they discovered Marxism *within themselves* long before they acquainted themselves with its literature. The situation, the social conditions, the misery of the people, and the futility of the war made them ready to accept without thought a system of ideas based on a radical change of the social order. Their experiences had taught them that this idea was right. Their yearning for a solution was so deep—and, it seemed to them, so hopeless, that when, in the course of their intellectual wanderings, they came upon a system which offered such definite, such final answers to all their problems, they at once accepted all its tenets and all its deductions. This system was Marxism.

The great and involved problems which occupied the mind of Hungarian youth (and of youth in general) became exceedingly simple and clear with the help of Marxism. In brief sentences, it rendered intelligible—and soluble—the extremely chaotic problems and interrelations of life and the world, of society and the soul. It restored the apparently unresolved mysteries of life and consciousness, of society and the individual. From the mystical and often unfathomable world of dualism, Marxism admitted youth into the simplified—and therefore intelligible—world of materialistic monism. The mystical secrets of life seemed solved: it was no longer an anarchistic, senseless whirl without beginning or end or purpose; it was, instead, a clear, unemphatic, raw, attractively unmysterious, limpid whole—a whole intelligible even for a child and from which those in possession of the key could read as in an open book.

They had, at last, that which they had always yearned for: an exact and perfect method to explain and change the world; a theory which, when translated into practice, righted all the wrongs. They soon created in their minds a complete picture

of that world: the world of concrete and glass buildings, spar-
klingly clean and ordered, and running as smoothly as if it had
been oiled—a perfect mechanism uniting society and the individual, and all rolling toward the blue dome of a faultless future.
This was at last the home of clear thinking, of rational harmony,
and of conscious freedom: the fatherland of man had released
the inevitable. Who could absent himself from the influence of
this beautiful vision? While the storm of fascism was reaching
its peak, demanding more and more victims, youth was simultaneously finding the end and the means—and youth's faith
blossomed like the flowers in spring. After all, the thoughts of
these youths were no dreams, no figments of the imagination,
no vain hopes! The armies bearing this theory (turned into
practice) on the barrels of their guns were approaching. The
armies had almost reached the borders. The hours of fascism
were numbered. And youth was happy, dreaming of the days
that would arrive after the war. It would be a new golden age—
the age of dreams come true, and of freedom and democracy.
Of this, they were sure. And when the great hour came, when
the units of the Soviet Army had chased the last German fascist
from Hungarian territory, they were received like emissaries
from a Promised Land.

These youths were young and enthusiastic. To them, Communism symbolized the freedom and the riches of which the
best sons of the people, its poets, have always dreamed. Youth
was equivalent to inexperience: they had never crossed the western frontier of their fatherland and they knew the democratic
institutions of the West only from hearsay. But these facts did
not bother them. What they cared about was that the Communist Party was declaring war on those classes which (and this
they knew from experience) had ruined the country and had
pushed it into a senseless war. For them, the "class struggle"
was not an abstract theory. It was a thoroughly justified living
reality—a struggle against those who had poisoned their youth,
plundered their best years, deprived them of perspectives, and
robbed them of the future. There was no more self-evident truth

in the whole world than this: if we want to build a country for the people and for ourselves, our first task is to defeat those who are trying to prevent us.

As far as the mental process is concerned, the origin and growth of this way of thinking was also aided by those who had nothing to do with the working-class movement and who had found their way to the Party only after the war's end. The young people who had their first taste of the omniscient theory of Marxism-Leninism in the first months after the termination of the war advanced more quickly along the road to discovery than did those of the contemporaries who had had at least a nodding acquaintance with the Maxist working-class movement during the war. These young people all came from the same kind of background. They were bourgeois or petty bourgeois. They were intellectuals who, in their search, never got farther than, for instance, in art, the slogan of *l'art pour l'art*. For these, we can safely say, the materialist philosophy and practice was a revelation altering their whole life. The nation not only needed a social change. It demanded one. And the change sprang from an ungovernable historical necessity. When the Communist Party announced the simple, clear, and attractive vistas of its realization, the overwhelming majority of the new generation fully identified itself with that Party.

These held to their faith sincerely and, what is more, they held to it the longest. Because of its inexperience, youth didn't even dream that, behind the sanctity of the Party, there was sacrilege, or that behind its unity there was disunity, or that behind its perfection there was crime. These youths were driven to the Party by the moral indignation caused by the horrors of fascism, and everything that fought against these horrors was automatically attractive to them. They had heard about democracy, but they had never experienced it. They believed that the lack of democracy was a higher form of democracy. To them, this contradiction was not only admirable and just; even the attempt itself to put it into practice was to them admirable. "There is no freedom for the enemies of freedom" was a slogan which sounded familiar; it was the slogan of the French Revolution, though on a much higher level! How simple it all was! There was but one thing you had to believe in: the Party's infallibility and the exclusive salutariness of the Soviet methods. For them, this belief was not compulsory; it was the *sine qua non* of happiness. It is certain that, had it been forced upon them, they would have abandoned it immediately—as they later did: their youth, all their experiences protested against compulsion. But they now accepted that which they found correct— and they obeyed it. Did they submit themselves to the iron discipline of the Party? Did they identify themselves with its program and approve its political line? Naturally. But, for them, this, too, was a sign of freedom, because they submitted themselves voluntarily and obeyed voluntarily.

The work of the Party was crowned with success. The forces of Hungarian democracy were expanding. The slogan—"The country is yours. . . . You are building it for yourself"—appeared true. It seemed as though everything were rolling smoothly along the rail laid down by the Communist Party. Socialism was no longer a distant phantom; it was a brightly shining, tangible reality. One had but to reach out to pluck its fruits.

In this war-torn country, life returned to normal within a miraculously short time. The ruins, instead of depressing the people, seemed to serve as a challenge. Within a few brief months, the whole country hummed like a busy beehive. Traffic came back on the roads in full force. A start was made toward rebuilding the blown-up Danube bridges—which thereby served as symbols of both destruction and reconstruction. In this new, fresh current, human relationships, changing, were renewed. People no longer felt responsible only for themselves and their families. They felt responsible for all society, too, because, now that they considered themselves a part of society, they did not mind working for it. It is only natural that this sudden blossoming should have had the by-products of black marketeering and speculation. Much more characteristic, however, was the com-

mon national effort which, beyond the reparation of war dam-
ages, attempted to construct a new country. Political life had
also changed. New, democratic parties appeared on the political
scene. A lively and promising interest in parliamentary affairs
evolved, though these affairs were not without initial difficulties
and shortcomings. An atmosphere of confidence prevailed in
the country. After the terrible inflation of the first year, national
economy became ever more stable and, though it was not easy
to eke out a living, one could safely hope for better days. And,
since everybody still remembered the war vividly, they thus appreciated the present and, which is even more important, felt
secure in their new society.

In those days, the Party was constantly gaining in strength.
After the war, this little sect, which had always lived and worked
underground and illegally, suddenly emerged from the shadow
and threw itself, with its large and efficient Party machinery and
boundless energy, into the political struggle. Its activities were
followed with close attention by the entire country. Although the
Communists were not exactly popular in Hungary, they won
seventeen per cent of the votes in the first free elections (forty-
five seats in Parliament), and they were strong enough to turn
this defeat into political capital—with, of course, the Soviet
Army standing behind them to help. The Communists' popularity grew, and this was due to a large extent to the fact that,
consciously and purposefully, they always presented programs
that served the interests of the poorest strata but, at the same
time, benefited the entire nation (or, at least, that is how it
appeared). They were clever enough to lay their hands on the
two most important ministries—those of the Interior and of
Agriculture—immediately after the liberation. The first of these
delivered the armed forces and the political police into their
hands; the second gave them an opportunity to create for themselves a real foundation among the masses. The Communist minister carried out the land reform—i.e., the parcelling out of the
large estates among the peasantry—free of charge. It proved to

be so popular a measure that nothing could compare with it. The name of the land-reform minister was Imre Nagy.

And this great, pure, and strong Party, "which gave heroes and martyrs to resistance," * which defeated, one after another, enemies stronger than itself † and "whose word was unshakable," now opened its arms to the young writers. It gave them tasks—literary tasks as well as Party tasks—and it gave a purpose and content to their lives. To a certain extent, it also took the place of the family dispersed by the whirlwind of World War II. Perhaps the young writers were spurred on by ambition. "The sky is the limit!" the Party promised, and where do young people not reach for the stars? But their wish to serve, to help, and to promote the cause of the people was stronger

---

* In this allegation, there was at least as much the conscious creation of a myth as there was truth. The Hungarian resistance was rather weak. Relatively few people engaged in active armed resistance against the Germans. Among these, there were Communists who carried out a few bold and sensational actions (they blew up a statue and they smuggled a bomb into a fascist mass meeting in Budapest); but among those who resisted the Germans there were also democrats like Bajcsy-Zsilinszki, a deputy of the Smallholders Party, who shot at the detectives who came to arrest him and who was executed by the fascists. He has grown into a symbol of Hungarian resistance, though his name was rarely mentioned, while the names of Communists possessing much less distinguished records were mentioned repeatedly.

† First among these enemies was the Smallholders Party, which had won an absolute majority in the elections of the autumn of 1945. The Communist Party (with the Soviet Army backing it) had formed an alliance with this party, but, at the same time, it constantly attacked it, saying—and there was some truth in it—that the Smallholders Party offered a haven and support to the fascists, to the reactionaries, and to the large capitalistic forces still existing in the country. Taking advantage of the weaknesses and intramural fights within the Smallholders Party and, at the same time, taking recourse to direct Soviet intervention (the Soviet Army simply arrested the party's General Secretary, Bela Kovacs, and deported him to Russia), the Communists succeeded in dividing the Smallholders into several small parties (by techniques which became famous as "meat-grinder tactics") and then, usually by various police measures, in liquidating them. In the fever of the struggle, the young Communist saw in this procedure not the smothering of the reviving democratic forces, but the actions of a tactical genius. He saw a successful battle in the war against reaction. And he saw tough and clever politics, all in the interest of socialism.

in them than was their ambition. This is why they took on the often tiresome, uninteresting, and always unpaid Party tasks. This is why they went out on "house-to-house agitation," did "cultural work," lectured on Marxism-Leninism, delivered election speeches, and sacrificed all their spare time for the Party. Those who think that this was mere careerism (though, indeed, there were careerists among the young writers) clearly ignore the feverish emotions burning in a young Communist. They also ignore his sense of responsibility to the people and his anxiety for the world-at-large—the two together being a comparable emotion only to love, to a solemn wedding where the bride is the community, the people, humanity.

The Party not only admitted these, but, in fact, it carried them on its wings. A "bold cadres policy"! This was the official line, and it meant that the young people who proved good Communists should be pushed into the foreground and placed in important positions, regardless of their lack of experience, their youth, and their entire lack of knowledge in the field in which they worked. A "bold cadres policy" meant, in essence, that the Party gave important jobs to young people who knew nothing of the work but were politically reliable. Using political reliability as a criterion was one of the means by which the Party won the young generation. Who would not be flattered if, at the age of twenty-three or twenty-five, he were to outrank old and experienced experts on the basis that he was politically reliable while the other was not? This is particularly true in literary life: the young writer usually scorns the older and more successful writer, rebelling against him and attempting to invent something new, because he always feels that whatever the older generation did is dated, even obsolete. Thus, he not only agrees, but actually believes that the Party is doing the right thing in relying on him.

Promotion in the framework of the "bold cadres policy" naturally improved the financial situation of the young writer. Formerly, a new writer had struggled for years (unless he came from a well-to-do family) until his name became known and he could make money with his writings. Frequently, he had to pay for the publication himself and then sell the copies, one by one, to his friends.*

Now, if the writer wrote something the Party considered useful—and, at first, the requirements were rather modest (such as a portrayal of the terrible conditions that had formerly existed in Hungary, or a description of the horrors of fascism)—he had no problems to face. His book was immediately published in an edition that had not, in the past, been dreamed of by any young writer. A number of young writers were appointed to well-paid, or, to be more exact, relatively well-paid cultural functions. A young provincial schoolteacher became secretary of the Writers' Association; a former clerk in a chemical industry became the man in charge of literary affairs at the Agitation-Propaganda Office of the Party; a former poet became editor-in-chief of a literary weekly; a short-story writer who also was a prospective secondary-school teacher became chief editor of a publishing house. These were rapid successes, the like of which was utterly impossible in the former regime. The incumbents never felt that they were doing their jobs for money. They considered their advance as the well-deserved recognition of their talents and their loyalty to the Party and to the people—and as a sign of changing times. They were flattered, very flattered.

The Party was not stingy. At the suggestion of the Communist Party in the spring of 1948, the Government introduced a system of prizes in literature, arts, and the sciences. Similar to the Stalin Prize, these prizes derived their name (in honor of the first centenary of the 1848-1849 Hungarian Revolution) from the internationally-known patriot, Lajos Kossuth. The Kossuth Prize was the highest award given to writers, actors, painters, sculptors, and musicians, as well as to scientists, engineers, doctors, and pedagogists, or even to workers and peasants

---

* Shortly before his suicide in 1937, Attila Jozsef complained in one of his poems that, although he had reached the ripe age of thirty-two, he had never yet been able to earn two hundred *pengoes* a month (then sixty-five dollars).

who achieved outstanding production records. The award included a large sum of money, country-wide celebration, and
fame and glory. The winners had the right to add to their names
the title of "Kossuth Prize-Winner" for as long as they lived.
After 1949, the youngest generation of writers was always represented among the ranks of the Kossuth Prize-winners, * even
though their literary products were often of far less value than
were the works of an older writer who was not, or had not yet,
been awarded the Kossuth Prize. In this respect, the Party was
much more generous with the young than it was with the Muscovites. One of the most significant among the Muscovite writers,
Andor Gabor, a truly gifted publicist, satirist, poet, and translator who gave up a rich and successful career and emigrated
to Moscow, became, upon his return to Hungary, editor of the
Party's comic journal *Ludas Matyi*. Financially, he was well-
off, but it was his secret hope and desire to win the Kossuth
Prize. Year after year, he scanned the magic list; but his name
was never on it. Young men whose talent could not even be
compared with his, were on it. But not he. In January, 1953, he
died. Two months later, on March 15, he was posthumously
awarded the Kossuth Prize. In his case, the Party was in no
hurry. He no longer had to be won over to the cause.

The young Kossuth Prize-winner became a member of the
"elite," the new aristocracy of the country. His name was added
to the protocol list, the list by which one could always judge the
momentary "standing" of a person. This protocol list was revised by the protocol department of the Prime Minister's office
before every celebration or important event. To be included on

---

* One of the authors of this book, Tamas Aczel, was awarded the
Kossuth Prize at the age of twenty-eight; the other, Tibor Meray, at the
age of twenty-nine. At the age of twenty-six, Tamas Aczel was chief editor of the Party's publishing house, "Szikra"; at the age of thirty-one,
he and an even younger writer, Sandor Nagy, were the first in Hungary
to be awarded the Stalin Prize. Tibor Meray was, at the age of twenty-
three, editor of the cultural column of the Party's daily, *Szabad Nep,* and
first editor of the Party's literary monthly, *Csillag*. At the age of twenty-
nine, he became Party Secretary of the Hungarian Writers' Association.
—ED.

it was a great honor. To be omitted from it was a very bad sign. However, not only one's presence on the list was significant, but also one's place. Whether one was invited to the first, second, or third section of the opera house at gala performances was of extreme importance. So was one's position on Section A, B, or C at the May Day demonstration. The interested parties were always carefully watching for changes. We do not pretend that these signs were absolutely reliable. Sometimes even the protocol department was not fully informed. But, at any rate, the list was highly significant and offered ample food for thought.

When his name was on the protocol list, a writer sometimes (on November 7 and April 4, the anniversaries of the Russian Revolution and of the liberation of Hungary, for example) even sat in the official box of the opera house with Matyas Rakosi, with the Soviet minister, and with other ministers and generals, and one ate and drank with them in the well-stocked dining room behind the scenes. He began to feel and think that he was one of the leaders—that he was one of those who directed the life of the country and of its people.

Then, in order to rid him of the last of petty-bourgeois remnants, and in order to turn him into a solid, unwavering, fully armed Bolshevik, the young writer was awarded the supreme honor which, though perhaps not for the public-at-large, was, in inner circles, equivalent to the Kossuth Prize: he was sent to the Party school.

On Karolina Avenue, on the right bank of the Danube, stood a large, modern stone building with a huge yard. The construction of this building had been begun under the Horthy regime, when it was intended as a pilot school. The building was given the last touches after the war, provided with a somewhat more primitive annex and, instead of a pilot school, it became the central Party school of the Communist Party. A member of the secret police stood guard at the entrance, but this was not what made admission to the school so difficult. Prospective candidates had to undergo a very severe political screening. To be accepted was equivalent to promotion. The section head of a ministry, after being sent here, left as a department head; the captain left as a colonel, the journalist as a columnist. The length of the course was carefully inscribed in the "cadre file." It might be a course of five months, or of one year, or of two years. Not even three university degrees were worth as much as a six-week "cram course" at the Party school.

Of all the Party schools, this one on Karolina Avenue was the most important. Characteristic of its importance was the fact that the director had to be a Muscovite. At first, the director was Laszlo Rudas, a Marxist philosopher. Later, Erzsebet Andics, a historian, became director of the school, and finally one of Matyas Rakosi's brothers, the pompous and stupid Zoltan Biro, took over. The instructors were not so "high-born." These were usually young Party workers—pedagogues who had only recently graduated and did not know much more than their pupils. But they took their jobs very seriously and maintained exemplary discipline.

The maintenance of such discipline was not always easy, since many of the "students" stood on a much higher step of the social ladder (i.e., the Party hierarchy) than did their instructors. Before classes began on Monday morning, more than one ministerial ZIM or Pobeda stopped before the entrance while the "comrade instructor" came on foot from the station of the No. 61 streetcar. The "student" knew that the minute he stepped out of the building (not to speak of the day when he would finish his course), he was more important than his instructor. The instructor could then thank his stars if his student as much as greeted him. However, within the gates of the school, they were respectful and polite. They owed such behavior, not to their instructors, but to the Party.

The students came from every corner of the country. There were Party secretaries of the various Budapest iron works, the commander of the southern frontier guards, agitation-propaganda personnel from the mining district, the working-class director of a textile factory, the chairman of the best village co-operative, a university lecturer, the headmaster of a country school, the head of a village council, and workaday members of the Party machinery. The writer who was sent here should have known, even if he had not been told in the festive speech delivered at the reception, that he was surrounded by the "elite" of the country, the best sons and daughters of the people. His main problem was not to become conspicuous by his silly, in-dividualistic artist's manners; it was to become one with them, or, as the Party jargon would have it, "to fit into the collective."

This was not as simple as he thought. Perhaps the actual studying was easiest. The main textbook was *The Short History of the Communist Party of the Soviet Union.* This three-hun-dred-page volume had to be learned almost by heart. You could wake any member of the student body from his deepest slumber and he could have told you when and where the Third Congress of the Party was held, what mistaken ideological tenets Plek-hanov had taught, etc. The other most important subjects were Marxist economy, the history of the Hungarian Communist Party,* and international problems and the People's Democ-racies. The tempo was quite exacting: lectures, seminars, read-ing, essay writing, study groups, examinations. The compulsory reading consisted of a little Marx, almost no Engels, much Lenin, and even more Stalin. Although, according to the rules, lights had to be out at 10 p.m., those from the factories and the coun-tryside often crammed all night in order to be able to digest the difficult and clumsily written material. It was usual for Party school students to "volunteer" some extra-curricular work, such as reading and making notes on Comrade Stalin's biog-

* The history of the Hungarian Party was taught without textbooks or notes. A textbook had been in the works for ten years, but it has still not been published because of the constant reevaluation of the past. In the first draft, for example, Rajk was one of the leaders of the illegal Party; in the second, he was a Titoist agent; in the third, after his re-habilitation, he was a martyr. The situation was similar in Bela Kun's case.

raphy,* in honor of a Party Congress or of some other festive
occasion.

Studying was not particularly difficult for the writer. After
all, writers are "men of letters." They made the required notes,
read not only the compulsory but also the "suggested" literature,
then helped the other somewhat slower workers and peasants
to understand and digest the "classics." The writers participated
enthusiastically in the discussions—for there were also discussions at the Party school at which the instructors encouraged the
students to speak up boldly and freely. Sometimes, when a problem was particularly interesting, the argument went on for weeks.
Thus, entire days and nights were spent in arguments to deter-
mine whether the Hungarian councils were equivalent to the
Russian soviets,† whether there had been an NEP era in the
People's Democracies,‡ or at what moment a People's Democracy became a dictatorship of the proletariat.§

---

* This is the biography which was torn to pieces by Khrushchev at the
Twentieth Party Congress when it was revealed that Stalin himself had
written into the text the lines dealing with "the brilliant Comrade Stalin's
unprecedented modesty."

† The Hungarian councils were organized in 1950. They followed the
Soviet pattern in that they were organized in the same manner. But, in
the Soviet Union, the councils had grown up spontaneously in the course
of the Revolution and, in Hungary they were imposed from above at the
order of the Party. Thus, they differed from the Russian soviets and were
much inferior to them.

‡ In the Soviet Union, the NEP (New Economic Policy), granting
compulsory concessions to the capitalists after the severity of war-time
Communism, had been introduced by Lenin in 1921. In the People's
Democracies, there had been no war-time Communism, and thus the
period leading to the nationalizations (1948) cannot be considered as
"a backward step" like the NEP. Yet, at the same time, the capitalist
elements were allowed greater freedom of action, and, in this way, this
period resembled the NEP.

§ After 1948, when the Communist Party had at last achieved full
power, an argument arose among the leaders of the Party as to whether
a People's Democracy was, or was not, a dictatorship of the proletariat.
The Pole Bierut said it was, but Rakosi and Revai argued that it was
not, because, according to Stalin, councils are a *sine qua non* of the
dictatorship of the proletariat. The dispute was solved by Stalin himself,
in that he decreed his own *sine qua non* and declared that "the People's
Democracy [was] a dictatorship of the proletariat without the Soviet
form."

After the Cominform resolution on Tito, one of the most passionately disputed questions was whether it was socialism or
fascism which had been created in Yugoslavia between 1945
and 1948. The school divided into two camps. One camp
argued that, though it is true that Tito, Kardelj, Djilas, Ranko-
vicz, and the others had been imperialist agents and thus had,
subjectively, promoted fascism, the majority of the Yugoslav
Party consisted of honest Communists; besides, there had been
the Soviet advisors. Thus, looking at it objectively, it was socialism that they had been building. This was all very well, the
other camp argued, but how could you build socialism even for
an hour when the Party was led by bloodstained dictators, by
people who, having been already in the service of the German
Gestapo during the guerilla fights, were simply imperialist agents?
Both sides referred to written proof. One waved the resolutions
of the Cominform, which said, in brief, that the Yugoslav
leaders had since 1947-1948 abandoned the road to socialism,
and thus, if they had abandoned it, here was proof that, for
a time, they had been following it. The other camp presented all
sorts of Soviet leaflets and *Pravda* articles which reported in detail the close contact that had, for a long time, existed between
Tito and Churchill, and between Tito and Hitler. The argument
was never really settled (even the instructors failed to see eye to
eye), and it was resumed every year.

Thus, discussions were free, though naturally within certain
limits. It was never disputed that Tito was an imperialist agent,
the question being only: "Since when?" * The instructors constantly encouraged the students in this manner: "Speak up,
comrades! Tell us frankly if you have problems, if there is something you don't understand, or if there is something you don't
agree with!" Questions or disagreements never got anyone into
trouble. Yet, it was better to raise one's problems carefully and
cleverly, for the instructor usually wrote down the question.

---

* In Trotsky's case, even this question was ruled out. *The History of the
Bolshevik Party* had set down the date in black and white: Trotsky had
been an imperialist agent by 1917.

Then, at the instructors' conferences, they discussed the problems raised by the comrades. If somebody had too many questions to ask and the questions all tended in one definite direction, he was judged to be a comrade who had "too many conflicts," or who was still burdened by "bourgeois influences," or who was "a little difficult." He was not punished for this failing. Nor was he removed from the school. On the contrary, more attention was paid to him than before. The Party school served not only to indoctrinate the students but also to help the Party know them better.

One of the writers of this book, being often "a little difficult," was asked into the room of the headmaster. The two had a long, friendly conversation. The headmaster praised him for the good work he was doing, and for helping the others with their work. The headmaster emphasized what a great thing it was, what proof of confidence, that the Party had sent him to the central school. Then he came down to brass tacks: "It would be wrong to attach too much importance to the question," said the headmaster. "Nevertheless, I should like you to realize that there are still a few petty-bourgeois remnants you will have to overcome in yourself. The Party values your talent, but you yourself know that talent in itself is not enough: your gifts can fully unfold only if you stand firmly on the foundation of Marxism-Leninism. . . . You remember the discussion we had on the employment of bourgeois experts. . . ? You mentioned the case of an engineer who, without cause and on the basis of false accusations, was dismissed from his job at the plant. . . . We are not saying that this couldn't have happened. We don't doubt your word. But, just think. Is it mere chance that you referred to this particular example? We don't want to offend you or suspect you. On the contrary, we want to help you here. Therefore, I think you should look into yourself and discover the roots of the impulse that made you bring up this example. You understand. The Party is great and strong. You are the problem here. It is you we want to help. . . ."

"Look into yourself" . . . "discover the roots" . . . "kill the

petty-bourgeois remnants in yourself. . . ." How often the writer
had to listen to these warnings during his period at the school!
Then the headmaster presented the question to the study group,
and the fellow students—to help him, naturally—"evaluated"
his entire attitude. For hours they discussed him, pulled him
to pieces, argued about him, and, in the end, it invariably turned
out that, "although he is a good guy, a decent comrade, he
couldn't *quite* fit into the collective." The working-class woman
whom, for long months, *he* had helped with her work, said that
he had helped her too much, thus preventing her from working
independently. The reason for it—she said—was quite obvious:
he undervalued the capabilities of the working class. The army
officer declared that, whenever the school marched together in
demonstrations, he had noticed that the writer never sang with
the others. This, beyond a doubt, was caused by some petty-
bourgeois bashfulness. They said that he often liked to be alone,
that he retired into himself, that he dreamed—as if he underestimated the others, as if he overestimated himself. The writer
felt that there was some truth in what they were saying: he still
hadn't developed enough; he still could not blend with the community. On some points, he tried to argue, but at the same time
he made promises to change his attitude, to overcome his shortcomings.*

When the young writer graduated from Party school, he
knew all of Lenin's and Stalin's most important teachings by
heart—and even most of the less important ones. In any situation that might arise, he knew the correct Bolshevik answer
—an answer that would hit the jackpot every time. At the same
time he knew—but it was only he who knew—that he was still
full of petty-bourgeois remnants, that he was still very far from
being a real Bolshevik. Six months or a year before he entered
the school, one pervasive feeling had dominated his entire being:

---

* Naturally, such "individual evaluations" were not restricted to writers.
Every student of the Party school had his turn. Some of them were so
badly "manhandled" by their fellow students that they walked around
in a daze for weeks. There were innumerable such cases of mild nervous
breakdowns.

that he was a good Communist, a Communist from top to toe, but that his ideological knowledge was rather poor. Now, on leaving the school, he felt that, though he had learned a great deal, he needed his Party more than ever if he were to become a truly strong and reliable militant Communist.

He set out toward his home along Karolina Avenue, his mind turbulent with contradictory ideas. Observing the passers-by he felt that he knew everything and was much superior to them. But, comparing himself to the wisdom and perfection of his Party, he had to admit that he knew nothing, that he was worth next to nothing.

BOOK I

DIRECTED INSPIRATION

An Aristocratic Communist

Gyorgy Lukacs always had a cigar in his mouth. Whenever he entered the door of Party headquarters, the Academy of Sciences, the University, or the Writers' Association, the inevitable cigar was always there, clamped between his lips. Smiling, he hurried with his short, rapid steps up to everybody he knew, shook hands, then sat down on a chair (usually placed as far as possible from the table) and continued, mostly unsuccessfully, to smoke his cigar. The cigar wouldn't draw. Its glowing end opened up like a rose, and a long tobacco stalk appeared in the middle. Lukacs shook his head, made another attempt or two, then threw the half-smoked butt into the nearest ashtray and took another cigar from his case. He lit it carefully and with great devotion, in that quaint mixture of science and enjoyment that was so characteristic of all his actions. The first puff was still his, his very own. He was fully occupied with it. He was excited and concentrated, perhaps also a little hopeful, as if he expected this cigar to be superior to the other one lying before him which was still smoky and smelly in the cheap synthetic ashtray. However, the cigar proved not one iota better than its predecessor. Disillusioned, he raised his head, and his attention, his active brain, were captured by the work of the meeting.

He was a shortish man, wrinkled and restless of face. He was over sixty, but his eyes frequently sparkled with childish pleasure and excitement—usually when he was explaining something. He loved to explain. The listener often felt that this strange, kind, and polite man considered the aim and purpose of his life to be the explanation itself, not the problems he was struggling so hard to explain. He spoke slowly, quietly, and articulately, the rhythm of his speech accentuating the rhythm of his thoughts. Sometimes he half closed his eyes, as if they were scanning vistas from that distant world which occupied his mind even at the moment when his lips were forming sentences about the most up-to-date problems. What he said was always interesting, informative, and methodical. Sometimes, when he felt he wasn't expressing himself with sufficient clarity, he interrupted himself with a fleeting, almost apologetic smile, then began his explanation from the beginning, bearing in mind the particular listener. He was fully aware of the range of his erudition, and he knew that the academic knowledge of his audience was almost always inferior to his own. He did not care, but neither did it make him vain. He was, on the contrary, tolerant and forgiving.

His knowledge was indeed staggering. The maturity attained during six decades of work and experience, the ceaseless activity of a sponge-like, eternally young brain sparkled in his searching eyes, which turned dull and anxious only when his passionate explanations fell on deaf ears. But even at such times he never became impatient, and his humor never left him, and his love of telling anecdotes helped him to overcome the unsatisfactory interruption of his trend of thought.

Gyorgy Lukacs' past was one of the most mobile Communist pasts in Hungary, yet he owed his prestige not to his past but to his treasure store of knowledge. In this, he differed from most other Communist leaders, and he differed also in never wanting to impose his opinions on those unwilling to accept them. He relied not only on his precise knowledge of facts but also on his judgment, although very often he was wrong. Yet, even in his mistakes, he remained self-confident, the discipline acquired in the difficult years spent in Moscow making him strong, almost superior. He was seldom angry, but, when he was, he was very angry and could, therefore, easily forgive. It was characteristic of his human patience that his calm never left him, not even when he was personally attacked. Amidst the storms raging around him, he could always work, think, teach, and create. He refused to squander his still-remaining strength and time on unimportant matters. His unbelievable capacity for work, his great mental activity remained unchanged in old age, spurring him on to ever new intellectual undertakings. He put up with everything so as to be able to work. He represented, lectured, wrote articles, and travelled a great deal as a member of the World Peace Council. He argued and debated, his head trembling a little, and the inevitable cigar was always in his mouth.

His *savoir faire* never deserted him.

Gyorgy Lukacs came from a well-to-do family and his aesthetic writing drew attention to him during the first decade of the century. His work grew from the positivist branch of the German history of ideas: he was among the first in Hungary to study and interpret Hegel. This, his first approach to dialectics, coupled later with materialism, turned him into the best-known Marxist aesthete and philosopher of his age. He soon disowned his early works: * together with a considerable number of Hungarian intellectuals, he became a left-winger and, in 1919, at the time of the Hungarian Soviet Republic at the end of World War I, he worked as Commissar for Culture. After the fall of the "Commune," he emigrated to Vienna, to Berlin, and, subsequently, to the Soviet Union. After World War II, he returned to Hungary as the exponent—in fact, almost the Pope —of Communist literary policies.

In many respects, his fame walked before him.

Rumor had it that this short, ugly, pock-marked, big-eared

---

* At the beginning of the century, when he was not yet thirty, he published his first large-scale essay on modern playwriting. This book alone brought him immediate fame among academicians. However, after 1945, he would not permit its republication in Hungary, saying that it was "a youthful, idealistic mistake," though many still consider it his best writing.

old gentleman was one of the few Communists who knew something about literature, and who studied and loved it, and his opinions were well worth listening to even by those who in other respects did not see eye to eye with him. Lukacs was an exponent of the policy of national democratic cooperation at the time when this was the Communist Party's tactical line. This premise determined his entire attitude: wise and calm, with serene devotion and with the patience of a medicine man in possession of magic potions, he explained to those young Hungarian writers who were deeply interested in all new ideas what Marxism and Marxist aesthetics meant, and he explained the Marxist interpretations of the relationship between poetry and politics. His lectures, articles, and writings were full of new expressions and new points of view which met either with approval or protest but which, at any rate, created a storm or at least inspired new ideas. He was immediately accepted as a leading authority. His books were published in quick succession, and it became apparent to all that he was a man of broad outlook and of unlimited scientific curiosity. His studies on Nietzsche, on Goethe, on Thomas Mann, on modern French philosophy and on the Russian classics (Chekhov and Gorki and Tolstoi) were highly interesting and significant. It was from him that many heard for the first time of Existentialism—and of Sartre—long before they ever read anything by this much-quoted (and later much-abused) author. Lukacs demonstrated the fundamentally false theoretical link between Nietzsche and fascism. He tore his former "pet," the German history of ideas, to shreds, and, with deep reverence, he analyzed the idealism of Hegel's dialectics as opposed to the materialism of Lenin's. In the course of three decades, Marxism became under his guidance a philosophical system rather than a newly-embraced religion.

With the pressing day-to-day problems between 1945 and 1948 in Hungary, the Communist Party had no time for methodical activity in the field of culture. It was too busy seizing power to bother about hacking an orderly path in the postwar jungle of thoughts and ideas. As a result, one can say with but little exaggeration that while the Communist Party, working with its organized discipline, its ruthlessness, and its purposeful action in the political and economic field, came closer to absolute power day by day, the cultural field was dominated by Gyorgy Lukacs with his clever explanations, his endless lectures, his gentle patience, his professorial detachment, and his cigar. The situation seemed almost ideal: the dynamic, militant young Party, active in the political field, and the wise old academician, in the cultural field, perfectly supplemented each other. In addition, Lukacs was never mixed up with the frequently soiled methods of everyday politics, so that he was more or less a symbol of the difference between exalted Marxist thought and down-to-earth Party politics. The reason why it never occurred to anyone that he might be acting a part, or that his attitude as a man and as a cultural politician was dictated to him by the Party, was that he was not acting. He was the man he appeared to be, and he felt happy—particularly, in thinking back on his Moscow emigration, he felt happy—in this freer, more pulsating, fluctuating, and somewhat chaotic atmosphere.

His thirty years' work in the ranks of the Party and his extended visit to the Soviet Union had taught him to appreciate thoroughly the degree of freedom still permissible in Hungary during those first years after the war. More than once, the returned Muscovites warned their young and inexperienced Communist friends to distrust Lukacs because Lukacs was not a real Marxist. There was a good deal of jealousy of Lukacs' international prestige in these warnings, and there was hatred because, with the exception of Gyula Hay, Lukacs despised his fellow emigrants, refusing to consider them as writers or even to meet them socially. There was a degree of truth in those warnings: after all, Lukacs was indeed no Marxist in the dogma-quoting and quotation-citing sense of the word; he was a creative Marxist, perhaps the last of the species, who had assimilated a good deal of the system's rigidity but had sunk to the belief that rigidity in itself was the system's greatest virtue.

The fellow emigrants were not mouthing mere generalities

when they spoke of Lukacs, for they knew a number of concrete
facts. In the course of the last fifteen or twenty years, there had
almost always been "trouble" brewing around him. He was repeatedly criticized by the Soviet "comrades," who pointed out
idealistic Hegelian remnants in his various works and, what is
even worse, his attitude as a Communist was not always unequivocal and correct. No one questioned his loyalty to the
Party. No such accusation was ever made against him. But his
confused and mistaken political ideas, which also manifested
themselves in his literary opinions, were suspect. Among the
many instances, there was one which had become rather widely
known among Communist writers in Hungary. It is no longer
interesting as a problem, but it forms part of the Party's history.
We are speaking about the so-called Blum thesis. Blum was
Lukacs' pseudonym during one period of the illegality. Back
in 1928, at the Congress of the Hungarian Communist Party,
Gyorgy Lukacs, then working underground, submitted a draft
of proposals in which he expressed the opinion that the tasks to
be fulfilled in Hungary were not those of the dictatorship of
the proletariat, but those of a democratic transformation which
should be accomplished by a democratic dictatorship of the
working class and the peasantry. His arguments were immediately torn to shreds by the sectarian Bela Kun group which was
then leading the Party and, since they did not demand an immediate dictatorship of the proletariat, the proposals were
branded as rightist deviationism. Gyorgy Lukacs, being defeated,
confessed his error. True, it was later "discovered" that Bela
Kun was an "enemy agent" and a "Trotskyite hireling," but this,
in itself, was not enough to rehabilitate the Blum thesis. The
shadow of rightist deviationism had fallen on Gyorgy Lukacs,
never, so long as he lived, to leave him again.

Lukacs' first self-criticism was followed by countless other self-
criticisms on his part, political, literary, and philosophical. There
was always something wrong with him, and self-criticism is the
lowest price to pay if one wants to avoid the consequences of
being wrong. How else could he have survived the years of the

great trials and of the "purifications"? Having been imprisoned for two or three months, as Lukacs was, is equivalent to having never been in prison at all. At the same time, however, these long, long years could not fail to leave their imprint on Lukacs' character. By the time he grew old, he had learned that tactics were all-important, that one had to keep smiling, that one had to ignore the things one did not like, and that one had to close one's eyes to horror and compromise, both in small and large matters, particularly if one wanted to survive and, more important still, to go on working. With his name and prestige, and with his presence and his attitude at international congresses, he not only spread the ideas in which he had faith, but he also covered up dreadful crimes about which he, if anyone, knew the truth. He kept silent about lies, though he knew they were lies, and he repeated slogans although he knew they were mere slogans. Unfortunately, "diplomacy" had become second nature to him, and he was patient not only with his debating partners but also with the injustices which were later committed not by himself but by his brothers in conviction—and which were committed against these same debating partners. There was a good deal of selfishness mingled in his concern for the community. It was the selfishness of experience, of disillusionment, and of old age, and this may be why (although he was greatly respected for his knowledge and admired for his "errors," the latter of which had indeed been castigated by the Party), he never became an integral part of the community from which, thirty years earlier, fate and his conviction had torn him.

Lukacs' "diplomacy" may also have been due to the fact that he wrote considerably better in German than in Hungarian. Even when speaking Hungarian, he conceived his sentences in German, and he could never rid himself of the Hegelian, highly involved style of the German history of ideas and philosophy. Yet, instead of being a disadvantage, this "strange" and involved way of thinking may even have added to his prestige; for, those who could not understand him did not dare to say so, and this snobbishness helped Lukacs greatly, though it was far from being at the root of his fame. This son of a rich family who had turned Communist, this expert on Western knowledge who had returned from Moscow, this Hungarian embedded in German culture lived in Budapest like a distinguished guest, an omnipotent intellectual aristocrat. He was, indeed, an aristocrat: he was selective and fastidious, and, though he was modest of manner, he was haughtily discerning in his taste. At the peak of his power, he proclaimed "great realism"—and not the official "socialist realism," about which he remained obstinately silent— as the leading literary trend. In his lectures at the political academies, and in his articles, he spoke of the German, the Spanish, the Russian, the French, and the English realists; he analyzed Dickens, Turgenev, Balzac, or Cervantes; he had a rather low opinion of Zola, and he never even mentioned the name of a mediocre writer. His comments on the new Hungarian Young Communist literature, which was just beginning to evolve, were not particularly complimentary. Mostly he ignored it, knowing that, from his own point of view, this was the best thing to do. But when he was called upon to express an opinion on some particular work, he was severe and straightforward.*

He called twenty-year-olds by their Christian names and liked them to call him "Uncle Gyuri" after a few meetings. He en-

---

* I can still remember the review published in Lukacs' popular-front literary magazine on my first book, which was entitled *In the Shadow of Liberty*. The book, which later won the Stalin Prize, was one of the first— if not the first—novel to portray the events of the first postwar years from the socialist-Communist point of view. In 1948, according to the Party, this was an act of revolutionary courage, and the book was very well received by the press. It was interesting that a Communist-directed literary magazine should attack and tear to pieces this not very pretentious and not very artistic novel. The review was naturally right on most points. The weaknesses of the book far surpassed its virtues—if indeed, apart from its readability, the novel had any virtues. The review raised quite a storm in Party circles. *Szabad Nep* attacked the review and defended the book. At a meeting of the "inner circle," Lukacs was hauled over the coals for the review. After listening to the argument, he made no reply. He had absent-mindedly made yet another mistake by judging the book according to its real—and not tactical—value. At that time, I saw in this Party attitude a defense of the new literature, and I was proud of it. To me, Lukacs' aristocratic attitude represented his rejection of Socialist literature.—T.A.

gaged in passionate arguments with thirty-year-olds against *l'art pour l'art* in literature, but he would never let fall a word of praise for a well-rhyming poem (which the young poets were just beginning to turn out by the dozens) written to the Party or about the Three-Year Plan. Paradoxically, he promised and demanded greater freedom and less recognition. although at that time these two goals seemed contradictory to each other.

Literary public opinion had it, although nobody knew where the rumor had originated, that Lukacs had been the original of Thomas Mann's Jesuit Jew, Naphta, in *The Magic Mountain*. Lukacs himself always denied this rumor, when the matter was brought up, and he protested that, when the book was written, he had not even met the great German writer with whom he had later had a long correspondence. But the legend persisted, and, since the not-too-complimentary elements of the comparison were forgotten, Uncle Gyuri remained a living Thomas Mann hero worthy of admiration in the eyes of all. The perfection of his thoughts outshone the imperfections of his face. The young writers forgave him his severity because of his delightful manners, and, since he never used it as a weapon, his power was never envied. The great theses and the endless sentences, the political slogans and Germanisms were dotted, as if by mischievous sprites, with new and plastic images, and, somehow, it was always these that remained imprinted in the consciousness of his enthralled public of writers and artists.

One of Lukacs' most original images—or, in this case, one of his most original ideas, was the so-called "partisan theory." The theory deals with the relationship between a poet and the Party. To Lukacs, it was natural and even self-evident that a poet, if he is a member of the Party, must not only accept and identify himself with the Party's world outlook and its tactics, but that he must also, in his own field, support these. In this respect, according to the teachings of Marx and of Engels, partisanship was an example to be followed by the poet. This partisanship, however—said Lukacs—was manifold and involved, being realized by the poet according to his temperament, and his background and his poetic nature, as well as by the strength of his impulses and the broadness or narrowness of his intellectual interests. The poet will accept or reject Party tactics (according to his own judgment), and, therefore, he is not a uniformed member of the regular army but a less disciplined fighter for the same aims. He is a militant fighting in his own particular way: i.e., a partisan. A poet is a poet. His weapons are different, and so is his attitude to reality. Therefore, he will necessarily serve the same aim *differently.*

Another problem that interested Lukacs was based on a short observation by Engels. This was the problem of the so-called "victory of realism." Here again, it was the question of the faithful, adequate portrayal of reality that occupied his mind. Here Lukacs, as the propagator and partisan of realism, tried to prove in his theory that there can be a contradiction between an author's outlook and the work which he produces—and to the latter's advantage. A really great writer (just because he is a really great writer and portrays reality) can be as reactionary as he pleases. The work will transcend the political barriers. The real artist's incapacity for falsehood will triumph over political prejudices. According to him, even a reactionary author can create objectively progressive works. Lukacs' classic example was Balzac. Balzac, Lukacs said, was subjectively a reactionary person. He was, in fact, politically a royalist; and yet the whole of his work is not reactionary but, on the contrary, progressive because, in analyzing and portraying the first half of the nineteenth century, he observed and described the victory of the advancing bourgeois forces over feudalism and the decline and fall of the feudal aristocracy. His heart was with the aristocracy, but his love of truth and his artistic conscience impelled him to write the truth. That is how, in spite of his political backwardness, Balzac wrote in support of progress.

Such a theory was, naturally enough, dangerous. It gave rise to the idea that someone might nowadays be a non-Communist or even an anti-Communist and yet be a progressive artist. Lukacs was compelled to add hurriedly the very unsatisfactory explanation that, since everything had been illuminated by the shining light of Marxism-Leninism, this was no longer possible. But even so, the first half of the theory was much more convincing than the obviously obligatory and much more shoddy second half.

To complete the picture, it may be worthwhile to mention another "Lukacsism" that has become famous: his image about the little rabbit and the elephant. The simile sounded almost like a fable, but, in spite of its innocent animal heroes, it was one of the boldest. If the little rabbit climbed the Himalayas and, from the highest peak, looked down at the world lying at his feet, he would still not be larger than the elephant standing at the foot of the mountain. The lesson to be drawn from this simile lay in the fact that if a poet was a bad poet, or even only a mediocre poet, he would never, though he was a convinced socialist, be greater than a great poet of bourgeois outlook. The rabbit remains a rabbit and the elephant an elephant, said Lukacs and thus he ranged himself clearly and unequivocally on the side of talent and great literature against the abundant Communist, but third-rate, literary crop. The simple little story which he told for the first time in a public lecture delivered at the political academy of the Party met, at first hearing, with approving laughter. Only later did his audience understand that what they had heard was not a facile joke but an act bordering on deviationism: they had heard an open condemnation of servile, utilitarian literature and aesthetics. Is it any wonder that the little old man with the lively mind and the gift of expression (and who was no empty-headed Party functionary, although one consents the epoch-making Party behind him) should have attracted the Hungarian intelligentsia, and particularly the writers and the artists? The older and more experienced of these were quick to discern how superior Lukacs was to the run-of-the-mill and the fearful ones among them; and so were the young ones, who feared his severity but who would like nothing better than to show him that they were not rabbits but, at least, baby elephants. If, today, one asks why so many writers embraced the

cause of Communism a decade ago, the reason lies, perhaps not
exclusively but certainly to a large extent, in the fact that the
Communist cause was expounded by the thin-fingered, wrinkled hands of a very intelligent, very erudite old man named
Gyorgy Lukacs.

Hegel and Self-Criticism

In the summer of 1949, the capital city of Hungary dressed itself in festive garb. It was a beautiful summer. It was hot and dry, but, though it was scorching, it was invigorating. It was the summer of youth. It was the summer of the young people who had assembled in Budapest to celebrate the Soviet-controlled Second World Youth Meeting, to have a good time, to make new friends, to laugh and dance, and to taste for a few days the delicious fruits of a foreign country.* Happy young men and women peopled the streets, exchanging greetings in Italian, French, English, German, Russian; and, where words failed, they used the international language of signs. Boys and girls, dressed in unknown national costumes, sang and danced on the stages of the various theaters, and the first performance of the Soviet Dance Ensemble at the Budapest opera house turned into a celebration lasting late into the morning hours. The young people exchanged ties, took snapshots of each other, and pledged never again to take up arms against each other. Notebooks were slowly filled with addresses ("Will you write?" "Of course,

---

* The First World Youth Meeting (the so-called "Festival") took place in Prague in 1947; the Second was held in Budapest in 1949; the Third in Berlin in 1951; the Fourth in Bucharest in 1953; the Fifth in Warsaw in 1955; the Sixth in Moscow in 1957; and the Seventh in Vienna in 1959.

I will"), and new love affairs flared high under the trees of City Park and of Margaret Island. The town lived and vibrated and was happy as it had never been since the war—and perhaps even before it.

This was the golden era. It was the epitome of the new system.

The shops abounded in goods. The bread shone white as snow. Red meat filled the windows of the butcher shops, and, on the market stands, the apples smiled, the pears, juicy in their golden-yellow skins, offered themselves, and multi-colored grapes stood in mountains. The war was far away. Peace was close by. There were almost no ruins left. The roofs of the new buildings sparkled in the sun. The standard of living rose steeply, and it seemed as though the road to socialism were running straight and sunny toward the not-so-distant pinnacles.

There were those who said that all this was but a "Potemkin prosperity" (i.e., an act put on for the foreign guests) and that it was better to see how things would work out after the meeting. But, since it was the summer when socialism had reached its highest peak of uninterrupted advance thus far, and since there was no sudden change in sight, such misgivings fell on deaf ears. Even those who had always mistrusted the regime were surprised and rather pleased.

By then, the Communist Party had achieved undivided power. That summer, it was this Party alone which ruled the political scene. The other parties had crumbled. Their leaders had left the country or were under arrest.

The happy crowds filling the streets of Budapest cared little about political party struggles. To them everything seemed perfect as it was. True, since not all the young people present were Communists, things did happen in this country that were not always attractive to visitors from the West. True, also, Ferenc Nagy, the lawfully-elected Smallholders Party's Prime Minister, had been forced into exile, and Cardinal Mindszenty had been in jail under life sentence for more than six months. And it was true also that, at the last elections, the voters could vote for only one ticket, and that the distribution of the mandates had been decided not by the voters but by the Communist Party. But these were rather obscure "internal affairs," and one could not interfere. Besides, all this was perhaps indispensable for creating such welfare and happiness in the country. Who could tell? The smiling faces and the overcrowded shops were arguments in favor of those who had now seized power and who were managing the country's affairs.

Yet, a large shadow that might well have blacked out the sunny ecstasy of the international meeting loomed over the country. Less than three months earlier, in the late hours of the night, on May 15, 1949, the wielders of power had arrested a man who was the Foreign Minister of the Republic and who was, in addition, a member of the Communist Party's Political Committee, one of the best-known leaders of the Hungarian Communist movement, a former political commissar of (and fighter with) the Hungarian Brigade in the Spanish Civil War. The man's name: Laszlo Rajk. Simultaneously, they had arrested innumerable well-known and lesser-known Communists. Rajk and his fellow prisoners were accused of participating in an imperialistic Titoist conspiracy against the leaders of the Hungarian Communist Party for the purpose of overthrowing the increasingly consolidated popular democratic order.

The Party press published long and edifying articles on the better-late-than-never unmasking of the Tito gang, denouncing the Yugoslav Party as a clique of international spies and adventurers with agents in all other Communist Parties. These articles explained that the class struggle had become more acute in the course of building up socialism and that the enemy had now transferred its central activity to the Party itself. The Party membership discussed the latest developments in meetings and in seminars, and every good Communist was deeply grateful to the Party Secretary, Matyas Rakosi, who complained at a mass meeting of the sleepless nights he had been forced to spend in order to perfect the plan for the liquidation of the Rajk gang. The loyal members of the Party increased their watchdog activities. They

locked their drawers at their offices and listened more attentively than before to every word said by their colleagues, vigilant against the enemy that had infiltrated the ranks of their
Party.

In the summer, however, the campaign became less intensive.
It was as if the Party had decided not to upset the happy celebration of youth by burdening them with the bitter and disappointing knowledge of Rajk's treachery.

The laughing young people dancing in the streets and singing
around campfires and swimming in the Danube knew nothing
of the one-time Communists, now traitors, waiting by the dozens
behind the bars of the Conti Street Prison and in the cellars of
No. 60 Stalin Avenue for their fates to be decided. The colorful
crowd walked in torchlight processions, singing songs of freedom
and victory to the catchy, if somewhat simple, music composed
by the Soviet composer Novikov. And the young Communist
writers, working in those weeks for the press, the radio, and the
periodicals, roamed the streets with shining eyes, their hearts
filled with a sense of triumph. The ecstasy of rapid and somewhat
unexpected success was present everywhere. A kind of dizzy
exaltation swelled the heart and numbed the brain.

But this numbness did not disturb them at the time.

They were busy with what they believed to be reality—the
colorful, exciting, invigorating, and manifold present. Poems
were written. So were short stories and articles glorifying the
successes of the People's Democracy, the friendship and cooperation between peoples, the triumph of peaceful, constructive work
—and cursing the enemy intent upon preventing all this.

In this atmosphere of good cheer, an article was published
in the periodical of opinion of the Party which contained a
passionate and unexpected attack upon Gyorgy Lukacs. The
article was signed by Laszlo Rudas, who was the founder of the
Party Academy, a well-known Communist of long standing, and
a Muscovite. At that time Rudas was one of the official "philosophers" of the Party, famous for his keen mind, his poisonous
tongue, his sarcastic comments, and his political rigidity. He was

not liked, nor was he held in particular esteem. His students were afraid of him because of his rudeness and because of the sadistic ruthlessness with which he pitched into those who, either out of ignorance or sincerity, brought up problems. They disliked him intensely, but they respected his mind and knowledge.

The article attacking Lukacs caused considerable excitement. Everybody watched anxiously for further developments, because the article hit hard. In tone, it was rude, supercilious, and unforgiving. It referred unmistakably to Lukacs' earlier errors—those errors repeatedly criticized by the Party and for which Lukacs had again and again repented in self-criticism (though always "formally" so). The article mentioned "ideological enemies," and "bourgeois tendencies" in Lukacs' works. Its openly sarcastic comments expelled the great rationalist from the realm of Marxism-Leninism. Though the article's claim to omniscience and infallibility caused great revulsion among the uninitiated, the unsuspecting believers, and the disciples of Lukacs (and almost all young people were disciples of Lukacs in those days), these at first thought that they were simply witnessing a personal controversy, or an outbreak of the latent hatred between the Muscovites, or a jealous attack on the part of a rival philosopher.

In the beginning, Lukacs stood up to the attacks.

The old and experienced professor who had graduated not only from the Comintern but also from the Lux Hotel school * sat watchfully but calmly among his innumerable books in his apartment on the shores of the Danube. He lit a new cigar, pushed his spectacles up his nose, and glanced at the manuscript lying before him. Then his eyes strayed to Mount Gellert oppo-

---

* The "Lux" was the international hotel where the leading Comintern officials lived after having returned to post-war Hungary. In their more relaxed moments, the emigrant wives paint a shocking picture of this hotbed of intrigues—of rivalries for power or love and of struggles for a higher place in the Party hierarchy. "Ulbricht," remarked one of the wives in speaking of the head of the East German Party. "And who is he, if I may ask? He lived on only the fifth floor of the Lux!" The altitude of his room betrayed a man's place in the hierarchy, and everyone watched the others' breakfast trays because those in favor were given eggs and bacon while those less favored received only a little bit of butter.

site and to the Statue of Liberty commemorating the liberation
—a winged angel holding up a palm leaf bent like an arc of
triumph and, at the angel's feet, a Soviet soldier holding a sub-
machine gun.

What were his thoughts?

Perhaps he remembered that this statue, the work of the old
and famous sculptor named Zsigmond Kisfaludy Strobl who
had served under every regime with the same enthusiasm, had
been made during the war as a tombstone for Miklos Horthy,
Jr., the then regent's son who, after a night of revelry, crashed
his plane on the Russian front and was burned to cinders. Strobl
had later sold the anti-Bolshevik hero's monument to the Communists, constructing an additional Soviet soldier on it so as to
keep up with changing times.

For a long time, Lukacs did not reply to the attacks.

Then he published an article in *Tarsadalmi Szemle,* in which,
diplomatically and cleverly, he refuted Rudas' accusations. The
article was couched in a tone that differed greatly from Rudas'
tone.

The outsiders believed that the argument would remain confined to the two philosophers. The more experienced, however,
were fearful. The whole situation looked rather bad for Lukacs.
In those days, Zhdanov had already expressed his decisive views
on the disputes among the film artists, the composers, and the
philosophers. These sharp and irrevocable judgments banished
any "kowtowing before Western culture" on the part of Soviet
intellectuals. They banished "cosmopolitanism" and modern
music and "naturalism." They pointed out mistaken symbolism,
and they unequivocally raised "socialist realism" to the throne,
for, so they decreed, socialist realist literature and art "educated
the people, portrayed reality in its evolution, emphasized the
future—and at the same time, directly served the interests of
the Party." All this was in sharp contradiction to practically
everything Lukacs stood for and taught. For the first time in
the life of the Party, it seemed as though it were possible to
talk of the same thing—of Marxism and Party leadership and
realism—and yet to interpret the words and the notions in two

different ways. The question was: Was Lukacs, or rather, was the Hungarian Workers' Party, in a position to give an interpretation to literary freedom and to the job of the writers that was different from the interpretation applied in Moscow? Did it make any difference that Lukacs was a figure of international fame? Had not Shostakovich and Prokofiev, whom Zhdanov so ruthlessly attacked, also been composers of international fame?

The World Youth Meeting came to an end, the celebration of the new, socialist Constitution was over, and life returned to its usual tempo. The flags disappeared from the buildings, the foreign delegations left, and, instead of carrying news of the day-by-day events of the World Youth Meeting, the newspapers carried long articles on the liquidation of the Rajk gang.

In early September, they published the text of the indictment and announced the date and place of the trial.

To stress the important role of the working class, the trial was not held in the court building but instead at the Magdolna Street headquarters of the Iron and Steel Workers' Union. Foreign correspondents arrived for the trial, and the Party distributed invitations among the workers of the industrial plants and throughout mass organizations. The radio broadcasted a running commentary on the trial, revealing unbelievable crimes.

Rajk admitted everything of which he was accused.

All the accused admitted everything.

The tens of thousands of Hungarian newspaper readers and radio listeners, to whom this sort of thing was, at the time, still entirely new, were horrified to learn from the fluently delivered self-accusations of these "dehumanized" Communists the details of the carefully planned conspiracy. The whole villainy unfolded before them, and it became clear to all how, with the help of Tito (that "leashdog of the imperialists") and the "advanced shock troops of international bourgeois reaction," Rajk had attempted to overthrow the People's Democracy and restore the hated bourgeois class rule.

Rajk and his fellow conspirators were condemned to death and executed.

It was at that time that *Szabad Nep* published the final blow dealt by the anti-Lukacs campaign. This final blow consisted of an article setting forth the Party's official opinion on Lukacs' work.

The article was written by a man who had hitherto participated only indirectly in cultural life because all his time was taken up with politics. Yet it was common knowledge that, although he kept in the background, he was the real ruler of Hungarian Communist cultural policy. This man, a member of the Political Committee, the editor-in-chief of *Szabad Nep,* an excellent publicist, historian, and literary historian whose books and essays on the various phases of Hungarian history were published and read in large editions, was a Communist leader whose opinions were considered authoritative and whose position in the Party leadership was undisputed.

His name was Jozsef Revai.

The writing in Revai's article was clear, energetic, and concise, as Revai's writing always was. Everyone knew—or at least everyone felt—that Revai's opinion represented the official opinion of the Party and thus ended all argument. The verdict had been pronounced, and it was up to Lukacs to admit his errors, to promise for the hundredth time in his life that he would correct them, and to wait.

And it was not small or unimportant errors that he was compelled to admit. With an incisive and yet stylish thrust, the Revai article inflicted severe wounds on the body of Lukacs' literary works. Recognizing Lukacs' virtues as a literary historian and praising him for the struggle he had carried on against modern decadents (and particularly against Sartre and the Existentialists), the article ran the point of its sword into the dominant problem of the day (dominant because of Zhdanov's denunciations): the problem of Lukacs' attitude to Soviet literature. Lukacs' work in Hungary was condemned as a whole. The basic error of his work as a historian of literature, said Revai, was his refusal to recognize the progress achieved by Soviet literature. Inherent in this error, so the article said, was an underestimation of Soviet literature, and such an error was closely related to—

and, in fact, it sprang from—Lukacs' fundamental errors. With the assurance of an inquisitor and the passion of a missionary, Revai, a past master in the creation of interdependences, listed Lukacs' errors in order to elaborate on a general theme. Lukacs' thesis on "great realism," behind which one could easily discern Hegelian remnants, presupposed that he esteemed old—or, as official Party slang has it, *critical* realism—over young Soviet literature. And this inflated evaluation of critical realism clearly underlined Lukacs' support of good bourgeois poetry over bad socialist poetry. Revai, however, argued that the premise was not so simple, since account must be taken of the fact that the class ideology of the bourgeoisie is essentially inferior to the class ideology of the working class. The man, who, like Lukacs, insisted on such parallels would, sooner or later, depart from the philosophical basis of the Marxist class struggle and, emphasizing the level of literature, would divert attention from the really important factor: content. Rabbit and elephant? This argument proved that Lukacs had forgotten the basic problem—the superiority of socialist ideology—and that he was thus facilitating the infiltration of a bourgeois (and therefore enemy) ideology into the young socialist literature. That is why Lukacs insisted on such high standards from young socialist literature—standards that, because of its youth, the literature was incapable of attaining. Instead of encouraging the young writers, he frightened them off, and, without encouragement or compassion, he trampled the first young shoots of the new literature underfoot.

It was impossible, added Revai, to maintain silence regarding Lukacs' ideas on the relationship between Party and poet. Said Revai: In referring to Engels, Lukacs considered tendentiousness to be the poet's principal task and from this concluded that the role of the poet is that of a partisan. It was obvious that, after Lenin's article in 1905 entitled "Party Organization and Party Literature," in which he wrote that the poet, if he wants to serve the cause of the class, must become "wheel and bolt" of Party work, Lukacs' ideas were subversive. Revai put class-angled literature in the place of tendentious literature, thus underlining what the Party demands from the writers: to be regular soldiers and not partisans, to reject Lukacs' liberalism, and to recognize the necessity to serve the day-by-day tactical requirements of the Party.

The roots of Lukacs' literary-aesthetic errors, as Revai clearly pointed out, were of a political character. They could all be traced back to the years following the liberation when Lukacs had elaborated a concept of the new democracy under construction which would differ from the Western bourgeois democracies because it would contain socialist features, but which would differ also from the Soviet system in that it would be a system permitting some bourgeois or even capitalist features. This was nothing but a vague and general democratic idea— a "middle-of-the-road" dream which by no means agreed with the aims of the Communist Party. To support his contentions, Revai quoted a number of paragraphs from Lukacs' earlier works, completely forgetting (and perhaps intentionally so) that quotations of a similar order could be collected from the speeches made by Rakosi and by Revai himself during the same years of 1945-1947. At that time, this was the official Party line, and Lukacs could be reproached only in that he really and truly wanted the Party to fulfill its promises, while the political leaders always considered such promises mere tactics.

If there had been room for argument, if Revai's article had not been an ideological judgment, Lukacs could easily have countered the Lukacs quotations by Revai quotations. But the time for arguments was over. The sun had set for the cigar-smoking old gentleman. The Party had pronounced its verdict, and, as Party member, Lukacs had but two courses to follow: either to oppose the Party and face all the consequences which that step involved, or to bend his head and exercise self-criticism. His three decades in the Party had rendered the old gentleman too experienced to choose the first course. He knew very well that the Lukacs debate was not merely a peaceful and comradely argument about the methods and development of literature, but the "ideological aspect" of the then current Rajk affair. He wanted to work. He still had much to say, if not for today, then for tomorrow. He was busy planning an important book—a book that probably would not be published by the Party publishers just yet but would remain in manuscript.

In his self-criticism Lukacs' judgment pronounced on his own earlier work was neither over-servile nor in bad taste, although, at the time, self-criticisms of such a distasteful type were already the order of the day. In cautious and involved sentences, he enumerated the obligatory points: he had failed to recognize the tempo and the direction of the progress of the Hungarian People's Democracy; he had failed to aid the unfolding of the new socialist literature; and, since he lacked the necessary erudition in this field, he had not paid Soviet literature the attention it deserved. He immediately set to work to make up for his shortcomings by writing two essays on two of the least offensive Soviet novels, Fadeyev's *Young Guard* and Kazakievich's *Spring on the Odera*. This accomplished, he considered the affair closed as far as he was concerned, and he retired from the difficult post of cultural leader to his quiet apartment on Belgrade Quay and to the cool lecture rooms of the University and the Academy. He felt, perhaps, even happy, for he preferred academic work to power, and, after all, the whole thing could have had a far worse ending. If his international fame could not save him from the verdict, it had, at least, saved him from its consequences.

As a matter of fact, Lukacs' self-criticism satisfied nobody. The "radicals" around Revai found it merely formal, lacking in depth and sincerity. They felt the old man was playing with them, that he was being diplomatic when his duty was to rend his clothes and, instead of excusing and explaining his mistakes, to recant and repent. Lukacs' most devoted disciples, his students, were, on the other hand, deeply disappointed that, instead of choosing death on the stake, their master had, like Galileo, chosen compromise. These young and enthusiastic future scientists, much more passionate but much less experienced than their aged master, had the temerity to ask him why he had agreed to exercise self-criticism.

"What do you mean?" Lukacs replied to their questions. "I did not exercise self-criticism on the most essential point!"

The students looked at him uncomprehendingly.

"What was the most essential point?" they asked him.

"Didn't you notice?" asked Lukacs, gravely. "In my article, I did not say a single word against Hegel. . . ."

A Communist Aristocrat

Jozsef Revai * always presided at the head of the table. From behind his flashing, gold-rimmed spectacles he watched the writers around him with a sharp, arresting gaze. Now and then he would run his fingers through his Prussian-style, short-cut hair, draw deeply on his strong cigarette (the doctors tried to make him reduce his daily cigarette quota because of his heart disease), then throw that cigarette away and light a new one.

The young writers observed him fearfully—and admiringly.

He had a restless face. His character was written in its lines. He was nervous, clever, witty, ironical, and stubborn. His features changed by the second, expressing indignation almost at the same time as serenity. Then, a moment later, they would combine contempt and malcontent.

He leaned back in his chair. He was bored. And he did not deign to conceal this offensive, shocking boredom. From time to time, he took off his spectacles to wipe them and, at such times, his face looked naked. His pupils contracted, his glance lost some of its sharpness, and he was more vulnerable, more human.

Then the gold-rimmed spectacles returned to their place, and the features resumed their original expression.

---

* Jozsef Revai was Minister of Culture from 1949 to 1953. He was replaced by Jozsef Darvas.

There was silence. An anxious, perhaps hopeful and curious silence. Everybody waited eagerly to hear Revai's opinion. Everybody was eager to learn from Revai his own opinion. And Revai made no secret of it. He didn't have to. He was opinion personified.

This "professional revolutionary," who had travelled through Europe and the Soviet Union, who knew the world and had a wide store of experience, was a man of fifty. He was the most erudite, the most complicated, and certainly the most interesting of the four-member clique of leaders who "owned" Hungary in those days. He was somebody. Both his disciples and his enemies often compared him—from different points of view, naturally—to the "foremost" master of postwar Soviet cultural policy, Andrej Alexandrovich Zhdanov, a pupil of Stalin's who had died an early death. The comparison was valid if one considered only their duties, but there was no resemblance whatsoever in their personalities or in their talents.

While Zhdanov was but an appointed Party official who was thereby an omnipotent cultural ruler, Revai was not only a scholar, but·a man who really loved and understood art and literature. The control of Hungarian culture was his, not only because he was entrusted with it but because he was born to it. In reality, he was a frustrated writer who, in his youth, had written poetry. He had once published a volume of verse, and one of the poems was for a long time frequently quoted in literary circles. The first line read: "Perish, father, perish, mother, perish, my first teacher!"

As with all "professional" revolutionaries, he had no life outside the political struggle. Party work, suffering, prison, exile —all these had filled his years. The study of literature and of history was only secondary. But this "secondary" work was much more valuable than was his primary work. Revai's articles and essays, and particularly those written during the war while he was in emigration or underground, belong to the treasures of the Hungarian history of literature and historical research, in spite of their Marxist-Leninist conception—or perhaps because of it.

His long essay on Kilcsey, one of the greatest Hungarian poets and thinkers of the nineteenth century, and his essay on Kossuth and on the 1848-1849 Hungarian Revolution, and his essay on Endre Ady, the foremost Hungarian poet of the twentieth century, are fine examples of analytical writing. Revai knew the craft of writing: his mind was active, his logic purposeful. The passion and purposefulness were due to the fact that these articles and essays were always written expressly for a political occasion and were always called upon to support some political action; but this did not detract from their value.

One of the greatest attractions of his talent—in contrast to Lukacs'—was its truly indigenous character. Revai's principal field of research was Hungarian literature and history, while Lukacs had studied German literature and history. Revai wrote outstandingly well in Hungarian; Lukacs' books had to be translated into the Hungarian by his students. Lukacs' greatest interest lay with Hegel; Revai's lay with Petofi and Ady. Lukacs was cold, objective, and circumspect; Revai was passionate and subjective.

The difference between them can best be judged by their theses. Lukacs preached "great realism," and he demanded from literature something noble, something beautiful: a perfection that took years or even a lifetime to attain or even approach. Revai assumed cultural leadership with a much simpler, much more militant thesis: "the cultural revolution." We have waged our struggle for power, ran his argument. Today, power is in the hands of the working class. The economy is ours. We have taken the land from its former owners, the banks from the bankers, and the factories from the industrialists. Now we must prepare for a new attack: we have to besiege the fortress of culture. In the past, science and art were reserved for the privileged few. In our time, we must make them available for the whole population. In the past, the gates of the colleges and universities were closed to the sons of the workers and peasants. Today, we must throw open these gates. In the past, only the well-to-do could afford tickets to the opera house and the theaters. Now we shall introduce the metal workers to Shakespeare, the textile workers to Verdi. Will you help us in this battle, comrades and writers?

There he stood on the platform of the Party Congress, a little pale, his thin body taut like a bow, his hands tearing nervously at the written text of his speech, his eyes blazing behind the gold-rimmed spectacles with a fanatical fire. His voice was a little rasping, but it had power. "The victory of socialism is impossible without the solution of the problems of the cultural revolution. What does cultural revolution mean? It means that we have to turn hundreds of thousands of unskilled workers into skilled workers. It means tens of thousands of new and highly qualified experts. It means that we must raise the general educational level of our working people, that we must broaden the cultural and political horizons of tens and hundreds of thousands of state and economic and Party officials. It means that we must harness every means at our disposal to the service of the socialist re-education of our people: the school, agitation-propaganda, art, film, literature—in fact, every form of the mass cultural movement. The cultural revolution is not mere schooling, or mere training, or mere political education. It is a composite of all these."

The young Communist writers were carried away by Revai's zeal. They felt they were being allowed to share in a task which was really epoch-making. The semi-feudal, backward, hitherto uneducated country of Hungary would soon be a cultured socialist country. And, though most of these writers came from a bourgeois background, they were warmed by the thought that they were called upon to break down the class barriers of a thousand years earlier. Passionately, with perspiring forehead, Revai enumerated the statistics of the cultural revolution: "In the school year of 1948-1949, only 1,118,000 children attended elementary and grammar school, but in 1950-1951, this figure had increased to 1,230,000. Two years ago, 71,000 children attended secondary school. Today, the number has risen to 95,000. At the universities and colleges, the number of students has increased from 23,000 to 33,000. The percentage of working-class children in the secondary school has increased from 17 to 41. And we are only at the very beginning. In 1948, we had 600 village libraries; in 1950, 1,600. But, by the end of the Five-Year Educational Plan in 1954, we shall have 4,000. As against seventy-four Homes of Culture in 1949, we now have 1,000. By 1954, there will be 2,500."

Cultural revolution! Perhaps we would never be great realists, but if we shirked this task, we would be heartless and soulless. And who knows? Perhaps in this way we shall create greater works than we could by applying Uncle Gyuri's outdated methods. This thin man with the face of a youngster (he never looked older than thirty or forty) was leading us on to exciting new vistas. Besides, his program was much more intelligible; his replies were much clearer, and his principles much less equivocal than were Lukacs'. He could do what he said. He had power. And, although he had power, he was much less squeamish, much less exclusive than the old gentleman.

The young people who harbored a justified feeling of guilt for having so quickly and easily abandoned Gyorgy Lukacs, held on to Revai's dynamism and principles as to a lifeboat. These justified their actions, their sudden infidelity. With these, they explained to themselves, it was not the road of lesser resistance or of rapid success or of greater opportunity they had chosen, but the principle of socialist realism, of the Party rather than of Lukacs. It was his principles which they loved, not Revai.

For there was, inded, nothing lovable in Revai. One could admire him, or honor his knowledge and authority, or accept his arguments. But one could not really like him. As a matter of fact, Revai had little use for such human sentiments as love. He was not given to liking people himself. He only used them. His erudition and artistic taste rendered his judgment infallible: he always knew what was good and what was bad, but this knowledge never influenced him, never kept him from praising, from supporting the less valuable experimental socialist realist works, for these works served the tactical aims of the Party and, thus, were useful. Nor did his erudition stop him from rejecting good writings which did not fulfill these criteria. He was not impressed by the zeal or excitement or the protests of loyalty on the part of the young writers: he considered them neophytes who, as he said, "had not as yet passed the test of brilliance." His good taste and inherent judgment attracted him to genuine literature. Whenever a new Thomas Mann volume was published in Switzerland, he immediately ordered it for himself through the Ministry of Foreign Affairs, and he read it in one night. But while he was Minister of Culture, not one single book by Thomas Mann was published in Hungary, and, in his speeches, he spoke of Babayevski and Azhayev as examples to be followed by the Hungarian writers.

He was fully aware of his power. He walked among the young writers, the journalists, the actors, and the Party functionaries as if he were a prince among his subjects; and all of them hung on his words. He did not talk to them, though he did sometimes condescend to address them. He never argued with them. It was he who made the law. He never asked leave to do so. Instead, he gave orders. He was, so to speak, "hovering above the water" with a disgusted grimace and an unconcealed disdain which expressed not only his superiority but also the absolute infallibility of his power. Everyone feared his displeasure. Because of his fits of fury and because of his impulsive, unpredictable moods, the writers called him the "crazy Count" among themselves.

His word was law. Woe to the writer about whom he let fall even one word of disparagement! It frequently happened that a thoughtless comment about a superficially read book or article or short story or scenario decided the success or failure of the work. Even if these comments were made in confidential, closed meetings, they trickled out through underground channels and were soon common knowledge. They were never disregarded. First, Revai's "opinion" was discussed only in the corridors of Party headquarters or of the Ministry of Culture. Then it passed on to the editorial offices of *Szabad Nep*. The editor considered the rumor a "directive," and when he went to see the film or read the book or article or short story, his opinion, whether he

liked it or not—in fact, whether he knew it or not—was precon-
ditioned: he saw not through his own eyes, but through Revai's.
After a while many of the authors no longer wrote what they
wanted. Instead, they wrote what they hoped would please
Revai. When Revai appeared at the first performance of a play,
the critics watched his expression, not the stage. More and more
of them began to compete in becoming the first to find out the
official attitude—i.e., the Party's, or rather Revai's, opinion.

Was Revai satisfied? Was he happy? His temperatment never
gave him peace, either in the physical or in the intellectual sense
of the word. To him, happiness was equivalent to complete victory over his opponents. Yet, he knew that his success was not
absolute. Although the young writers were prostrate before him,
the older generation fell silent and drew back; and there was a
stratum, or rather a group, that showed itself equal to him. This
impressed him. But it was also a source of constant irritation to
him.

Who were these writers or artists who showed themselves equal
to him? Mainly, they were those who had deep roots in the soil
and the people and the past of Hungary, and whose reputations
were firmly established long before Revai came to power. Poets
like Gyula Illyes, painters like Aurel Bernath, and composers
like Zoltan Kodaly remained untouched by the hubbub around
Revai and assumed the (to him) unbearable rank of equality.
He could never break nor defeat them. They resisted him. And
that impressed him.

He was very prone to the Muscovite's nostalgic longing to be
really Hungarian. True, his main concerns were Hungarian
literature and history, and, true, he was more deeply identified
with Hungarian tradition than was Lukacs. Yet he never felt
completely or sufficiently Hungarian. For Revai was a Jew who,
even in the guise of a proletarian revolutionary, could never cross
the borders of Hungarianism. He yearned nostalgically and ro-
mantically to be one of the people—someone whom the Hungarian people would accept as one of their own. Often he went
out of his way to use peasant expressions and country proverbs

in his speeches and in his conversation in order to prove how deep his Hungarian roots had become.

This yearning influenced not only his attitude toward politics, but also his attitude toward human beings. He felt absolutely self-confident when he was dealing with those who were non-entities before his arrival and who had become personalities only through him. But, in spite of his haughtiness, he lost his self-assurance when he was dealing with those who had been well-known before him and who would continue to be so even without, or even in spite of, him. Though he had won many a victory, he never triumphed in this battle: the "Hungarians" never accepted him as one of them. They feared him, esteemed him, and often admired his erudition. But this was not enough. Perhaps that is the reason why he never ceased to woo them, why he preferred their "sins" to the virtues of his disciples. While a Communist could never permit himself sharp or ironical or—heaven forbid!—openly contradictory remarks, Revai was almost happy when Illyes or Peter Veres crossed swords with him. Once, while he was still Minister of Culture, Revai called a meeting to discuss a scenario on which Illyes was then working. He sharply criticized the scenario, but Illyes disagreed. What is more, during the entire meeting, which lasted for about an hour and a half, Illyes addressed Revai as "Your Highness." "I see, Your Highness," he said. "Your Highness is right," "By your order, Your Highness!" Revai smiled. He did not protest.

Naturally, Revai never gave up his "right" to attack these writers, although everyone knew that they were the only ones he considered real writers. But his criticisms were, in spite of their frankness and "ideological consistency," the lamentations of a hopeless lover who repeats his protestations of love all the more furiously the more often he is rejected. How different this was from the tone he used toward his disciples, his admirers, or toward those who offered themselves to him or whom he had already conquered! These no longer interested him. He was interested only in the unattainable. He would not tolerate contradiction; yet he despised those who never contradicted him.

True, he needed only to make one of his ideas known, and the mass production of "artistic" treatments had begun.

In addition—and this is only natural—the disciples soon "went one better" than the prophet, not only fulfilling but over-fulfilling their tasks. And that was when the enchanting, magically misleading moment arrived—when Revai's sharp brain came near to genius, when at last he carried away even those whom hitherto he had been unable to win. In spite of his good taste and his erudition and his broad intellectual outlook, this man was the personification of sectarianism, of quasi-religious intolerance, and of haughty despotism. With one flick of the hand, he condemned dozens of writers to years of silence, forbade the publication of hundreds of books, withdrew hundreds of other books from circulation, and banned innumerable plays and films. He determined how many films, both historical and current, should be produced this year and the next year, or what poems should be left out of the poet's next volume. *He* decided whether the role of the Party secretary was positive, or whether the role of the kulak was negative enough, in a new play. Then, when everything was beginning to run smoothly, and when the authors and producers knew the routine by heart, and when the Party secretaries were as positive and the kulaks as negative as it was written that they should be in the Communist Bible— then suddenly he, Jozsef Revai, began to protest against exaggerations, against over-zealousness, against sectarian narrow-mindedness, and against schematism. The Communist dictator of the National Theater, Tamas Major, directed a performance of *Macbeth* in which the actors unmasked in that mass-murdering king none other than Marshal Tito. "How idiotic!" exclaimed Revai. "You want to turn Shakespeare into a class-conscious militant? Who ever heard of such a thing!" He went to a meeting of film directors and reprimanded them for having completely banned the kiss from Hungarian films of the last few years. "The class struggle does not mean," he said, "that we must be ceaselessly waging it from morning till night. Or, what is worse, from night till morning." He gave the teachers a piece of his mind because they mixed politics in with the curriculum too much, and because they talked politics during the mathematics and geography classes instead of teaching their pupils fundamental arithmetic and geography. He abused the Party propagandists and officials for speaking in a distorted and synthetic Party dialect—a bureaucratic jargon that is "without color or smell, is tortuous and lifeless and drives off the masses."

He was sharp and witty and ruthless and courageous and brilliant. For who else would have had the courage (or rather, who could thus have permitted himself) to discuss and deride all this so openly and mercilessly even after having noticed and condemned it? The "Party jargon," the "class struggle," the "political interpretation" were so many holy notions, so many taboos. Revai, however, knew no taboo. He dared to name the errors, the mistakes, and the absurdities even more forcibly if they manifested themselves within the Party or within the Party's life. To him, good intentions were no excuse. Nor was the little red membership card any protection. He was fearless, merciless, and just.

At the First Congress of the Hungarian Writers' Association, in the spring of 1951, Revai launched this slogan: "The foremost peril of our literary life, the greatest threat to progress today, is *schematism.*" What was this schematism? It was the uniformly grey and overly simplified portrayal of life, the dismal and mediocre, politically correct but artistically dreary, scribbling. Schematism gave to literature a certain official, government-issue character that was neither courageous nor sincere, and, instead of showing up shortcomings and errors, sang praises and licked boots. Schematism allowed of no imagination, no poetry in writing. It was full of earthbound commonplaces. Schematism meant that the authors identified human life, which is rich and colorful, with the life of the Party and with the problems of the Party officials. Schematism portrayed the heroes as anemic, cardboard figures—as shadows, not as characters.

The young writers, entranced, listened to him with beating hearts. He was, in fact, abusing their work, and yet they were almost happy. They, too, had lately felt that something had gone wrong. What they were writing sounded empty. It was true to the Party line, but it lacked authority. Improbable people lived their never-never lives in synthetic, artificial stories. They gushed because they had no enthusiasm left. They roared, but they had forgotten how to speak. Yes, the young writers, though not devoid of self-satisfaction, had had their doubts. But it was themselves they had doubted. It was their own ideological weaknesses and their petty-bourgeois remnants. They had believed that they were on the right track, that this was the way to do it because this was what the Party demanded, and the Party knew best. And now the Party itself had come forward to say that it was all wrong, that the artificial pathos, the ceaseless feverish enthusiasm, the political over-simplifications, the Party agitations put into rhyme, were all wrong. The Party said so. Revai said so. And now they wanted art. Rich, textured, living art. The young writers were a little ashamed of themselves for not having realized this beforehand, but they were also proud of their Party and its wisdom for having understood and expressed what had always been there at the bottom of their hearts. It was characteristic of the enemy to call this Revai sectarian and to say that he had made Hungarian literature shallow, insipid, and dull! This Revai, who now proclaimed the fight against schematism!

Indeed, in this respect Revai differed from any of his colleagues in the other People's Democracies. But, chiefly, he differed from his Soviet counterpart, Zhdanov. Nowhere in any of the People's Democracies had anyone openly denounced schematism. It was characteristic (and it must have given Revai food for thought) that the fight against schematism was passing entirely unnoticed in the Soviet Union. Moscow, which had so enthusiastically approved the campaign against Lukacs and which had even encouraged Fadeyev, the chairman of the Soviet Writers' Association to write an article on that matter, was maintaining silence toward the campaign against schematism.

Why, then, had Revai engaged in this struggle? Had his good

taste revolted against the onslaught of ever more dreary, ever more mediocre "socialist" writings? Had his sense of beauty, his literary education, rebelled against the monotonous psalm-singing, the outpourings of loyal trash? Undoubtedly so. He came to realize that, though he had defeated Gyorgy Lukacs, that defeat had turned into self-defeat. He had opened the sluices for that avalanche against which Lukacs had warned—an avalanche which Lukacs' prestige and cultural policies had hitherto prevented from flooding artistic life in Hungary. Here were the little rabbits which danced their little dances to the melody of primitive little songs on the peaks of the Himalayas. For a while, Revai watched them patiently, but then he pulled the trigger of his gun to chase them away. At the bottom of his heart, he, too, loved elephants.

But there was also something else. This was a conception that, at the time, nobody realized and that, paradoxically, again proved the acuteness of Revai's mind and his instinctive horror of the mediocre. It was 1951. A war was being fought in Korea. Border incidents between Yugoslavia and Hungary were the order of the day. The outbreak of a third World War appeared more imminent as the days went by: or, at least, feverish preparations were being made for it. Revai, the old Bolshevik, one of the founders of the Cominform, one of the four who "owned" Hungary, was fully aware of this fact. And he knew something else: he knew that war, or even the preparations for war, demanded sacrifices and caused suffering. In the new Five-Year Plan, transformed at the Second Party Congress into a "stepped-up" plan, the Party decided to accelerate armament, to industrialize more rapidly, and to force collectivization—all of which meant a lowering of the standard of living. Revai knew very well that a literature which praised the successes of socialism and which glorified the beauties of the new life would fall on increasingly deaf ears and would lose even the remnants of its prestige. And it would be less and less capable of mobilizing the tired, disappointed, disillusioned people for new and even more difficult tasks.

The writers who were listening to the outstanding orator sounding the war cry against schematism never for one moment realized that this movement for the protection of literature was but an integral part of the preparation for a new World War. They should have listened a little more carefully. Revai was not a secretive man. He insinuated clearly enough—as clearly as it was possible—what it was all about: *"The building of socialism is not a smooth, simple matter. It abounds in difficulties, struggles, conflicts. To educate our people for selflessness and courage and heroism, it is necessary that our literature portray difficult situations. . . . Our literature must study Hungarian life more deeply, and then it will find the heroic types that are today heroes of production but might tomorrow turn into entirely different heroes."*

Yes, the writers should have listened a little more attentively. But all they understood was that the Party wanted them to write better, deeper, truer, and more artistic works. They threw themselves enthusiastically into the battle and thanked Fate that it had given them a cultural leader who, though he may have been bad-mannered and ruthless, or hard and incalculable, knew his job and gave voice to their secret desires.

And Revai sat at the head of the table, deeply satisfied with himself. He had won another battle.

Dies Irae

Tibor Dery never wore a tie. In the winter, he buttoned his white shirt at the neck. In the summer, he wore its collar open, turned down over that of his jacket. At such times his thin neck became visible. So did his Adam's apple and the soft, somewhat sagging skin. He was no longer a young man. His hand, in lifting a glass to his mouth, sometimes shook, and his narrow lips twitched nervously. His strong, fleshy nose sniffed the world with excessive curiosity, and this curiosity was reflected in his eyes. These eyes were gay, childish, almost innocent. Their look was usually open and sincere; but sometimes it was self-assured and severe, and sometimes reproachful and nervous. Yet, even under the greatest seriousness, there lurked a shadow of mockery, of derision. Anyone looking into those eyes was immediately arrested by the deep sympathy that was one of Dery's chief characteristics. True, this sympathy was often mingled with a touch of resolute superiority, or an affected resignation, or the cool impartiality of the writer, or a sudden suspicion (and this was particularly so when somebody tried to persuade him that bad writing was good), but in his heart Dery loved humanity. He was deeply interested in the behavior of the world's living beings, and he never considered life to be mere literary raw material from which to distill his works. To him, life was a more or less amusingly strange hodgepodge. It was an exciting adventure. It was a thrilling, though stupid, Grand Guignol, worthy of both curiosity and disdain. But it was an adventure he enjoyed.

He loved life. Mainly, he loved women, money, and cards; but he loved also literature.

In his youth, he had roamed the highways of Europe, and everyone knew that he had lost his inheritance (a block of flats in Budapest) in one night at the card table with absolute nonchalance, as if it had been no more to him than a pair of gloves lost in winter on the bus.

Numerous members of his family despised him because of his Communist principles. He had joined the Communist movement in his early youth when revolution broke out in Hungary in the spring of 1919.

He had been unfaithful to many things, to many people in the course of his life. To women, friends, money. But never to his beliefs. During his entire career as a writer, he had seen the world as battlefield where the rich fought the poor, where justice struggled against injustice, light against darkness. This conviction was the driving force of his restless life. It was its tragedy, and its fulfillment.

It was as if his refusal to wear a tie were at the root of all the trouble. The shirt without a tie, the turned-down collar, symbolized that apartness not only felt but also realized by the writer. Did he despise tie-wearing society? Or did he simply consider that strange habit uncomfortable and superfluous?

Probably both.

He had no need for a tie in a Berlin seeking refuge from the *danse macabre* of fascism in the fox trot, or in the battle of the Communist workers of the Marx Hof in Vienna, or on the island of Majorca or under the magnolia trees of the Dalmatian coast where, for four years, he worked on the great novel of his life, the trilogy entitled *The Unfinished Sentence*. Nor had he needed it in prewar Budapest, in the Cafe Japan. Then, though the great novel was in the bottom drawer of his desk and the bow-

ties behaved as if the world was theirs, it had appeared that the
future belonged to the tieless.

But the war came to an end.

The Unfinished Sentence was published. With dignity and
moderation, Lukacs called it "one of the greatest creations of our
century"; and Dery, an old Communist, continued living in his
native town with the confidence of a great pioneer. Fame and
glory surrounded that head of his—that head with the slowly
thinning hair. And one morning, on March 12, 1948, he was
informed by telegram that he was one of the first to be awarded
the newest and the most important literary prize in the history
of the country: the Kossuth Prize.

This made Dery proud and happy. The days of the tieless had
at last arrived. He went to the celebration to receive his Prize.
Everybody was wearing a tie.

Everybody had a white shirt and a silver-gray tie except him,
the writer.

Freshly shaved, solemn faces observed him disapprovingly.
Wasn't it time to stop being eccentric? From that day on, he
was often accused of being eccentric. And, to tell the truth, Dery
was indeed fond of eccentric people, eccentric stories, and eccentric situations: In a certain sense, he, too, belonged with these:
he not only observed but also portrayed the world. And that, as
everybody knows, requires a good deal of eccentricity.

But those who had for years shared the fate of the tieless with
him, now suddenly became strangely traditional and well-dressed
and severe. This, in itself, would not have mattered; Dery knew
that power brought with it responsibilities, and now that the age
of torn shirts and of ragged trousers had ended, it was only
natural that the leaders of the new world should dress decently
and be impressed with their authority. What mattered was that
they were beginning to look upon him as upon someone who
underlined—who dared to underline—his own eccentricity.

Suddenly they were beginning to discover strange things in his
past. His eccentricity. His solitude.

In the late thirties, Dery translated André Gide's *Return From the U.S.S.R.* into Hungarian. This book, which the Comintern circles would have liked to erase from the surface of the earth, was a faithful and unprejudiced report on the author's travels in the Soviet Union, written with much tenderness and, no doubt, with criticism—particularly with criticism against the cult of Stalin which was just beginning to form in the Soviet Union. One thing, however, was obvious: whatever Gide disliked in the Soviet Union, he disliked *for the Soviet Union's sake.*

In those days, the Communist Party was banned in Hungary, being forced to carry out its activities underground. Only books containing bloody revelations about the Soviet Union were permitted to be published.

Dery agreed with the critical aspects of the Gide book. He said he thought that such a book was better than no book at all. But he did not get away with it. The judges of the Horthy regime sentenced him to three months in jail for having translated it.

He was jailed for his convictions; or, at least, that was what he believed.

But he was proved wrong. In the Soviet Union, the Communist regime decided that his having translated the Gide book qualified as a crime—the crime of diversionism. He had slandered the great Soviet Union. His Communist past was no longer unmarred. There was a shadow of Trotskyism.

After the war, Dery wrote a book about the siege of Budapest. This garland of short stories depicted the life of the capital and its liberation from the fangs of the fascists. Dery went even further than that. He showed how Soviet soldiers had liberated the Hungarian capital.

This was true, said the official critics. But Dery's portrayal of history was somewhat strange.

Strange? In Dery's short stories, the Soviet soldiers wore no halos around their heads. They were hungry, dirty, tired, exhausted. Sometimes they put a piece of bread into a child's mouth. Sometimes they caressed a little girl loitering in the street because she reminded them of their own little daughter. But, at other times, they shouted rudely in their strange language, and

they robbed (for this, too, was mentioned in one of the stories)
and violated women. This was a delicate problem about which
no Hungarian writer was ever permitted to write. When, at a
writers' conference, the matter was brought up before Rakosi,
Secretary of the Hungarian Workers' Party, he replied: "Can't
you leave this idiocy alone. What is there to write about? In
Hungary, there are, let us say, three thousand villages. Let us
say, they violated three women in every village. Nine thousand
in all. Is that so much? Do you have to make such a fuss about
it? You writers have no idea of the law of large numbers!"

One of the Muscovite writers denounced Dery's book to the
Soviet censorship, and, not much later, the book was seized and
sent to the pulp mill because it slandered the Soviet Army.

Strange, wasn't it?

Dery, however, said nothing. He continued to work. Perhaps
he thought that the people who said he did not view things
correctly were right. Perhaps he thought: "Although what I
write is true, it may not be typical. After all, the Soviet Army
liberated the country and defeated the fascists. Perhaps I am
wrong."

But, perhaps, he was not so pleased with the whole procedure.

He wrote a play with a judge as its hero. The judge, a hard,
just, very attractive person, faces the gravest problem of his life
because, according to the law, he ought to sentence a Communist, whom, in his heart, he would rather acquit.

The play received very severe reviews. It was accused of bourgeois objectivity. In other words, Dery sympathized with the
judge: instead of showing up the wickedness of this servant of
the bourgeoisie, he portrayed him with understanding.

Then he wrote another play in which a former Horthy officer,
returning from a prisoner-of-war camp, was portrayed in a sympathetic light. Sympathetic? The play portrayed a man who,
immediately upon his return from the camp, finds himself in
conflict with the Communist hero. This Communist protagonist
had, though he had fought in the Spanish Civil War, seduced

the wife of the prisoner-of-war officer. This play was entitled *At Home*, and it was banned.

Dery continued to go without a tie.

He proclaimed with deep conviction that literature must strive for absolute truth and that truth can never harm progress, or the working class, or the future.

His respect for works of art was deeper than was his respect for authority. He spared no effort in making everything he said and wrote complete and true and effective. Perhaps the effort was too obvious and perhaps that is why—at least for a while—the young writers considered him a bug-hunter of style, a self-adulating old writer intoxicated with words. Yet, in his case, the style was identical with the man: truth, to him, was always beautiful, however merciless.

Dery was—and he remained—the interpreter of that merciless truth. In vain, they attacked him, criticized him, and tried to change his very essence as a writer. But, instead of giving up his principles, Dery became more and more convinced of his correctness. Then, suddenly, something great and unexpected happened: Jozsef Revai appealed to the writers to create works that would be richer, more beautiful, more complete, and more true to life. When the "struggle against schematism" became the central problem of literature, Dery felt that, at last, he and his Party understood each other—that, at last, he could show them what real Communist literature of the highest standards should be. Now, at last, he had been proved right. The time had come for him to put his ideas into writing.

After the trilogy *The Unfinished Sentence,* he set to work on a novel, a four volume *roman-fleuve* entitled *The Answer.* He wanted to describe the career of a working-class boy named Balint Kope from the thirties until 1948. Balint Kope, this intelligent, clever, nice-looking, and sensitive worker, was intended to represent the Hungarian working class, to symbolize that working class with which Dery, the writer of bourgeois background, had for decades identified himself. The book reflected all the tenderness and the experience and the knowledge of men which the aging writer possessed. All his desires that had never been fulfilled, all the loves that he had missed, the games he had left unfinished, the pain and suffering, the joy and resignation were gathered here. It portrayed the great economic crisis of the thirties, the chaos of fascist police, the strength and spirit of demonstrating workers. Balint's fate was a fate inseparably linked with the Revolution. Dery had planned to end his novel with the moment when this militant working-class boy, matured by experience, becomes the director of the nationalized factory where he had worked for years. Here, again, was a symbol: Balint (i.e., the Hungarian working class) seizes power and creates a truer and better future. This, Dery thought, was socialism.

It was to be the portrait of an era, the epic of a class, with delicate details. He worked on it with unbelievable perseverence. His preparations lasted for months. Night after night, he talked to factory directors who were once workers, coaxing them to reveal their lives, their youth, their struggles. He visited factories, studying the scene and filling notebook after notebook with his fine writing; and only then did he sit down to write in the little flat in Buda, behind the windows of the little house overgrown with vines. He not only knew that he was creating something great; he believed that he was fulfilling a duty. He was creating something beautiful and something also necessary—something useful, although he had always protested loudly against the subordination of artistic work to narrow-minded utilitarianism. But now he wanted to be useful. He wanted to be useful to the Party which, for long decades, he had served as a soldier and which he loved and could still criticize. For, with him, love and criticism, welded into a human attitude, formed the unity of creation. This was his essence.

The first volume was rather well received. Official opinion praised it, though with moderation and circumspection, and for this there was some justification. After all, it was difficult to judge a four-volume work by the first volume. But there was a good deal of suspicion present in this moderation. In this book, too, Dery had remained true to himself. Here, too, strange people appeared, amid strange and sometimes extreme situations. Besides, there had been so much trouble with Dery that, if he began anything with such enthusiasm, that in itself was suspicious.

Soon after the publication of the first volume, he set to work on the second. He worked eight to ten hours a day, or rather a night, writing only very little in all that time but laboring with unflagging attention and diligence. This was his method. Sometimes he sat for hours over the white paper, turning and chewing his pen, seeking for the best solution, the supreme, the mature, near-perfect. But when he had written it down in his spidery, disorderly letters, there was nothing left to correct. He never wrote more than a page a day, but he wrote a page every day.

The second volume was published early in 1952, and the readers took it in hand with avid curiosity. They were eager to learn what had happened to Balint Kope and to the second most important character in the book—the brilliant, independent, dissipated, and anarchistic professor of chemistry, Zeno Farkas.

This time the critics were silent.

The Party, too, was silent, and this boded ill.

Soon rumors began to spread. Gossip circulated by telephone, presaging the arrival of a storm.

Then the storm broke. *Szabad Nep* and *Tarsadalmi Szemle* published Jozsef Revai's long and merciless "Comments on the Margin of a Novel" that dissected Dery's great work ruthlessly.

A few weeks later, invitations were mailed to the homes of the best-known Communists and fellow travellers. The invitations announced a debate at which the participants would discuss the "state of our literature," but everyone knew that Dery's book would be the only subject.

Even Dery himself knew it. In the Hungary of the old days, it would have seemed strange that a novel should be discussed and argued about for weeks and months by Government officials and Party leaders at special meetings. But, by 1952, this seemed entirely natural. It did not even occur to the invited guests that they should ask themselves whether the Party or the Government had the right to initiate such debates, nor whether these impassioned meetings were self-evident and ridiculous.

The meeting started in the usual frightening manner at the Academy Street headquarters of the Party. The writers, who were aware that they had been convened to preside at Dery's "execution," sat at long tables. When they were all there, Revai's rapid, nervous steps were heard in the corridor, where he stopped to exchange a few disgusted words with a few writers who were loitering there in the hope of speaking to the great Comrade Revai himself. Then the excited hubbub subsided, and Revai took his place at the head of the table. He glanced around, pushed up his glasses, and spoke a few words to his neighbors. Then the debate began.

The beginning was bad, but characteristic. On that same day *Szabad Nep* had published a review of the first volume of a trilogy written by the Muscovite writer Bela Illes. The book was entitled *Conquest of the Fatherland* and dealt with the battles fought in Hungary by the liberating Soviet army. It was flat, uninteresting, and gave no evidence of Illes' quality as a storyteller: it was a gushing, artificial report of a world which existed only in Party propaganda. However, the subject was good. The subject was socialist realist, and topicality was often stressed by the Party, according to Rakosi and Revai. And, according to the holy teachings, the content was of primary importance at the initial stages of socialist realism, and not the artistic form.

And Miklos Gimes * had praised the book enthusiastically— and undeservedly—in his paper. Those sitting near the head of the table heard Revai's angry words to Gimes who, as writer of the "theses" of the debate, was sitting next to him. "What

---

* Later, Miklos Gimes was among the first who were instrumental in bringing about the Revolution of 1956. In 1952, he was still a stubborn Stalinist and one of the editors of *Szabad Nep*. According to an official statement, he was executed with Imre Nagy on June 16, 1958.

balderdash, that article of yours!" said Revai. "That Illes book is undiluted rubbish, not a novel!" But those sitting far down the table did not catch the demigod's words, and this circumstance was the cause of grave trouble right at the beginning of the debate.

The first speaker was Istvan Kiraly. He was a Fascist turned Communist, an Existentialist turned Marxist, and the most servile bootlicker of Communist cultural policies. He was also, by the way, a lecturer attached to the chair of the history of literature at the University, and he knew what was expected of him. He knew who Revai was and he knew that *Szabad Nep* was the one and only catechism of the Party.

Therefore, he began with the following words: "I fully agree with Comrade Gimes' article in today's issue of *Szabad Nep*—."

He got no further. Like an old circus pony at the sound of the trumpet, Revai threw back his head and, with his usual brutal tactlessness, yelled at the blushing Kiraly: "You couldn't do worse."

Muted laughter rippled along the table. Kiraly enjoyed the ceaseless and undivided hatred of all who knew him or who even knew of him, and now a malicious glee improved the mood of all present. Yet Kiraly maintained his composure. After learning from the interruption that Revai's opinion differed from Gimes' and that, therefore, his own did also, he continued:

"—although I must confess that there are serious shortcomings in the review."

This about-face was received with frigid indignation. But Kiraly was not worried. In a lengthy address which was insufficiently motivated because he had been prepared to uphold the opposite point of view, he elaborated in detail how wrong Gimes had been and how right he himself now was. Revai did not reply. His face betrayed a deep contempt. He knew all about Kiraly, although this knowledge had never kept him from accepting his collaboration.

The debate went on, and not without surprises. There were a number of speakers who, despite threats and accusations, and despite the fact that they knew they spoke in vain, more or less openly defended Dery's novel. The leader of the pro-Dery faction was, of course, old Professor Lukacs. He himself restricted his remarks to generalities. But his disciples behaved with great courage and determination. They tried to prove that Dery's book was an important weapon in the fight against schematism (a fight launched by Revai himself) and that its standard was considerably higher than that of most novels. The poet Zoltan Zelk declared that "those anxious to see the development of a good socialist literature side with Dery's novel." Istvan Eorsi, a very gifted young poet and literary critic, stressed, in contrast to Revai, aesthetic points of view.*

Tension and excitement grew in the room. Revai had frequently criticized Dery. At the Second Party Congress in February, 1951, he had declared: "We should be pleased if our outstanding novelist, Tibor Dery, would give up his position as a 'fellow traveller within the Party' who, though a Communist, maintains an aristocratic attitude and who in his works and behavior never fails to stress his individuality, even his eccentricity." A few months later, at the Congress of the Hungarian Writers' Association, where Dery warned the young writers to pay more attention to artistic form, Revai replied by saying: "We tell the writers: be the spokesman and helper of your age, your people, your state, your Party. Let this be your main concern, and not artistic form." But these had been only preliminary skirmishes for the decisive battle which was now to follow.

The two almost constitutional old antagonists, Revai and Dery, were now, at last, face to face. Both listened to the debate, but neither participated. Dery was nervous and a little absent-minded. It was obvious that this pointless verbosity exhausted him, for he knew beforehand what the consequences would be.

Revai fidgeted restlessly, made notes, snatched his glasses from his nose, wiped them, put them back, made remarks to one of

---

* The attitude of these two excellent poets foreshadowed their future fate. Eorsi is still in prison (sentenced to eight years). Zelk was recently released, after two years in jail.

his close collaborators (Marton Horvath, then editor-in-chief of *Szabad Nep*) and, with ironical glances and interruptions which were intended to influence the debate, emphasized his own attitude and, even more, his power.

If there had been an unprejudiced observer in the room, even he would have watched the as yet wordless duel between the two men with breathless attention.

There was, as a matter of fact, much that was comparable in the two men. Both were thin, restless, and nervous. Both were stubborn and persevering. Both were unwilling to change their opinions. Revai was stubborn because, to him, power meant infallibility. Dery was stubborn because he knew he was right and because he believed that truth would sooner or later triumph.

There were also other similarities in the two men:

They were approximately the same age.

Neither could reproach the other for his background: both came from the "decadent" cultured bourgeoisie and both, in addition to their intellectual heritage, had inherited worldly goods.

They had become Communists at about the same time, and for similar reasons.

Both were convinced that the liberation of the working class was equivalent to the liberation of humanity.

Both loved great literature. Their idols: Thomas Mann, Attila Jozsef, and Tolstoi.

Both despised such bootlickers as those who served unconditionally, or those who were humbly proud of having no opinion, or those who were the manufactureres of literary hack work.

And yet, how different they were!

Revai loved power. Dery loved truth.

Revai subordinated truth to power. Dery subordinated power to truth.

In the course of his career, Revai had become familiar with the mechanism of the Comintern. The subject had, in fact, taken up practically all of his time during his emigration.

But Dery had familiarized himself with the world during his emigration, and had travelled and worked, writing always about what moved him most.

Revai loved to command and demanded absolute obedience. Dery had no desire to command, but was ready to obey in the interest of justice.

Revai wanted to change the world by violence. Dery wanted to portray violence.

Revai was supported by the entire state and Party machinery. This was what he relied on and what gave him power.

Dery relied on nothing except a few books, a few friends, and the knowledge that he was right. It was this which gave him self-confidence.

Revai was never more conscious of his power than when he could refuse. Dery was never more conscious of power than when he could give.

Nobody loved Revai. Everybody loved Dery.

Revai was determined to educate men; Dery to understand them.

The two called each other by their first names and each condescended to the other. But each feared the other (though for different reasons) and each stood aside to let the other precede him through the door.

Revai stood aside for tactical reasons. Dery stood aside out of politeness.

Revai sat on the platform with his assistants and disciples. Dery sat at the end of the table, alone.

It was a frightening comedy.

In those days, Communist criticism had already developed a certain pattern: when criticizing somebody or something, it was obligatory that one also recognize the good points of the person or thing criticized. Such recognition was intended to stress the educational tendency of the criticism. The aim was not disparagement but objectivity. Thus, following the obligatory procedure, Revai praised the novel that he was about to tear to pieces. "There is no lack of talent, or writing skill, or truly artistic portrayal," he said. "The second volume of *The Answer* has qualities that raise Tibor Dery to a position among the foremost novelists not only of the present, but also of the past. However [and here follows the first bloodcurdling somersault] the fact that the book is good only aggravates the situation. What makes this novel particularly dangerous is its high literary level."

After the obligatory and summary praise, Revai came down to brass tacks. His criticism of the novel centered around two cardinal points.

One of these was Dery's portrayal of the Communist Party. In Dery's second volume, the youthful working-class hero of the novel reaches the age of seventeen or eighteen. Dery takes this young boy to every scene of the working-class movement in contemporary Hungary: Balint Kope takes part in the famous demonstration of September 1, 1930, acquaints himself (through his uncle, who is an old worker) with every shade of the Social Democratic Party from the right wing to the left, and meets Trotskyite factionists and a police spy disguised as a Communist Party member. With the help of a young student and friend, Julia Nagy, he is even in contact with the Communist Party underground. Dery portrays this Party as it really was: a Party fighting courageously against the existing Horthy-semifeudal-capitalist system, but at the same time suffering from many shortcomings: from over-suspiciousness and from sectarianism. This portrayal was not only correct but, though it was not flattering, it was also sympathetic. Yet it was this very portrayal which made not only Revai, but also the entire Communist Party leadership, rave with fury.

"The second volume of *The Answer,*" roared Revai, "is a complete distortion of the Hungarian working-class movement in the 1930's. . . . This interpretation is not only false but also mendacious, and we can safely say it slanders the Communist movement of the early thirties. . . . The Party that Balint meets in Dery's description does not attract. It repels.

It frightens. . . . The failure to expose Balint to the educational effect of the Party, the refusal to allow him to become a member of the Party until 1945, shows an anti-Party tendency. . . .

Thus, plainly speaking, the trouble was that the author had allowed Balint to join the Communist Party only in 1945—and not earlier, since the underground Communist movement was not sufficiently attractive in the thirties to working-class boys like Balint. Dery could have argued—and he did so argue—that young workers like Balint never, or at least very rarely, joined the sectarian, hardly active Party which recruited its members mainly from the petty-bourgeois intelligentsia. Why, then, was his book slander? Where was the anti-Party tendency?

It soon became clear that what Revai and the Party leadership demanded was not a faithful and true portrayal of the Communist Party of the thirties. The Communist Party was not missing from Dery's novel, only the Communist Party as Revai and the others wanted to see it.

"Dery," Revai repeated the accusation, "wants to save Balint, to protect him until 1945 from the influence of the Communist Party. *This is anything but typical even though it is a hundred times true* that, in the days when the Party was illegal, hundreds or, at the most, thousands of young workers like Balint Kope joined the Party, and that only liberation brought about the joining of tens of thousands." Still, the portrayal of society in the early thirties could not be true, if the revolutionary party of the Hungarian working class, the then illegal Communist Party, did not figure in it with sufficient weight, in accordance with historical truth and with a consideration not only of its momentary situation bus also of its growing, future-forming strength.

The requirement was obvious. Truth was not that which was true, or, what was more, a hundred times true. The writer should not describe a given situation or fact or force as it was at the time described. He should portray it according to some "historical truth," taking into account not the momentary situation but some undefinable "future-forming" force. The argument in its simplest form was: Dery falsified by telling the truth; but he would be telling the truth if he falsified.

The other dominant error of the novel was its so-called "petty-bourgeois moralizing." In his description of young Balint, Dery had made the character face up to various moral conflicts. To this, Revai did not object, for he knew too much about literature to do so. He did, however, object to the examples of moral conflict which this intelligent, sensitive young worker had to solve in the course of the story. From the many examples quoted at the meeting, one will suffice. There was a beautiful and moving place in the novel where Balint hides Communist tracts in his room. The police find them and arrest the tenant of the flat, Balint's godfather, the old Social Democrat Neisel. After great inner conflict (i.e., "moralizing"), Balint gives himself up because he cannot bear having anyone else suffer for him.

To this scene, Revai raised severe objections. According to him, Balint made a senseless sacrifice out of personal loyalty. It would have been much better if he had thrown himself into the battles of the Communist Party, since thus—though indirectly—he would have been of far more help to his godfather. The way Balint thinks and acts in the novel was, Revai said, a way in which "no brave, intelligent proletarian youth would have thought or acted. Only a self-centered bourgeois intellectual [i.e., Dery], who sees moral problems in the socio-political problems and who tries to solve them by moral means [would have thought or acted thus]."

The accusation was clear: it was a grave political mistake that Balint should listen to his conscience, that his heart and soul should protest against permitting someone else to be questioned and tortured in his stead, and that he should expose himself to prison and torture in the hope that, by giving himself up, he might save his godfather. The political answer, Revai was saying, could not be the same as the moral answer; the correct political answer considered only usefulness and purpose and effectiveness. Thus, briefly, his argument was: politics is one thing, morals another, and no moral answer can be given to political questions.

Revai added, naturally, that the Party did not object to morals in general. It objected only to individualistic, petty-bourgeois moralizing. Where was the difference between the two? The "political basis" of the moral preached by Dery (for, of course, everything must be translated into the language of politics) was, at bottom, sympathy with the enemy or, at least, it led to such sympathy. Said Revai: "Our morality, our humanism is: Don't sympathize with the enemy. Hate him. Liquidate him!"

The participants in the debate could not fully understand why the moral problem was so strongly stressed in the criticism of Dery's novel. Why was petty-bourgeois moralizing such a terrible crime? Why was sympathy with the enemy such a crime? This was the point where, unlike elsewhere, Revai's answer was somewhat obscure. He pointed out that the Western "renegade Communist" literature is full of such moralizing elements and that this was the blind alley he was trying to prevent Dery from entering. He mentioned that this moralizing was one form of the ideological pressure exerted by the bourgeoisie upon the intellectuals. His argument was clearest where he went on to say that this question had particular importance today "when the imperialists are hypocritically preaching a 'super-class' moral as a weapon against our revolutionary national interest, against the measures dictated by that national interest, and against the needs and requirements of the class struggle."

Revolutionary national interest! Measures dictated by the national interest! The needs and requirements of the class struggle! These notions were unusually general. They were almost too subtle and inexact. What measures? What needs? What requirements did he mean? The participants of the debate were in the dark concerning the heart of the matter. It was 1952. It was not until a year or two later that they would fully understand the meaning of these words in all their nakedness.

After analyzing the principal faults of the novel, Revai could have stopped. But he did not. Now he had been speaking for hours, and it was hot in the room, and the small bottles of soda which were lined up on the table for every important Party meeting had all been emptied. Now the gold-rimmed spectacles of the "crazy Count" were covered with vapor, and there were large spots of perspiration on his white silk shirt. But he went on. Whether he was intoxicated with his own voice or was simply fulfilling his duty as a Communist (a duty not only to criticize but also to show how to correct mistakes) was almost immaterial. He cut deeper and deeper towards the innermost nerve centers of the novel. Suddenly, the novel was no longer Dery's. Instead, it belonged to Revai and the Party; and in Revai's hands, it was beginning to lose its original form and to assume a new shape.

The participants in the debate were permitted to witness something entirely unprecedented in Communist cultural policy. There, before his select public, Revai began to rewrite Dery's novel. If Balint's development took the wrong course, if he had not joined the Party much earlier, it was not the novel that was responsible, nor the character of Balint, either, but he, Dery, alone. "Had Dery permitted Balint to develop according to his own wishes and temperament instead of doing him violence," said Revai, "Balint's life would have taken an entirely different course from the one chosen for him by Dery in the second volume." It was, by this interpretation, obvious that the Party's education would have proved far better and more useful to Balint.

Fortunately, it was not too late yet. Balint could still be given the necessary Party education. He could still be saved—and so could the novel, from its unworthy, stubborn, and unnatural father, the author. And now—partly buried under ideological statements and partly quite openly in the form of directives— Revai outlined the changes to be made. That Balint should join the Communist Party in the second volume was a basic requirement; and so was it that the class struggle, and not love and psychology, nor poetry and friendship, should figure in the fore-front of the novel.* The instructions were exact and detailed. Even Balint's adherence to the Communist Party would not be enough. Revai decided that there must be another Communist —a better one—in the book. Balint would remain the hero, but the other Communist must influence and educate him.

There was a love story in the novel. It portrayed the tragic love between a Communist student, Julia Nagy, and a progressive bourgeois professor, Zeno Farkas. Revai was deeply dissatisfied with this relationship, which was often humiliating to the Communist girl, and he proceeded to give detailed instructions as to how this love story should be altered. It turned out that not only Balint, but also Professor Farkas should join the Communist Party, or, at least, that the professor should become a fellow traveller,† since otherwise the Communist student's love for him would become—to use Revai's words—"unnatural and rotten."

It was difficult to establish where the Communist cultural activist stopped and where the thwarted writer began in this criticism. It seemed as though Revai, who could never become a Dery, but who was now considerably more highly placed in the Party hierarchy, was unconsciously taking revenge on Dery for his own unrealized dreams, for everything Dery had achieved

---

* Dery refused to accept this outlook. Nothing could be more characteristic of his courage and stubbornness than a cartoon which was drawn in those days and put on exhibit for weeks in the building of the Writers' Association. This cartoon, which was entitled "After Many a Year," shows an old and bearded Tibor Dery in 1990. Kneeling before him is one of Revai's henchmen, also old and bearded. The latter begs of Dery that, if Balint Kope persists in his refusal to join the Party, he should, at least, join the Hungarian-Soviet Society, which was one of the Party's mass organizations set up to popularize Soviet culture in Hungary.

† "Let us understand each other," said Revai. "I am not saying that a Communist can and should fall in love only with a Communist. She can fall in love with a non-Communist, but with a real Communist the two feelings of love and devotion to the Party cannot run parallel. One can love only a person who shares one's thoughts and ideals and who, if not today, then tomorrow, can become one's partner not only in love but also in the struggle for the new world."

and he had not. It was as if Revai were desperately trying to prove that he, too, could have written *The Answer*—and better than had Dery.

A father always fights for his children. Dery attempted to explain why he had written the novel as he had. At the end, unable to contain himself any longer, he broke out: "The writer is trying to defend his right to write what he wants to write." But Revai replied explicitly and with finality: "In our world, the writer does not have this right. His rights are much greater: he can write the truth freely, but only the truth. We give no license, no so-called freedom to the writer to distort the realities of life. We do not accept the aesthetic thesis that the writer's taste and judgment are the highest criteria of how his works should be written and of what he should write about. The taste and judgment of the writer may be in conflict with the judgment and interests of the people, the state, and the Party. It isn't the people or the state who should adapt themselves to the taste and judgment of the writer. It is the writer who must, by work and study, become one with the interests of the building up of socialism."

The argument was closed. And, in order to warn Dery that he should not even try to reopen it, Revai dropped a few undisguised threats. He said that Dery was, by permitting representatives of the multifarious false and harmful trends to line up behind him, becoming, willy-nilly, the leader of a highly dangerous movement. "Be careful, Tibor Dery!" Revai cried, "that that conflict between talent and attitude should not turn into the conflict between the writer and the working people."

This cry was no longer that of the cultural politician. It was the voice of the policeman of literature.

Revai then paused and drank a little water. He was pale with exhaustion, and he seemed to have lost several pounds in a few brief hours. The Party officials sitting close to him exchanged worried glances, as if to say: "Let's hope he isn't in for another heart attack." But nothing happened. For him, the realization of complete victory made up for the efforts of concentration, of

supposedly clear and logical thinking. His eyes shone, not only
with excitement and exhaustion, but also with the awareness of
a unique accomplishment. His merciless, omnipotent, omniscient
and burning passion continued, after a brief moment of rest, to
flow like lava, destroying everything Dery had built up with
the work of many years.

There was silence in the room. You could have heard a pin
drop, providing a dangerous weapon like a pin could have been
introduced into the carefully guarded building of Party headquarters. For a moment, the writers thought that they could now
continue the debate among themselves. But this was not so. Revai
continued. He knew no limits. He attacked, he cudgeled, and he
smashed at everybody he could, no matter whether it was friend
or enemy, a Communist or a fellow traveller. The peasant writer
who, at Revai's command, had written a satire on bureaucracy,
was abused because his satire reflected only the peasant's instinctive distrust of all authority. He hit out at the old Communist poet who had written that growing old is a lonely business.
Under socialism, said Revai, nobody needed to grow old alone.
He attacked a writer who, in a short story, described a love affair
without love. The writer should have known that this was nothing but the "glorification of prostitution." Poets who had declared that one had to be sincere when writing poetry were told
that, though sincerity had its points, it was absolutely out of
place as principal requirement of poetry. The poets who had said
that one should write about the life of the people were attacked
because they wanted to lower poetry to the cheap level of everyday political tactics. The Party members present were abused for
not being sufficiently loyal. The fellow travellers were abused
for being too slow in adhering to the Party.

But it was his last attack that closed the entire debate. This
was his attack against the Communist poets, who were Revai's
most reliable disciples but who felt that the atmosphere was
getting more and more oppressive and who, fearing that difficult
days might follow, had written poems on the moral courage they
were pledging themselves to show in eventual danger. One mem-

ber of this group, Laszlo Benjamin, who was perhaps the most
gifted of living Hungarian Communist poets, had written a moving and beautiful poem on this problem:

> This is why I prepare the balance in advance . . .
> When caught between the thousand crazy horrors of dagger,
> whip, thumb-screw, tearing my flesh like snakes,
> how shall I bear the laughter and the torture?
> For it is easy to face death bare-chested,
> pit iron against iron, as here among heroes . . .
> But how shall I, if needed, face hordes of human monsters
> left to myself, alone, without gallant companions?
>
> Be my witnesses, brave partisans,
> now in dead silence among the distant birches,
> that unafraid of torture I'll be among the first,
> when we must die for you, beloved fatherland.

The poem was a Communist oath of loyalty and an example
of its writer's dedication. But Revai did not approve of it. "In
this poem," he declared, "Benjamin is talking of the devil. We
cannot teach bravery and moral courage by depicting the possibility of an isolated and lonely struggle with the enemy and its
horrors. . . . The poet must never face the enemy alone. He
must face it together with his entire people. In the mood that
permeates this beautiful poem, we read that the poet not only
foresees the struggle with the enemy but has already discounted
the defeat."

The writers exchanged shocked glances. Then they looked at
Revai. Why this destructive flogging? Why did he offend and
repel everybody? This was no longer a display of power or of
strength. It was an irrational rage—a madness. Yes, more and
more of them were beginning to believe that this man was not
simply a fanatic or a maniac, but a madman! Yet the demigod
ignored these uncomprehending, horrified glances. Calming down
a little, he acknowledged with a tired and condescending smile
the admiring approval of those who formed a group around him,
replying irritably to the forward ones among them. Then he

exchanged a few words with his assistants, instructing them to tell the perspiring stenographers that he wanted the text of his speech by tomorrow or by the day after that at the latest. He knew, as everyone knew, that a new masterpiece had been created, a new basic text, a hitherto unknown treasure trove and catechism of socialist realism which would have to be translated into the somewhat despised language of the new literature. The interpreters, the explainers, the analyzers, and the developers were happily sharpening their knives. They had been given enough ideas to last them for months. They would have nothing to do but to reformulate Revai's text, to spice it up with new quotations, to supplement it with a few turns of phrases that looked new and original, and then to show it to the world as the new creation of a fertile mind.

When the writers looked around, Revai had disappeared.

The writers walked silently down the dark and deserted streets of the city. Buses and streetcars had stopped running hours ago. Some of the group decided to walk home. Others, who lived near each other, decided to share taxis.

But there were no taxis.

And, although it would have been pleasant to swill down a cup of coffee in the excitement, the coffeehouses were closed.

So they simply set out for home.

They remained silent for a long time. They were deep in their frightened and uncertain thoughts. What was there to say?

Their thoughts were cold and dark like the streets. As a matter of fact, they felt nothing but fear and uncertainty and the desperation of self-analysis. While listening to Revai talking, many of them had delighted in the clarity of his thoughts, in the elegant points of the sentences born of passion. They had sat there like rabbits charmed by a serpent. But in the depths of their souls now, there was a strange and frighteningly disagreeable anxiety. Something must be wrong here. Dery's book was not as Revai wants us to believe. Benjamin's poem did not say what Revai read into it. But they tried to ignore the irritating contradictions. They tried to ignore them with all the might of their Communist consciousness and their Party discipline. Revai was always right.

The great speech had come to an end, and there was silence under the excitedly humming surface. It was the empty, deserted silence of the soul, which had hoped to get answers to great questions but has received in reply only chaos, only a formless mass of emotional falsehood.

The writers crossed the Chain Bridge on their way to Buda. Dery, too, was silent. After a while, he asked for a cigarette. What had happened to them?

Everything that had seemed clear and pure only two short years ago—the fight for a new literature, the struggle against schematism, the desire for a rich and textured portrayal of life which the Party itself had awakened and which (so Revai said) was their duty to the people—had become muddy and unclear, like a pond covered with dust and weed and time. What they had just heard had been a complete and unanswerable annulment of all that had two years ago been sacrosanct—an annulment of the demand for artistic standards, of the battle against schematism, of everything which they had believed they understood because of that knowledge and faith which comprise the two indispensable qualities of a Communist.

What they were not supposed to do was relatively understandable. Their heads were filled with an endless procession of taboos.

They were not supposed to admire decadent Western literature, its formalism, or its cosmopolitanism. They were not supposed to kowtow to cosmopolitanism, but neither were they supposed to err towards nationalism. They were not supposed to engage in bourgeois objectivism, in naturalism, in instinctivism, or in inner struggles ("because the private sorrows of the individual soul were uninteresting"), nor were they to engage in sorrowful poetry (because that meant "a desire to quit the building up of socialism"), nor in self-analyzing lyricism ("because that is unproductive digging into the soul"), nor in a poetry of moral courage (because that is, in the ultimate analysis, "a poetry of fear"). Nor were they to engage in bourgeois melancholy nor in syrupy optimism. The Party wanted neither idyll nor tragedy. It wanted no truth unless that truth were typical (and nothing was typical unless it was Party-minded, and nothing was Party-minded if it were schematic). It was bad if poetry showed no inspiration; but it was worse to leave everything to poetic inspiration, since inspiration must also come from the Party and be directed by it. They were not supposed to define the characters of their heroes too exactly, nor to circumscribe their heroes' shortcomings and virtues (but there should not be too many shortcomings in the "positive hero"). They were not supposed to portray the enemy as an inhuman beast but he must never, for a moment, be sympathetic. In addition, they were not supposed to indulge in conversativism, nor in modernism, nor in individualism, nor in collectivism. Nor were they to indulge in self-criticism nor self-satisfaction, nor in lack of imagination nor myth, nor in lamentation nor overenthusiasm.

But what, exactly, were they supposed to do?

Our Example: Soviet Culture

They knew well enough what they must do.

Had not Revai told them so clearly and unequivocally? "Soviet literature," he had said, "is the example which we draw on and from which we learn; and the perfection which we strive to attain is embodied in it."

The youth of Hungary, as well as the best part of the older generation of the Left, had lived without any—or, at least, with very scanty information about Soviet literature. During the Horthy regime, the publication of Soviet works had been forbidden in Hungary. The exceptions had been a severely abridged version of Sholokhov's *And Quiet Flows the Don,* and two satirical books—*The Soviet Millionaire* and *Twelve Chairs*—co-authored by Ilf and Petrov. In addition, at the time of the Ribbentrop-Molotov Pact, one of the largest Budapest cinemas had advertised the showing of the Soviet film entitled *Peter the Great,* a number of stills from which were exhibited for months in the hall of the movie house though the film was never actually shown.

After the war, the writers themselves had been avid to discover and study Soviet art. There had been no need for a Party appeal or order. They had gone to see every Soviet film, and they had read every Soviet novel they could lay their hands on. There had been no shortage of these works. They had arrived by the dozens and the hundreds: volumes of poems, of music, of artistic reproductions, of films, novels, and ideological works. At first, this flood had been understandable. The omissions of a quarter century had had to be made up for; and, later, the flood had become even more understandable because, as Revai said: "We must first draw upon the culture of that country in which socialism has been victoriously founded and which is now on its way to Communism."

The first Soviet films were a great success. They dealt with the war. They were films like *The Battle of Orel* and *Tovarich P.*, and it was not so much their artistic virtues that carried away the spectators, but rather the fact that, in them, the fascists, being shown as villains, were defeated and persecuted. After the propaganda of Hitler, it was refreshing to watch films in which Nazis were defeated, even though the films were filled with propaganda. The second "wave" of films was equally interesting. Here were the great Gorki trilogy portraying Gorki's childhood and university years, the Maxim trilogy depicting the 1905 and 1917 revolutions, and the Lenin trilogy, which portrayed the life and struggles of the Party's founder and first leader. All these films had been produced in the mid-thirties with the collaboration of outstanding directors and of excellent artists, and they portrayed a world that, to the majority of the Hungarian spectators, had hitherto been completely unknown. It was difficult to judge the truth of their content, or their historical reliability. Those who had been there during those years probably wondered why it was Stalin, and not Trotsky, who always stood by Lenin's side in these films. But to the public-at-large, the details were less interesting than were the chief historical scenes in them—the siege of the Winter Palace, the proclamations of the Soviets, and the enthralling mass scenes.

Or were these films so interesting? It must be said immediately that these films attracted fewer and fewer spectators as the weeks went by. The writers, the artists, and the experts continued to watch them and to discuss them and to learn from them. But the ordinary people became less and less willing to pay to see them. "We've had enough of war," these people said. "We don't want to watch this constant shooting on the screen!" Or, "There is too much politics in them. I want to have some entertainment for my money!" These were the most frequently voiced objections. The majority preferred—as they had before the war—the American, the French, and the British films which were not by a long shot always masterpieces, though one could at least laugh at the comedies, or thrill to the mystery films. And the same was true of literature: the Soviet novels could not stand up in free competition against Steinbeck or Maugham, or even against Agatha Christie or *Forever Amber.*

The more that power became concentrated in the hands of the Party, the less the Party was able to tolerate this situation. It was no longer a cultural question that was involved when crowds queued in the streets to see Rita Hayworth while films of the great Soviet actor Cherkassov were shown to a handful of an audience. It was a political question. The Party resorted to "administrative" means. At the end of 1948, it simply stopped the import of American films and reduced the import of other films from the Western nations to a minimum. At the same time, side by side with Soviet films, the Party increased the import of Czech and Polish and East German films. This forceful interference was, of course, supported by an ideology. After all, the fact that the Western novels and films and plays attracted a larger public did not mean that these novels, films, or plays were better. The reason lay in something quite different: namely, that the past quarter century had debased the taste of the Hungarian people, that readers and movie audiences were full of bourgeois remnants, and that they were as yet incapable of deciding what was good and could not, therefore, understand the products of superior Soviet art. This situation could be changed only by radical interference, by a thorough operation: the masses were to be taught what was good and what was real.*

Between 1949 and 1953, the Hungarian public had no Western books to read, and no Western films or plays to see, except for the works of a few Communist or fellow-travelling writers and playwrights. One or two neo-realist Italian films were permitted to get by the censorship because these had, with reservations, been well received in the Soviet Union. But even with these, there were problems. It was their great virtue that they mercilessly and ruthlessly unmasked capitalist society. But it was a shortcoming almost as great that they showed not a ray of hope, that they were not optimistic as far as the future was concerned, and that they never introduced the social force that would one day change life in Italy: the Italian Communist Party. They were "critical realist" films and not "socialist realist." Therefore, in a few cases, administrative measures had to be taken regarding even these films. Most characteristic was perhaps the fate of the famous and indeed excellent Italian film, *The Bicycle Thief*. The last sequences of this film showed the poor and miserable Italian worker, whose means of subsistence, the bicycle, had been stolen, and who, when unable to find this irreplaceable treasure, had, in attempting to steal one himself, been apprehended and beaten, and who had walked away into the void, broken and embittered. In 1950, no film was permitted to end this way in Hungary. The head of the Film Department of the Ministry of Culture made a few ingenious changes in De Sica's almost classic creation, working into it that which, due to the ideological limitations of the Italian artists, was missing from it. From an Italian newsreel, he cut out shots of a mass meeting of the Italian Communist Party, a meeting at which the leader of the Party, Palmiro Togliatti himself, spoke. He added

---

* There were, naturally, also vulgar foreign trade reasons for this step, but these are too involved to be discussed here.

these newsreel excerpts to the tail of the film. Thus, the hero of the film no longer walked into uncertainty. Instead, he walked straight into the arms of the Communist Party.

Fortunately, such problems never arose with Soviet films. These films were ideologically intact. They radiated optimism. They pointed toward the future. And, in them, the leading role of the Party was invariably properly stressed.* The trouble lay elsewhere. The artistic level of these films—and not only of films, but also of novels, plays, and other artistic creations—sank from year to year with amazing rapidity. These were the years following upon the Zhdanovist Party resolutions, and it suddenly seemed as though the creations of the thirties, in spite of their old-fashioned methods and their outmoded techniques, were still more alive and possessed more depth and truth than did the well-appointed, technically-improved works then being created in the Soviet Union. But such things were unmentionable. The critics were seeking avidly for something, for anything they could praise in the Soviet works of art, because only with full

---

* It was completely impossible, even if there had been technical reasons for doing so, to tamper with a Soviet film. It is generally known that these films are usually too long and too slow, and that certain political conversations are repeated three or four times. It is also probable that the temperament and sense of timing of the Russian and Asian spectator differs from, let us say, the Hungarian spectator. Therefore, to improve their chances of success, the Hungarian film experts would have liked to cut them a little. But, according to a provision in the Hungarian-Soviet cultural treaty, they were not permitted to cut them even by so much as one millimeter of film. It may be interesting to contrast the other side of the picture with an example that really happened. The opera house of Novosibirsk put on the classic Hungarian opera entitled *Bank Ban*. This tragedy of love and nationalism ends with the heroine drowning in the river. The Soviet comrades, however, found this ending too pessimistic and rewrote the ending of this almost 200-year old masterpiece so that it ended happily. The ideology in this case (though it was naturally left unexplained) must have been something along these lines: "One can safety change the creations of an 'inferior' people." Thus, the Hungarians could alter the works of the Italians, the Russians could alter the works of the Hungarians—but never the other way around.

praise and full enthusiasm was it permissible to mention anything Soviet.*

Naturally, there was much that deserved not only praise but also admiration. The Russians are a great people, and they possess great gifts. One after another, the brilliantly talented ballerinas of the Moscow and Leningrad ballets—Ulanova, Struchkova, and several others—visited Budapest to enthrall not only the experts but also the lay public with their dancing. When Ulanova danced the Dying Swan, the audience trembled and sobbed and raved in delight. This performance needed no forcible organization of the audience. It needed no loud-mouthed propaganda. People swarmed to the ticket office and made use of every trick or "connection" to get tickets. The outstanding musicians came to Budapest, too: David Oistrakh, the violinist,

---

* In 1948-1949, at the editorial offices of *Szabad Nep,* one of the film critics had written an unenthusiastic review of an earlier Soviet film. Revai, who was then editor-in-chief of the paper, sent for the young man and gave him a piece of his mind. "Let me tell you," he shouted, "that even the worst Soviet film is better than the best American one!" That was the opinion which prevailed in Hungarian cultural politics in the five or six years that followed. But we should not be fair to Revai if we permitted anyone to think that he really believed his own opinion. He was, fundamentally, a man of two souls. The ideological basis of his remark was that even the worst Soviet film radiated a socialist spirit while even the best American film grew from the capitalist soil of the United States. At the same time, Revai's every nerve protested against the artistic mediocrity and valuelessness of the Soviet film. In 1950, I was a member of the film delegation which attended the film festival at Karlovy-Vary. Upon our return we were received by Revai, who was then Minister of Culture, and we told him in detail of our experiences. In the course of the conversation, I told him what I had heard from Deputy Minister Semjonov, the leader of the Soviet delegation. Semjonov said that Soviet film production would shift from quantity production to quality production. This meant that, although the capacity of their studios permitted the shooting of several hundred films a year, they would shoot only eight or ten. The scenarios, the direction, and the photography of these would be so carefully supervised that every film would be outstanding. I was at this point in my explanation when Revai, practically foaming at the mouth, interrupted me. "And you believed him?" he screamed. "You fell for this? Can one know in advance whether a film will be good or bad? . . . This is art! This is not shoemaking! . . . What utter, undiluted rubbish!"—T.M.

Gilels and Richter, the pianists.* And Budapest adored them.
People argued whether Oistrakh was greater than Menuhin
(many swore by the Soviet violinist), but they fully agreed that
there was no greater pianist than Richter in the entire world.
This opinion was not Party-inspired. It required no Party resolution. Communists and anti-Communists were in full agreement.

Obrascov's puppets and the great song-and-dance ensembles
had the same frantic success. Each year another of these ensembles visited Budapest, bringing with it the color and magic of
the Soviet peoples' cultures. The Moiseyev ensemble brought
vigor and fearlessness, the Piatnitsky chorus the tenderness and
sadness of the ancient melodies of the Russian people. The Ber-
yozka ensemble brought the poetry of the vast Ukranian fields,
the Alexandrov ensemble the military hardiness and the courage
of the war years, and the Georgian State People's ensemble the
passionate lyricism of the Caucasus. These ensembles were large
and rich. There were choirs a hundred-strong. There were orchestras (some with ancient music instruments) of sixty pieces
and choruses of dancers, bursting with youth and good cheer,
of forty-five. They usually performed at the largest theater of
the capital, the Erkel Theater, which seated 2,000 people. Then
they went on to the most important industrial towns and areas
of the country. These performances lasted until late into the
night because, when the official program had ended and the
public still refused to leave, the Soviet guests gave one encore
after another.

In all this, the Russians were beyond compare, and where
they were beyond compare, there was nothing to worry about.
The Hungarian people appreciated and enjoyed these achievements. The trouble was that the Russians considered themselves
peerless even in areas where they were not. There is not a single
nation in the whole world that can call itself perfect in every

* Gilels and Oistrakh are known and admired by Western music lovers.
But Richter, believed by experts to be perhaps the greatest pianist of
the age, has not yet received permission (perhaps because he comes from
the Baltic states and is, therefore, politically unreliable) to perform before
Western audiences.

field—in industry and agriculture, in statesmanship and commerce, in politics and diplomacy, in music and the fine arts, in films and literature, and in sport and science. The fatal error was that the Soviet leaders declared that their people, their country, and, last but not least, that they themselves were beyond comparison; and they expected everyone to acknowledge their uniqueness. As if it were no longer enough for them that the 1917 Revolution had started a new historical era, they were anxious to prove that there had, before then, been no history at all. Not satisfied with the significant successes of thirty to thirty-five years in industry, in technique and culture, and in warfare, they declared that their achievements were unequalled —that they were, in fact, perfect.

As a result, Soviet forms and Soviet methods were no longer propagated in Hungary, but were instead forced upon practically every manifestation of Hungarian life. A host of Soviet experts beleaguered the ministries, the large industrial plants and offices, the army, the police, and the State Security Organization. Their will was law, regardless of whether they were better or worse qualified than were the Hungarian experts. But even when they knew more, as was true in certain technical fields or in the field of military affairs, it was clearly offensive and unhealthy that they were trying to reorientate Hungarian life as a whole in order to fit it into a Soviet reality—a reality which differed from it in a multitude of shadings. The fields in which they knew less are hardly worth mentioning. Yet the reorientation extended to these fields also because, although they knew less, they knew, "officially speaking," everything better. They were not hesitant to crush underfoot the most precious symbols of the Hungarian nation. In designing the uniforms for the new Hungarian Army, they had to imitate the Soviet uniforms; and the historic Hungarian emblem was taken off to be replaced by a monstrosity, a servile imitation of the Soviet emblem. To be just, it must be admitted that Soviet tyranny was only one of the causes of these changes: the other cause lay in the servility of the Hungarian leaders. But, since even this servility sprang from the knowledge that the Soviet comrades demanded such servility, it is difficult to establish the exact proportions of the responsibility.

Sovietization extended to every walk of Hungarian life. But let us, for the time being, restrict ourselves to culture. From the elementary school to the university, everything was changed according to the Soviet pattern, including even the system of grading the students. As a remnant of Latin culture, the best mark in Hungary had for several centuries been a "1," and the worst a "5." But this system was now completely disregarded. Now, a "5" was to be the best mark and a "1" the worst, as in the more "scientific" Soviet system! It was an equally old Hungarian tradition that the physicians, the jurists, the economists, and the secondary school teachers received at their graduation the title of "doctor." This title was now done away with, and, instead, the scientific grades of "docent," "candidate," etc., were introduced, exactly as in the great exemplary nation, the Soviet Union. The Hungarian Academy of Sciences, which was more than 150 years old, was reorganized on the pattern of the Soviet Academy of Sciences. The publishers and theaters were given a "new facade" (the old, traditional theaters becoming the "Army Theater," the "Youth Theater," etc.) just as they had in Moscow. And the same was true for the press: *Pravda,* the organ of the Soviet Party, had its parallel in *Szabad Nep; Trud,* the organ of the trade unions, in *Nepszava;* the semi-official *Izvestia* in *Magyar Nemzet.* Moscow had one evening paper called *Vechernaya Moskva.* So Budapest had to have one, too, called *Esti Budapest.* The Hungarian writers were given a weekly magazine named, in exact translation of *Literaturnaya Gazeta, Irodalmi Ujsag.* Budapest humor, which remained inexhaustible to the end, originated a joke about this phenomenon. In a school attended by children of various nationalities, the teacher, according to this anecdote, asked his pupils to write an essay about an elephant. The title of the French child's essay was: "Sex Life of the Elephant." That of the German boy's essay was "The Reich and the Elephant." That of the American boy's was: "The

Atom Bomb and the Elephant." That of the Soviet Boy's: "The Original Home of the Elephant was the Ural." That of the Hungarian boy's: "Our Example—the Soviet Elephant."

It is difficult to decide where form ends and content begins. If one cites only the emblem placed on Hungarian Army uniforms, here form is identical with content. But even if we had accepted the supposition that all these compulsory changes were merely formal, the changes nevertheless affected more important matters. Not only the names (not to speak of the content) of the newspapers were changed, but even their styles of writing began to be imitative of a Soviet style which was based on entirely different traditions. Not only the structure of the Academy of Sciences was changed, but the dubious as well as the real achievements or opinions or quackeries of Soviet science became obligatory in the study of the sciences in Hungary. Those were the years when the ill-famed but celebrated Michurin-Lysenko theory of biology had reached its peak in the Soviet Union. This scientific humbug, which simply rejected a series of results achieved by classic biology and which declared that the Mendelian theory of propagation was a bourgeois degeneracy, and which promised apple trees and orange groves in the deserts of Siberia (and which, since then, has been dethroned even by Moscow) also became sacrosanct in Hungary. Woe to the Hungarian scientists who dared raise their voices against it! The fact that Marxism-Leninism had become the official ideology of the state (in five years, 530,000 copies of *The History of the Soviet Party* were published in this country of 9,000,000 inhabitants, and the successive volumes of Stalin's collected works in 100,000-copy editions) was easily explained by calling it political expediency. But the mind revolted when a Hungarian professor of medicine, who had become famous throughout Europe, had to look up to a mediocre Soviet colleague as to his master, and when the Hungarian linguists were forced to accept the senseless and impossible theories of a Soviet linguist named Marr, until Stalin in his well-known series of articles published in the summer of 1951, finally put an end to "Marrism." After that, of course, Stalin's linguistic dilettantism became law, and the Academy of Sciences held a series of festive sessions to apply his brilliant directives to all branches of science. In 1949, on the occasion of Stalin's seventieth birthday, a fat volume was published in Moscow (and soon after in Budapest), entitled "Stalin and Soviet Science." In this volume, the representatives of the most varied branches of science reported what their science owed to Stalin. The volume clearly showed that there was not a single branch of science, from meteorology to hydrodynamics, or from philosophy to anthropology, whose successes and results were not due to Stalin. What is more, there was not a single scientific thought or idea, or result or discovery that could not be traced back to one or another of Stalin's brilliant theories.

In 1917, the year of the October Revolution, Hungary stood on a much higher industrial, agricultural, and cultural level than did Czarist Russia. This difference remained constant during the subsequent twenty-five years. In addition, Hungarian culture was linked by traditional ties to the West.* French and German influences leavened the country's intellectual life, too. But Hungary's ties with Slavic culture have always been very loose. Between the two World Wars, these ties had been further loosened by the Horthy regime's anti-Bolshevism, its irredentism, and its complete isolation from the Soviet Union. The foremost representatives of Hungarian culture had drawn from the Hungarian soil and from the various "isms" fashionable in the West. The best were: Bartok among the composers, Attila Jozsef among the poets, and Gyula Derkovits among the painters. All were modern artists in the European sense of the word, and the intellectual elite identified themselves with the most advanced world culture. Thus, apart from a few admirable exceptions, Soviet art and Soviet taste had been considered highly prob-

---

* It is characteristic of these ties that the Hungarian literary monthly, which was published in the first decades of the century, and which gathered around it the greatest and the most progressive writers, and which broke with revolutionary courage and modernism into the stagnant and conservative literary life, was called *The West*.

lematical, not only in regard to its level, but also in regard to its forms—forms which seemed to have been learned in nineteenth-century museums. There is an old Latin proverb which holds that one cannot argue about taste, and in this case the saying was true. Everything that pleased the Russians or the Ukranians had to please the Hungarians as well. And this enforced taste also manifested itself in other fields of everyday life. The Hungarian women were accustomed to follow the Parisian or Viennese fashions; but the Hungarian textile mills now produced only fabrics of Soviet pattern and of Soviet color combinations, and the fashion magazines contained only models of Soviet design. The young women dared no longer use lipstick or red nail polish because this was considered a petty-bourgeois remnant. More and more, they began to wear kerchiefs around their heads, in proletarian fashion, instead of hats. A "good" Party official did not wear a hat. Instead, he wore a cap like the Moscow officials wore (except for the leaders who wore Russian fur caps), and male fashion—if one can talk about fashion at all—consisted of wide trousers and straight-shouldered jackets. Whenever a new pastry shop was opened in Budapest, the design of the curtains and even the pattern of the wallpaper was something never before seen in Hungary, though these imitations of Victorian England have survived in every Russian town since the days of Alexander III.

This dominance of backward influences became stronger and stronger as the visits of Soviet artists and cultural functionaries increased in number. In both 1948 and 1949, a "Month of Hungarian-Soviet Friendship" was observed in Hungary. During this month, lectures were given on the Soviet Union, Soviet films were shown, Soviet plays performed, and large Soviet delegations arrived in Budapest and toured the larger towns. In exchange for the hospitality accorded them, the guests from Russia considered it their duty to give the representatives of Hungarian culture basic instructions in the fundamentals of their superior Soviet culture. The boldness and self-assurance of these people, when they gave their opinion on Hungarian art, of which they knew hardly anything, was simply astounding.

Had, let us say, Shostakovich come to Hungary and given good advice or explained his method of composing, this might have been useful. But at that time Shostakovich was in disfavor, having been accused of being one of the promulgators of formalism; and thus he never came. Hungary did, however, receive a visit from the Secretary of the Soviet Composers' Association, a composer of cheap popular music and accordionist by the name of Hrennikov. This Hrennikov criticized Bartok tactfully and praised Kodaly *—with reservations, of course. He sat in one of the studios of Radio Budapest and listened to the recordings of the latest compositions of the Hungarian musicians. The excellent young composers, as well as those no longer so young, waited anxiously for Comrade Hrennikov's judgment. Would he find their compositions melodious enough, intelligible enough, popular enough? Or would he discover decadent remnants in them? To a large extent, Comrade Hrennikov's judgment determinated whether their works would or would not be performed, what kind of reception they would receive, and whether or not they would be published by the State Music Publishers. In a few short years, even the social standing and the income of the composers were to be determined by Comrade Hrennikov's opinion.

The painters and sculptors were instructed in Soviet wisdom by a sculptor and art critic named Finogenov, who repeatedly visited Hungary. Nobody knew what Finogenov had produced, or what gave him the right to interfere in the affairs of the Hungarian artists. But this fact did not distress Finogenov. Accompanied by his interpreter and by an official of the Ministry of Culture, he visited the exhibitions and the studios of the

* Zoltan Kodaly, the greatest composer living in Hungary, was constantly under fire from "disguised" criticism. Though his greatness was recognized by the Soviet "experts," these blamed him for "having become stagnant" and for "sticking to the Hungarian folk-song motifs instead of progressing in the direction of socialism."

artists, expressing opinions, passing judgments, praising, or making long faces. Due largely to French influence, Hungarian painting had, in the twentieth century, a brilliant, modern period, the so-called "School of Nagybanya." Comrade Finogenov decided to remove this "obstacle" from the path of "progress," just as he decided to remove Gyula Derkovits, the foremost proletarian painter. He advised the Hungarian painters to drop their "formalist" aberrations and to return to the road followed by Mihaly Munkacsi, because that road would ultimately lead to socialist realism. Munkacsi had, indeed, been a great painter. But he had been a great painter not of the twentieth, but of the nineteenth century. In 1950, the Hungarian artists, who had for years known Soviet painting only from reproductions, were given an excellent opportunity to study it "in the flesh" at the first Soviet exhibition of painting in Budapest. The material for this exhibition was carefully selected. It consisted mainly of the Stalin Prize-winning canvases of the foremost Soviet painters. The effect was horrifying. The majority of the paintings portrayed "Stalin at the Front" (where he had never been), "Stalin in the Kremlin," "Stalin in Front of the Kremlin," "Stalin with Mao Tse-tung," "Stalin with Molotov," and "Stalin among the Children." Even more amazing was the primitiveness of the color effects and the childishness of the composition. "Academicism" was too complimentary a word to be used in describing these paintings. The whole exhibition reminded one of those so-called "painters" who sell their daubs in rich, gilded frames in the streets. It was in vain that tens of thousands of people were herded into the exhibition and that the press foamed at the mouth with enthusiasm. The exhibition turned into the most disappointing failure suffered by Soviet art in Hungary.

The Hungarian film people were the luckiest: their "tutor" was inded an artist. He was Vsevolod Pudovkin, who came to Hungary three or four times, participated in the shooting of several films, directed scenes, instructed the actors, rewrote scenarios, and taught and inspired his pupils. Everything he did and said was brilliant. He knew how to move mountains and, with tiny little changes, he raised entire scenes to a high artistic level. But, like most film directors, he was a violent man, imposing his will upon his Hungarian colleagues. At times, this violence was useful. More often, however, it was harmful. After all, though Pudovkin was a great director, these films were *Hungarian* films, and he was not sufficiently familiar with Hungarian conditions. There was also another reason why Pudovkin was not too successful in Hungary. The fact was that he was no longer what he once had been. It was not his age which had made the difference, for he was not yet sixty and he was still full of explosive energy. Nor was it his heart, nor his lungs. There was something else that must have gone wrong with this world-famous master of the Soviet films. One of the present authors met Pudovkin several times. His enthusiasm was enthralling, his wit charming, and his love of story-telling delightful. The eyes, above the broad, Mongolian cheekbones were small and searching, and their glance was sharp and observant. His face was covered with a net of small red blood-vessels that almost glowed when he was excited. He was impatient and irritable, prejudiced and devoted. His two great passions were to tell anecdotes and to teach; and one could learn a great deal from him. Yet, the fire emanating from him was not quite real. One had the impression that he himself was fanning it artificially. True, he was unrestrainable and inexhaustible, like a perpetual motion machine. But it was as if some small screw were broken somewhere in his make-up.

There was a scene involving Pudovkin which took place in the Budapest film studios in the course of his first visit to the city. At the Gyarmat Street Studio, they were showing a few hundred meters of a new Hungarian film to the Soviet director and to a small group of Hungarians. The action of the film, which took place in a Hungarian village, showed the formation of a new agricultural cooperative. The scenes that were finished portrayed the difficulties the new cooperative was facing. And Revai, who had seen the finished reel, had forbidden the continuation of the shooting because, as he said, it was condensed pessimism which, instead of encouraging the peasant, would frighten them. The money and work invested had been lost.

At the showing, everybody was eagerly awaiting what Pudovkin would say. It was not that they hoped he would countermand Revai's orders. They only wanted his expert opinion, and it was quite obvious that Pudovkin liked what he saw and that his praise of the director and of the script-writer was sincere. But this was not the important point. The important point was that Pudovkin declared that the Party (i.e., Revai) had been right. The conception of the film was a mistaken one, he said. Shooting should be discontinued.

In order to dispel the impression that he was trying to interfere with the Hungarian film-makers so soon after his arrival, Pudovkin told a story to show that such things happened even in the Soviet Union—and that, furthermore, they had happened to him.

"During the war," he began, "I was making a film on Admiral Nahimov [Nahimov was the commander of the Russian fleet in the Crimean War of 1853-1856]. The film was to illustrate the excellence of the Russian military leaders and the courage of the Russian soldiers, and it dealt, in approximately the same proportions, with Nahimov's great love for a woman and his great feats as an admiral.

"When the film was finished, we arranged a showing for Comrade Stalin. You can imagine, comrades, how anxiously I watched for his reaction when the lights went on again.

"For a little while, there was silence. Then Comrade Stalin sought me out with his eyes and slowly began to speak.

" 'Vot, Pudovkin,' Comrade Stalin began. [The word 'vot' means 'well,' but it can be used only for a subordinate. It symbolizes a certain familiarity and condescending friendliness, and it immediately determines the relationship between the two people.] 'You were once a very gifted director. . . . How did you come to make this film? Such a bourgeois Western film! Half of it shows the intimate details of Nahimov's love life. . . . This, Pudovkin, is like an English film on the love affair between Ad-

miral Nelson and Lady Hamilton. . . . Our public is not a
bourgeois public. . . . Our public is the Soviet people, who are
not interested in Nahimov's love life. . . . Our public wants
to know what kind of soldier this Nahimov was, how he prepared
his military plans, what his strategy and tactics were, how he
behaved towards the plain seaman, etc., etc. If you, Pudovkin,
want this film to be a success, this is how you will have to redo
it. . . .'

"You can imagine, comrades, how I felt. I was broken. I
was annihilated. No one likes to be criticized, even if the critic
is Stalin himself. I could not grasp the essence of the criticism.
I struggled and thought, but something in me resisted.

"Then, a week later and now much calmer, I thought it all
over. And a little while later, I thought it over again. And again
and again. I don't even know how many times. And, thinking
it over again and again, I discovered, comrades, that Comrade
Stalin was right.

"I went to work and remade the whole film. From beginning
to end. Now Nahimov the *admiral* was the center of the story,
and the love affair was barely mentioned. I worked for months,
for months. . . ."

Here Pudovkin looked around him and raised his voice:

"And what do you think happened, comrades?"

Nobody answered, for nobody knew. Pudovkin pushed back
his jacket over his shoulders (one of his favorite gestures), stuck
his thumbs into the two straps of his suspenders, and announced
triumphantly and with a smile:

"I got a Stalin Prize for it."

The fact is that the Hungarian film in which Pudovkin had
most actively participated—a large, two-part epic of the 1848-
1849 Hungarian Revolution—was one of the least successful
of Hungarian films, though many months of hard work and
many millions had been spent on it, and though the best actors
had been engaged for it.

The manner and degree of interference by the visiting artists
may have differed. But the ideological basis of the phenomenon

itself was always the same. The Russians' constant, condescending interference rested on the assumption that at home, i.e., in the Soviet Union, everything was perfect or, at least, everything was better than in Hungary. The Russians had been building a socialist state for thirty years, and therefore they knew everything, really everything, better than did the Hungarians or anyone else in the entire world. This outlook—an outlook which, in the case of any other people, would simply have been called nationalism—led to tragicomical extremes, particularly in the scientific and technical fields. The Russians were no longer satisfied with proving that they were more advanced at present than was any other nation; they had to prove also that even in the past (i.e., in the times of Czarist Russia), it was they who had given to humanity its greatest talents and its greatest discoveries. True, Czarist Russia did have a few outstanding scientists. One would have to mention only the mathematician Lomonosov or the biologist Pavlov. But the Soviet propaganda machine was not so easily satisfied. The Russians suddenly announced that almost all the important discoveries of modern civilization had been made by Russian scientists. The Western notions regarding the beginnings of the airplane and electricity and the telephone (and, of course, the Western notions about such inventors as the Montgolfier brothers and the Wrights and Edison and Marconi) were all the products of loud bourgeois propaganda, if not outright fabrications. The real inventors, who had, of course, appeared long before their Western colleagues, had been nameless Russians, who had remained nameless because the criminal politics of Czarist Russia had prevented their names from becoming known. There may have been some truth in this assertion, since any people can produce half-finished designs and half-baked inventors by the dozens. But Soviet propaganda now acclaimed all manner of unknown geniuses. There was the "Father of Air Travel," the "Father of the Radio," etc., etc. It has to be pointed out here that even the most loyal Hungarian Communist intellectuals were rather appalled by this phenomenon. Their only defense lay in the fact that they believed the movement had resulted from the fringe actions of some leading Soviet ideologists and that it would soon be noticed by the Party and stopped.*

It was not these details, however, that were the most oppressive. It was the continuity and the extent of the campaign. It was impossible to imitate the nationalist exaggerations. It was, for instance, impossible to say that the "Father of Air Travel" was Hungarian and not Russian, because this would have been considered a serious chauvinistic error. But it was compulsory that Hungary imitate the "achievements" of the Russians in the fine arts or in music.† Tens and hundreds of pictures similar to those of the exhibition of Soviet painting were produced; so were songs like the *Stalin Cantata,* and poems and novels and films like the works of Sukov and of Malcev, of Dolmatovski and of Piryev. Now Hungarian exhibitions of fine arts had to be (and were) arranged each year, and their material resembled more and more that of the Soviet expositions. Now not only Soviet films were shown in Hungary, but also Hungarian films in Soviet Russia. For, there was nothing to fear from the Hungarian films. They were certain not to smuggle a bourgeois world outlook across the well-guarded frontier.

It was, naturally, impossible to explain everything in terms

---

* I remember that, in or about 1951, Miklos Gimes, who was then a staff member of *Szabad Nep,* explained to me indignantly and extremely naively in a private conversation that Malenkov or some other officious Russian must be responsible for this idiotic affair, but that if Comrade Stalin discovered it, there would be no end of trouble. The people of Budapest reacted to the whole affair with much more simplicity and with greater realism: they made a joke of it. Here is the joke:

Professor Kuklin is delivering his inaugural speech at the Soviet Academy of Sciences. Says this great scientist: "The X-ray apparatus was not invented by that typical representative of German imperialism and bourgeois decadence, Roentgen. It was invented by a plain Russian soldier called Ivan Ivanovich. I have irrefutable evidence to prove this fact, because in the Moscow military archives I found one of Ivan Ivanovich's letters written to his wife, Anna Semyonovna, in 1769. The letter begins with the following words: 'I can see through you, you dirty slut. . . .' "— T.M.

† It must be stressed here that the musicians to be imitated were not Shostakovich, Prokofiev, Khachaturian, or even Muradeli, but the "official" musicians like Novikov, Hrennikov, Alexandrov, etc.

of Soviet influence. There were many Hungarian artists who
had long since outgrown this Soviet outlook and this Soviet
level, and who now fell back to the "level of their youth." There
were those who immediately and enthusiastically proclaimed
themselves priests of the "new art"; and there were others who
surrendered to the "new art"—but slowly, arguing and struggling all the while. There were those who believed in the "new
art" sincerely, and there were those who could no longer resist
the pressure. There were those who served it for the sake of
their own careers and their own success; and there were those
who hoped to earn a piece of bread by it. There were those who
believed the "new art" meant progress; and there were those
who thought to themselves: "If this is what you want, this is
what I shall do." There were those whose eyes popped with
excitement when they looked at the creations of the Soviet artists;
and there were those who, instead, made abstract drawings or
composed "unmelodious" music and hid it in their desk drawers.
There were those who cheered, and there were those who sobbed
—depending on their responsibilities toward themselves and
toward the Muse. But the number of the honorable few who
could swim against the tide and who dared to do so, no matter
what the consequences, became increasingly small.

Yet, even those who followed the "great" examples were not
yet considered ready for paradise. Whatever branch of the arts
they belonged to, those Hungarian works which were produced
on the Soviet pattern were nevertheless considered no equal to
the Soviet works. Or, to use the official wording: they were not
yet socialist realism. A strange new system of grading was integrated into the system of values and of art criticism: everything
that came from the Soviet Union was socialist realism; Hungarian work could, however, only "approach" that distinguished
standard. A mediocre Belorussian poem was without fail socialist realist; but a somewhat better Hungarian poem was not yet
up to the standard. Young writers and poets told each other
enthusiastically and confidently: "You know, old man, I am
working on something that, I am sure, will be considered social-

ist realism." When the work was finished, it turned out that it was not. It simply could not be socialist realism *yet*.

Again and again, the writers asked themselves uncertainly and curiously: "What, then, is socialist realism?" The question was not born of doubt but of ambition. The young people were eager to solve the riddle, to lay their hands on the philosopher's stone so as to reach perfection.

The answer took many forms: it was contained in short essays and in thick volumes, in Zhdanov's speeches and in Malenkov's congressional report, in numerous Fadeyev articles and in the statutes of the Writers' Association. Every artist knew about these answers. In fact, they knew them all by heart. They knew that socialist realism was not a style but a method. They knew that its basic elements were the faithful portrayal of life, the depiction of reality in terms of progress, of Party loyalty, and of revolutionary romanticism. They studied carefully the exact description of these basic principles—principles that were different from any hitherto known teachings on art. But the whole was still neither clear nor comprehensible enough. They still did not know *what* made a work of art socialist realism.

It is easy to imagine the delight of the writers who, late in 1950, were elected members of the writers' delegation which was to visit the Soviet Union. At last, they would quench their thirst at the source of wisdom, and they would receive all the answers. At last, all their misunderstandings would be dispelled. Preparations for the First Congress of Hungarian Writers were already under way. How fortunate that all ideological problems would be solved before it would take place!

The writers' hearts were filled with awe and joy as they crossed the frontier. One of their most beautiful dreams had become a reality. They were standing on the soil of socialism. They were filled with love for their great friend and liberator, Soviet Russia—and for the wonderful example it had set.

Their hotel rooms were comfortable enough, though not too well heated. The food was good, though the service left much to be desired. And, though the people in the streets were rather

badly dressed, the performances at the Stanislavsky Theater
were excellent. The delegates visited art galleries and factories
and museums and schools. Though they repeatedly asked to be
allowed to visit the homes of ordinary citizens of Moscow, they
were never allowed to do so; * but at this, the Hungarian writers
simply shrugged their shoulders. The defects and the ungranted
requests were soon forgotten. What they had found good and
beautiful, they praised to the sky. They walked around the big
stores which were filled with poor goods, and then they reported
to each other on all the wonderful things they had seen. No,
they were not lying. They were only good Communists, who
were determined to find in the Soviet Union a country of mir-
acles and to see what they wanted to see.

After days of preparation they were granted their most fervent wish: they were received by the elite of Soviet literary life.

The meeting began at four o'clock in the afternoon in the
building of the Soviet Writers' Association on Vorovski Street—
the very house in which Natasha Rostov, Tolstoi's heroine in
War and Peace, had once lived.

The best-known Soviet writers arrived in quick succession:
Fadeyev, creator of *The Young Guard;* Azayev and Nicolayeva,
who had only recently earned great fame with their novels *Far
from Moscow* and *The Harvest;* Malcev, author of the Stalin
Prize-winning book, *The Yugoslav Tragedy;* Katayev, the "old
fox," known for his youthful book about the Revolution of 1905
and for an earlier "error," the satirical *The Embezzlers;* and

---

* The Russian translation of one of my books had only recently been
published. The translator of the book was our interpreter, a charming,
dark-haired young man who had soldiered in Hungary during the war.
He spoke Hungarian well enough, and he did his best to give us a good
time. I told Alyosha—for that was his name—that I should like to get
better acquainted with him and to meet his family. I told him I would
like to visit them in their home. Alyosha smiled. He replied that there
was nothing he would like better. Naturally, however, nothing came of
the visit. I learned his address only at the last minute before we left. I
wrote to him, but received no reply. When, two years later, I visited
Moscow again, it turned out that he had never received any of my letters.—T.A.

Bezimenski, the old Bolshevik militant who could recite his own poems so beautifully.

The Hungarians were interested chiefly in Fadeyev. This was not only because he was the only writer on the Party's Central Committee nor because he was Chairman of the Writers' Association. Nor was it because they considered him the best Soviet writer (literary public opinion granted this distinguished title to Sholokhov), although they did think him good. They were particularly eager to meet him because Fadeyev was the foremost literary ideologist of socialist realism. He had written at least twenty essays on the subject in *Pravda*, in *Bolshevik*, and in *Literaturnaya Gazeta*, and in one of these he had criticized Gyorgy Lukacs' opinions for not being socialist realism.

In fact, the Hungarians had only one question to ask. It was a question which they all asked, though in different words, some cleverly, some clumsily, some shyly, come openly. The question:

What is socialist realism?

Fadeyev rose to reply. He smoothed back his greying hair, looked into his notes, and then began to speak.

He enumerated all the characteristics of socialist realism and pointed out that nowhere in the world was there a method that would give the creators greater opportunities or help them more. He talked about revolutionary romanticism, which satirizes the present and the present in the future; and, a little reluctantly but kindly, he mentioned himself as an example of the importance of Party loyalty and Party leadership in literature. *The Young Guard*, he said, became a good novel (perhaps, he said, it did not sound too immodest if he called it a good novel) only after he had completely rewritten it according to the Party's advice, stressing the leading role of the Party in the young partisan movement of the Donets Basin—something he had not sufficiently underlined in the first version of the book. . . .

He was clever. He was systematic. He was cool. Perhaps, too, he seemed a little tired and constrained. But the Hungarian writers were diligently taking notes. They did not want to miss a single word, and what they heard seemed clear, complete, and convincing.

Not much later, Fadeyev asked to be excused. He had much to do, though he would always be glad to meet with the Hungarian guests again. If there were more questions now, however, others would be glad to answer them.

Then more speeches were heard. Azayev spoke, followed by Nikolayeva and Kateyev.

The little notebooks were overflowing with words and sentences.

It became very late.

On the way back to the hotel, the Hungarian writers discussed what had been most useful of all the things they had been told. There, in the snow-covered Moscow street, they felt that all their problems had been solved for them. Though it was very late, they sat down in the Hotel Metropole and looked through their notes. And, suddenly, they felt cold and desolate. They felt almost like stone. The notes were clear, complete, and convincing. But there was nothing, absolutely nothing new in them. There was nothing that they had not read or heard a million times before.

The writers thought of the reception they would receive at home, of the many questions they would have to answer concerning their experiences and concerning the new wisdom they had acquired in the Soviet Union.

Next morning they sat quietly at the breakfast table, wondering what had happened to them. Were their notes incomplete? Had they asked the wrong questions? Had their attention wandered when the answers were given? Impossible! The notebooks were full. The questions had been ready for weeks, and some of them had been submitted in writing to the Secretary of the Soviet Writers' Association. And they had listened with such concentration that they had become exhausted.

Then, what was the reason for this failure?

They compared notes. Impossible! After all, Fadeyev must know what he was talking about! But the pages were filled with truisms. "Study life. . . . Study Marxisms-Leninism. . . . Progress beyond critical realism. . . . Fight against cosmopolitanism. . . . Discover the new in the germ. . . . Stress that which points ahead. . . ."

The empty slogans grinned a wry, toothless grin, and the writers looked back mutely and listlessly at the lifeless nouns and verbs and adjectives encouraging them to a faithful portrayal of life. There was a little of everything in these words except an answer.

What, after all, was socialist realism?

A few years later, on April 19, 1958, there appeared in an issue of the Czechoslovak *Literary Noviny* a speech made by the noted Soviet writer Mikhail Sholokhov to the Czechoslovak writers. Sholokhov's Czech colleagues asked the author of *And Quiet Flows the Don* his opinion of what socialist realism was. "Let me tell you the story of my last meeting with my friend Alexander Fadeyev," answered Sholokhov. "It was shortly before his death. I asked him approximately the same thing. I asked him what he would reply to the question of what socialist realism really is? 'If someone asked me that question,' Fadeyev replied, 'I would have to tell him quite sincerely: the devil knows what socialist realism is.' "

BOOK II

THE EARTHQUAKE

Two Programs

The building where Hungary's fate had allegedly been in the balance for so long a time stands on the Danube. It is a solid and dignified-looking building. Its dome rises high above the city, and its towers, its porticos, its balconies, and its entrances almost form a separate little town. This Gothic building is one of the architectural monuments of the capital. It is part of the very air of Budapest. It is part of the town's body. It serves, in fact, almost as the town's head. For decades, it has also been the head of the entire country. It is from this building that the country's politics, or, as the Hungarians say, "the gentry's mischief," emanate.

The main entrance opens onto a huge Square that has witnessed many a historical event. On two sides of the Square stand statues of the two great figures of Hungarian history: Lajos Kossuth, world-famous leader of the 1848-1849 Hungarian War of Independence, and Ferenc Rakoczi II, the legendary leader of the insurrection against the Austrians and the "greatest Hungarian of the eighteenth century." At the foot of the equestrian statue of Rakoczi are engraved the following words: *"Recrudescunt vulnera inclitae gentis Hungariae,"* which is to say, "The Wounds of the Noble Hungarian Nation Have Reopened."

This, too, is a part of the symbol.

The inside of the great building vies in pomp with the outside. There are tortuous corridors, and grand assembly rooms, council chambers, offices, lounges, restaurants, and buffets. The person who enters the building for the first time without knowing his way must surely feel that, after walking through the maze of endless, tortuous corridors, he will, by turning a new corner, suddenly come face to face with himself. The building reminds one of the days when there was still life and excitement within these walls—when there was a Government political party and an opposition, and when loud arguments and silent intrigues abounded.

The most beautiful part of the building is the large assembly room. Seeing the empty benches, the visitor cannot help remembering the men who have filled these seats in the past half-century—the men who have sat in the ministerial velvet chairs on the right side or the left, with the Government party or with the opposition. The straight-backed, ornamental presidential chair, rising serenely above the semicircular benches, conjures up the memory of those who have presided over the debates. In the silence of the room, one can almost hear the loud bell clanging to restore order among the passionately arguing deputies.

After 1949, there was no more need for the bell. True, the corridors of Parliament were peopled by men who had never before entered here: by workers and peasants and writers and engineers. But behind this facade, the essence of parliamentary government—discussion and debate—was banned forever. Even in the old days, Hungarian elections had not always been beyond reproach, and even then the sittings of Parliament had not always been dignified, nor had everybody had the real interests of the nation at heart. But, even during the most difficult days, there had always been a few courageous and responsible men who had dared to express their opinions.

Today, there is no Government party. Neither is there an opposition. It makes no difference who sits on the right side, or who on the left—for all belong to the Patriotic People's Front.

And, instead of with the Speaker's bell, the hall resounds with rhythmic applause and loud cheers.

The mechanism is now quite simple.

The deputies are assembled each year at a given time.

Bills which have been carefully prepared and worked out and already approved are submitted to them as proposals of Party and Government.

Instead of arguments for or arguments against, solemn speeches are made which have previously been submitted for approval to Party headquarters, or to the competent departments of a ministry where each word is weighed and checked and double-checked.

These speeches enthusiastically approve the bill, and the deputies vote, without exception, in its favor.

From this fact, the press invariably draws the conclusion that the population of the entire country stands "as one man" behind the Party, behind the Government, and behind the Patriotic People's Front.

Then the bill, prepared, elaborated, and approved in advance, becomes law.

The Speaker announces the adjournment of Parliament.

The deputies return to their homes, and silence descends on the assembly room for four, five, or six months.

As far as the outward forms were concerned, there was no change on July 4, 1953. At that time, the new House, elected hardly six weeks previously, consisted almost entirely of the same men as before. Again, the deputies assembled from every corner of the country. Then they applauded and approved.

Yet, there was something strange about the whole performance.

The deputies present had been elected on the basis of a carefully worked out and quite unequivocal program. This program was known to everyone. It had been widely discussed in the press and on the radio. It had been explained at length at mass meetings. It had been "supported" by newsreels.

But that Saturday, the deputies approved unanimously and enthusiastically the exact opposite of the program which had been the basis of their return to office.

In the middle of the front bench, with a microphone in front of him, stood a short, portly man with a moustache and a pince-nez, who read aloud the Government's program in a calm, agreeable voice which only rarely betrayed any emotion. He was Imre Nagy. Since the previous day, he had been the Prime Minister. The deputies, who had unanimously elected him, knew little about him. They knew he was an old-time Communist and a well-known figure of the Muscovite emigration. They also knew that he was one of the heads of the Kossuth Radio and that he had worked in Moscow during the war. After the war, he had been Minister of Agriculture, then for a brief period Minister of the Interior, and then Minister of Public Supplies. They had heard it whispered that, as member of the Political Committee in 1948-1949, he had come into a conflict over principles with the Party leadership and that, as a result, he had been expelled from the Political Committee, relieved of his post, and appointed Professor of Agriculture at the Budapest School of Agriculture. Later, he had again been reappointed a minister, but with a very subordinate portfolio—that of collecting surplus agricultural produce. Yet, the subject of his past conflict within the Political Committee was known to very few. At the time, rumors had circulated about the "right-wing deviationism" of the expelled Political Committee member, and it was said that this had not been the first time that he had opposed the Party line. It also was said that he had several times been reproached for this opposition and that he had always been ready to submit to self-criticism.

And, lo, here stood this little man with his beautiful language, as the head of the Government and as the proclamator of a new program.

There was silence in the assembly room—an excited, tense, almost oppressive silence. The boxes were crowded with foreign correspondents, members of the diplomatic corps, guests, and journalists.

Nobody knew, and Imre Nagy least of all, what a turning point this day was to be in his life and in the life of the nation. Nevertheless, everyone felt that they were witnessing a grave and significant event.

Fully aware of the importance of his message, the Prime Minister spoke slowly and deliberately. Perhaps he wanted to give his audience time—time not only to take note of what he was saying, but also to remember and to discard the "old" program on the basis of which they had been elected.

It was easy to remember this "old" program.

Barely six weeks before, it had been announced by the then Prime Minister of Hungary and Secretary of the Hungarian Workers' Party, Matyas Rakosi. It had been announced from this very building to hundreds of thousands who stood under a multitude of banners fluttering in the wind in the Square outside. Who would have thought then that, in fifty days, everything would be changed?

The words and phrases of the two programs swam side by side in the heads of the deputies, and the narrow path of time that separated the one from the other widened and deepened into an unbridgeable gulf.

This is what Matyas Rakosi announced from the steps of Parliament on May 10, 1953:	*This is what Imre Nagy said in Parliament on July 4, 1953:*

On the general situation:

"Four years are a short time in the history of a nation, and yet in these short four years our fatherland has advanced and changed more than it did in long decades of the past."	"We are facing grave and responsible tasks if we want to make good the grave mistakes committed in the past by the Government and to restore law and order and assure full legality."

On the Five-Year Plan:

"We have appropriated thirty-five billion *forints* for the investments of our Five-Year Plan. This sum seemed so exorbitant that we had to prove to· the doubters and to the sceptics that the plan is well-founded and realistic. Since then, we have had to raise that amount repeatedly, because we found that our possibilities and our reserves were far greater than we thought."

"We have had to realize and to tell our people openly that the targets of the stepped-up Five-Year Plan exceed our abilities in many respects. Their realization would exhaust our sources of energy and hinder the growth of the material basis of prosperity. What is more, they have lately led to a reduction of the standard of living."

On industrialization:

"It will be one of the major tasks of the new Parliament to enact the second Five-Year Plan of the Hungarian people's economy—a plan with which we intend to build a socialist society in our country. Our basic aim is to double the output of coal, iron, steel, and electric power by 1955-1959."

"The Government will reexamine the economic plan both in the field of production and of investments, and it will submit suggestions concerning an adequate reduction.

"We must change the direction of our economic policy considerably by reducing the speed of heavy industry and of heavy production, and by accelerating the production of consumers' goods and food."

On agricultural policy:

"An increasing part of our working peasantry is engaged in socialist large-scale production. Four years ago, only 15,-

"The unfavorable trend of agricultural production was, no doubt, influenced by the exaggerated drive for coopera-

000 families worked in producer cooperatives. This spring, 340,000 families worked in cooperatives, and the number of cooperative members is nearly half a million.

"During the agricultural working season last autumn and this spring, the superiority of socialist large-scale production became obvious.

"Clearly the Government's policy of insisting on the principle of volunteer recruitment of members of the cooperatives and of refusing to allow any pressure or coercion in their formation was right. While our enemies have proclaimed that we are forcing our peasantry to join the cooperatives, we have, on the contrary, slowed down the growth of cooperatives.

"Today, the rapid development of the cooperatives is fully assured."

tives and the undue haste to increase the number of cooperatives—as a result of which that portion of the cooperatives in which the necessary conditions were absent never gained sufficient economic or organizational strength.

"It is a well-known fact that our agricultural production is based predominantly on individual farming. . . . The acts of violence and the offenses against the voluntary principle have caused unrest among our working peasantry. . . . The government considers a "go slow" policy for the cooperative movement correct and necessary, and, to ensure the principle of voluntary adherence, the Government will make it possible for those cooperative members who want to return to individual farming to leave the cooperatives at the end of the agricultural year. In addition, we shall permit the dissolution of cooperatives, if the majority of its members should so desire."

On the intellectuals:

"The overwhelming majority of our intelligentsia is united in the belief that the People's

"Unfortunately it still happens —but the Government is resolved to change this—that in-

Democracy can raise the nation from its ruin, that it appreciates and values the work of the loyal intellectuals, and that it offers them opportunities for the development of their talents that could not be dreamed of in a capitalist society."

tellectual work and the intellectuals in general are not properly appreciated. Due to mistrust or during the course of senseless purifications, the Government has acted in a way unworthy of the People's Democracy toward honest intellectuals and has deprived them of the opportunity to put their knowledge in their own field to use for the benefit of the country."

On public education:

"Today, there are three times as many students at our universities and in our colleges as there were in Horthy times, and we can proudly say that in this field we have progressed far beyond such advanced capitalist countries, as England, France, and Holland."

"With tremendous sacrifices, we have imposed university education, practically by force. Now we shall have to be much more modest in this field, too. Let us not build castles in Spain. At the same time, we shall have to pay increased attention to the elementary and secondary schools, which, because of our exaggerated attention to university education, we have sorely neglected."

On legality:

"Due to the successes of our People's Democracy and the progress of building socialism, the class struggle is becoming even fiercer. The remnants of the capitalist system have less

"One of the most urgent tasks of this Government is to restore law and order. Our authorities have frequently failed to respect the constitutional rules that protect the rights,

and less scope for action in the towns as well as in the villages. However, they are waging an ever more bitter fight for the fields that are still theirs.

"Let us be vigilant in every field of the People's Democracy, and let us act ruthlessly against those who want to sabotage the building of our happy future! Our People's Democracy must ceaselessly watch for conspiracies, for sabotage, and for espionage, the organizing and financing of which is without exception in the hands of the United States."

the personal freedom, and the security of citizens.

"The Government will cease internment and dissolve the internment camps. Thereby, it wants to make it possible for the amnestied and the interned to return to their homes and their families. . . .

"This Government also intends to regularize the position of those banned from the capital by permitting them, within the statutory provisions valid for each citizen, to select the place where they want to reside."

On the tempo of work:

"We all know that there is still much to be done in the field of work discipline. We can still considerably increase the productivity of labor."

"So as to protect the health of the working people, this Government will reduce all unnecessary and unmotivated overtime work, as well as Sunday work. . . . We shall discontinue fines as a disciplinarian measure against workers and employees."

On the most important task:

"The realization of the second Five-Year Plan will mean that Hungary will surpass most of the advanced capitalist coun-

"The new road on which the Government desires to advance will be on a broader basis, with the whole people, at first per-

tries in every sphere of activity. . . . Are the preconditions
for the fulfillment of the plan
present? Yes, they are."

haps more slowly, but all the
more surely toward the same
aim . . . socialism. . . . The
basic principle of our new economic policy is the constant
raising of the population's
standard of living."

The overwhelming majority of the deputies were Party officials; the minority were reliable fellow travelers, the so-called
"peace priests" loyal to the Party, and the collaborators who
were more disciplined and better indoctrinated than the Party
members themselves. Not a ripple showed on the composed faces.
Every deputy behaved as if the thoughts Imre Nagy expressed
had always been his own most cherished ideals. It was as if
everything that Imre Nagy had said was self-evident, and as if
the new program differed not at all from the one which had been
announced at innumerable election meetings. But, behind the
calm, almost serene faces, there was a churning chaos of terrible
doubts and fears. No, they were not afraid that their constituents
might blame them for not having stuck to the Rakosi program
in Parliament! They did not have to be particularly astute to
realize that the vast majority of the electorate would not protest
against the dissolution of the internment camps, against religious
tolerance,* or against the higher standard of living. There was
no doubt in their minds that Imre Nagy's program would be
considerably more popular in the country than that of his predecessors had been. But the deputies had other preoccupations. It
had been pounded into them in Party schools and seminars that
the most popular program is not the best program, and that the
Party must never follow in the wake of the masses.† Everything

---

* Imre Nagy declared: "We must be more tolerant in religious questions. The former practice of administrative interference in this field is
intolerable. This Government condemns such measures and will not permit them."

† Every Communist has read in the Party history the Russian name
of this grave political mistake. It is called "*hvostism*" and is a deeply
despised phenomenon in the ranks of the Party.

that had now been said about alleviating measures, about the easing off of the class war, about the abolition of the "kulak list,"* or the dissolution of the cooperatives, or the slowing down of production in heavy industry, or about trade with the capitalist countries,† left an odd taste in their mouths and filled them with an uncomfortable suspicion. Luckily, the speaker did not forget to mention with great warmth the liberating and powerful Soviet Union‡ and neither did he forget to condemn such hostile elements as the war-mongers and the imperialist provocateurs.

The question that worried the deputies was this: What would all this lead to? What would be the outcome of this sudden reversal, of this rejection of former programs and former proud slogans, of this sharp criticism and this proclamation of a new policy? And behind this question was hidden the ghost of a second, even more exciting, even more incomprehensible question: What had brought this about? How had this whole change come about? Only a few days ago, everything had been running smoothly and without a hitch. There had not been a breeze to announce this storm. What was behind this whole thing?

About fifty or sixty of the three hundred deputies were members of the Party's Central Committee. They knew that, on June 27, the higher Party leaders had met for a discussion. At this meeting, Rakosi had been the speaker, and he had reported on the political work accomplished by the Party. The discussion that had followed had contained essentially the same criticism of the Rakosi program that was in Imre Nagy's program—but in a

---

* Each village had its own "kulak list" consisting of the names of the well-to-do peasants who were subjected to the most diverse forms of persecution. Imre Nagy announced the abolition of this list.

† Imre Nagy stressed increased participation in international trade and the importance of an interchange of goods with the capitalist countries.

‡ Said Nagy: "It was the Soviet people, who, by sacrificing their sons, brought us our freedom in order that we may create a free and independent country and a prosperous, happy life for our working population. That is how the Soviet Union became the source of all our successes and achievements. The Soviet Union is a selfless friend to small nations and is the fortress of liberty and peace."

cruder and more severe form. The meeting had then adopted a resolution which had begun with the following words: "The Central Committee of the Hungarian Workers' Party condemns the leftist adventurist policy of Matyas Rakosi, Erno Gero, Mihaly Farkas, and Jozsef Revai—a policy which has driven the country to the brink of a catastrophe." The deputies had then made personnel changes in the Political Committee and in the Secretariat. The "foursome" had been dissolved. Mihaly Farkas, Minister of Defense, and Jozsef Revai, Minister of Culture, had been relieved of their posts and their ranks. A number of other leaders had also been relieved of their posts and replaced by young, unknown men.*

This was what the members of the Central Committee knew. But nobody knew—although, as usual, this was where the key to the riddle lay—that exactly ten days before Imre Nagy's announcement in Parliament, the Presidium of the Soviet Communist Party had summoned to Moscow these leaders of the Hungarian Party: Matyas Rakosi, Erno Gero, Mihaly Farkas, Chairman of the Presidium, Istvan Dobi, Imre Nagy, and an unknown young man, named Bela Szalai, who was one of Rakosi's secretaries. The resultant meeting in the Kremlin had been rather loud and stormy. The leaders of the Soviet Party had given the leaders of the Hungarian Party a sharp lashing and had declared that the irresponsibility of Rakosi and his friends had driven Hungary to the brink of utter ruin. One after the other, Malenkov, Beria, Molotov, Mikoyan, Khrushchev, and Kaganovich, had risen to speak. And, without exception, they had attacked Rakosi, Gero, and Farkas.

Beria had been particularly ruthless.

---

* Apart from Revai and Farkas, those expelled from the Political Committee were: Antal Apro, Karoly Kiss, and Marton Horvath (all three old Communists from the underground days), Jozsef Harustyak and Sandor Ronai (who represented "the absorbed Social Democratic Party" in the leadership), and Laszlo Piros, Minister of the Interior and Chief of the Political Police. The new members were: Lajos Acs, Bela Szalai, Istvan Bata, and Mihaly Zsofinecz.

"Listen to me, Rakosi," he had said, turning to that "beloved leader and wise father of the Hungarian people." "We know that there have been in Hungary, apart from its own rulers, Turkish sultans, Hapsburg emperors, Tartar kings, and Polish princes. But, as far as we know, Hungary has never had a Jewish king. Apparently, this is what you have become. Well, you can be sure that we won't allow it."

The Jewish question played a very important role in the criticism. The Soviet comrades highly disapproved of the fact that in Hungary, where anti-Semitism has such deep roots, all four leaders of the Party should be Jews.

Yet, the Jewish question was only a side issue. The principal subject of the criticism had been the stepped-up Five-Year Plan— that unreasonable and unfounded plan of forced industrialization that demanded greater and greater sacrifices, that caused a lowering of the living standard and that (according to Soviet experts who had visited Hungary) would drive the Hungarian state to bankruptcy if nothing were done to prevent it.

"If the situation is not immediately and radically changed," said Khrushchev, "you'll be chased out of the country with pitchforks."

At first, Rakosi attempted to defend himself. He was an experienced politician; he had no difficulty in discerning behind this concentrated attack the events in Berlin. Only a few days had passed since the East Berlin uprising of June 17, 1953, and, also, since the demonstrations in Czechoslovakia. The members of the Politburo had seemed to take fright at these uprisings. There was an atmosphere of panic in the Kremlin, and an effort was being made to prevent similar occurrences in the other People's Democracies. There had also been sudden riots in a few villages in the Hungarian lowlands, and Moscow must have heard of these. What Rakosi could not quite understand, however, was the unprecedented rudeness of the criticism. What was the reason for that tone? Antipathy toward himself? The well-known anti-Semitism of Malenkov, of Beria, and of the others?

Or was it that, in the previous year's bad harvest, he had asked the Russians for grain and they had been disinclined to help, or unable to do so?

Not even in Horthy's law courts had they talked to him in this manner! There was nothing he could say in his defense. No one knew better than the men who were attacking him that the now-denounced Five-Year Plan had been worked out with the assistance of Soviet experts and that, what is more, it had been approved by the same Politburo in the Kremlin that was now abusing him for it.

It was, of course, the same Politburo. Except for one difference. Then, there had been one additional member present: Stalin. Should Rakosi say so? No, this was something he could never say. It would have meant his end. Besides, he was fully versed in Party practice. He had applied it himself. The superior body always had the right to blame the subordinate body for all the mistakes and errors and stupidities ordered by it. It had the right to pretend that this was the first time it had heard about the whole affair.

The verdict was passed very rapidly. Gero and Farkas were not even allowed to speak.

The Politburo unanimously resolved that Rakosi was to be relieved of his post as Prime Minister (though he would remain as Party Secretary in order to correct his mistakes), that his place would be taken by Imre Nagy, and that a new Government program would be inaugurated for bringing relief to the present difficult situation.

They had selected Imre Nagy for these reasons: first, because he, too, was a Muscovite; second, because he was not a Jew; and, third, because, in 1948, he had been the one Hungarian politician who had opposed the official Party line, who had opposed the policy of accelerated industrialization and collectivization, and who had wished for a realistic plan that would take Hungarian conditions into consideration and that would be based on the land reform that had been carried out in 1945 under his leadership. The leaders of the Soviet Party had re-

habilitated Imre Nagy. They had entrusted him with the realization of a new political line.

Imre Nagy came to the end of his Parliamentary speech.

The deputies applauded a little uncertainly, a little shyly.
There was no rhythmical applause in unison. The deputies had
been warned before the opening of the session to disregard this
ingrained habit. They knew that in the future they would have
to applaud more discreetly, more moderately. But this was almost all that they knew with any degree of certainty about the
new situation.

They knew for sure only one other fact: during Imre Nagy's
speech, Matyas Rakosi, the beloved leader and wise father of
the Hungarian people, the hero and veteran of the working-class
movement, and their infallible and unerring previous leader, had
been sitting in the second row of the benches—an action unprecedented in the history of the Hungarian People's Democracy.

"The People's Wise Father"

Nobody could tell exactly how many Rakosi portraits were
in circulation in Hungary at a given time. Were there six hundred or three thousand or a million and a half? All that we knew
for certain was that there was not an office, or a schoolroom, or
a shop or shop window, or a railway waiting room, or small inn,
or coffeehouse without that portrait on the wall. Neither was
there a local Party office, nor a trade union center, nor an editorial room, nor a factory workshop or gate, nor dressing room,
nor sports field, nor hospital room, nor ship's cabin, nor health
service consulting room, nor tractor station, nor cinema, nor
cloakroom, nor open-air theatre, nor supermarket, nor garage,
nor museum in Hungary without a portrait. In the room of a
true Communist, or in the room of a clerk suspected of being
politically unreliable, there were usually two portraits rather than
one: a large photograph on the wall and a small picture on the
desk.

These photographs, usually with some slogan or other bearing
Rakosi's signature beneath, were of three or four varieties. One
showed only the head, in all its baldness and roundness and enlarged to giant proportions. Another, approximately six to ten
years old, was a bust of the man, with a Party emblem in his
buttonhole. The third, which was a little less common, portrayed

Rakosi from top to toe, and in this pose he held a little girl on his arm. The most ubiquitous photograph, however, showed the "people's wise father" in the middle of a wheat field, holding a couple of ripe stalks in his hand, his infallible eyes scrutinizing the quality of the expected harvest.

This picture—so the faithful thought—expressed with the utmost concentration and perfection all the benevolence that radiated from Matyas Rakosi toward the people, whether the people desired his benevolence or not. All these qualities were evident: the serenity emanating from the man standing in the middle of the wheat field; the strength and tenderness with which he grasped the tough, yet fragile stalks; the serenity promising a secure future; the solicitude and responsibility for the new bread, the new future; the goodness of heart with which, with the loving eye of the farmer, he scanned the stalks; and the expert knowledge he had of the crop, because it was quite evident in the photograph that, apart from being deeply moved by the stalks of wheat, his quick eye had immediately noticed the quality of it and had calculated the quintals per acre and added up the quintals to get the national average. And beyond all that, this picture summed up in its straight-forward symbolism, the important truth that this man had deep roots in the Hungarian soil, as deep as the wheat itself, and that this soil fed him and made him strong as steel, so that he was at once son and father of the Hungarian land and the Hungarian village.

As far as this last attribute was concerned, there was some truth in it. Rakosi was indeed born in a tiny South Hungarian village, at Ada, County Bacs, on March 9, 1892. If he was not the son of wheat-growing peasants, he was at least the eldest son of the village grocer. His parents wanted to bring him up as a decent and honest man and as a useful member of society, and, although they had seven more children to take care of, they made every sacrifice to give their eldest a good education.

The boy was good at school. He was intelligent and interested, and his astute cunning and cunning astuteness made up for his funny, gnomelike appearance. At the High School of

Commerce he learned correspondence, bookkeeping, and calculation, and to these he owed his later tenacity and love of systematic work. It was here that he began to study languages, for
which he had great talent. Encouraged by the excellent results he
had achieved in his studies, his parents sent him to the Eastern
Academy to prepare for a career in foreign trade.

Foremost among his gifts was his phenomenal memory. His
almost completely round head was a veritable warehouse of
frighteningly exact memories, brought forth at the right moment
in the form of exceedingly apt little stories and surprising analo-
gies. The effect was always disarming. Rakosi belonged to the
type of man who can make excellent use of a natural gift. He
soon discovered how very effective a well-placed quotation, a
tilting poem, or an axiom rising like a warning finger, could be.
When, during his time as head of the Hungarian Workers'
Party, he invited writers for a conference, he recited poems,
quoted from the classics, and gave evidence of great erudition.
When he spoke to mining engineers, he amazed them with his
expert knowledge. He knew how to fit together the prefabricated
parts of mining combines and was as much at home in that
technical maze as if he had spent his whole life studying them.
Now and again, he threw covert glances at the men sitting
around him to make sure they had swallowed the bait and not
noticed the trick. In most cases, they did not notice his pretenses.
When the church delegation that visited him to discuss the
social problem of the church came out of his room, the members
of the delegation stared at each other in amazement. It was not
that he had quoted from the Bible or from the gospels according
to Matthew and Luke or even from the Apocalypse with a self-
assurance that convinced them that the corpulent gentleman
knew his Bible better than they did. It was, instead, that Rakosi
had also quoted *in Latin* from Pope Pius XI's *De Rerum No-
varum,* which deals with social injustices, and this was more than
the priests could bear.

The writers, the mining engineers, and the priests had no idea of how diligently and circumspectly Rakosi prepared himself for these meetings. True, his memory was excellent, but he spared no effort to refresh it. The underlined text of the Apocalypse, the gospels according to Matthew and Luke, and the papal encyclicals were there among the piles of documents lying on his desk, and it was when, now and again, he glanced at his notes (or rather at the Biblical "statements" to which he was to refer a few minutes later) that he was refreshing his memory—a trick that not only saved him in the course of disagreeable and uncomfortable discussions but that also enlarged to a legendary figure his rather ridiculous little body.

He was always preparing for something. It was as if all the years of his past—the risks, the sacrifices, and the sufferings—had served only to prepare him for the coming glory, the pomp, and the power.

He had joined the working-class movement in his early youth. In World War I, as a prisoner-of-war in Russia, he joined the Communist Party, then returned to Budapest toward the end of 1918. After the defeat of the first Hungarian Soviet Republic (in which he was Deputy Commissar for Trade) he emigrated to Moscow, and later he worked as trusted member of the Third Internationale as an agitator and organizer in Italy, France, and Austria, under an alias and with false papers.

Then he returned to Hungary again.

In 1924, he was arrested by the Horthy police as an underground organizer of the Hungarian Workers' Party.

Everyone knew he would be condemned to death.

An international campaign was launched to save his life.

He was spared a hanging, but he was not spared a prison sentence. He spent sixteen long years in Horthy's prisons, at Vac, at Szeged, and at Budapest.

In 1940, at the time of the Ribbentrop-Molotov meeting, there was a certain improvement in the diplomatic relations between Hungary and the Soviet Union. The two countries made a bargain, according to which the Soviet Union returned the flags of the Revolution of 1848-1849 that had been captured by the Russians and taken to Moscow. In exchange, the Hungarian Government handed Matyas Rakosi over to Moscow, plus several other Communists detained by that Government.

So, after sixteen years, he was again free. From that day on, he worked in the Soviet Union as one of the leading members of the Hungarian Workers' Party. He spoke at meetings. He lectured to the Hungarian prisoners-of-war at the prison camps. He learned every little trick of Party life, and he prepared himself for the role for which the Soviet comrades then cast him: that of Hungary's Number One leader.

And, indeed, who could have been better suited for that role than the man who had given all his life to the cause—the very cause whose armies were now occupying Hungary? When, after the war, he returned to Hungary, he was witty and clever and cunning in his dealing with the leading Hungarian politicians. He was thinner and even more energetic than he became later in the years of unlimited power. He still argued, but he could also command. He still asked advice, but he no longer accepted it. And, though there loomed behind him the superior force of the occupying army, he but rarely imposed his will on his opponents. There was no need to crack the whip. He could even be generous at times. It was enough that everyone knew what he knew: that, according to the treaty of Yalta, Hungary belonged to the Russian sphere of influence.

Very soon, his name became well known in Hungary. Articles and pamphlets proclaimed his struggles and his heroic deeds for the Hungarian people. The story of his life was taught at Party schools and seminars, so that everyone might rejoice that here was a man whose work would give wings to industry, unprecedented yield to agriculture, and a new and wonderful inspiration to the arts.

It turned out, gradually, that Rakosi, as Deputy Commissar for Trade, had been the real leader of the Hungarian Soviet Republic in 1919, because the name of the man who had in fact been its leader, Bela Kun, had become absolutely taboo.

Kun, of course, was a Trotskyite traitor and his name represented sacrilege and villainy and baseness personified.*

Then came the glorification of Rakosi's prison years. On the basis of "authentic" data, the story of his trial was published in book form. The book was compiled by the staff of the Institute of the Working-Class Movement, a group of Party-appointed "historians" whose loyalty and reliability were the only "scientific training" they had ever received. Like every historical personality of note—from Napoleon to Frederick the Great to Augustus to Philip of Macedonia—Rakosi hired himself a court historian to write the story of his life for the edification of present and future generations. This tall, skinny, nervous, falsetto-voiced, moustached and bespectacled man called Laszlo Reti grew, in the course of several years, into the official expert on Rakosi. Busy as a bee, he collected and "integrated" all sorts of material that added brilliance to Rakosi's already brilliant past. It did not particularly disturb him when he could find no historical document to support some point or other. At such times, he resorted to a well-known method: he made the details up himself or had someone else make them up, and the missing detail fitted in exactly with the rest—which is small wonder, since most of the picture had been put together from such details. He corrected and deleted and rewrote court minutes, or he invented or removed articles from the archives of history if their existence interfered with his "line."

The finished work was a huge success. It had an unprecedented sale in the annals of Hungarian political book publishing: 235,000 copies. Though it was not read by all the people who purchased it, they knew that to have that imitation-leather book with the simple but promising title of *The Rakosi Trial* in a place of honor on their bookshelves was not a virtue but an obligation.

---

* Two contemporary newsreels showed Rakosi in action in 1919. In one, he was seen for a second only at a mass meeting. In the other, he was seen in uniform at the North Hungarian front. But these scenes were sufficient to make him the hero of several novels and plays.

Rakosi's dumpy little figure grew to giant proportions, and, as the leading politicians who at first surrounded him disappeared behind the scenes or surrendered to him unconditionally, he began to resemble that hero of Chamisso's who lost more and more of his shadow.

There he stood at the increasingly frequent gala performances at the opera house, triumphant in the middle of the stage, in the focus of the floodlights, apparently oblivious of the deafening storm of applause. Then, after a while, when he felt that the audience had had sufficient opportunity to give way to its boundless enthusiasm, he too, began to clap, in a manner learned from Stalin, as a signal that it was time to calm down. Enough of the celebration. It had already been perhaps even too much. His modesty would not stand for more. Though he could understand their adoration and approve of it . . . still, one should not exaggerate. . . .

He sat down.

But this touching, delicate modesty served only to fire the audience to renewed outbursts of ecstasy. Besides, nobody would have dared to be first to stop applauding. Who knew who might have noticed it, and who knew in what form this lack of enthusiasm might live on in the secret and mysterious files of the Party headquarters' filing department? The hysterical applause, now rhythmical and unending, broke out with new force.

It was like some sort of religious trance which turned dutiful homage into intoxicating ecstasy, or into happiness and gratitude on the part of the masses to the man who had relieved them of the heavy burden of thinking for themselves, who was prescribing every action for them, and who was staking his life on their liberation—a man whose strength, power, and knowledge was far beyond that of ordinary mortals and whose touching simplicity and moving modesty betrayed intelligence and strength, superiority and humility, unwavering faith and absolute certainty.

Rakosi rose again.

It was impossible to watch this celebration, this thanksgiving service, sitting down, and, though one had the impression that it really was an effort, one must bear up bravely, carrying this burden in the interest of the community, smiling with the slightly apologetic (but at the same time self-assured) smile which simultaneously rejected and invited this triumph. One must smile with that slightly painful smile of earthly transubstantiation—a smile lit with joy and bitterness, reflecting the past and the future.

To be exact, this was the People's Democratic Paradise.

Generals' uniforms rubbed elbows with well-cut black suits, the chests of the former covered with a multitude of decorations recalling the self-sacrificing work carried on for the benefit of the people. Ministers smoked their cigarettes in the corridors during the intermission, talking with charming and sincere and almost apologetic condescension to those sparkling-eyed women in national costumes who were the real representatives of the people and who could never before have entered the opera house and who were now occupying the boxes reserved for the bourgeoisie, watching and enjoying themselves and walking around as living proofs of the already accomplished future.

Here, everybody was a son of the people.

There were the generals and the ministers, the department heads and the writers, and the carefully prepared protocol list numbering only the faithful and reliable—i.e., those who could be trusted to stand by in difficult times and who knew that the Secret Police messenger arriving on a motorcycle was bringing a ticket to Paradise in the carefully sealed envelope.

It was a serene, self-satisfied crowd, well-balanced and happy like a big family, whose members meet but rarely because there is much work to be done and a hard struggle to be waged against a cunning enemy. They shook hands, slapped each other on the shoulder, drank a few glasses together, and, in this sparkling mood, they all became accomplices. They merged into one group. Everybody became more equal among the equal. Everybody became part of the festive ecstasy, of the brotherly world. With their glasses in their hands, they all shared the power and the

security of power—a power and a security that they were holding
and would continue to hold as long as they protected it well.

Suddenly, the huge room was filled with an excited hum.

"Comrade Rakosi is coming," the people whispered on all
sides.

And there came the dumpy little man, advancing between
two walls of people with a gay and interested smile on his
face, dressed in regulation black, with the regulation silver tie,
and half a step behind him followed two unknown men, one
on either side of him and their hands in their pockets.

In a few seconds, Rakosi is surrounded by a huge crowd. The
more fortunate stand near enough to touch him. The less fortunate stand on tiptoe on the outer edge of the circle, trying to
catch his eyes. He shakes hands with the people he knows (and,
because of his excellent memory, he knows a good many), and
he speaks a few words to them, betraying not only the excellence
of his memory but also his interest in their work and achievements. He asks the writers what they are working on at the moment, or, in order to make them realize how well informed he is,
he quotes a few words from their last writings. Sometimes, he
praises. At other times, he criticizes or voices such a delicate
and modest order as: "We are still waiting for the novel you
promised. Why don't you work on it? Is anything disturbing
you?"

Invariably, Rakosi spoke in the first-person plural as if he
were royalty. But *his* royalty was the Party, the great "one-man
collective"—a term intended to express the perfectly condensed
reality of the unity of will and action.

They listened to him with starry eyes. They were the adorers
listening to the saint.

It was a strange kind of adoration. For, though it filled them
with a mad ecstasy during the half-hours of rhythmical applause, there was an undercurrent of inexpressible and unex-
pressed fear in it. A brilliant chemist would be needed to deter-
mine the exact proportions of acids and of alkalis in the souls
of the most faithful adorers. There were hundreds, perhaps even

thousands, who would gladly have given their lives for Comrade Rakosi or who would have jumped at his command from the top of Mount Gellert right into the Danube. Yet, the same people shook with fear when they heard over the telephone the voice of the adored chief—that voice with a broad, somewhat Slavic accent, sounding sometimes like its own echo.

Why were they afraid?

Everybody knew (and Rakosi himself made no secret of it, which was again something to admire in him) that he was cunning and ruthless toward his enemies. It had been he who had crushed all the "bourgeois" parties in Hungary. It was he who was the international expert on "meat-grinder tactics." It was he who began his good work by tearing to pieces the country's largest party, the Smallholders Party, frightening and blackmailing its members and inciting its leaders against each other and who then, by driving its leaders into exile or by jailing or paying them off, had swallowed up the Social Democratic Party. True, the fraternal Soviet Army had been there to back him up—a fact which somewhat facilitated his task. But the brilliant plan had been his work. It was he who had removed from the scene the two heads of the Roman Catholic Church, Cardinals Mindszenty and Groesz, even though the Church was very strong in Hungary; and it was he (and this again is something he boasted of) who had unmasked and liquidated Tito's bloodhounds, the Rajk bandits. It was he who would have had no compunction about wining and dining with a man whom, on the very same night, he would have arrested and sent to the gallows as a confirmed enemy of the people, of progress, and of socialism. Yes, so thought the faithful to themselves. But, so they thought, these had really been enemies who had wanted to slow down the tempo of construction, who had wanted to push the country back into the mire of the past, and who had planned to sell their country's independence to foreign powers. These had deserved their fate. These had deserved to be treated roughly, and, if necessary, hypocritically and mercilessly. But this was no reason for Rakosi's *disciples* to be afraid of him.

Those, however, who knew him more closely, and who had met him at work, when reporting to him, or who had been summoned in front of the Political Committee, knew only too well that this round and serene face was not always a smiling face. After all, the fierce class struggle could not be waged with a smile. This was no May Day celebration. Nor was it a county ball. This was something that not only the enemy, but also the comrades, had better understand! At work, Rakosi was serious. He was often nervous or impatient or morose, with his left brow constantly raised as if he were asking a question to which he already knew the answer. There was no subtlety about him. He was not polite. He expressed his opinions roundly and coldly. He composed his sentences with axiomatic exactitude. When he was dissatisfied, these sentences, though they were rarely rude, were all the more cutting and painful and destructive to one's self-confidence. With an apparently polite remark, he could humiliate even his most devoted disciples. The last sentence with which he dismissed his visitor could be like a parting gift, the traveller carrying it in his luggage until the next meeting, trying to explain it to himself, analyzing it, finding out what Rakosi had really intended to say. Gay or bitter, this last sentence sometimes became the leitmotif for a very long time.

Those who knew him were afraid that he would not speak to them or that he would ignore them, for he was a past master in looking through people. And they were equally afraid he would stop and talk to them, for one never knew what consequences such a conversation might bring. Even if he had no intention of poisoning the atmosphere of a reception, he nevertheless managed to do so. It was enough if he jokingly reminded a minister that he was still waiting for the promised report. As a result, the minister had a sleepless night. Or if he mentioned to a general that, according to certain information, the regiment's food was bad (a thing unheard of in a people's army), the general had a sleepless night. Or if he asked a film director whether some color film had arrived from the Soviet Union, and, if it had not, he would immediately see to it, then the film director had a good night. It was impossible to argue with him. It was even difficult to carry on a conversation with him, not only because he would not tolerate arguments, but simply because he gave his companion no time to speak. He spoke fast, changing the subject suddenly, telling anecdotes or making demands, threatening or cajoling. But he always spoke in such a way that his partner had to content himself with a "Yes" or a "No" until he realized that his opinion was of no importance at all and that Rakosi was not interested in it—all the less so, since he already knew what the other would say.

They were afraid of his capacity for work and of the super-human—or perhaps inhuman—tempo of work that he imposed on the entire country even without official proclamation. His car arrived in front of the gates of Party headquarters at 7:30 in the morning, and the light was on in his room until late into the night. The tempo he dictated for himself was fairly stiff, and he was no longer a young man. But, behind his study there was another room, a small room with a couch and a liquor cabinet and a bathroom where he could retire when he was tired, while his collaborators, who had no hidden rooms behind their offices, worked incessantly and dared not leave the building until Rakosi left. As a result, it became habitual for the department and sub-department heads of the ministries at Party headquarters to remain in their offices until late at night, for what would happen if Comrade Rakosi telephoned, let us say, at 10:30 and they had already left, deserting their sector of the class struggle because of their shameless, petty-bourgeois love of comfort.

Slowly a situation developed in which the deputy ministers watched the ministers, and the sub-department heads watched the department heads. Nobody dared to go home, although all were exhausted. Their rooms were filled with cold, sour cigarette smoke. The desk, the tables, and the armchairs were strewn with ashes and cigarette butts. The secretaries had gone home, and there was nobody to make a cup of coffee, and, anyway, they had had at least five strong black coffees since noon. Yet they stayed on, their tired foreheads resting on their fists, their unseeing eyes on a column of figures or an uninteresting report. They were too tired to work. They only knew that the wife was already asleep, and that she would awake at their arrival and give them one of the usual reproachful looks. And they knew that they had not seen their children for weeks, that they had not been to a cinema or a theater or read a book for ages. Yet, what could they do? They had to build socialism.

And Comrade Rakosi worked on with unflagging energy.

They were afraid of his memory. They were afraid of the convolutions of the brain in the disproportionately large skull and of that frightening store of filed-away data and material which seemed to contain information on all the nine million inhabitants of the country. They knew that he could always refresh his memory from the files and the reports and the denunciations of the State Security Department. But that did not alter anything. It was all there in his head. All that figured in the files in the form of tiny notes or in a few words underlined in red, all the more or less important slips committed in the past (a little fascist infection, a relative who had absconded to Australia, a passing adventure, a contradiction in the curriculum vitae, financial troubles, a desk drawer that had once remained unlocked—for, after all, nobody is perfect and everybody has made blunders) was known by Comrade Rakosi; or, to be more exact, one never knew whether he knew or not and, therefore, it was safest to suppose that he did. It often happened that, in a conversation, he suddenly dropped a half sentence or a veiled insinuation referring to some old blunder that the culprit would gladly have forgotten. Thus, one never knew when that blunder would suddenly gain utmost importance, or over what political task or change of policy one would stumble after having gone through the first screening as an excellent officer. It became increasingly evident that everyone's fate was in that strong, fleshy, stubby hand—a hand that knew how to caress, but that knew even better how to break necks.

In reality, they feared the totality of his power. For who

was there to control or to check or to limit that power? Everybody knew—and Rakosi took good care that there should never be any doubt about it—that Stalin was greater and more powerful than he. But it was equally evident that Stalin relied on him and trusted him fully, for it was with good reason that they called him "Comrade Stalin's best Hungarian disciple." They knew that one of the telephones on his desk had a direct line to the Kremlin. Rakosi liked nothing better than to weave into his conversations with people little remarks like: "As I was told yesterday by Comrade Molotov . . ."

Those who were fortunate enough to travel to the Soviet Union were frequently told by some gossiping clerk of the Intourist Agency of the Kiev or Lvov air terminals the news that never reached the papers: "Comrade Rakosi passed through here yesterday en route to Moscow in his private plane. . . ." "Indeed?" asked the surprised Hungarian visitor, to whom the Soviet clerk would reply with the superiority of the initiated: "Of course. He often comes this way. A very polite comrade. . . . He always has a glass of lemonade. . . ."

At such times, the Hungarian visitor's thoughts ran something like this: Rakosi had certainly been invited by Stalin for a friendly little conversation. And what would the visitor do if Rakosi became angry? Turn to Stalin for help? Ridiculous! He could perhaps turn to the other three members of the "foursome"—to Gero, Revai, and Farkas. But it was certain that Rakosi was infinitely superior to them, for these three men not only accepted but proclaimed this fact—and they never even tried to compete with Rakosi. There was absolute unity in the leadership: his three partners completely subordinated themselves to Rakosi.

He who crossed Rakosi's path was lost. His ruthlessness towards those who earned his displeasure was notorious. Whatever he did, he did in the interest of the *cause,* but it was he who decided what the interest of the cause was, and nobody else. No matter who you were, no matter whether you were the General Manager of the Csepel Iron Works or the Ambassador to Norway or a university professor or the Chairman of the County Council—if you did not fulfill your plan in time or behaved clumsily at a reception or did not apply Soviet methods or made some equivocal remark among friends, then you found out the next day that you had lost your job at Rakosi's order and could not even work as a messenger boy or as a laborer in your field. A respected critic had written a review on a play which he found mediocre but which, for political reasons, was approved by the comrades at Party headquarters because it incited hatred against the kulaks. Rakosi had then picked up the telephone. As a result, the critic had been compelled to criticize himself publicly; he had had to write that he had made a grave mistake, that the play was not bad but good, and that it was his own fault that he had not fully appreciated its beauties or understood its depths. Then, after he had obeyed Rakosi's order, this same critic was kicked out of his job. A Party official had remarked to someone that the customary rhythmical applause which greeted Rakosi was not an absolutely necessary requisite of the building of socialism. He was not jailed, but he was shortly transferred to an insignificant job where he was superfluous, and in his new environment everybody avoided getting in touch with him. Neither past merits (nor high rank nor distinguished decorations) sufficed as a protection. What counted was always the most recent achievement or the most recent mistake. For, Comrade Rakosi was just. Terribly just.

And yet, the fear that filled the souls of even his most faithful disciples comprised only a part of their devotion. It comprised a strange, cold current under the waves of passionate ecstasy. Its unbanishable presence served only to make happiness more poignant, delight more exciting, fulfillment richer in content. There was something overpowering in it, almost like intoxication or like standing on a peak near the blinding sun, from which it was so easy to tumble into the depths. This fear multiplied the importance of every little word, of every condescending gesture. One could "live on it" for days, for weeks, for months, recalling it again and again and telling one's friends about it. "Just imagine," one could say, "recently the telephone rang in my office. I picked it up. 'Hallo, Rakosi here,' he says. 'Well, comrade, all I wanted to tell you is that, though that suggestion you submitted could have been worked out in greater detail, it was not bad, not bad at all. I shall personally recommend you for a decoration. How is your wife? . . .' I was so moved, I couldn't even reply. Anyway, he didn't wait for my answer. But that is not important. It is a great thing, old man, that he finds time to ring me up and even inquire about my wife, what with all the work he has to do, with the worries of an entire country on his shoulders. If you stop to think of it, he is doing everything in this blessed country."

The figure of Rakosi became more and more legendary. It became invested with superhuman, almost supernatural, powers. He hardly slept, it was whispered: not more than three or four hours a day. But he read four or five hundred pages of political literature and fiction alike, and of poetry and science. He finished with the newspapers by 9 a.m.—not only with *Szabad Nep* and *Pravda*, but also with the *Manchester Guardian* and the *New York Times,* not to speak of *Le Monde* and *Unita.* He had eyes like an eagle. He immediately noticed the essential thing in every book or article. Like the Greek gods, he appeared unexpectedly in the most unlikely spots: early at dawn he was at the market hall to ask the amazed housewives whether they were satisfied with the potato supply, whether there had been enough tomatoes on the market, whether the price of the carrots was not too high, and whether this year's cabbage was leafy enough. Then he emerged in a village where he had agreed to stand as godfather for a poor peasant's tenth child. Nobody had hoped that he would arrive for the christening, but there he was, and he had even brought a present.

Rakosi liked to be kind. He was proud of his kindness. After all, his brilliant mind had devised the principal slogan of the system—his system!—in the immortal words: IN OUR SYSTEM, MAN IS THE GREATEST VALUE! This slogan served to inform the world at large of the basic motive of his activities, of the source of inspiration of all his thoughts, of the quintessence, so to speak, of his ideas. Because—and let no one be misled by the plural—"our" system meant "my" system, and in my system, comrades, man is the greatest value, and I have to watch over man, if for no other reason than that I have risen above those whom the noun includes.

This superhuman status permitted him a certain liberty, of which he made full use. Which of his disciples was not moved to tears watching Rakosi kiss the ladies' hands (although it was understood that kissing hands was a despicable bourgeois remnant)? Oh, Comrade Rakosi could do what he pleased! Such things befit him. They rendered him more attractive, more human, more real. For, behind this somewhat old-fashioned gesture, behind the Old World politeness of the professional revolutionary, one perceived, as in a haze, past love affairs with women who must necessarily have adored this perhaps not handsome but irresistible man.

Oh, yes, everything was permitted to Comrade Rakosi that was strictly forbidden to ordinary mortals. For, was it not charming when he said: "Well, comrades, with God's help we shall have an excellent harvest this year"? Or was it not natural, when he said, turning to the disciples who were figuratively on their knees before him: "Even God loves our Party. Doesn't He always give us good weather on May 1st?" Had anyone else mentioned God, he would have been accused of being under "clerical influence." But Comrade Rakosi could say what he pleased. Who knows? Perhaps he was really on good terms with God, or in some kind of comradely relationship, or in a sort of gay complicity.

Yes, he was different from anyone else.

His rules were different, and so were his limitations, his thoughts, his cerebral convolutions and—probably—many other of his qualities. There would have been nothing to be surprised at if it had turned out that Comrade Rakosi was also biologically different from the other mortals above whom he towered.

The faithful were indescribably proud and happy that a gracious fate had given them and the country a leader like Matyas Rakosi. True—or so they whispered to each other— Comrade Gottwald and Comrade Gheorghiu-Dej were excellent men and excellent Communists. Still, our Comrade Rakosi was by far the most outstanding among the people's democratic leaders. Officially, this kind of talk was severely censured at the Party schools and seminars, being branded as nationalist diversion. But, invariably, the censure was compounded with a grain of tolerant complicity, because, though it was strictly forbidden and in bad taste to talk about it, there was some truth in it— and had the comrades noticed that, at the great festivities in Moscow on the occasion of Comrade Stalin's seventieth birthday, only one people's democratic leader had sat in the first row: our Comrade Rakosi? If the Communist Party of the Soviet Union had, after Stalin's death, turned to Rakosi for leadership in those chaotic days, the faithful would have felt honored—but not surprised.

Is it to be wondered that the legends told about this wonderful man were approved and fostered and, as they proved useful, spread and enlarged upon? Can it be ascribed to vanity and not political utilitarianism that, after a while, every photograph taken of Rakosi had to be submitted to Rakosi for his approval, and that only those that showed his moonlike face and his short, neckless, and obese body to advantage were printed? From that day of his complete seizure of power, an entire literature dealt with the story of his life and brilliant deeds. In March, 1952, on the occasion of his sixtieth birthday, a red leather-bound volume was published under the title of *Hungarian Writers on Matyas Rakosi*—a volume in which the foremost writers and poets of the country, both Communist and non-Communist, paid tribute in prose and verse to the wise father and great leader of the Hungarian people. An old and gifted painter painted a portrait of Rakosi, with his wife * at his side, talking to the simple children of the people. A moving play was performed at the Army Theater. The play proved with absolute authenticity that Rakosi had been the most heroic soldier of the 1919 dictatorship of the proletariat.

The official opinion of the Agitation-Propaganda Department was that these artistic creations were a necessary and useful means of educating the people to socialism, and there was no doubt that Rakosi was very pleased with them. On March 15, 1953, after the festive distribution of the Kossuth Prizes, some writers stood around talking to Jozsef Darvas, the writer and the then Minister of Education, and Peter Veres, Chairman of the Hungarian Writers' Association, when Rakosi unexpectedly joined them. After the mutual congratulations, they began to talk about the first volume of Peter Veres' latest novel, which described the life of a peasant boy in the first decades of the century.

"I read your book, Peter," Rakosi began. "It is a good book. A beautiful book. But do you know what your trouble is?"

Peter Veres looked at him curiously.

"That you have a heart as soft as butter," said Rakosi.

"What do you mean by that?" asked Veres.

"Listen," said Rakosi, "your book deals with life in the Hungarian village, but there is not a word in it about the kulaks. It is as if there had been no kulaks at all in your village."

"Well, there weren't any," replied Veres.

---

* Rakosi married in the Soviet Union. His wife, a lawyer, was an almond-eyed, rather ugly Kirghiz or Uzbeg, who was secretary of the committee that had been formed for his liberation at the time of his imprisonment. The woman was noticeably embarrassed by having to play the part of Hungary's first lady, and she did her best to remain modestly in the background. But Rakosi insisted on taking her with him to every reception and every public appearance, introducing her to everyone, and making her sit with him in his box at gala performances. Obviously, all this was intended to show the people what an exemplary family life he led.

"You can't tell me that," Rakosi rebuked him. "I was a village boy myself. There were kulaks in our village. They were haughty, disgusting exploiters, who sucked the poor peasants' blood and were hated by them. Your trouble is that you refuse to mention this. You don't want people to hate the kulaks."

It was easy to see that Peter Veres was simply fuming with rage. He was a proud old man who was convinced that no one knew the life of the Hungarian village better than he, and now here was this grocer's son teaching him how to give an authentic picture of peasant life. Yet, unless he wanted to appear to be a defender of the kulaks, he could not give free rein to his feelings. It was through his peasant cunning that he soon found a way to hit back at Rakosi.

"That's not where the trouble lies," Veres said, looking anxiously at the "wise father." "I am working on the second volume but I got stuck."

"Why," asked Rakosi. "What is the problem? Perhaps we can help."

"You know," the old peasant continued, "I have come to 1918-1919. In those days, dozens of socialist tracts were sent to us in the village. We read them, studied them, and were enlightened by them . . ."

"Well, what is wrong with that?" asked Rakosi.

"What's wrong with them," Veres replied with sarcastic calmness, "is that you Communists later declared that one tract had been written by the Social Democrats, the other by factionists. Now, what the hell am I to do about it?"

"Oh, that?" Rakosi dismissed the problem. "You don't have to worry about that! You can safely say that they had all been sent by the Party."

"All right. But there is also something else. Something more serious. You know, when we were fighting against the Rumanians with the Red Guard, the commander of the entire front down there at the Tisza was Vilmos Boehm."

Hearing this name, Rakosi's face clouded. This Social Democratic Party leader was on the list of those who had been branded

the vilest right-wing traitors to the working class—a list of people
whom only emigration had saved from prison.

"Well," said Veres, "we believed in Boehm. We considered
him an honest man and a good leader. Now, what am I to write
about him?"

By then Rakosi knew what to say.

"Look," he said. "There's no point in making such a fuss
about this. Your best course would be to transfer the whole
action from the Tisza to the northern front. There, it is all
clear sailing. There, I was the commander. You could write
about me."

Peter Veres nodded approvingly.

"You are perfectly right," he said. "And I should be more
than glad to do so if I could. But you know how it is. There
are certain difficulties. Because, in reality, it was not there that
the important things happened."

Instead of lessening Rakosi's prestige, Stalin's death only increased it. The faithful felt that he should now be supported even
more fervently, since, with the death of the Great One, he had
clearly risen in the hierarchy of the working-class movement.
When, on May 10, 1953, on the eve of the elections, he appeared on the steps of the Parliament building to announce the
program of the Party to the masses, his power had become
greater than ever before.

"The huge, gaily decorated Square overflowed with the masses
of Budapest workers," wrote *Szabad Nep* the following day.
"The endless columns, singing and carrying flags, had to stop
in the side streets. On the gala platform raised on the steps
of the Parliament building were the pictures of Lenin, Stalin,
and Rakosi. To the left of the platform, on the facade of the
building, were the pictures of Comrades Malenkov, Beria, Molotov, and Voroshilov. To the right were those of Istvan Dobi,
Erno Gero, Mihaly Farkas, and Jozsef Revai. Cheers of wild
enthusiasm and storms of applause greeted the first candidate of

the Hungarian people: Comrade Matyas Rakosi. . . . The Square resounded with cries of "Hurrah," acclaiming Rakosi. . . ."

Istvan Dobi, the head of state, introduced the speaker with the following words:

"All our great achievements are linked with Comrade Rakosi. His name is the banner under which the entire Hungarian people rally in a single camp. Comrade Matyas Rakosi is deeply loved and highly esteemed by the Hungarian people, because in him they see a great fighter for peace—a peace which guarantees our free and independent life, the greatest treasure of our people. . . ."

Only then did Rakosi appear on the platform. "The flags," said the newspaper account, "were raised high. Thousands and thousands of hands held up Soviet and national flags to salute Comrade Rakosi. Enthusiastic cheers and applause filled the Square, and these quieted down only when Comrade Rakosi began to speak. . . ."

This was the great moment of fulfillment.

Only six weeks later, the very same man was called in Moscow a political adventurer and a Jewish king by the supreme leadership of the Soviet Communist Party.

And on July 4, 1953, the very same man sat in the second row at the session of the Hungarian Parliament.

The Hungarian Village

The first symptoms of the Nagy landslide made themselves felt in the Hungarian villages. The capital, which was usually a highly sensitive seismograph of events, felt only that "something was up"—something extraordinary and new, though life went on undisturbed, without excesses, without serious anxieties. Naturally, the direct effect of Imre Nagy's speech was very apparent in Budapest: the terrible pressure that had weighed down on people for years now lessened. Everybody breathed more freely. Nightwork at the ministries and at the various offices ceased from one day to the next. Suddenly, it became obligatory to go home after work hours, and an adequate time for leisure, which had previously been considered a petty-bourgeois love of comfort, became the duty of every citizen. The turnover of the pastry shops, of the coffeehouses, and of even the nightclubs doubled. Old "bourgeois" tunes were heard on the radio, and new American numbers were added to the repertory of the jazz orchestras. People danced, not only at trade union fêtes, but also in public places; and the narrow streets of the city's shopping center, where the creators of fashion had once lived and displayed their models, hummed with new life. Modern, colorful shop windows bloomed in famous Vaci Street, bringing to mind a past which was naturally much less brilliant than it seemed in people's memories

—a past transformed into a fairy-tale world under the pressure of the difficult more recent years. Heaven knows how it happened, but the best dressmakers suddenly presented their clients with the latest Western fashion magazines. Women used lipstick in daring colors, and men wore ties of a bold pattern, for such acts were no longer punished by severe criticism nor even by loss of work. All this was permissible now, and the new freedoms were happily, a little flauntingly, enjoyed. The barbers, the pastry-makers, the art dealers and opticians and photographers who had worked for years in the scarcely profitable cooperatives now dreamed—as promised by the Government—of reopening their own shops. They applied for licenses and, to their amazement, received them in a very short time. Old names appeared on new billboards. They were familiar old names, and the passers-by stared at them curiously and happily. Those who had been banned from the capital planned to move back to their old homes. Those who had moved into those homes thought anxiously of the time when the former owners would suddenly appear and claim their apartments.

Everything was still a little hazy and uncertain. There was a strange atmosphere of hope and, at the same time, of distrust. Everybody was waiting curiously for developments, and, in the meantime, the capital lived the gay, pulsating, bustling life that had in the past attracted so many foreign visitors.

No storm raged. All was peaceful and quiet, although it was rumored that in certain parts of the country there were disturbances among the peasants and that (with a cry of "Communism is finished!") the old police uniforms were being fetched down from the garrets (uniforms that had always been and still were an object of loathing to the peasants, because the cock feathers waving on the *chako* had always been symbols of persecution and terror). It was also said that in certain places the kulaks were trying to reclaim their land, which had been expropriated for the cooperatives. But these rumors caused no undue excitement in the capital.

It was not so much among the people as among the Party

officials that these stories were spread. And the discerning ear could easily distinguish the purpose behind them. It was natural that it should be so, for it was in the Party machinery and among the Party officials that the new program was meeting with the greatest resistance. The policies which Imre Nagy had proclaimed in his speech were new and extraordinary and almost unbelievable to those who had for years grown accustomed to believing in Rakosi's ideas. By this time, the Party officials had completely identified themselves with routine. Their ears had grown accustomed to the empty slogans (to the very slogans which were the foundation upon which they stood and worked) and, even worse, they had absolutely divorced themselves from the real life of the people, even though they lived in the very heart of the factories, the offices, and the ministries. After a while, they had even come to believe their own reports which, as presented in summarized form at conferences and congresses, had turned into simple "Bulletins of the Progress Achieved by the Working People."

The Party officials had lost contact with real life. But the workers and clerks and engineers had lost contact with the Party officials. After a certain time, the Party official stood alone, or, at most, flanked by one or two of his disciples, on a lonely island removed from the swift current of life—a life which, in reality, was entirely different from his conception of it. He lived in a world of his own. He breathed in an atmosphere of his own. And it was suddenly brought home to him that everything he had done and that everything he had believed in (if he had believed in it), and that everything he had pretended to believe in, had been false, mistaken, harmful, and wrong.

The first thing the Party official had to face was the calm but openly ironical smile that lighted up the people's faces after the announcement of the new Government program. This smile contained contempt, pity, scorn, and hatred—all the feelings that had always been there, but which the people had not dared to act upon. The Party official sensed that the milieu in which he had lived and in which his command had hitherto been obeyed blindly and unconditionally, had suddenly changed. Although the machinery had not yet turned upon him (though even this now occurred in some places), it was undeniable that a screw had come loose in the perfect machine and that a strong vibration, the source of which could not yet be established, was shaking its entire body. The official, who had long since lost the habit of hearing and understanding the sounds of real life, now sensed the full force of that vibration, and he knew that it held unknown dangers for him unless an outbreak was prevented in time. Yet, it is obvious that, with only a handful of exceptions, most Party officials determinedly resisted any relaxation of control.

This resistance was strongest in the central Party machinery, where stood the supreme fortress of Party life. The mass of leading officials, being completely detached from life and reality, considered the new program an attack upon their very existence and watched the rapidly moving events with deep anxiety. They expected and demanded that the highest Party leadership take action to prevent a "disintegration."

The emphasis, however, was on Rakosi's speech.

This speech made it clear to the officials that the situation was not quite as bad as they had thought. Rakosi declared that—on the basis of Party unity—he fully agreed with Imre Nagy's program. But, he said, it had become clear during the last week that it had been a mistake to allow the Government, rather than the Party, to announce the new program. His admission implied that leadership would remain in the hands of the Party (i.e., of Rakosi), and that thus the officials had nothing to fear from an eventual change.*

Rakosi's speech reassured the anxious Party officials, particularly when he declared that excesses in the villages would have to be suppressed with an iron fist and that, though the "kulak

---

* It was learned the day before Rakosi's speech that Beria, the man who had most sharply attacked Rakosi at the meeting of the Politburo in Moscow, had been arrested. Rakosi immediately referred to this arrest in his speech, warmly approving of it. It was obvious that he was prepared to use this event as the motivating reason for eventual changes which would later take place in Hungary. The participants of the meeting, who knew nothing about the Politburo meetings, did not quite understand Rakosi's elation, but later he took good care to spread word of his motivating reason among the highest Party officials.

larly when he declared that excesses in the villages would have to be suppressed with an iron fist and that, though the "kulak list" was no longer in existence, a kulak was always a kulak. The officials beamed: Comrade Rakosi had not changed and they had nothing to fear, for a proper answer would be made to these newfangled ideas!

As far as the Communist writers were concerned, they were, in general, happy about the program. Their reaction to it was not identical with that of the Party officials who feared for their positions: for them, the problem was not primarily a materialistic one. It was, rather, an ethical problem—a problem of an attitude toward reality, of how to judge their own work, of where the truth lay in literature. In general—though there were a few exceptions—the writers had never really known what was going on in the country. The Party literary work they had been doing, and the struggle for socialist realism, had either obscured reality or had transformed it into a sham. Now they greeted the Government program as the Party's effort to disclose the full truth. They fully and unconditionally approved of the measures involved in the program (i.e., the end of deportations, the dissolution of the concentration camps, the rule that no evidence could be used against a peasant in order to make him join a cooperative, etc.). And they made a sincere effort to admit and to correct their own mistakes.

At the same time, however, the Government program gave rise to a certain growing nervousness and fear among the writers that, in the last analysis, coincided with the nervousness and fear of the officials: the writers feared that the upheaval endangered the results achieved, that it endangered the Party's prestige, and that it might, in its consequences, become an obstacle to development. Some of them held that the Party's own self-criticism made the difficulties and faults appear more severe than they really were.*

---

* Special mention must be made here of the Muscovites, who were from the very first moment violently opposed to the program. They started rumors about Imre Nagy's "Bukharinist" past, and Bela Illes ironically called Imre Nagy's Government the "Provisional Government."

The ideological foundation of the newly developed—or per-
sisting—attitude was *solicitude* for the Party. This was the feeling
that while, on the one hand, one should help the Party correct
its past mistakes, one should on the other hand defend it against
the attacks of its enemies, who had founded a new platform in
the Government program. It is characteristic that a writer like
Tibor Dery, who had enthusiastically approved the Government
program, considered it necessary to declare his loyalty to the
Party in its difficult days.

The situation was further complicated by the fact that, immediately after the announcement of the new program, the Communist writers were severely reprimanded by the Party for not
having called the attention of the Party—as good Communists
should—to the difficulties and mistakes pointed out by the Government (i.e., the Party) program. In the official Party lingo, it
was the writers' fault for not "giving signals," for not having kept
up with reality, and for not having fulfilled their duty to the
Party—to the Party which was, thus, compelled to solve every
problem alone, without the help of its writers. This reproach was
as hypocritical and demagogical as it was unjustified, because
everyone knew that prior to July 3—i.e., one day before the
"official" launching of the Nagy program—it had been completely impossible to publish a line or even a word which did not
fully support Rakosi's Government program.

The best example of this fact lay in the case of Sandor Csoori.
Csoori was a very young poet of peasant origin who had been
enabled to attain a university education by the good offices of the
regime. He was an enthusiastic glorifier of the new world until—
in the course of repeated visits to his village—his friends and
relatives had convinced him by their very example that the realities of life were the exact opposite from those proclaimed by the
propaganda in Budapest. Csoori had then written a few poems
which had suggested that something was wrong in the Hungarian
villages. The poems were written months before the new Government program, but there was naturally no question of publishing them. They were locked up in his desk drawer, and it needed
Imre Nagy and the new era to get them published.

Although the writers knew (and they knew the Party knew) that the criticism had been unjust, they firmly resolved never again to lose touch with life. They resolved to be the first to "discover" truth and thus to contribute to the Party's successes.

In the countryside, the situation was much more exciting—and much more critical. It was late September, the season when the "agricultural year" was approaching its end, and, as a result of the new program, the problem arose as to whether or not the cooperatives would disintegrate or survive—i.e., whether the members would leave or still maintain the cooperatives. What passions, conflicts, and interests were now at war in the distant villages? The Hungarian Writers' Association made it possible for twenty-five or thirty writers to observe this war on the spot, and, at the same time, to help the local Party organizations to save as many cooperatives as possible. This group of writers went forth, not for a day or two, but for weeks. They were driven by a newly blazing passion: the passionate desire to get acquainted with reality.

It happened that two young but nationally known writers decided to roam the country together.

One was a Communist. The other was not.

The former was a tall, somewhat bent, tousled, long-legged young man who not only carried a Party card in his pocket but considered himself first and foremost a poet of the Party. No, he considered himself more than that: he was the Hungarian Mayakovsky!* Both in his appearance and in his writing, the young poet stressed his resemblance to Mayakovsky. Emerging a few years after the war, he had soon become known for his shrill

---

* Vladimir Vladimirovich Mayakovsky is the poet most valued by official Soviet history of literature. He was, no doubt, a very gifted poet who devoted the last ten years of his life wholly to the Communist Party. He called himself a Party agitator-propagandist. His poems dealt with the actual problems of Soviet life. In his early youth, he was a futurist. Later, he created a staggered verse form that he used to the day of his death. Lenin did not like him; Stalin, however, called him "the greatest poet of the Soviet period"—but after Mayakovsky's suicide. The circumstances of that suicide are not quite clear. Some said the cause was an unhappy love affair. Others said that he was driven to death by the persecution of the Trotskyites.

poems of propaganda agitating for the Party's causes. He had written about labor competition, about collectivization, and about there being less worry and more sugar than ever before in the country. He had written a series of poems on the struggles of the Hungarian Soviet Republic of 1919. He had belonged among those who devoted all their time and energy, all their faith and enthusiasm, to the cause they believed to be good. He was a gifted young man. His poems had told the world loudly and unequivocally of the things he believed, and consequently his career had been meteoric. The Party had immediately recognized him as the man it needed. Soon he had been put in charge of Hungarian literature at Party headquarters. From here, he had been transferred to the Hungarian Writers' Association as secretary of the local Party organization. Many disliked him for his rigidity, his vanity, and his stubbornness. His poems had become ever weaker, for all his time was taken up with politics, and he considered writing poems a secondary occupation. To be more exact, he had continued to write poems only to "support" his political activities. He had become one of the foremost "schematists"—so much so that, at the First Congress of the Hungarian Writers' Association, Jozsef Revai himself had warned him of his "leftishness," and of the fact that poetry deals not only with the progress of heavy industry but also with flowers, clouds, the sky.

This young poet's name was Peter Kuczka.

The other young man was a very gifted novelist who enjoyed good living and whose hair was thinning at the top. His specialty was the portrayal of peasant life, and he had always had certain reservations about the official Party line. Still, his books had been published and his plays had been performed, though the books and plays had always been received with "instructive" criticism on the part of the reviewers. Without exception, the Party's pet critics had pointed out the young writer's "peasant outlook," as well as his "Narodnik" limitations,* all of which indicated that he had not fully realized the leading role of the Party in the

---

* A notion borrowed from Soviet political and literary life, meaning that one doubts the leading role of the working class and idealizes the peasantry.

transformation of society, nor the importance of the cooperative movement in agriculture.

This young writer had spent much time in the countryside. He knew the life and the mind of the peasant of the lowlands, and, more than that, he knew conditions as they really were.

His name was Imre Sarkadi.

The two friends decided that they would have a look at reality —together.

Kuczka thought that he would keep an eye on the other who, because he was not a Communist, might lose his head in an upheaval which was merely superficial and which, as everybody knew, could be assessed correctly only with the help of Marxism-Leninism.

Sarkadi thought that here, at last, was his opportunity to show his friend that, now as before, it was he, Sarkadi, who was right.

They selected one of the most backward and poverty-ridden areas of the country as their destination: the northern part far from the capital, a region which abounded in sand, in dusty acacia trees, in potatoes, in houses without electricity, and in poor and narrow-minded peasants. The region was County Szabolcs.

It was a mild, tender Hungarian autumn. Plums and grapes were ripening, and nobody who walked across the peaceful, hilly landscape guessed the conflicts raging in the hearts of the villagers.

The poet started out on the journey with a mysterious, meaningful smile on his lips which was intended to inform the world that he—although he had no intention of boasting—knew more about what was going on than did ordinary mortals who remained in ignorance of the great secret. Although he liked his friend, he was also a little sorry for him, particularly because of the impending disappointment, for he was certain his friend would discover his mistake: the peasants were with the Party and, if there were still some who had not realized where their own interest lay, the majority could distinguish good from bad and right from wrong. He believed this stubbornly and unwaveringly, for such was his nature.

For weeks, the two roamed the sandy, melancholy roads of the Nyírség. They stopped in the villages, talked with the peasants, and went to meetings of the cooperatives in order to listen to the arguments.

The poet was all ears. He had been in the villages before. The Party had often sent him to deliver a lecture, to read his poems, and to write a report; and he had always returned to the capital happy and smiling, filled with the solemn and majestic knowledge that everything was exactly as the books had foretold.

Now, however, he met a different situation. What he saw was not only different; it was shocking, disappointing, and frightening.

He saw huge potato fields with potatoes left to rot—a fact about which nobody cared. He saw maize fields, with the maize yellow and dry and unbroken. He saw acres and acres of hard, unplowed land which the peasants had forsaken in order to flee to the towns. The fields were overrun by weeds, and vermin built their nests in the furrows.

Then he talked to the peasants and learned the cause of the terrible situation.

For, suddenly, the peasants had begun to talk. On previous visits, it had been necessary to have time and patience in order to coax them to talk at all (well, the Hungarian peasant had always been a laconic breed!) and when they had spoken, they had talked of nothing but generalities. Now, silence had been broken like a dam, and the peasants flooded him with their complaints. They told stories of pain, of humiliation, of disappointment, of bitterness, and of resignation.

A new world opened before the poet. It was the world of the past few years, which he had ignored and which, even had he known about it, he would not have believed.

He learned that the fields had been left unplowed because the peasants had felt that there was no sense in plowing, since they never knew when the fields would be requisitioned for the cooperatives. He learned that many peasants had fled from the soil because it did not give them a livelihood and was, instead, a terrible burden, a worry, an uncertainty, and a frustration. The smallholder was being driven from his land by heavy taxes, by obligatory deliveries, and by regroupings of the farms. But he had not been excused. The obligations had to be fulfilled at any price, and the peasants were threatened by the council chairman. In turn, the council chairman was threatened by the village Party secretary, the village Party secretary by the district Party committee, the district Party committee by the county Party committee, the county Party committee by the emissaries, instructors, and inspectors sent out by Party headquarters, and these by the department heads sitting at headquarters, who were threatened by the Secretariat, which was, in turn, threatened directly by—Matyas Rakosi.

All the plans had to be fulfilled!

And what a lot of plans there were!

There was a meat-delivery plan, an egg-delivery plan, a fat-delivery plan, a potato-delivery plan, and a grain-delivery plan. There was a plan for the levying off of oleaginous plants, of flax, and of jute as contracted by various state enterprises, and, whatever happened (be it flood, frost, or drought), the quantity prescribed in the contract was ruthlessly extracted from the peasants. It frequently happened that the peasant, who was unable to fulfill his contract, had to sell his own wheat to the state delivery authorities at the official price and to buy flour at three or four times the price on the black market in order to be able to provide his family with bread.

There were rigid plans not only for deliveries, but also for production. The National Planning Bureau made exact estimates as to how much wheat, oats, rye, sunflower seed, and alfalfa had to be produced by each county, each district, each village. It was the task of the council chairman to see to it that the plan be fulfilled in his territory. No matter whether the soil was suited to a particular crop or not, the plan was law, and the farmer who did not fulfill it had to face legal proceedings. The peasant had to produce whether he could or not, and whether he wanted to or not. There were areas where the peasants had specialized in one particular farm product for decades, for centuries. With that produce they supplied the entire need of the country and assured large exports, as, for instance, Mako supplied the onions, the Szeged area the sweet red peppers, etc. The plan, however, changed all that. Following the example of the great Soviet Union, cotton was sown in the onion fields, though cotton had never before been produced in Hungary because neither the soil nor the climate were favorable to its growth. In the end, there was neither cotton nor onions. The discouraged peasants shrugged their shoulders. They had foreseen it all.

The plan was the master. The plan was God. Its letter was the law. It spun its thick web over the entire country, smothering incentive, ingenuity, ambition, and initiative. There was not a single province of life which the state did not occupy and strangle with its ruthless fingers. The plan was "protected" by an army of state employees who were hired and paid for that purpose alone.

Hungary, a country which had always abounded in agricultural produce, began to look like an empty larder. Where had its treasures disappeared to? First of all, to the Soviet Union; then to East Berlin, which had to be well provided for so as to be able to keep pace with West Berlin. In the summer of 1953, the peasants of the lowlands, home of the famous Hungarian wheat fields, stood in line for bread, because the Ministry of Deliveries had robbed them of even those rations to which they were legally entitled. They had no bread, and they had no grain to sow. In the famous vineyard counties, the fields lay barren because there were no chemicals to be had, and no vine props. The ministry had forgotten to provide for the production of these necessities. In addition, the grape growers were not interested in producing wine, for the state bought up the grapes and the wine for tiny amounts, and all their work was thus in vain. In the homelands of Tokay and Eger and Mecsek and Badacsony wines, the wine lovers were served some horrible inferior liquid made of corn cobs. In Tokay, new Government-sponsored quarries destroyed the volcanic soil producing the best wine in the world. Those who sometimes found sufficient courage to protest against this van-

dalism were immediately accused of being enemies of socialist
Hungary, the country of "iron and steel." Fewer and fewer
protested. The grape growers and the onion farmers left the land
and went to the towns to become turners or welders, which was
more profitable and less dangerous than working in the fields.*

There was also a precisely timed plan of "cooperative development." Now that the large estates had been banned from Hungarian agriculture, the time had come to ban the dwarf holdings,
too. Hungarian agriculture "had" to be collectivized, since Soviet
agriculture was already in *kolkhozy*. The plan prescribed in great
detail and to the minute by what date certain counties, districts,
or villages had to be fully collectivized, and when every peasant
would have had to join a cooperative. Woe to the Party secretary
in whose territory the plan was not fulfilled on time! In case of
disobedience or resistance, "administrative measures" were in-
stituted:

First, the resisting farmer was punished.

It was easy to punish him. He was punished if he did not
deliver in time. He was punished if the quality of the pork was
inferior. He was punished if his dog was not properly chained,
or if his well was not properly covered. One punishment followed
the other. The farmer was called every day to the council house
to see the Party chairman or the Party secretary.

Then, it was no longer the council chairman or the Party
secretary who reprimanded him.

He was summoned before the commander of the local police.

Then came the state security officer of the district.

People disappeared during the night. Sometimes entire fam-

---

* Let us tell here one of the bitter jokes born in those days. The
Minister of Transportation asks the stationmaster of Zahony, a border
town between Hungary and the Soviet Union, to make a report on the
freight that had passed between the two countries during the last six
months. The stationmaster begins: "To the Soviet Union, 4,000 wagons
of wheat, 5,000 wagons of pork, 100,000 wagons aluminium, 3,000 wagons
fruit, 600 wagons leather . . ." "All right, all right!" interrupts the
Minister, nervously. "But what came in?" "The Moiseyev Ensemble,"
answers the stationmaster, without batting an eye.

ilies disappeared. Large, black lorries stopped before the houses, and the families were bundled in and carried off. After thirty or forty miles, they were made to get out and, by the time these desperate, frightened people had walked back to their village, they had nothing. Their house had been occupied by the council or by the AVO. Their land had been given to the cooperatives, their cattle driven away.

Most peasants preferred to avoid this fate.

Peasants who had worked their own fields all their lives, and peasants who had all their lives dreamed of having a piece of land of their own and who had at last been granted their wish by the land reform, were driven into the "collective," to be bossed over by ignorant cooperative chairmen and dictatorial "brigade leaders." The state did not care. All it cared about was that the proud inscription "Cooperative Village" should be nailed up at the entrance to the village as soon as possible.

Thus, the peasants joined—voluntarily.

The state went all out to support the cooperatives. There were cooperatives that soon became famous for their outstanding results. When the dividends were distributed at the end of the agricultural year, the peasants received large sums of money— from the state funds, as it turned out later. As a matter of fact, the fame, the good work, and the high dividends were in most places creations of the state. All the foremost cooperatives lived on subsidies from the national income, part of which they were supposed to supply. These were all "Potemkin" villages; and behind the enthusiastic reports, the newsreels, the wonderful "results," the orders, and Kossuth Prizes won by the chairmen, there stalked the *deficit,* which, instead of decreasing, kept on growing as the years went by.

The more modest, weaker, and more neglected cooperatives, on the other hand, were near starvation. The peasants were in no mood to work. And if they did, they worked on the tiny strips of land given them after they had joined the cooperative as "household gardens." In the middle of 1953, Hungary, whose peasantry had for centuries fought for the land, had

1,000,000 Hungarian acres of arable land uncultivated—which was 10 per cent of all the arable land of the country.

There was also another plan, which supplemented the agricultural plans but which was more important than any of them: the plan to intensify the class struggle in the villages.

At the heart of this plan—which showed a complete ignorance of Hungarian conditions and a servile imitation of the Soviet example—stood the fight against the kulak.

The word "kulak"—a Russian word—had hitherto been unknown in Hungary. Now everybody who possessed over twenty or thirty acres of land (depending on the quality of the soil) or who worked his land with hired help, qualified as rich peasant—i.e., a kulak. The kulak, together with his family and his relatives, was a constant target of persecution. He was fair game. His land could be taken from him. He could be chased from his house. He could be spit upon in the street. Furthermore, anyone who had a father or some other relative who was a kulak was branded. A son of a kulak was always open to suspicion. He was not admitted to the university or to any form of higher education. He was not drafted for military service. Instead, he was put into the most humiliating labor battalions. The AVO had a wonderful time hunting for kulaks. To beat up or torture a kulak was a revolutionary deed. It was a heroic feat for which one was praised, not punished. The kulak was the villain. He was the cause of all ills. When there was no bread in the towns, official propaganda broadcasted the story that the kulaks were feeding the bread to their pigs. Where there were no kulaks, they had to be created, because the plan prescribed that the class enemy in the villages had to be liquidated. Anyone who offended the Party secretary or the council chairman (perhaps only by arguing with him) knew that his name would be added to the kulak list, even if he had never had enough land to qualify as a kulak. It needed no more than a painful sigh of "No rain again. Even God has turned from us"—and the helpless, unprotected peasant was lost. He was made a kulak.

In the past, the poor of the village had looked with envy, mixed with hatred, upon the well-to-do peasants who gave their children a university education (because there had always been conflicts—though much less violent ones—between the rich and the poor peasants). But now, they began to feel pity for these fellows. Now, the artificially whipped-up class struggle had an opposite effect: it engendered sympathy. The peasants were sorry for the kulaks. And they also feared for themselves. For almost everyone had kulak relatives or friends or acquaintances, or went to school or played with one or the other of the sons of kulaks, and in the course of the years the natural family and emotional relationships of the village, which had been healthy because they were natural, had become unhealthy and dangerous. An atmosphere of terror now smothered the villages. Nobody knew what humiliation was in store for him. There was no protection. There was nobody to turn to. And, once a man was branded with the shameful name, he bore its consequences as long as he lived. The accusation of having been influenced by a kulak could be raised against anyone at any time. The peasant lad whom the Government sent to Denmark in 1947 for a year to study the cooperatives became suspect when he explained how those cooperatives were organized, even though he did not say they were better than Hungarian cooperatives. At this point, the AVO appeared and began to investigate the affair as a case of "incitement against the Soviet Union." It did not take long before they discovered that the lad was wooing a kulak girl and was, thus, subject to kulak influence. He was arrested. So was the kulak girl. So were both their families. Sometimes, such people were never heard of again. Sometimes, they were released after many months to discover that they had nothing left in the whole world except the clothes they wore on their backs.

The prisons were crowded with peasants, with kulaks, with "kulak hirelings," with peasants who had failed to deliver on time, and with those who were accused of having incited against the cooperatives. Those who were given prison sentences in

1952-1953 went home and waited until summoned. There was simply no place for them in the prisons.

In the forced labor camps attached to the steel mills and the power stations that were under construction, kulaks, with a red stripe across their backs, worked without pay on the "great socialist projects." Workers were badly needed, and if there were not enough to be had, there were the kulaks—who were even cheaper.

On the walls of the village council houses, there was a "guilt board" with the names of the kulaks. The bearers of those names had to stand on one foot for hours in one or the other of the offices, or to crouch on all fours and bark like a dog as a warning to other kulaks who did not fulfill their delivery plan. That same afternoon or evening, the "culprit" was visited by the AVO. There was no search warrant. No one would have dared ask for such a thing. The family was awakened and made to stand in the yard, guarded by a youngster holding a tommy gun while the others searched the house from top to bottom. From one of the haystacks, an old German rifle was fished out. Here was the evidence! The kulak was planning to overthrow the People's Democracy! The family was deported. The head of the family was brought to trial and either hanged or put away for life for hiding arms.

Two days later, in the garret of another kulak in another village, the AVO would "find" the very same German rifle, and a brief news item in the press would then inform the country that another kulak had been sentenced to death for hiding arms.

There was silence in the villages then—a deep, stonelike, deathly silence. The Party secretary and the council chairman, who were usually workers who had never before seen a village and had offered themselves "voluntarily" for these jobs, would send in reports in which everything was reported as in the best order: in which collectivization went according to plan, in which the struggle against the class enemy was intensifying, and in which the peasants were happy.

Nobody contradicted these reports.

Fury and hatred and despair blazed high in the people's hearts but, in the course of centuries, the peasants had learned how to behave toward the oppressors on their backs. They had said nothing. When they were asked, they had smiled or mumbled something under their mustaches and excused themselves. They had so much to do.

But now this silence came to an end.

The village drew a deep, sighing, sobbing breath.

From day to day, the poet's face grew darker. His heart beat more painfully. Though he did not notice everything, and though he did not discern the hatred behind the sighs and though he was not yet told the story of the hidden arms, what he saw was enough to inspire one of the great poems of that era. His honesty and his decency protested. He was a poet. He had to cry out. In this poem were contained the germs of the storm of indignation that was to break out later. It was entitled *Nyirseg Diary*.

The strength of the poem lay in its content of truth. Here, inspiration had fed on two sources: on indignation and on the desire to help. There was no flaming enthusiasm here, no Fata Morgana which was believed to be reality. The picture conjured up by the poem was dark and cruel. For the first time in years, the bitterness and despair of the peasants was given tongue in a poem. The contrast between the official description of the village and the terrible truth was reflected with painful brilliance.

In the poem, the poet meets, under the dust-laden acacia trees of the highway, a little old peasant woman and listens, aroused and helpless, to the volcanic outbreak of her fury and despair. He drops in at the meeting of a cooperative, where they are counting the "ayes" and "nays" which will decide whether the cooperative is to be dissolved. In the poem, autumn brings the answer to this great problem: although the regime introduces a number of measures to prevent the peasants from leaving the cooperatives, **they are not given back their land;**

they are given back only part of their animals, and are faced
with heavy taxation—and thus, though the Government succeeds in keeping a relatively large number of cooperatives, the
liberated emotions of the peasants break the chain of many a
kolkhoz.

Kuczka, however, was not only a poet. He was a *Communist poet.* He had to write about the suffering of the village.
His conscience compelled him to do so, but at the same time he
felt obliged to watch, lest he be carried away by the masses
and "toe the political line" of the peasantry. The cooperative
is dissolved? All right, he writes, the fault lies with forced collectivization, with a mistaken economic policy. But the peasants
are also responsible, because, since their souls are torn with
"unhappiness and private ownership" and since their feet "are
caught in the iron-toothed trap of the past," "they do not know
that the country is theirs down to the last blade of grass." The
poet is still filled with the conviction so characteristic of the
official ideology: that, though mistakes were committed, the
people themselves are still unaware of their future happiness,
and it is up to the Party to show the way.

Most characteristic of Kuczka's Communist conviction is the
part which describes his meeting with a local Party official. This
official, who has been spit upon and beaten up by the hitherto
silently suffering peasants following the announcement of the
new Government program, expresses what the entire Party apparatus and Rakosi himself think, without, however, putting the
thought into words. He says: "Everything went well . . . and
then that speech of Imre Nagy . . . they danced until dawn . . .
it drove them out of their minds. They liked me . . . and now
they spit on me . . . they wielded cudgels, pitchforks, and
hoes . . . Is this what I deserved, comrade? You tell me . . ."

Kuczka does not agree with this argument. According to him,
it is not the Imre Nagy speech that caused the trouble, but
the mistakes committed in the past years. He does not agree—
but he understands. Of course, he does. His problem—that of

the Communist poet—has much in common with that of the Communist Party official. He, who has always proudly called himself a Party poet and still remains one, can blame the Party official. Fundamentally, he still feels that the Party's and the people's fate and task are the same. Yet it is here that the roads irrevocably diverge. The official wants nothing except to return to the old ways, to the old methods, to the hand of steel. He blames the new political line. The poet wants something else: he wants correction, atonement, work, restitution.

But does the official listen to the poet? Does he believe that they can work together? Does he believe that, together, they can separate the good from the bad and correct the faults they have made? The poet believes they can. The future will show.

Nyirseg Diary was published in *Irodalmi Ujsag* on November 7, 1953.

And immediately the storm broke.

No, nobody doubted the talent, nor the poetic fire, nor the good will of the poet. And the critics admitted that, in its composition and its poetic level, this poem was a milestone in Kuczka's work.

The argument turned on entirely different questions.

The first attack hit the poet in his weakest spot: What was the cause of this sudden change of opinion? How did it happen that he, who had always painted everything red (too red), suddenly saw everything in black? What had happened to him, the militant Communist who had gone with his friend, Imre Sarkadi, to convince the latter of the falseness of all accusations against the Party? Had he, too, come under the influence of those accusations? The answer was clear. Kuczka had gone from one extreme to the other, and his instability was due to his petty-bourgeois origin and to his ideological weakness.

The other attack was more theoretical. It argued that perhaps Kuczka had indeed seen what he described, but that this had nothing to do with anything. What he had seen was not the truth, only part of the truth. It was a part which, because

of its very character, contained a falsehood. From things seen
in one village or one district, one could not draw general conclusions that would be valid for the entire country. For, what
is true in one place is certainly not true in another. What is
more: even if it were supposed that the general situation were
as Kuczka described it (i.e., if his poem reflected the general
situation), the picture would still be neither characteristic nor
typical, because it lacked the progressive tendency that, in spite
of many mistakes, is still inherent in the work of the Party.

General, but not typical. True, but true only in part. False,
because it does not illustrate the tendency toward progress. These
words were familiar to the poet who had returned, crushed, from
the countryside. They belonged to the ideological armor of
Jozsef Revai. Kuczka, who had in the past frequently used
them himself in arguments, replied, at first patiently, then with
growing anger, to the repeated attacks. Again and again, he
explained that he had written only what he had seen with his
own two eyes, and, even though he could not pretend to infallibility, he had the right to write about what he had seen. If
someone else should see something else, let him write it, without regard for what had been written in the past. He admitted
that it was wrong to have portrayed everything in the same
shade of black. But was that a reason for not saying in the
future what he thought? Hitherto, every time he had gone to
an industrial region or a village, the Party had expected him
to write what he saw: how the labor competition was developing,
how the cooperatives were multiplying; and he had always done
so with sincerity and with love toward the Party, for, that was
how he had seen things then. Now, however, he had seen another
aspect of life, and he believed that it was his duty, his Communist duty, to write about it. They were telling him that it was
not he, but the Party, that had revealed the mistakes in the
new Government program, or that had courageously admitted
its mistakes to the entire country. Well and good! He honored
the Party for its courage, but if the Party had the right to

talk about its mistakes, why couldn't he, the Communist poet? He and his friends had been taught by Stalin to write the truth. He had written the truth, and he could do no differently.

It was during these days that more and more of the writers travelling throughout the country returned to the capital. What they had to say agreed generally with what Kuczka described in his poem. At the meeting organized by the Writers' Association, they told of terrible experiences and depicted conditions in the villages in bitter words.

Sharp and ever more easily discernible conflicts were taking shape between the various groups of Communist writers. Kuczka and those who agreed with him declared loudly and unequivo- cally that the only attitude worthy of a Communist writer who also wanted to help the Party was to express his opinions clearly and sincerely and to reveal the mistakes without waiting until reality again became divorced from his work and until the Party again blamed him for having roamed the world with closed eyes in these difficult times.

The opinion of the other group was that the Kuczka-Sarkadi group had panicked and was falsifying reality and betraying the Party in this difficult situation by stressing only the gloomy side of life—thus making improvement more difficult, though an effort was being made all over the country to rectify mis- takes. Kuczka and his friends were, naturally, first attacked by the Muscovites. These were also joined by such other Hungarian writers as Laszlo Benjamin and Zoltan Zelk, and, to a certain extent, by Tibor Dery, who feared a renaissance of nationalistic, anti-Semitic, and provincial trends. For entirely different reasons, Laszlo Benjamin, too, replied to *Nyirseg Diary* in a poem. True, he said, there was much to worry about and much to correct. But that was no reason to become hysterical like a man who runs for the axe to chop down the whole tree because he had seen a caterpillar on a branch. The poem was published in *Szabad Nep,* and it heralded the ever more sharp, the ever more clearly outlined split.

New and terribly real conflicts took the place of the former clashes between cliques and personalities.* These new conflicts were concerned with openly political problems of outlook and portrayal. Naturally, too, the new rift also involved the deepening of personal conflicts, and so anger and mistrust sprang up between the two groups, and neither believed the other and each was convinced of its own rightness and of the fact that it was serving the Party better than the other did. Those who had set out on the new road suddenly despised those, their former brothers in sectarianism, who argued about conditions in the villages in their editorial rooms and could not or did not want to leave their comfortable offices and their comfortable delusions. Simultaneously, the latter considered the former cowardly and faithless and inconsequential petty bourgeois who were plunged into despair by the laments of an old peasant woman and who now noisily defended a fictitious truth. Gradually, as all ties were cut between the two groups, they stopped each other in the street and continued to launch wild attacks upon each other.

The battle was in full swing when, suddenly and unexpectedly, an illustrious guest, Alexei Surkov, appeared in Budapest. Surkov was a Stalin Prize-winning poet who was secretary of the Party organization of the Soviet Writers' Association. He was apparently familiar with the contents of the arguments and, like the good Communist he was, immediately offered his services to help solve the problems that had arisen.†

----

* In 1951-1952, so-called "clique battles" were waged chiefly among the young Communist writers. In these, the differences did not touch political issues. They raged around the question as to which group served the Party more sincerely and with the greater talent. True, when filled with their greater "sincerity," the young poets sometimes touched upon the ills of the country. But these had been mere indiscretions compared with the present rift.

† One of the principal subjects of argument was an article by a very gifted Communist writer, Istvan Orkeny, published in *Irodalmi Ujsag*. Without beating about the bush, Orkeny raised the question of what should be done if, as at present, a chasm should again open between the Party and the people. Should the writers stand on the side of the people or on the side of the Party? He answered his own question by saying

Surkov talked to the Communist leaders of the Writers' Association, delivered a lecture to the full membership, and ranted with equal energy against both those who painted everything red and those who painted everything black. However, it was to Kuczka that he talked at the greatest length. He had known and liked the young, tousleheaded poet who was the Hungarian Mayakovsky for a long time and—admitting the poet's absolute honesty—he now proceeded without any waste of time to convince him of the deep truth, not of what Kuczka had seen in the countryside, but of what he *knew* in Moscow. Kuczka tried to argue. He told Surkov of everything he had seen and experienced, and he attacked that other group of writers who were attacking him. But, then, he fell silent. He smiled, his head bent with a mysterious, forgiving smile, secure in the knowledge that he was right. Surkov talked, argued, begged, and demanded. But it was in vain. His mission—probably for the first time in a People's Democracy—had failed. Kuczka remained unyielding.

It seemed that the Communist writers had irrevocably divided into two hostile groups.

---

that, in such a case, the writers must be the *bridge* connecting the two shores of the chasm and thus restore unity. The opposing group considered this theory wrong and defeatist. They said that there was no chasm, that there were only mistakes, that the Party was one with the people, and that Orkeny was crying wolf and thus putting arguments into the mouths of the enemy.

The Council of the Gods

The Political Committee of the Hungarian Workers' Party met every Thursday on the first floor of their building on Academy Street, to the left of Rakosi's room. The list of the invited was handed in good time to the state security guard standing with his tommy gun at the entrance. Each new arrival showed his Party membership card, which the guard politely checked, ticking off the name on the list and, after asking whether the comrade was carrying any weapon, permitting him to enter the building. The visitor was again stopped, after a few steps, by a glass door, also guarded by an armed AVO soldier, but here there was no further red tape. The guard asked whom the comrade wanted to see, and then he very politely gave the directions.

The building, which had once been the headquarters of the Horthy political party, the Hungarian Life Party, had the atmosphere of a church. Its halls were cool and calm and extremely clean and silent, and one could almost smell incense in the echoing corridors and on the sprightly but silent secretaries who, whizzing from one door to another, reminded one of choir boys. The headquarters building was a relatively small, three-story building; the other building—that of the central Party executive, which had, in the course of the years, extended over an entire block—differed greatly from the first building. In the second building there was a more plebeian bustle, and there was loud talk and a smell of food coming from the dining rooms downstairs. Here in the first building, however, elegance and awe reigned supreme, as if the very air had divested itself of all vulgarity.

The guest walked up stairs which were covered with a deep, red carpet and entered a smallish room on the first floor. The Political Committee was already in session, discussing the next to the last item on the agenda; and the guest and his companions had to wait until their problem came up for discussion. The tables of the little room were laden with rich sandwiches, with smiling Jonathan apples, and with the indispensable small soda bottles. Anyone who was hungry was welcome to help himself. Most guests were, however, far too nervous to swallow even a bite. They were also too busy putting their thoughts into order and deciding what they would say when, at last, they were face to face with the "comrades."

Their items on the agenda would be a nineteen-page memorandum bearing the title of: *The Situation and Tasks of Our Literature.*

On the bottom of the last page appeared the date "February 1, 1954" and the signature "Marton Horvath." Horvath was then head of the Agitation-Propaganda Department of the Central Committee.

It was a great thing—and it had never before occurred in the history of the People's Democracy—that the highest body of the Party, the Political Committee, should discuss the problems of literature with the writers themselves participating in the discussions. But the time was ripe for such a discussion, and it could not be put off any longer. The Party Congress was approaching, and, in this new situation, the Party had to define its political principles in the field of literature. Yet, even had there been no approaching Congress, a meeting with the writers was more than necessary, because the Party could no longer remain silent on the new phenomena manifesting themselves in literary life. Order had to be restored. The Party's attitude had to be clarified.

The fact that the Communist writers now formed two camps was in itself sufficient reason for the Party to step in. But there were also other, if less acute, difficulties. New theories attacking the very roots of the Party's teachings on literature were being advanced practically every day. Some writers were going so far as to talk about the *vates* role of the writer, saying that, instead of following Party directives, it was the writer's task to be prophet and to show the way. For—so they said—the Party might err, and why should the writer identify himself with such errors? Was it not the writer's mission to encourage the Party, to help it along the road to progress, and, by revealing all mistakes, to urge it and warn it to correct such mistakes? Other writers were beginning to say openly that the Dery debate had been all wrong, and that it is the inalienable right of the writer to draw his heroes the way he wants to draw them, and that nobody has the right to prescribe how a writer should portray the past or the present. Still other writers were declaring that it was a grave mistake to silence certain outstanding writers by "administrative" means. It did not satisfy these writers that some of the "silenced" writers—for instance, the outstanding novelist Aron Tamasi and the poet Ferenc Jankovich—were again being published. They demanded that the doors also be opened to certain writers with a fascist past who had hitherto had to "confess their errors" before they had been permitted to publish their works.

These theories were beginning to leave their imprint on written works. Gyula Illyes, who was almost unanimously recognized as the greatest living Hungarian poet, had written an article for *Irodalmi Ujsag* about man's right to sadness and sorrow and about the poet's right to speak in his poems of approaching old age, of death, and even of the fear of death. As an illustration, Illyes had appended two poems to the article. The one was concerned with love and death. The other even included this slogan: *"Doleo ergo sum."* This latter poem contained a warning as well as some advice for the Party leaders: "He who knows only joys/Lives in a world of dreams!"

It was an entirely novel thing: a poet advising the Party, rather than the other way round! In addition, only the deaf could fail to notice the undisguised challenge of those articles and poems which were now directed at Jozsef Revai—a man who had less than a year earlier declared that "our poetry needs nothing less than the absolutely uninteresting private laments of individual souls!"

The National Theater of Budapest produced a new play by a young Hungarian author named Erno Urban, of whom it was generally known that he was a friend of long standing of Imre Nagy. The title of the play was *The Cucumber Tree*, and it was a satire. It was not its literary quality, but, rather, its content which made this play into a hit. Its hero was a ne'er-do-well who, by some quirk of fate, becomes managing director of a provincial enterprise, the Fur Surplus Collecting Enterprise. He knows absolutely nothing about fur. All he knows is that if he exceeds his quota, he will get a considerable reward and his career will be assured. Therefore, he torments the peasants and the animals, for, instead of collecting the surplus, he wants to *produce* fur. Every animal that crosses his path, be it sheep, pig, goat, or even dog, is shorn to the skin. As a result of his "beneficial" activity, disease breaks out among the animals in the villages of his "empire," but he doesn't care. He cares only for success, for bonuses, and for the approval of his superiors. At last, the peasants can no longer tolerate this state of affairs. They take to pitchforks, cudgels, and hoes, and they drive the managing director and his accomplice, the council chairman, away like a couple of mad dogs.

The play was performed to crowded audiences night after night. Nothing like it had been seen in Budapest for years. In it, there was a scene which took place in the council chairman's room. The action of the scene was unimportant. What was important was that the walls of the room were hung with the chairman's *own portrait*. The audiences watched with bated breath, but when "the representatives of the Party and the state" were finally chased from the stage with cudgels and pitchforks, the walls of the theater shook with applause.

It was not surprising that writers should write plays like this one, and it was not extraordinary that this one had been written by a man who was one of the most faithful of Communists and who had, barely a year before, been awarded the Kossuth Prize for another play which—contrary to his satire—had glorified the amazing progress of the villages and had unmasked the base maneuvering of the kulaks. The really surprising thing was that such works were allowed to reach the public either in print or on the stage.

Suddenly, it seemed as if the Party machinery, which had hitherto exercised an iron hand over the ideological "purity" of literature, had grown weaker or had vanished entirely. Heretical new ideas were beginning to find a fertile soil in even the highest spheres directing literary life—i.e., in headquarters and in the Ministry of Culture.

In the course of the personnel changes following the announcement of the new Government program in July, 1953, Jozsef Revai, the god of Hungarian literature, was left out of the Political Committee and relieved of his post as Minister of Culture. He was given the entirely unimportant and more or less nominal function of Vice-Chairman of the Presidium, and, sick, angry, and offended, he retired into the background. His "dethronement" had been suggested by Rakosi,* who said that Revai was "mad," and that his work was no longer satisfactory because of his illness and moodiness.

---

* In reality, Rakosi wanted to get rid of Revai (who was thus the first to be dismissed from the "foursome") because he considered Revai the only dangerous rival who might replace him if his own power should wane—and particularly if the problems concerning the "infringement of legality" were raised publicly. Imre Nagy approved of Revai's dismissal, not only because he disapproved of Revai's cultural dictatorship, but also because he, too, had had a personal clash with Revai in Moscow and later again at the time of the debate in 1948-1949. In his book published in Moscow, Revai had accused Imre Nagy of rightist views and, in 1948-1949, he had attacked Nagy most sharply as a "Bukharinist."

Now the supreme Party authority on literature was Mihaly Farkas, who had previously been the Minister of Defense.

In the course of the Moscow conferences at the end of June, Farkas, too, had been dismissed from the "foursome," partly because he was a Jew and partly—so it was said—because he was the embodiment of haughty terroristic methods, of an inhuman driving of his subordinates, and of a self-satisfied loss of contact with the masses. For many years, this apprentice printer who had been turned into a general (and who had taken part in the Spanish Civil War as a political commissar and who had attended the Comintern school as a youth leader) had appeared at all gala performances and military parades, behaving like a little Napoleon in his brilliant uniform with the innumerable decorations on his fat chest. Entire regiments had been accustomed to standing stiffly at attention in the burning sun, listening to his orders of the day, which he screamed at the top of a squeaky voice betraying a speech defect. If his piglet eyes had discerned the slightest movement, woe to the enlisted man and the commander! The entire army had trembled before him: he had torn the rank off the shoulder band of any officer, and he had slapped the face of any general who caused him displeasure. And then, in June, 1953, from one day to the next, he had become a nobody. He had not even been given an inferior post, as had Revai. He had run from pillar to post, yelling, ranting, storming, and cursing the political change, the Government program—but in vain.

And now, from one minute to the next, the scene had changed again. Farkas had had an old friend from the "good old days"— a drinking and hunting companion who was the Soviet Ambassador to Budapest, Fodor Danilovich Kisselev. In the end, it was to Kisselev that the dismissed commander-in-chief had gone in order to air his grievances. Kisselev had taken pity on him, though he had also explained to him that he would get no results by opposing the new trend. This trend was Moscow's creation, and nothing could be done about it. If Farkas were shrewd, Kisselev said, he would pretend to be sorry for the mistakes he had committed, and he would become the most enthusiastic supporter of the new political line. And, since Farkas cared little about the political trend and cared only about climbing back into power, he had promised henceforth to be a convinced partisan of the new line—and Kisselev had gone to see Imre Nagy.

This had happened a few weeks after the announcement of the new program, but by that time the Premier had gained some experience and had learned how difficult his situation was. It was upon these experiences that Kisselev built his case. He called Imre Nagy's attention to the principal difficulty: the resistance of the Party machinery. In this situation, said Kisselev, Rakosi was not to be relied upon. On the contrary (as was proved by his speech to the Party activists on July 11), Rakosi was the most determined opponent of the new program, and it was Rakosi who now stirred up the officials from behind the scenes. Imre Nagy was rather lonely at the top, said Kisselev, and this might endanger the entire program. Nagy urgently needed some help in the Party, someone who had the knowledge and the energy and know-how to keep Rakosi in check— Mihaly Farkas, for example. True, Farkas had committed many mistakes in the past. He had been haughty and rude and dictatorial and unpopular. But Farkas was sorry now and was ready to atone for his mistakes. Kisselev added that Farkas was very enthusiastic about the new program, and he suggested that Farkas should be given a new post. Not in the Army, naturally. The Army had been only too happy and relieved to get rid of him. But why didn't Imre Nagy reappoint him as Party executive? Perhaps he could be one of Rakosi's secretaries. After all, Kisselev argued, Farkas had had a great deal of experience, and he was an excellent organizer who would go to any length to be of help to Imre Nagy. He, Kisselev, personally guaranteed that Farkas would conduct himself well.

Imre Nagy argued and protested. But, in the end, he made one of the greatest mistakes of his career: he agreed to Kisselev's proposal. On the one hand, he really needed help. On the other, he believed the Soviet ambassador to be a sincere partisan of the new political trend because the ambassador had been among those who had prepared the report that had caused Rakosi to be so rudely abused in Moscow. So, Imre Nagy overcame his personal antipathy, and, a few days later, a short communiqué was published in the press announcing that Comrade Mihaly Farkas was once again a member of the Political Committee and one of the secretaries of the Central Committee. The over-fed, vain little general discarded his uniform and donned a grey civilian suit. Yesterday, he had been the country's fore-most military expert. Today, he was the supreme authority on literature and the sciences.

The surprising thing—or, depending on how much one knew about Farkas, the natural thing—was that he seemed to have taken his promises seriously. He became a loud supporter of Nagy and a front-rank militant of the new program. And even his behavior reflected the change. He tried hard to be more modest and more distinguished. He tried to convert the hitherto soldierly expression of his rubber face into a smile. He talked about the mistakes the Party had committed in the field of literature. He made Erno Urban, author of *The Cucumber Tree*, his friend and, though he did not fully approve of them, he pretended to understand the new literary trends.

Two of his closest collaborators were men who had also been Revai's closest collaborators. These were Marton Horvath, who decided on questions of literature and of art in the Party appa-ratus and who had for ten years been Revai's First Deputy, and Jozsef Darvas, who had taken Revai's place as Minister of Culture. These two men, whose principal job it had been for ten years to explain, to popularize and to "apply practically" Revai's theories, now set to work, slowly and circumspectly, to "reevaluate" the activities of those ten years.

The first argument they advanced was that, though the Party had committed grave mistakes in the field of politics and economics, its cultural policy had been essentially correct. It was the *methods* employed in applying this policy that had not always been proper. It had been wrong of the Party to employ so frequently "administrative" measures to ban periodicals, to close publishing houses, and to condemn writers to silence—instead of trying to win the writers over by means of persuasion. And there had been other methods that had hindered progress. There had been "the repeated violation of the principle of democratic leadership." There had also been "the exaggerated sharpness of tone and the violence of attacks and the emphasis on mistakes that failed to take into consideration that we are not facing an enemy, but, instead, confused writers in need of persuasion." These methods had repelled the writers.

Clearly, this "reevaluation" was a personal attack upon the discarded Jozsef Revai. But Revai's two former faithful disciples did not stop at this. They soon discovered that their former master had also made other grievous errors, for, so they found, Revai had erred not only in his methods but also in his principles. They gave him credit for having launched the battle against schematism and against the oversimplified, colorless, unilateral portrayal of life. And this, they said, was proof of his genius, for, in contrast to Rakosi and Gero, he had sensed something of the unhealthy and nerve-wracking tempo that the other leaders had imposed upon the country. But, they pointed out, even Revai himself had failed to understand the essence of it all; and thus they wrote in their report: "We saw the symptoms, but we were unable to realize that the ideological root of the errors committed lay in the Party's political line, in the exaggerated tempo, in the excessive haste."

This was nothing less than calling the Hungarian prince of Marxist ideology a "vulgar" Marxist. For, to discern only the symptoms, to instruct the writers, and to seek the cause of a distorted portrayal of life in the artistic weaknesses and the ideological incompetence of the writers and not in the given reality—all this had nothing to do with Marxism or with materialism. It was nothing but the harmful, unforgivable, petty-bourgeois subjective idealism so often condemned by Revai. Without expressing all this openly, the two disciples were hanging the hangman. Not only Revai's methods had been wrong but, so they declared, "his violent whippings [had] turned into a war against everybody a struggle in which the Party remained, so to speak, alone." Finally, they concluded, Revai was not even a good Marxist.

This was the essence of the memorandum submitted to the Political Committee by Marton Horvath. There were, naturally, also other points in the memorandum. It rejected rightist tendencies; it criticized certain "exaggerations" of the Kuczka group; and it set forth the need for maintaining Party guidance and for increasing ideological work. Yet the really new element in the memorandum was its demand for greater literary freedom— in moderation, of course, and couched in the basic teachings of Marxism-Leninism. The memorandum, in fact, gave definite form to a hitherto somewhat hazy hope: that the new literary leaders favored the renascent realistic and truthful trends and that they disapproved of the old, so-called sectarian line.

After an hour's wait, the discussion turned to the writers' item on the agenda. At such times, it was usual to scrutinize the faces of those departing guests who had been discussing with the Committee the previous item, in order to prophesy the mood of the "comrades" on the Committee. Now industrial experts were leaving with long faces.

But the writers were given a friendly reception. In this rather small room, the leaders of Party and of country sat around a square formed by green-topped tables. Or, rather, they sat on three sides of the square. In the middle sat Rakosi. To his left was Erno Gero, to his right an empty chair. Then came Mihaly Farkas, and, in both directions in the order of the hierarchy, the leaders of lesser rank.

The guest writers took their places on the fourth side of the square, opposite Rakosi. Solicitous hands had placed paper and pencil before each of them, in case they wanted to make notes.

They had also placed before them the traditional small bottles of soda.

Matyas Rakosi called the roll. Then he welcomed the "literary comrades." He had, he began, an announcement to make. Comrade Imre Nagy was very sorry, but he would be unable to participate in the discussion because of an important engagement.*

Marton Horvath was the first to be given the floor. He said a few words in favor of his memorandum, explaining why it was important—and even essential—that the Party should make known its position in regard to the questions raised therein.

Then came the writers. At such meetings, it was always the guests who spoke first. They were expected to express their thoughts without knowing the "great secret," without being let in on what the "comrades" (i.e., the Party), thought about the issue under discussion. In most cases, the "council of gods" listened to their speeches without batting an eyelid. In vain did the guests try to read from a smile or a frown what the outcome of the discussion would be.

The Communist writers represented the two different trends of thought concerning the Kuczka poem, concerning actual conditions in the countryside, and concerning the correct portrayal of reality.

The "right wing," which believed in a long process of liberalization (i.e., in the "thaw"), was represented at the beginning by the poet Lajos Konya, who was Secretary of the Writers' Association, and by the ruthless and opportunistic critic Istvan Kiraly, who was editor of the literary periodical *Csillag* (meaning "Star"). These two confined themselves to backing up Horvath's memorandum. They said that there was at present a new buoyancy in literature, that the writers were writing

---

* It is improbable that Imre Nagy's being "busy" was a mere excuse, since, as it was proven later, he could have had no reason for not wanting to participate in the conference. The Party was getting ready for its Third Congress, and Nagy was to be one of the principal speakers. The time was short and he wrote all his speeches himself. It is very probable that he was busy working on his speech and that this is why he had excused himself from participating in the conference.

with more gusto and more freedom and more courage. They had to admit that the reevaluation of the full truth increased the literary value of poems, of short stories, and of essays and that, instead of being a hindrance, this new trend was helping the Party to accomplish its work.

The "left wing," which sympathized with the old and rigid Revai trend, was represented by the Muscovite Bela Illes, by Tibor Meray, Party Secretary of the Writers' Association, and by Sandor Fekete, head of the literary section of *Szabad Nep*. All these men were much more passionate and more angry than were the members of the opposing group of writers. Their main concern was solicitude for the Party. There was, they said, a certain petty-bourgeois wavering in the ranks of the Communist writers, some of whom were frightened by the current troubles and difficulties. They said that practically everything the right wing called the "authentic" portrayal of reality was nothing but narrow-minded lamentation, distortion of reality, or cowardly panic. For this state of affairs, they added, it was not only the writers who were responsible. The present literary leadership of the Party was also responsible, including first of all Marton Horvath, the writer of the memorandum, because, in his weakness and his indecision, he had encouraged harmful and confused tendencies.

The sharpness of the attack against the right-wingers was motivated not only by political sectarianism. It was also motivated by more human considerations—by loyalty to Revai and by a strong personal antipathy toward Farkas and Horvath and Darvas. The left-wingers listened with hardly disguised contempt to Farkas' "understanding" phrases, knowing only too well that, only a few months previously, Farkas had been notorious for a rudeness, for an inhumanity, and for a sectarianism that far surpassed the left-wing writers. They found it in extremely bad taste that Horvath and Darvas, who had been Revai's foremost bootlickers, were kicking the wounded leader to make themselves look more important. They admitted that there had been certain mistakes in Revai's methods. After all, they had never particularly enjoyed the screams and hysterical outbreaks of the "crazy Count." But, as far as basic principles were concerned, they refused to make concessions. A hundred times rather Revai than Farkas, they thought! A hundred times rather than this bloated idiot who had never read twenty books in his whole life, or than these cowardly careerists like Horvath and Darvas! To them, the fact that these people represented the new trend was sufficient argument against it.

Thus, the situation was clear-cut. It remained to be seen whether the right- or the left-wingers would win the Party's approval.

Farkas was the first "god" to speak. He spoke with moderation and circumspection, declaring that, though there were a few shortcomings in the memorandum and some parts of it which would have to be clarified, he was essentially in favor of Horvath's arguments.

The next "god" was Istvan Bata, the new Minister of Defense. Nobody quite understood the point of what he was saying, but it gradually emerged that his empty phrases, his clumsy sentences, and his appalling grammar were meant to convey that literature was a beautiful and important thing. This short, scared little man had been a ticket collector before he became a general, and the writers of both factions thought how amazing it was that this ridiculous figure was supreme commander of the nation's Army when, if anyone had asked them to do so, they would not even have entrusted him with a bus.

Next came Erno Gero, the same creator of the "speeded-up" Five-Year Plan and inventor of the idea of a "country of iron and steel" who had been relieved in Moscow of his economic leadership and who was now acting as Minister of the Interior in the new Government. He spoke clearly and briefly, and it did not take long for everybody to understand that Gero opposed the memorandum. It was obvious, he said, that Horvath had put a great deal of work into it and that there were numerous useful points in it. Yet, as it now stood, the memorandum was raw and unpolished and not fully thought out. The Party was not willing to make concessions where Marxism-Leninism was at stake. "More freedom to literature" was a phrase which sounded well. But there were two kinds of freedom in existence. The two freedoms: a bourgeois and a socialist freedom. The Party—and this was something the writers had better realize— would not tolerate any bourgeois freedoms. In the memorandum, certain comrades had complained of too many administrative measures in the past. Gero openly stated that he considered the present administration too lenient. As an example, he cited the affair of *The Cucumber Tree*. Undoubtedly, its author, Erno Urban, was a gifted and a well-meaning man, Gero said. But the play, as it stood, was politically scandalous. And, instead of being more vigilant, Comrade Horvath now approved of it, and the Minister of Culture, Jozsef Darvas, had praised it in *Szabad Nep* instead of banning it from the stage. This tendency must be brought to a halt. The time had come for the Party to show its hand and restore law and order.

Here the Muscovite Bela Illes interrupted the speaker. Said Illes: "And these writers, my dear comrades, will come and kiss our hands."

Mihaly Farkas, who had been morosely listening to Gero, took this opportunity to argue. It was not with Gero that he argued, however, but with Illes.

"The Party," sputtered Farkas, "has absolutely no need for hand-kissing on the part of writers. . . . We want a literature that is strong, not humble. . . . The trouble with you and your kind, Comrade Illes, is that you can think only in terms of kissing hands and of bludgeoning. . . ."

Farkas' words were followed by silence. Everyone thought his own thoughts. It was rather strange that this should have come from Farkas, of all people—that it should be he, of all people, who should raise his voice against currying favor. On the other hand, what he said undoubtedly sounded well.

The atmosphere in the room was tense.

Everyone looked at Rakosi. He was the chairman. As always,

his was the last word. What would he say? Whose side would he take? How was the argument to be decided?

The Party leader lifted the tension in a few seconds. He was in excellent spirits. There was no trace of the defeat suffered in Moscow six months ago, nor of the defeat in the Hungarian Parliament. It was obvious that he enjoyed the debate and that he enjoyed not only the debate but its subject. For, this time the subject was not statistics, nor the fulfillment of plans. The subject was literature. It was as if the whole conflict had been invented for his amusement. After the passionate seriousness of the speakers, he, Rakosi, was careful to emphasize the relative unimportance of the whole affair. In the course of the debate, one of the writers had said that it was up to the Party to calm the storm raging in the literary world.

"Storm?" asked Rakosi, smiling wisely and serenely. "What storm? It is a storm in a teacup!"

He needed to say no more. This told the excited opponents that the Party was ready to lend a hand to the writers to help them solve their problems. But it also told them that there were much more important matters at stake. Rakosi himself, he indicated, would always be glad to offer advice. Not for a moment, however, would he lose a sense of proportion and take this little literary "rebellion" too seriously!

It was in this mood that he discussed the problems raised. He joked. He told anecdotes. He related his prison adventures. He remarked that he had received a letter in prison from Romain Rolland, the French writer, in which Rolland had assured the prisoner of his admiration and support; for the famous and gifted writers had always been on the side of progress and had never stumbled over the problem of how to portray reality, or over the question of the revelation of the "whole truth," as had our good comrades. "Reality" and "truth" were indeed very important, and the Party absolutely implored the writers never to forget this fact. But was reality to be portrayed as it really is? No! Reality was often ugly and disgusting. It could do no harm for the writer to embellish it a little.

Now he was speaking of the vital issue. For, this was the principal issue dividing the writers. Listening to his jokes and his anecdotes, it became more and more obvious to the guests where Rakosi stood. It became even more obvious when he referred to *The Cucumber Tree*.

In Horvath's memorandum dealing with the new satirical writing, there was a paragraph* which referred to this play. In a very involved, long-winded, and loyal Party manner, Horvath had suggested that the writers should write fresh, critical satires supporting the system, yet sharply attacking its mistakes.

Rakosi did not approve of this paragraph. "Why should we

---

* The full text, which Rakosi disapproved of, was as follows:

"The political line of the new phase offers an extraordinarily wide field to free, truly democratic criticism. A strong weapon of that criticism is the satire which unmasks and eliminates everything that is obsolete, rotten, and base. Our new satirical writing is still in its early stages. The Party gives it every support, knowing that the evolution of socialist satire is a pioneer task, both politically and artistically, and a difficult task demanding a great deal of courage. The satire may be directed at hostile elements or at remnants of the hostile classes, or it may also be directed at the mistakes in our progressing social system, its retarding forces and absurdities. Naturally, there will be negative phenomena in the focus of the satire because of the laws of an exaggerated art form. We shall have to reject every criticism that is intended to stifle satire in the bud, or that demands automatically that the good and the bad should figure in the same proportion as in our society as a whole, or that demands in the satirical work the same predominance of the positive element as we find in reality in every field of our society. The basic trouble in socialist satire is that our writers have not, as yet, fully understood the difference between the old and the new satire. In the past, the satire was directed at an exploiting society as a whole, at the rotten, and at the oppressive system and characteristics which resulted naturally from it. The new satire is aimed against the *mistakes* in a system which assures the freedom and welfare of the people. Satirical writers must make clear to their readers and audiences that these negative phenomena are alien to the nature of our system, that the negative figures move in an alien sphere, and that they are doomed to failure. Only thus will satire be true to reality and mobilize the masses to fight against mistakes and absurdities which still exist. It must be emphasized that Party loyalty in the new satire will manifest itself not only in its unequivocal partisanship toward the new system, but also in its passionate hatred for everything which hinders the advancement of the people. Not the .dulling of the blade of criticism but the sharpening of rightly directed criticism will show how consistently the writer stands behind his people and behind the cause of progress."

encourage our writers to mock our system?" he asked. "Is there
not enough to mock in the past—in the Horthy regime? Why
not criticize the past? Have they said everything there is to say
about it? There are plenty of remnants of that past among us
today: there are aristocrats, bankers, gendarmes, and kulaks.
Why not unmask these? Why make a sport of mocking our
good comrades, our council chairmen, our Party secretaries?
Our system is too young! The shoots are too delicate. . . . We
cannot allow writers to trample it underfoot lightly. . . .

"And then"—and now he was speaking very seriously—"why
is it so certain that what the writers see really exists? Why do
our writers believe that they are more clever than anyone else?
And if they erred, if they attacked good and healthy elements
in our society"—and then he repeated what he had said to the
Director of the National Theater after having seen *The Cucumber Tree*—"one had better be careful about satires. . . . 'Scissors,
knives, and forks are not toys for children'."*

Thus, Horvath's thesis failed. Without asking the others for
their opinion or putting the question to vote, Rakosi declared
that the Political Committee could not in this form accept the
suggestions, and he returned them to Horvath and Darvas for
further reflection. Two weeks from today the matter would be
raised again. Until then, he advised the comrades to work on
what they had heard here. "Let us speak more about the tasks
of the writers and less about the Party's tasks," he said.

The visitors were dismissed. They folded their notes, bowed
to the Political Committee, and left the room. The left-wingers
triumphantly, the right-wingers dejectedly. There was no doubt
of who had won.

In the two weeks that followed, nothing happened. Erno
Urban rewrote his play. The self-portraits were taken off the
wall of the council chairman's room and replaced by small red

---

* A little nursery rhyme which Hungarian parents are wont to repeat
to their children.

flags;* and, instead of the peasants armed with cudgels and pitchforks, it was the honest Party secretary who chased the tyrannical director and his accomplice from the stage. The play continued before crowded houses because, even in this form, it was more courageous and less schematic than were the others.

Not much was done to the memorandum which had been returned by the Political Committee. Horvath and Darvas poured over it, deleted a sentence or two, and added another sentence or two. But they wrought no essential changes. These two Revai fledglings, one the erudite son of a rich family of art dealers, the other a schoolteacher turned writer, were constitutionally closer to the new and freer political line than Revai. They had suffered at his hands. And whether they knew something the writers did not know or whether, for once, they were trying to overcome their weaknesses of character, they made no essential changes in their memorandum in spite of the warning and the unequivocal criticism. Like gamblers ready to risk all on one throw, they went two weeks later to the "council of the gods" once more.

The meeting began in exactly the same way as did the previous one. There was the same guard at the entrance. There was the same question: "Is the comrade armed?" There was the same little room with the sandwiches and apples, and the same waiting before admittance to the temple. The routine was unchanged.

Even the debate was the same. The writers of the memorandum and the writers of the right-wing and of the left-wing repeated the very same arguments. Nobody had changed his attitude. It was as if the same film were being shown for the second time.

Yet, there was one difference: in this meeting of the Political Committee, Premier Imre Nagy participated.

Nagy sat on Rakosi's left, silent and serious. There was not

* The Party was wont to reward the winners of labor competitions, elite workers, and Stakhanovites with little red silk flags.

even a smile on his face throughout the debate. True, there was nothing enjoyable in it this time, and none of the "gods" were as cheerful or as vivid as the last time.

Farkas reiterated that the memorandum was good and should be accepted as it stood. Gero—yes, something appeared to have happened to Gero. The very same document was lying before him on the table, and yet his attitude toward it had changed. He was neither firm nor determined. Instead, he was quiet and moderate. After the corrections, he said (as if he had not noticed how unimportant these corrections were), the memorandum was all right. It was obvious that Comrades Darvas and Horvath had put the advice of the Political Committee to good use. There was no point in arguing back and forth about it. The memorandum should be passed as a resolution. The others—Lajos Acs, Antal Apro, and Bela Veg—spoke in the same vein.

The writers simply sat there, not knowing what to think. They did not understand how the memorandum which had been rejected two weeks before had suddenly become acceptable as a resolution. The left-wingers were breathless. They had been ready to explain to the Political Committee that the changes in the memorandum were utterly insignificant, that Comrades Horvath and Darvas had persisted in their mistaken ideas, and that the Committee should not be fooled by a few purely formal changes. But all their principles, which had been so fully approved by the Political Committee two weeks previously, were now discussed as so much nonsense, and the comrades did not even listen to their speeches.

What was behind all this?

Imre Nagy was the next speaker. He took off his little pince-nez and put on spectacles. Then he took from his pocket a sheaf of pages and began to read. He had prepared his speech beforehand.

The speech was neither brilliant nor particularly witty. There was no color in it. There were no anecdotes. There were no reminiscences. The speech was dry and grey, but it was an unequivocal statement of his attitude. Horvath's memorandum was entirely correct. It was high time that the Party sanctioned the memorandum without reservations. There had been many errors and mistakes in the cultural policy of the last few years. It was high time that these be corrected. No longer should writers be treated like juvenile delinquents, with mistrust and suspicion. Literature should be given absolute freedom. Naturally, this did not mean that the Party relinquished its leadership. It meant only that it would henceforth trust the writers and give them greater independence. It seemed—and here his voice became sterner—that in the editorial offices of *Szabad Nep* and in the Party organization of the Writers' Association there were certain comrades who still had not understood the new political line of the Party nor the new program of the Government. As these places were hotbeds of resistance, organizational measures would have to be introduced. The Political Committee would decide on that question today. The main thing, however, was that Horvath's memorandum should be accepted as a Party resolution and should form the basis of the future cultural policy.

Imre Nagy did not speak for long. His speech lasted no more than ten minutes. But those who listened to him knew that it contained a well thought-out and a well-formulated outlook, and that the man was not playing with words or tactics. From his voice, from the way he held his head, it was clear that not only was he certain of his own mind, but that he was also certain of the importance of his opinion.

The amazement of the left-wingers knew no bounds. Not a single word had been said in their favor during the entire debate. And there was no doubt that when Imre Nagy mentioned organizational measures, he was referring to their dismissals from their posts.

They had but one hope left: Rakosi.

The closing speech was again delivered by the Party's First Secretary. Again, Rakosi spoke calmly and without notes exactly as last time. But he seemed to find a little less enjoyment in the situation and in the subject and in his own voice. He began by

saying that he had again carefully perused Horvath's memorandum and that he could only repeat what Gero had said: that
it had been worthwhile to discuss it all with the Political Committee two weeks ago, that the comrades had learned a great
deal from that discussion, and that now, since the memorandum
had been rewritten on the basis of the Political Committee's
advice, there was no obstacle to its being accepted. . . . He,
personally, fully agreed with Comrade Nagy. . . .

The writers, both left-wingers and right-wingers, began to see
light. It was not that Rakosi and Gero were too dense to see that
the memorandum before them was substantially the same as it
had been two weeks previously. Nor was it that something of
importance had occurred during those fourteen days. The difference lay only in the fact that Comrade Nagy had not then been
present—and that now he was.

Two other hitherto obscure points became clear also: 1.) that
Imre Nagy's opinion was decisive in this body; and 2.) that
Rakosi and Nagy did not see eye to eye—or, at least, not in
questions of literature and of cultural policy.

This discovery shook the ground beneath the feet of the left-
wingers. There had been rumors—and the right-wing of the
Communist writers had often spoken of them lately—that, since
the announcement of the new Government program, there had
been no complete unity in the Party leadership, or rather that
there were two lines, Rakosi's and Imre Nagy's. When the left-
wingers had heard this rumor, they had shrugged their shoulders
contemptuously. They had been convinced that this was but a
pipe dream of the enemy, that it was a cheap and superficial
deduction, and that the Party was continuing as unitedly and as
solidly as before the new program. They had believed that the
personnel changes that had been made were only tactical steps
intended to win the masses, that the country was led by Rakosi
as before, and that Imre Nagy was but a figurehead who, because
of his origin, his genial appearance, and his beautiful Hungarian
speech, had been given the popular role of announcing the
milder, more liberal tactical line of the Party. They had held too

high an opinion of Rakosi's capacities and too low an opinion of Imre Nagy's capacities to imagine that the latter could have an independent political opinion and an outlook of his own.

This debate convinced them that they had been wrong. One brief episode was enough to dispel all their doubts.

The episode occurred during Rakosi's closing speech. Rakosi was saying that—as Comrade Nagy had said—the writers should portray life more profoundly, speak more freely of the phenomena observed, and criticize mistakes. But, naturally, he added, they were not to forget the tremendous achievements attained by the Party in the last eight years. It would perhaps be right if this were emphasized a little more in the memorandum.

When he got this far, Imre Nagy interrupted unexpectedly.

"There were plenty of mistakes in these eight years," said Nagy.

"But there were also achievements," replied Rakosi.

"No doubt," said Imre Nagy in a voice that meant, "Let's not argue, my good man; I know what I know."

Rakosi was obviously disturbed by this interruption. It was most unusual in the Political Committee that its members should betray a difference of opinion before strangers or guests or ordinary mortals. They had always been very careful about a show of unity. Until then, they had never said: "I do not agree with Comrade X. or Comrade Y." Even if they had violently disagreed, they had presented their opinion as a whole and never as an argument. This little clash of words lasted only a few seconds, but Rakosi disapproved of it.

"I," he continued quickly and zealously, "should like to remind those present that it was I who encouraged Comrade Horvath to prepare this memorandum, and when I asked him to come and talk to me on this matter, he was still convinced, at most, that we had made mistakes of method in our cultural policy. I told him that it was absolutely impossible that we, having committed such serious mistakes in our political line, should have erred only in the methods applied in cultural policy. . . ."

Whether this was true or not was no longer important. But it was extremely interesting now to see how the omnipotent leader of yesterday retreated with his tail between his legs, how zealously he explained himself, and how he emphasized the mistakes committed. Writers have sensitive ears. It was impossible to ignore the signs of change expressed in this tiny incident. There were indeed differences of opinion within the Party leadership, not only as far as literature was concerned but also in fundamental matters—as, for instance, in the valuation of the Party's activities in the past eight years. The left-wingers had to give up the hope that Rakosi had remained the same and that he differed from Imre Nagy only in the role he had to play.

Yet, Rakosi made another effort to protect his disciples. In reply to Imre Nagy's demand for organizational measures, he turned with great warmth and understanding toward the left-wingers, declaring that they were decent, well-meaning comrades and that the Party should now give them time to understand and to accept the new political line fully. This was, however, small comfort to the left-wingers. It was clear that they had lost.

What they were worried about was not a loss of position or a personal failure. They felt as if an invisible corpse—Revai's cultural policy—were lying on an invisible bier in the middle of the little square of green tables. They felt as if people were still walking on tiptoe around this corpse and whispering words of praise about the immortal virtues of the deceased. But they also knew that the dead was dead and that nothing could ever resurrect the corpse again.

The situation was not altered by the fact that the corpse would have liked to live. As a matter of fact, Revai, who had been the first to see the minutes between the two sessions of the Political Committee, had written a letter to the Party leadership, protesting vehemently against the Horvath memorandum. (He had not "officially" seen the minutes, for he was no longer a member of the Politburo, but was shown the minutes only out of respect for an old comrade who had shaped cultural policies for a long time and who had not been completely shelved and whose opinion was always respected in important matters.) The tone of

Revai's letter had been too rough even for him: he had called Mihaly Farkas an ignorant idiot and Horvath and Darvas spineless careerists. But his accusations had been of no avail. The letter was not even mentioned during the second session. Only Farkas spoke of it, and even he did so only once, and with hypocritical sympathy, saying how painful it was that Comrade Revai had apparently misunderstood the essential problem and had persisted in his mistaken attitude.

On March 15, 1954, a full-page editorial appeared in *Szabad Nep*. The editorial was based on the resolution which was passed at the second session of the Political Committee. In a text richly seasoned with Marxist-Leninist quotations (and without abusing the left-wingers by name or fully approving of the right-wing exaggeration), the editorial supported the new objectives. Greater freedom and greater responsibility! This was the basic plea of the article. Writers should be given greater freedom, but it was up to them to use it properly in the interest of the Party.

The article was so diplomatic that no Communist writer could take offense. There was nothing objectionable in it, and it permitted both sides to agree with it. And so, that was exactly what happened. The right-wingers received it with enthusiasm because the Party resolution justified them. The left-wingers pretended to agree with them on this point. After all, a Party resolution is always right and, considering the debate with the Political Committee, the article could have been much worse as far as they were concerned.

Yet, beneath the surface calm and the unanimous approvals, the differences persisted. The Political Committee discussed the problem twice. The "council of the gods" passed a resolution. In reality, nothing had been settled, and the Communist writers remained as divided as ever.

BOOK III

THE PURIFYING STORM

The Wheels Turn On

The summer of the year 1954 promised to be quiet, peaceful, and calm. The dark clouds on the international political horizon were beginning to dispel. A whole year had passed since the truce in Korea. Peace bulletins replaced war bulletins in the press. The newsreels showed Khrushchev's smiling, bald head, Eisenhower's bony, somewhat bent figure, Eden's polite smile and famous hat. The foreign ministers sat together in Geneva. Toasts, declarations, and statements emphasized the general desire for peace and the new hopes for an international agreement. In Indo-China, the guns fell silent. It seemed as if the world were at last coming to its senses: the fearful felt more secure, the hopeful more hopeful still. Even though nothing was yet quite settled, the "spirit of Geneva" reigned supreme and calmed the stormy waters.

The effects of the changed European atmosphere made themselves felt in Hungary, too. Although the summer was unusually cool, windy, and rainy, the political meteorologists forecasted good weather and a fruitful future. Life had perceptibly improved in the last year. The 15 per cent increase in the living standard—which had been promised in the new Government program—was even more noticeable. The Party Congress held in May had apparently assured smooth progress: the speakers had praised the achievements of the past ten years, but they were unequivocally in favor of the "new phase." Rakosi and Imre Nagy appeared to work together in full agreement. Less was said about the mistakes committed in the past; more was said about the ways and means to assure further improvement. People looked less worried than a year or two before. In spite of the bad weather, the holiday resorts were crowded. Men flirted more boldly. Women's dresses grew more daring. It was as if the *Treuga Dei* was favorable to the birth of new love affairs; and thus, there was also a larger number of divorces. A rendezvous in the dark corner of a hidden little pastry shop no longer involved the risk of losing one's job. People began to enjoy long forgotten pleasures again. Literary debates became less frequent and, though the conflicts remained unsolved, there was a certain rapprochement between the two camps. Both the right-wingers and the left-wingers, convinced that they would have to prove the correctness of their theoretical attitudes in a practical way, had retired into their studies to work. Nothing worth mentioning happened at the conference of the Writers' Association at the end of June.

Imre Nagy, head of the Government, who had done a good job both in Parliament and at the Party Congress, went to the Soviet Union for his vacation.

Yet, in reality, things were not quite as simple as they seemed. The country faced serious unsolved economic difficulties, particularly in the field of international debts. The mistaken and harmful economic policy dictated by Erno Gero, which concentrated exclusively on the development of heavy industry, was making itself felt in every sphere. The increased imports and decreased exports caused an acute shortage of foreign currency, and the creditors were demanding payment more energetically all the time. The Czechs and Poles, who had supplied the country with coal and iron ore on credit, declared that, due to their own economic difficulties, they could deliver in the future only for cash. The Western creditors were also pressing for payment.

Even within the country, production could not keep pace with the improvement of the living standard. On the contrary, there was a certain retrogression. "Reconversion," which aimed at the progress of light industry rather than of heavy industry and at the modernization of agriculture, caused extraordinary difficulties. And everywhere in the country stood half-finished construction jobs and buildings, the remnants of stepped-up investments. The half-finished tunnels of the subways of the capital sagged and crumbled (their maintenance alone cost millions). Columns of concrete reached toward the sky all over the countryside. The frames of a ball-bearing plant in Szeged, of a power plant in Kazincbarcika, of a chemical works in Tiszapalkonya, and of a steel works in Stalinvaros stood as half finished constructions, all of them stopped by the new Government program. Naturally, all this was a result of the Rakosi-Gero "adventurist politics" which had failed to take the limited possibilities of the country into account. The situation was made more acute by the enemies of the new phase (very numerous among the officials who, on the one hand, did everything to slow down "conversion," and, on the other, blamed the dismissals—which hit the industrial workers first of all—on the new policy and on Imre Nagy personally).

Behind the padded doors of Party headquarters, the economic leaders worked out a plan of "counter-attack" against the new program. Imre Nagy was on vacation in the Soviet Union, and the population lived a little more comfortably in the hope of better times—and Gero and his accomplices gave birth to a new (but oh, so old!) theory, according to which the sudden increase of the living standard was at the root of all trouble. The conclusion was clear: in order to relieve the situation, a further rise of the living standard had to be prevented, or else it had even to be lowered to restore the balance.

The Government began to work out measures to lower the living standard, or, as they called it, to "restore economic balance." One of the basic necessities was the reduction of the top-heavy and, indeed, unwieldy army of civil servants. Thus, the idea of so-called "rationalization" was launched.

The civil service was indeed gigantic. No country would have been able to support it. Only forty out of every one hundred men engaged in productive work really produced, the other sixty simply augmenting the unproductive bureaucracy. Thus, the reduction of the civil service was indeed necessary and objectively correct. But, in attempting this correction, Erno Gero and his partisans had forgotten to mention that it had been they who had been responsible for the past bad state of affairs, and now, with this sudden change, they put the blame for this past state of affairs on Imre Nagy and the new political line. Losing no time, they set to work to carry out their plan. Storm clouds were gathering on the blue summer sky. The fear of the concentration camps (which had been dissolved by Nagy) was replaced by the fear of want and the fear of unemployment. Rationalization was in full swing. Thousands upon thousands were removed from their jobs, and rationalization became the main topic of conversation. But the press and the radio never mentioned it, basing their censorship of such news on the principle that that which is not mentioned does not exist.

A new wave of fear and bitterness flooded the country.

The only stratum which regained its old power as a result of the new measures was the Party. The Party officials decided who should be dismissed and who should retain his job, and the Party officials decided who should live and who should die—and the Party officials were thus again busy at a job they liked. The situation filled the Party officials with new hope. There was again one boss and nine million employees, as people were wont to say jokingly—or bitterly—in those days.

However, rationalization was not all. Gero and his general staff worked out other measures that were to be introduced in the autumn. This general staff consisted of a Muscovite economist by the name of Istvan Friss and a half-politician, half-economist young Party functionary named Bela Szalai, who had risen from a position as Rakosi's secretary to membership in the Political Committee.

These three evolved a new system of taxation for the peasantry.

A year previously, the Imre Nagy Government had given its solemn word that the new decrees regulating taxes and deliveries would remain in effect for at least three years, partly to relieve the terrible burdens borne by the peasantry and partly to increase the peasantry's incentive to produce. Gero's plan, had it been carried out, would have again confused the people and destroyed Imre Nagy's popularity.

Gero's plan did not forget the working class either. It was established that the norms* prescribed by the state had become obsolete and that a new system of norms was necessary. This propensity for changing the system of norms was a favorite pastime of the Soviet People's Democracy. It meant the increase of the norms—i.e., the reduction of wages, and this simple form of pressure which, in every capitalist country would have been called exploitation, was always introduced by a large-scale campaign. The press was full of articles explaining that this measure had been requested by the workers themselves and that, fundamentally, it meant an increase in wages (though perhaps not directly but indirectly) because the resulting increase of production benefited the working class. That not a word of this was true, and that the accelerated tempo of work never improved the conditions of the working class, was well known in the factories, where each change in the system of norms was received with passionate hatred.

Erno Gero now published a carefully worded article in *Szabad Nep*, in which he announced the introduction of these measures. The title of the article was: "Let Us Prepare for the Winter."

He explained that "we were living too well" and that it was time to "tighten our belts" because the rise in the living standard had been "too rapid" and was out of proportion to the increase of production. He announced that "we must save," because there was great extravagance throughout the country, and saving was the only way to solve the economic problems. By this time,

---

* A norm was a centrally determined unit of work which the worker had to fulfill in order to receive his basic wage.

the people were fully familiar with Party jargon, and they knew exactly what "saving" meant.

A wave of bitterness swept the entire country.

People had quickly become used to the relative freedom of the past year. Now, since they no longer kept their mouths shut, Budapest resounded with complaints. In every public place, loud arguments could be heard about rationalization, about the old and the new restrictions, about whether or not one should believe in the promises of the Government. Apparently, this Government was not any better than the other had been. In vain had Imre Nagy promised this and that. He was no different from the rest. A stone had been dropped into the stagnant water of the peaceful, calm summer, and the ripples were traveling outward in larger and larger circles.

Something else happened that summer, too. It was not a very significant event and it was an absolutely nonpolitical one, but it is still worth mentioning because it was not without its repercussions on later events.

It was the year of the world soccer championship game, which took place in Switzerland, and the Hungarian team, at the top of its form, had excellent chances of winning this championship. In those days, the Hungarian team enjoyed world-wide fame. It had played every European team and had always come out victorious. It had won the championship at the Olympic games in Helsinki in 1952. It had also beaten the invincible British team on its own ground 6 to 3 (and in Budapest 7 to 1), and it had beaten the Swedes, the Rumanians, the Yugoslavs, the French, and the Italians. The whole country was convinced that the team would easily defeat the best teams in the world again.

In other sports, too, Hungarian athletes—both men and women—were making excellent records. The Hungarian fencers and water polo players and amateur boxers had always been famous, and, after 1945, the Party had begun attributing exaggerated importance to sports—or rather to outstanding international victories. The Party spent huge amounts of money for this purpose. It proclaimed that, in Hungary, sports were a mass movement, though, in reality, the money was spent not on the masses but on the outstanding few who were called upon to devote their achievements to political propaganda. The Party launched the theory that the excellent results were not due to the quality of the Hungarian sportsmen but to the superiority of the socialist over the capitalistic system. It said that the achievements were necessarily an evidence of the superiority of the Hungarian social system. The most money of all was spent on soccer, the most popular sport in Hungary. The famous players were the spoiled darlings of the country. Their incomes exceeded those of the best-paid factory director, although they were "officially" amateur players. They were the richest people in the country. They were the happy exceptions who could travel abroad, who flooded the country with foreign goods at astronomical prices (through the black market, but with the tacit approval of the Party, although not of the public), and who had cars, who built themselves luxurious villas, whose names were surrounded with legends, and who enjoyed all the glory due to heroes.

There was purpose behind this pomp and noise. It was the People's Democracy's variation of *panem et circenses*. The Party offered ever larger portions of sports victories to be spread on the ever smaller portions of bread. The masses were feverishly interested in the sports results. Half an hour after its appearance at 11 p.m. every night, the only sports journal could be bought solely at black market prices. Whenever a great game was played in the most beautiful stadium of Central Europe, which seated 100,000, tickets were sold out weeks in advance. The soccer players who returned victorious from abroad were met at the railway station by the representatives of Party and Government and by the loud cheers of the population.

As far as the masses were concerned, a soccer game was a ninety-minute escape from a depressing reality into an exciting dream. It was a drug which brought forgetfulness, an elixir which turned anxiety into exultation. But, chiefly, it was—and of this the Party was aware—a relatively harmless outlet for accumulated tensions. For, after ninety minutes of mad excitement, of yelling and raving, people were too tired, perhaps also too satisfied, to think of any other kind of madness.

Not only the team, but the entire country was preparing for the world championship for weeks in advance. The press was full of articles explaining the chances and attempting to guess the outcome and telling the population that victory was not "quite certain." Yet, it was impossible to conceal the near certainty that the Hungarian team would win. And the Hungarian team did indeed win many a victory. During those days, a whole country sat before the radio (there was no television), and, during the broadcasts, it forgot rationalization, the new system of norms, and the troubles of taxes and deliveries. The Hungarian team defeated its most dangerous opponents, the Brazilians and the Uruguayans. And then came the decisive battle for world championship with the West German team.

The Hungarian team lost that battle.

That same night there were demonstrations in the streets of Budapest. Instead of calming down, the restlessness increased during the following day. The rioters broke the windows of shops in which photographs of the members of the team were displayed. They marched to the house of the team captain, Gusztav Sebes, who was the dictator of Hungarian soccer, and threw stones at his windows. The street resounded with a cry of "Down with Sebes!"

Thousands and thousands marched up and down the main thoroughfares in demonstration. Opposite the building of *Szabad Nep*, there was a pari-mutuel office, and there, too, a group of demonstrators assembled. They marched to the editorial offices of the sports journal and made a bonfire of the latest issue of the paper.

The whole thing began to assume a strange and frightening aspect. Such riots, with people shouting slogans and breaking windows and putting fire to newspapers, had not been seen in Hungary for years. True, they were crying "Down with Sebes," but who knew what they might shout tomorrow? It was quite clear that these people were driven by something else—by something more than mere indignation at the loss of the world championship. The police interfered. The demonstrations were broken up. And some of the rowdiest demonstrators were arrested.

Yet, although the entire country knew about it, the press kept silent over the matter. Rakosi personally forbade the editors of *Szabad Nep* to mention it. Then, the excitement calmed down in a few days. People resigned themselves to the loss. The "national sorrow" lifted. Yet, everybody felt that something had happened—something that had a certain significance, although it was too early to see exactly what, and something that should not be talked about, because it was different. It was an outbreak, an expression of discontent, a demonstration. It was something forbidden that tasted good—something that people suddenly loved and that reminded them of a distant era almost forgotten during the last few years.

At least, the sports craze decreased.

"It Is My Crime to Have Believed in Yours . . ."

The door of the editorial room flew open with a bang. Blown in by the sudden gust, his face pale, his lips trembling, his hand clutching his summer hat, stood Bela Illes, the Muscovite writer. Tiny beads of perspiration covered his bald head. He sank into an armchair.

"What's the trouble, Comrade Illes?" asked the editor of *Szabad Nep,* knowing that the elderly writer often suffered from heart attacks.

With trembling fingers, Illes lit his cigar. He drew on it deeply, and the blue smoke obviously calmed him down.

It was an unusually warm September afternoon, and the soft asphalt of the avenue clung to his shoes. But curtains kept out the sun, and the editorial room was cool and peaceful.

"Trouble?" replied Illes. "Trouble, my friend? Do you know whom I met in the street, here, in front of your door?" He seemed more calm now, and he appeared to enjoy the situation.

The editor had no idea whom Comrade Illes had met.

Illes rose from the armchair.

"I was on my way to see you," he said, "and suddenly a man passed by. Then he turned, looked at me, and came closer. 'Don't you know me, Comrade Illes?' he asked. 'Don't you remember me? We have met often, here and there, and worked together. But that was a good many years ago. . . . ' "

Illes' face darkened again.

"Do you know who that man was?" he asked. "Janos Kadar! What is going on here? Will you explain it to me?"

This is how the editorial offices of the Party's central organ, *Szabad Nep,* learned on a September afternoon that Janos Kadar, a former underground militant of the Communist Party and a former Party Secretary of Budapest, who had been arrested without explanation in March, 1951, and never heard of since, was once again walking with his wife in the streets, a free man.

It was staggering. It was hardly believable—and all the more so since there had been no warning, no explanation. True, as a result of the dissolution of the concentration camps, more and more people who had disappeared for years were reappearing. The "non-people" became people again.

Yet, Janos Kadar and those like him did not belong in the category of the interned. When they had been arrested, there had been no communiqué. It was whispered that they had been a part of the second, less ostentatious act of the Rajk case. But, since there had been no public trials, no leading articles in newspapers or magazines, and no admissions of crimes, it had, in fact, been advisable not to talk about such people. They had been cloaked in the black mist of an unproved—though strong—suspicion that they were enemy agents and enemies of the people. They had been there, and then suddenly they were there no longer. They had lived, and then they lived no longer. They had conspired against the state, and then they conspired no longer. Their memory was shrouded in horror and contempt, and the mass mind was reassured that these men had received their well-deserved punishment.

Nobody had known exactly what their fate had been.

And now, suddenly, it turned out that they were alive. They walked the streets, visited the cafes, entered editorial offices, and gave friendly greetings to old friends and acquaintances, even though they knew that during the years of their imprisonment they had been denounced by these friends and acquaintances.

Yet, suffering had made them forgiving.

Now they came back, these old militants of the underground Communist Party who had disappeared years ago. One after the other, they came back, both those who were well known and those who were lesser known. These were their names and their pedigrees:

Geza Losonczy, member of the underground Communist Party and former Deputy Minister of Culture.

Sandor Haraszti, one of the founders of the underground Communist Party, Secretary of the Hungarian-Yugoslav Society, and Editor-in-Chief of the Party organ, *Szabadsag*.

Ferenc Donath, member of the underground Communist Party, former secretary to Rakosi, and Deputy Minister of Agriculture.

Gyula Kallay, militant of the underground Communist Party, former head of the Party's Agitation-Propaganda Department, and former Minister of Foreign Affairs.

Szilard Ujhelyi, militant of the underground Communist Party and former deputy head of the Hungarian Radio.

Istvan Szirmai, militant of the underground Communist Party and former head of the Hungarian Radio.

Bela Szasz, militant of the underground Communist Party, writer, and former deputy head of the Information Department of the Ministry of Foreign Affairs.

Gyorgy Paloczi-Horvath, militant of the underground Communist Party, writer, and editor.

Sandor Sala, militant of the underground Communist Party and Chairman of the National Film Bureau.

Endre Rosta, militant of the underground Communist Party and former head of the Party's press department.

Laszlo Zigmond, militant of the underground Communist Party and former director of the publishing offices of *Szabad Nep*.

Frigyes Major, militant of the underground Communist Party,

fighter in Spain, and former director of the *Szabad Nep* publishing offices.

Gyorgy Adam, militant of the underground Communist Party, economist, and university lecturer.

Gyorgy Heltai, former head of the Political Department of the Ministry of Foreign Affairs.

Vilmos Tariska, militant of the underground Communist Party, physician, and former department head of the Ministry of Public Health.

Lajos Csebi, militant of the underground Communist Party, fighter in Spain, and a major general in the police force.

Gyula Oszko, militant of the underground Communist Party and a major in the police force.

Janos Reismann, militant of the underground Communist Party and cultural attaché at the Hungarian legation in Paris.

Peter Erdos, a young Communist journalist.

Geza Seres, militant of the underground Communist Party and Moscow correspondent of the Hungarian Telegraph Bureau.

Peter Mod, militant of the underground Communist Party and of the French resistance, and former head of the department of the permanent undersecretary at the Ministry of Foreign Affairs.

The list is incomplete. Others came, too. There were men who had been dragged away in the middle of the night, men who had been sentenced to life imprisonment, men who had been sentenced to death. There were men blacker than the devil, who, disguised as angels, had infiltrated that controlling force of the people, of progress, and of revolution—the Communist Party—in order to destroy it and its leaders.

All these were returned, and they were exactly the same as everyone else. They enjoyed their freedom and the pleasures of a life which they had long ago given up as lost. At first, not many people dared to talk to them, for, even though they had been released, who knew what crimes they had committed and, particularly, when they were going to be arrested again? But the released prisoners did not care that few people talked with them.

And when the official rumor was spread around that they were really guilty but that the Party, in its unbounded mercy, had forgiven them and given them amnesty, they simply shrugged their shoulders.

They knew better.

Then they began to talk. Calmly, quietly, watching for their listeners' reaction (for they had learned circumspection in prison), they told of their experiences.

At first, their friends listened in amazement, hardly believing them. The reason for this amazement had nothing to do with the attitude of the returned, for the newly released ones did not seem to have changed at all during these years. In fact, they seemed, if anything, younger, except for the grey hairs and the deep lines etched on their foreheads and around their mouths. They seemed younger, not in body, but in heart and soul. Before their arrests, most of them had been hard and dry and cold and haughty and reserved (and those who had then tried to get close to them had been repelled by their air of superiority, by their self-assurance, and by their self-imposed discipline). They had lived even then under the spell of the cause that later threw them into prison. Most of them had been high-ranking officials with all the advantages and isolation of the privileged. All of them had belonged to one caste: the caste of Communists. Gradually, the former partisan, the poor university student, the former bank clerk, had built up in themselves the feeling that they belonged to the Stalinist category of "people of a special type."* Thus, they had come to believe not only that they were different, but they had also acted accordingly. They had pretended they were not only different but that they were much superior to anyone else, knew more, had greater experience, had stronger arguments, and held the key to every problem of the world. Thus, they had become estranged from their friends and their former brothers-in-arms, and, while the slogan of "Everything for Man" had withered on

* From Stalin's famous oath at Lenin's death: "We Communists are people of a special type. We are carved out of special matter!"

their lips, their hearts had offered fertile soil for Horace's "*Odi profanum vulgus et arceo.*"

Now, however, they were indeed different.

They knew how to smile, and their hearts were serene. They had become kinder, less remote, more direct, more truthful. Instead of hardening them, the injustices they had suffered had made them more human. Now, long forgotten sentiments broke through the frozen surface of their souls. Torment had killed the evil which had formerly inhabited them: the evil of power. They felt that their most important task—if indeed they still had a task in this life—was to pass on their experiences so that never again should such things happen.

Thus, it was for other reasons that these friends were reserved in their approach to these newcomers.

Had they looked into themselves, these friends would have had to admit that they were *afraid* of the newcomers—or, rather, of themselves. For, when they faced the newcomers for the first time and listened to their words, they themselves felt as if they were sitting face to face with their own consciences. It was as if the quiet, calm words, the mild humor, and the little prison stories merely added to the churning chaos already in their minds.

For a while, the people did everything to avoid long and involved conversations with the former prisoners. But such conversations could not be put off forever.

And, then, they learned what had really happened.

They learned how these men had been arrested in the early hours of the morning and how they had been taken to the cellars of the AVO on Andrassy Avenue. In those first hours and days, even the arrested ones themselves had not fully understood what was happening. They had been convinced that they were the victims of some misunderstanding that would be cleared up in a few hours, or, at most, in a few days. They had had nothing to hide. Their consciences had been clear, and they had believed that innocence was a protection. They had thought of the Party —of that friend of the poor, that torchbearer of truth, that fortress of revolution. They were Communists, and their first thought had been what Comrade Rakosi would say about this "incident."

Then they had been questioned, by higher- or by lower-ranking AVO officers, depending on their importance. Some were questioned by the head of the AVO, Gabor Peter himself. The officers did not beat about the bush. They came out with the accusation: the prisoners were spies of the Western imperialists; or they were Titoist adventurers or agents. They had penetrated into the ranks of the Party to destroy the power of the working class.

These had been the days of the sharpening of the class struggle. The prisoners had denied the charges. They had protested.

Days and nights had merged into one endless nightmare in the darkened, smoke-filled little offices. Proof was put before the prisoners. The proof: confessions signed by their friends and acquaintances describing how, when, where, and by whom they had been enlisted as agents of the imperialist spy ring. Readymade statements were put before them in which they were to confess the crimes they were accused of. The prisoners refused to sign.

Then had come the first beatings.

And the tortures. They had stood facing the wall for days, without food, without water. Their nails had been pulled out. Their teeth had been knocked out. Their testicles had been caned. The tortures had been exactly the same as those in the Fascist prisons.

When this was of no avail (and in many cases it was not), mild persuasion was used. They were told that it was their duty to the Party to sign the confessions, that it was of primary importance to the Party, and that it was to the interest of the international working class movement. They were told that Comrade Rakosi himself had asked them to accept this role, that he knew they were innocent, that he knew they were good Communists, that nothing would happen to them, that there would be a public trial, and that they would be sentenced, but that this would mean nothing. They were told that they would be kept in prison in comfort, with books, cigarettes, and decent food for a year or two, and that they would then be released, be rehabilitated, and be able to return to life, to their former jobs, and their former functions.

But they must first sign the confessions because they would, thereby, deal a terrible blow to the imperialists.

Could this really benefit the Party? The bleeding, emaciated, tortured men had begun to see clearly. No, they were not victims of a misunderstanding. They were the tools of an all-embracing, horrible, carefully worked-out, devilish plan. They were but links in a chain of horror, the beginning of which they had ignored and the end of which they could not see.

That was when Janos Kadar had visited Laszlo Rajk in his cell to ask him, in Rakosi's name, to play the role for which he was cast—in the interest of the Party. And then it had been Kadar's turn to stand accused before his former subordinates of being an agent of a foreign power.

Kadar had denied the charges.

Mihaly Farkas' son, Vladimir, who was a colonel of the AVO and a bald, tired young man of thirty, had questioned him. Vladimir had but one argument: blows. They had begun to beat Kadar. Then they had smeared his body with mercury to prevent his pores from breathing. He had been writhing on the floor when a newcomer had arrived. The newcomer was Vladimir's father, Mihaly Farkas.

Kadar was raised from the ground. Vladimir stepped close. Two henchmen pried Kadar's teeth apart, and the colonel, negligently, as if this were the most natural thing in the world, urinated into his mouth.

Everybody had laughed.

It had indeed been an amusing sight: a bleeding, helpless man half drowning in urine.

The telephone had rung on the table. Mihaly Farkas had picked up the receiver. It was Matyas Rakosi. The wise father and great leader of the people was nervously inquiring whether Kadar had confessed.

Farkas' answer was negative. He had not yet confessed.

Kadar had heard an angry rumbling at the other end of the line. The kind father of the people was giving his orders: "Beat him. Beat him until he talks. These are my orders."*

Farkas had put down the receiver.

Vladimir had proceeded. He did not have to be told to do so. His father and he understood each other without words.

Kadar was beaten. There was no one who would have stayed the hands of these monsters. They felt they could do what they pleased. Nobody would ever call them to account.

In the end, Kadar had "confessed."

And so had most of the others who were thus accused. After a while, there was no point in refusing. The officers had grown tired and had begged their victims to sing out the statement because then, at last, they would be permitted to sleep, and so would the torturers. If they had continued to refuse, they would have been allowed to die, and the officers would not have earned their well-deserved advancement.

Statements were signed. Every word they contained was a lie, every sentence a falsehood. But the victims had grown tired of protesting and, when they had reached the last limit of human endurance, they had given up. They had reached the last gasp, the "nihil," and they had felt that they would never get out of there alive.

The AVO had made no secret of this. Every questioning had begun with the words: "Something you should know is that we don't have to account for you here!"

Gabor Peter, head of the AVO, had said these words openly to Gyorgy Faludy, an outstanding Hungarian poet who had returned from the United States and who was, naturally, arrested: "If you were stupid enough to come back from America to this dunghill, you deserve your fate."

After the confessions came the trials, the sentences, the hangings. What had happened to the promises that all would be well, if only they confessed?

---

* The story comes from Kadar himself. It was a close friend of his, Bela Kelen, present Party secretary of Budapest, who told it to me.—T.A.

There had been hangings. Morning, noon, and night, there had been hangings. Never had an executioner hanged so many Communists, not even in the days of the bloodiest "white terror" of the Horthy era. The regime had hanged its best Party workers, its outstanding underground Communists, its most experienced soldiers, its most talented public servants.

But those who had received prison sentences were also lost to life. They had received no letters, no parcels; neither could they write to their families. They were given ten, fifteen, or twenty years. But the length of the sentence meant nothing. They knew their lives had come to an end and that only a miracle could save them. They were given almost no food. They were allowed almost no sleep. The guards were cruel, the cells cold. Every few minutes, an eye appeared in the Judas-hole and, if they were not lying on their backs with their hands above their blankets or if they were not facing the glaring light over their heads, they were beaten.

Sometimes, the guards had wakened them just for fun.

Sometimes, they had been told that the following morning they were going to be hanged.

In the morning, the guards had then told them, laughing heartily, that it had been a joke.

The guards had never tired of this game. Their job was boring.

Fathers had known nothing about their families. The women who had been pregnant when arrested were robbed of their babies after delivery. Mrs. Rajk's son had been renamed in the nursery where he was raised. Ferenc Donath had to seek his son for weeks after his own release until they told him "as a favor" where the child was hidden.

There were those who had gone mad under the tortures. The poet Endre Havas, who had been secretary to Count Mihaly Karolyi, one of the leaders of the 1918 Hungarian Revolution, and the Hungarian Ambassador to Paris, had screamed until he died: "Long live the Party! Long live Comrade Rakosi!" There had been those who had contracted tuberculosis in the damp, cold cells. There had been those who had become completely apathetic. And there were those who, though they were not many, had hoped.

Now, the writers, particularly the young Communist writers, listened to these newly released men with amazement. The tortures, the hangings, the suffering faces of those in the cells unrolled before their inner eyes like a film. The most shocking part of the whole picture was not what these men, sitting opposite them over a cup of coffee or a little glass of cognac were saying, but the fact that so many were not there to tell their stories. These missing ones had been executed.

Official sources made strenuous efforts to explain what had happened: they reaffirmed the accusation against Laszlo Rajk and the others who had been executed, and they declared that the innocent had now been released. But the mind had broken its fetters, and now nothing could stop the thoughts of the listeners from running free. If those who had been released were innocent and could tell the story of their experiences, then it was evident that those who could no longer speak had also been innocent. This realization filled the listeners with burning indignation and bitter hatred, plus another, perhaps even stronger, feeling: shame. For, there was the question of responsibility.

A face emerged before their eyes. It was a kindly, smiling face. It was the face of the great and wise leader whom they had admired and loved and feared and honored, and whose sixtieth birthday they had celebrated by writing sentimental odes. It was the face of the man who had come to them like a Messiah, fulfilling great dreams and defending the right of the people. Now, suddenly, this man stood naked before them—naked and bloody as the possessor of a voice at the other end of a telephone line, ordering his henchmen to torture, beat, and kill. There stood Matyas Rakosi, the fearless "unmasker" of the people's enemies, who had personally discovered and thwarted the devilish plans of the Rajk "gang"—as it had, at the time, been loudly proclaimed in Party schools and seminars, and in the entire press. Was he the man who had been responsible?

No doubt, he was. In vain did the official propaganda scream and rant against the already arrested chief of the AVO, Gabor Peter, saying that it was he who had been responsible for the "violation of socialist legality" (as they liked to call it in Party jargon) and not the wise father, Matyas Rakosi.*

Gabor Peter? The writers asked themselves and each other whether he could have been responsible. Yes, perhaps. But, then, how could that wise and experienced leader of the country, Matyas Rakosi, have permitted such things to happen?

That squat little man stood firm and unshakable. It seemed as though the thoughts and doubts churning about him did not disturb him in the least. Perhaps he was already busy preparing the arguments in his defense. "It was not my fault," he would say. "I did it on Soviet orders. It was Stalin's idea, and what can one do against Stalin? And, anyway, I knew of nothing. I saw only the finished reports. Mihaly Farkas managed the affair. . . ."

Soviet orders? It was true that the officers of the Soviet State Security Organization had cooperated with the AVO from the very first moment and that nothing had been decided without Soviet "counsellors." But it was also true that Rakosi's zeal had known no limits. His zeal had been the price the "leader of the Hungarian people" had to pay for being permitted to sit, on Stalin's birthday, beside the "leader of humanity." It was no small price, but apparently Rakosi had not minded paying it. Though there had been similar trials in Poland and Rumania, Rakosi had been the first to "complete his plan." Hungary had produced the first big show trial. Hungary had been the loudest

---

* Major General Gabor Peter was arrested early in 1953. His arrest was a result of the great purification campaign carried on in the Soviet Union: the campaign against Jewish doctors who were participants, as the official propaganda had it, in an imperialist Zionist conspiracy against Stalin. As usual, this example had to be followed in Hungary, and it was obviously the best course for the Hungarian leaders to arrest the man who, in addition to being a Jew, held in his possession the complete documents and the false confessions of the Rajk trials. A great number of Jewish AVO officers were arrested at the same time. Later, Rakosi and his disciples tried to make the country believe that these arrests were not part of a new campaign of terror, but that, instead, they were a punishment meted out to those responsible for the Rajk trials.

voice in the chorus denouncing the Yugoslavs. And who had been at the head of the Party? Not Gabor Peter, nor Mihaly Farkas, although they, too, were depraved gangsters. It had been the bald father of wisdom, the smiling, polite, and erudite leader who had proudly complained how many sleepless nights the unmasking of the Rajk gang had cost him. It had been Matyas Rakosi.

Now, it suddenly became clear what it was that had caused these sleepless nights. It suddenly became clear—and now it was the writers' turn to spend sleepless nights—what it was that had worked behind the smooth, almost unbelievably well-oiled mechanism of the Rajk trial and behind the endless succession of self-vilifying confessions which had surpassed even the invectives of the prosecution. What had worked there was a well-constructed machine of terror, at the lever of which had sat the man who had always been adored as the very image of infallibility.

This suddenly liberated power of thought drew the young writers, including the authors of the present book, deeper and deeper into a new perception. Everything that had hitherto appeared obscure and difficult to understand and that (they had once reassured themselves) emanated from men who better knew the whole truth and who *better* knew what they had to do about that truth became at one stroke clear and understandable in this whirlwind of awakening souls. They now understood what Revai had meant when he had explained in the Dery debate that it was a mistake to raise social problems in isolation or in abstraction or in a moral context, "particularly today, when the imperialists are hypocritically comparing the demand for a 'super-class' morality with our revolutionary state interest, with the measures dictated by this interest, and with the expedient necessities and requirements of the class struggle." In the light of the stories told by the former prisoners, all this seemed almost blindingly self-evident. State interest? Measures? Expediency? From behind the words emerged Revai's clever, bespectacled face, together with the sharp brilliance of the arguments and the final and witty, but unanswerable, definitions.

Now the words regained their original meaning. The brilliance of Revai's logic could no longer prevent the feverishly busy minds from translating the thieves' lingo into straight talk. "State interest" really meant ruthless dictatorship. "Measures" really meant arrests, sentences, and executions. And "expediency" actually meant the uninhibited raging of a bloody reign of terror.

For everything could be explained. One could, of course, understand the speeded-up plan, the murderous tempo of work, and the exploitation of agriculture. After all, a terrific effort was needed to achieve the sublime aim: socialism. But it was completely and absolutely incomprehensible why the murder of innocent people was necessary and even expedient. Here arguments and witty definitions and clever thoughts and pleasing formulations of words were of no avail.

The real content of even the famous Dery debate of two years ago could now be understood. "It is not ethics that are important, but the class struggle," Revai had announced, looking down mockingly upon the multitude of admirers. Now the time had come for the admirers to reply. What Revai had most feared had happened: the writers were moralizing. Revai had proclaimed proletarian humanism. Was this proletarian humanism? Revai had, in those days, branded as base slander the following lines by an excellent poet, Anna Hajnal: "A cart pulls up/The silent house draws a deep, sobbing breath./ A car stops. Here comes the henchman:/ Death for us."

The writers now understood that Anna Hajnal had told the truth about the nightly arrests and the oppressive fear of inquisition. One had not been permitted to "moralize." One had been forbidden to "feel sorry for the enemy" at a time when the prisons were not full of the enemy but of the sons of the people.

The writers understood. "Moralizing" meant thinking for oneself. Thinking meant raising one's voice. Raising one's voice was equivalent to rebellion against the murder of innocent people, against the trampling underfoot of humanity and democratic rights and progress—and the Revolution. This was the blind alley. This was the downward path from which Comrade Revai had attempted to "save" the writers.

The writers had no doubt that Revai had not only known of

these things but that he had contributed to them by his vote in the Political Committee. There was a rumor that, in 1949, he had been the only one in the Political Committee to vote against Rajk's execution. Whether that was true or not, one thing was certain: that the indictment against Rajk had been written from the first word to the last by Revai himself and that, after the execution, Revai had kept silent and had continued to give his full support to Rakosi. He had watched without lifting a finger while his closest friends and comrades had been arrested and executed. (His own brother-in-law, Laszlo Gacs,* was arrested in 1950 and released only when Imre Nagy became Prime Minister in 1953.) He had loudly proclaimed the superiority of Communist cultural policies, while knowing all the time what was going on behind the scenes. It was no extenuating circumstance in the eyes of the writers that Revai had himself been in danger, that his name had figured in the list of those to be arrested in the Rajk case because, among the Muscovites, he had been Rajk's best friend.† He had been under observation by the AVO for several months, the AVO occupying the middle room of a three-room apartment opposite his, the window of which opened on to Revai's front gate. Ultimately, however, he had been saved by his loyalty to the Party and by his Muscovite past; and he had continued to serve, within the "foursome," the system which then held a knife at his throat. But all this had, as far as the writers

---

* Miklos Gimes, a journalist who was executed at the same time as Imre Nagy, told me that he was in the room of Jozsef Revai, editor-in-chief of *Szabad Nep,* when Gabor Peter telephoned Revai to tell him that his brother-in-law, Laszlo Gacs, had been arrested. Revai's hand, holding the receiver, shook, and his face turned a pasty white. But all he said was: "That was a pretty close shot, Gabor."—T.M.

† Rajk and Revai were the patrons of the so-called "People's Colleges Movement." These colleges offered board, lodgings, and recreation to students of working-class and peasant origin, and they were organized for the purpose of creating a new intelligentsia. There were an art college, a music college, a technical college, etc., for students of the various faculties. After Rajk's arrest, the movement was branded Titoist, and Revai himself, one of its patrons, announced its dissolution. The principal accusation against the movement was that the college youth was trying to "become independent of the Party," creating a state within the state and thus endangering the power of the Party leadership.

were now concerned, increased his responsibility. To them, Revai became a striking example of how completely power, which is not only the master but also the slave, can debase a gifted, capable, and valuable man.

To the writers, Rakosi was now the head of a criminal gang, and Revai, Gero, and Farkas were his accomplices, and the picture grew ever darker. Yet, this was not the most unbearable aspect. There was a more unbearable one: when the young writers asked themselves the question of who was really responsible for everything that had happened in the country, they had to admit, with aching hearts and disturbed minds, that they, too, had been accomplices, and that they, too, had been responsible.

Looking back on the past years and on their own attitude in those years, the writers saw with horror not only that they had had faith in the Party but also that they had been helpers, agitators, and propagandists in all that had happened. A great Hungarian poet, Mihaly Babits, once said: "Among criminals, the mute is an accomplice." Oh, if they had only been mute! But they had not, and now, suddenly, they began to hate themselves in a surge of shame and guilt. They did not know which of the two feelings was stronger: shame for having been blind for so many years, or guilt for pretending to lead when they themselves had been blind. They were not ashamed of having believed and of having been convinced that a new world had to be built in place of the old. They were ashamed of having believed *blindly* and in glaring contradiction with their past, their inner feelings, their upbringing. This, they could never forgive themselves. They could never forgive themselves for having been so stupid, so dehumanized, so harmful.

Looking back, they saw only bare rocks. They saw only years of barrenness. They glanced through their works and were shocked by the lies they had written, and by the silly, unconvincing, empty slogans. All that they had written in giving everything of themselves in their effort to help the Party had suddenly become valueless. They recalled Revai's upbraiding them in a thunderous voice: "No writer should consider himself infallible.

Let him accept the Party's guidance!" And they had accepted it. And what had happened? The poet who had written passionate poems against the white-coated "murderers" of the Stalinist "doctors' plot" now discovered painfully and bitterly that every word he had written was a lie. The poet who had written an epic poem of several hundred lines on the border incidents provoked by the Yugoslavs now discovered that what he had written was a lie from beginning to end. The novelist who had written an enthusiastic novel on the beautiful and happy new life now turned the pages of his book nauseously. There was not a word of truth in it. The writers who, in early youth, had pledged to devote themselves to the cause of justice in order to help the Party and the Revolution with their literary work now pronounced sentence upon themselves. They had lied, lied, lied. And why? Not because they had wanted to lie, but because they had listened to the infallible and powerful Party and had allowed it to tell them what their mission was. They had wanted to describe how right the Party was—and now they discovered that it had been wrong. They had been the literary wardens of their country—wardens whose faith had been contaminated by haughtiness and by the bugaboo of omniscience.

How self-assured they had been! How proud and how vain! They had sometimes thought with secret anxiety that what they wrote was, perhaps, not so very good. But, then, the Party had praised them, and, sunning themselves in that praise, they had silenced their own doubts. Without really noticing it, they had become distorted souls. The poets' delicate reactions had become blunted. The novelists' probing, analytical minds had become shallow. The dramas were no longer centered on sharp or bold or real conflicts, but on artificial problems discussed in seminars and on artificial conflicts between cardboard figures. They had no real subject and no real theme. Instead, they were propaganda displays of uniformly flat theses in a literary form. Their authors had not known how the workers really lived. They had only known how the Party depicted their lives. In fact, the playwrights had been turned into nothing but hacks and rhymesters because they had listened to their Party. Their lives had become grey and anaemic and empty—and they had considered this fact natural and worthy of a loyal and militant revolutionary.

Now the writers had smothered in themselves everything they had once loved and admired. No new friendships were born, and no old friendships were continued. Old friends became estranged, and though they felt that, on the surface, the attachment still held, they knew in the depths of their souls that they no longer needed each other. There were no walks in the silent streets until late into the night. There were no endless conversations about matters either concrete or abstract. Everything was as it should be, and that was that; and they began to have secrets from each other. Strange feelings awoke in their innermost hearts. They had doubts and questions that they concealed even from themselves, as well as from their friends. The result was that they feared that their petty-bourgeois remnants remained strong and that they were not yet good enough Communists. How could they have told their friends about such feelings and their innermost struggles when friendships no longer existed and when an atmosphere favorable to such conversations was a thing of the past?

Even the air around them was dead, and in that air they had petrified. It had been a luxurious death, with automobiles and villas and social recognition and money. It had been a death in which they had long forgotten the years when they were poor and unknown—in which they had long forgotten the days when, in order to be able to go to the movies, they had checked every telephone booth along the boulevards in hope of picking up pennies which had fallen from the slot. Now, they were opulent and, therefore, uninterested in money. And this they had found natural because they had belonged to the privileged group whose mission it was to manage the country's affairs. Deep inside themselves, they had known, of course, that in the lower strata there were large working-class families subsisting on ridiculous wages— but, after all, the building of socialism was no picnic. The building of socialism was a hard struggle. Thus, these champions of justice and democracy had explained to themselves that they had the right to live well. They had also explained to themselves that it would be entirely wrong to demand "equalitarianism." The large and productive social classes simply had to wait a little longer for prosperity. For themselves, the writers had proclaimed "thriftiness" and "modest living" in the interest of the future—at the same time that they themselves had become less and less thrifty and had led a rich and thoughtless existence.

They had lived somewhere near the pinnacles. They had been high above the masses for whom they had "worked," for whom they had "argued," and whose bread they had eaten. Even their own families had been far beneath them. They had not been able to put up with fault-finding uncles, nor with fathers-in-law who had asked uncomfortable questions and had repeated the complaints of the "petty-bourgeois" masses to them. At first, they had argued with these people. They had explained that their relatives' thinking was all wrong, that it was polluted by fascism or by the past, and that these had been voicing the opinions of the enemy and had been agitating against the People's Democracy. For, how could they have dared to say that this system, which was the very embodiment of justice, had arrested innocent people? How could they have dared to insinuate that the police— the police of the people!—were beating people? Why could the people not understand that it was still too early for everyone to live equally well, but that, nevertheless, it was a brazen lie that in the new Hungary anyone had to starve! No, it was all lies! And when the meat disappeared from the butcher shops, when there was no potato to be had for love or money, and when the prices rose from day to day, they had explained, ever more loudly—perhaps to convince themselves—that patience and tolerance were needed in the interest of the future. What they had never talked about was that they themselves had that happy future *in the present* and that the airy promises to the masses were realities only to the writers.

For a while, the uncles and the fathers-in-law, the cousins and the old friends, had continued to visit uncomfortable news upon them, but they had soon lost courage. They had seen that arguments and proof were of no avail, and they had felt that there was no point in starting family quarrels every time they met. They had fallen silent.

By that time, the writers had felt that it was best to sever all contact with the "reactionary" members of their families. Their families were too stupid and stubborn to recognize that the reality *they* saw had nothing to do with the exalted reality hovering above them. By that time, the writers had been living in the rarefied atmosphere of success, completely divorced from everyday reality. They had been living in a fuller and truer world, on a more dignified and more sublimely moral level. They had, of course, concealed this fact. Yet, everyone knew that they had not liked the "backward" relatives who had badgered them with news from an earthly life of small tragedies and joys and who stank of disbelief, of doubts, of slander, and of hatred for the Party.

Their marriages, too, had cooled off. Yet, everything had gone on as before. There could be no new love affairs, for one had to be careful of scandal, and Communist morality disapproved of divorce—though perhaps the real reason had lain in the fact that in these last few years the writers had lost their capacity for deeper feelings. They had considered themselves writers, but, in reality, they had not been too interested in literature. In these barren years, they had comforted themselves with the thought that their only passion was their love for the people— i.e., serving the Party. Not only would the dissolution of a marriage or the involvement in a passionate love affair have hindered them in their "work for the people" (after all, it would have been petty-bourgeois to spend time on the "individual sorrows of the individual soul"), but these would also have made questionable their position as Communists, and would have lowered their position in the Party, and would have been a black mark to be recorded in their file. And this, they had feared more than anything.

For they had not been able to deny even to themselves that they were afraid of the Party. When the telephone had rung in

the morning and they had been told to appear the next day at
the personnel department of Party headquarters, they had trembled and had searched their souls feverishly for the reason for
that summons. Perhaps the Party had discovered one of their
insignificant minor slips: a fleeting love affair, a new acquaint-
anceship made in a coffeehouse—a possibility they really disapproved of, but could not always resist. Perhaps the personnel
department had overheard a remark concerning a not too important aspect of Party politics—a remark which, though they
had known it was not advisable to do so, they had made in
public. They were impregnated with the cold and damp air of
an all-pervasive fear. The distinguishing factor of this fear had
lain in the fact that it had been a different fear from the fears
known to ordinary mortals—that it had had different causes
from the fears of the ordinary people about whose free and
happy lives they had written so much in the last few years.

The truth was that they had feared *themselves* most. They
had feared the petty-bourgeois feelings concealed in their hearts.
They had feared the enemy which was attached to them by
invisible ties, and they had feared their own weaknesses, which
prevented them from becoming the one hundred per cent Communists, the determined and ruthless class fighters like so many
in their environment of whom they were a little jealous and
whom they admired and whom (and they confessed it to themselves in their sincere moments) they thoroughly disliked.

Yet, they had always sought the fault in themselves. Yes,
they themselves were very imperfect men. They were unable to
applaud for a half hour in thoughtless, happy ecstasy when the
wise father of the people said something witty, and they had
considered the three cheers and the endless *"Vivats!"* superfluous stupidities. At the same time, they had felt that their ties
with the Party were too loose, that their critical attitudes were
due to their individualistic, bourgeois "apartness," and that
those who accused them of not merging with the collective
and of maintaining their individuality and apartness, were right.
Therefore, they had decided to go to work on themselves and

to weed out of their souls all the silly remnants of the past, of the petty bourgeois, of the enemy, and of the family and education. Thus, they had become more enthusiastic than the loudest enthusiasts and more collective-minded than the collective. They had known that they were insincere, and thus their fear had grown to terror, lest someone should discover the unreliable individualist in the madly applauding, wildly cheering, gushingly enthusiastic super-Communist.

Their souls had been split. When they had feared that they were unable to hate as passionately as they were supposed to hate, or that they felt pity for the "class enemy," they had risen at Party meetings and launched violent attacks against the doubters and the weaklings and the fainthearted in order to prove to themselves and to the Party what determined and merciless fighters for the class struggle they were. Gradually, they had reached a point at which they had known in advance who the enemy was—and a point at which they were not at all surprised when this or that person disappeared, or when people were arrested, because, as paid agents of the imperialists, these persons had tried to stick a knife into the back of the working class.

Naturally, it had also happened that people were suddenly arrested who had never been touched by suspicion and whom they had known very well and whom they had honored. At such times, a tremor had gone through the writers. No, they had never believed that these people were innocent. Even if such a thing had occurred to them, they had shaken away the pinpricks of doubt and had again blamed themselves for being bad Communists; and they had blamed themselves for not having been circumspect or vigilant enough and for not having noticed the enemy's subversive activity, although it had been going on under their very noses. Then they had become ashamed of themselves. They had begun to search their souls, to put their relations with the person arrested into a test tube, and, very soon, they had come to the conclusion that evidence was indeed abundant, that he really had been an enemy all the time, and that, if they had been more vigilant or less naïve or less trusting (i.e., better Communists and class fighters), the enemy's activities would never have remained unnoticed. Sometimes, when they could not sleep, it had occurred to them in flashes that they, too, could be arrested one day, and then who would worry or who would try to prove their innocence? But these had been ridiculous thoughts to them then. Why should they be arrested? They had known that they were absolutely blameless and that the Party punished only the guilty.

And thus they had lived on. They had become cogs and screws of the giant machinery of which they had understood neither the mechanism, nor the methods, nor the aims.

And now, as if a blinding light had cut through the darkness, they found out what had been going on behind their backs and yet with their own collaboration. They learned of the secrets of the torture chambers, of the merciless reality behind the lofty phrases, and of the underground swamp pullulating with crime from which there was no way out.

And yet they had become Communists because they had believed they had found in the theory of Communism the sacred ideals for a changed society, and because moral indignation caused by the injustice and the poverty and the crimes of fascism had driven them straight into the Communist camp.

Now, the writers wriggled desperately in the throes of a deadly shame.

They were ashamed of their inhumanity, and of having preached the love and liberation of man while they themselves had become insensitive and vile sub-human beings—sham human beings subordinating the most sacred human sentiments to an illusory cause.

They were ashamed of their privileges, and of having accepted and enjoyed advantages that the millions had to go without, and of the price they had paid for these privileges.

They were ashamed of their stupidity, and of having believed and of having become the propagators of the most revolting lies. Now they took from their bookshelves the blue book about the Rajk trial, and they reread the accusations and the confessions. How transparent and crude it all was! How could they have been blind enough not to notice the glaring contradictions, and not to discern the carefully prepared and mechanically repeated text behind the too smooth and too willing admissions of the accused?

They were ashamed of their self-defense: that they had known nothing of this; that they, too, had been misled and cheated. It was a terrible realization that, not so long ago, the fascists had used the same arguments in self-defense. Now the writers stood before the severest judges—their own consciences—and they could not acquit themselves.

They were ashamed of what they had written and of what they had not written. Now they looked with disgust upon the volumes that they had once upon a time caressed with their eyes—the volumes that had won them the recognition of Kossuth Prizes; and they had no other desire than to unwrite them. They were tortured with shame for not having written about subjects worth writing about: love and happiness, flowers and the spring, the beauty of the sunset and the bouquet of a red wine. And they were ashamed of having ignored in their writing the *real* life of the people.

They were ashamed (they who had held themselves to be the heroes of liberty and of the intellect) of having become the mere tools of a ruthless power and of having worshipped false gods and of having been guilty of compromises and cowardice. For, now, though they could not indeed know *everything* nor understand the mysteries of the fabricated trials, they had seen sufficient mistakes and sufficient anomalies against which they should have protested. They had not protested because they had been afraid of being taken for petty bourgeois. They remembered the deportations. Had they had the courage to protest? No. They had reassured themselves that this was a hard measure, hard indeed, but what was there to do? This was the class struggle.

They were ashamed in front of their friends and relatives,

whom they had silenced so often and with such superiority and who, as it turned out, had been right all the time. And they were ashamed of themselves before the larger family, the nation, which they had offended and betrayed so violently that nobody knew whether they would ever be forgiven. They were ashamed, and they knew that their shame would cling to them as long as they lived.

They were ashamed, and they felt that, unless they wanted to be sucked in the mire of their lost consciences, they had to do something. The moral indignation that had once driven them to the Party and which had been lulled to sleep for years, awoke and pushed them forward. They were writers, compelled by inner forces to express the aches of a chaotic soul, because, unless they expressed themselves, they could not continue to live. "It is my crime—to have believed in yours," one of the most gifted poets of the young generation of Communist writers, Laszlo Benjamin, now wrote to a friend released from prison, Sandor Haraszti, and in the same poem he pointed out the only imaginable road which he and his companions could follow:

> To fight to death for the impossible
> And to atone for the inexpiable . . .

To atone for the inexpiable! This was the "foundation," the most sacred and urgent duty of the generation returning from Party life into moral life. Those who had for years been the cherished darlings of the system now threw themselves with frightening passion into the battle of "expiation."

Perhaps it was in this attitude that there lay the greatest difference between the writers and those who had been responsible for the murders and the other crimes in the first place. The writers—who, by virtue of their profession, were moralizing beings—took upon themselves the crimes so completely ignored and minimized by the real criminals. Rakosi, Farkas, and the others preferred to remain silent about the happenings of the past, or, if they could not avoid speaking about it, they brushed aside all responsibility. But the writers were ready to assume responsibility for the crimes of others, in order to be able to atone for their own.

The process which fundamentally changed the minds of the Communist writers was very brief. It lasted but a few days, a few hours; for, the moment it became evident that the Party had committed the basest crimes behind their backs and yet with their cooperation and with the use of their names as a shield and with their faith and their passion and talent, they drew their conclusions with a swiftness that surprised even themselves.

In this atmosphere, there remained not a trace of yesterday's split between the various groups of "right-wingers" and "left-wingers." On the contrary, those who had so bitterly criticized *Nyírseg Diary* became—as if to make up for the delay—more passionate attackers of the regime than did those who had a year and a half previously set out on this road. The storm of indignation brought about the absolute unity of Communist literature. Thus was accomplished exactly what the Party had for long years tried to achieve by persuasion or by threat, what the resolutions of the Political Committee could never accomplish, and what official cultural policy could never attain. Now, in October and November of 1954, there were no essential ideological differences among the Hungarian Communist writers, with the exception of a few Muscovites and a few mediocre careerists. The two camps were reconciled, and the former opponents became loyal and affectionate brothers-in-arms.

With absolute and irrevocable finality, they turned their backs on the Stalinist system and on its father, the Georgian mail-coach robber, who, with the ingenuity of a thief turned policeman, had built up in Russia and perfected in Hungary that system of absolute enslavement called the People's Democracy.

The writers had lost all their illusions, and, if there was still hope, that hope centered around the one man who, they knew, had not been an accomplice of the murderers and who was a true champion of a new way of life. That man was Imre Nagy.

The Rebels at *Szabad Nep*

In October, Imre Nagy returned from his holiday in the Soviet Union. He was rested, in excellent health, and full of energy. Immediately, Rakosi and Gero submitted to him their economic proposals: 1.) the lowering of the living standard, 2.) the continued dismissal of public servants, 3.) a list of new taxes to be paid by the peasantry, and 4.) a system of increased norms in the factories. These economic measures, so they said, were absolutely necessary; otherwise, foreign debts could not be paid, nor the budget balanced.

Imre Nagy knew that enforcement of these measures would mean neither more nor less than a return to the old economic policies and would, as a result, annul his program and completely destroy the confidence the people had shown in him. His anger knew no bounds. And the fact that some of the measures had already been introduced without his knowledge served only to increase his fury.

The news he received from various parts of the country and from his friends and acquaintances revealed that the atmosphere was heavily charged. Everywhere, people were embittered and were openly saying that apparently Imre Nagy was not to be trusted either—that his promises were mere words, just as had been those of Rakosi.

Since he could not overcome Gero's opposition in the Political Committee, Nagy decided to deviate from the usual Party procedure and to submit the problems in question to the Central Committee. The Central Committee met in the middle of October to decide which road the Party was to follow: the so-called "June road" or the old Stalinist road. As if he knew that this meeting would be a very stormy one, Gero did not participate. Using his bad health as an excuse, he went on a vacation to the Soviet Union.

The speech delivered by Imre Nagy before the Central Committee in October, 1954, was one of Nagy's most brilliant political achievements. Tearing Gero's economic plan to pieces and showing it up for what it really was, he submitted instead a plan that seemed well suited to bring the country out of bankruptcy and put it on the road to prosperity. The living standard is too high? Some are living too well? Yes, said Imre Nagy, perhaps some are. But certainly not the Hungarian workers or peasants. Thriftiness? Yes, said Imre Nagy, that may be necessary, but it is by no means of prime importance. Much more fundamental changes were needed. It was, for instance, absolutely necessary that everything set forth in the Government program of June, 1953, be carried out consistently and unwaveringly. The trouble was not, as Gero pretended, that heavy industrial investments had been stopped and replaced by light industrial investments; the trouble was that this had not been done rapidly and energetically. The trouble was not, as Gero pretended, that the peasants had received too much support; the trouble was that they had not received enough. A very simple calculation would show how much easier it would be to repay all foreign debts by restoring the once famous but now completely ruined Hungarian wine export business—as well as the exportation of onions, of poultry, and of goose liver—instead of putting more money into the construction of the large foundry at Stalinvaros that had always operated at a complete loss.

In this speech, Imre Nagy did not mention Gero or the others by name. He simply spoke of them as "the resistants." He emphasized the necessity for the following tasks: breaking the "resistance" to the new trend, putting an end to "sectarianism" within the Party, doing away with "leftism," and setting out with new spirit on the road pointed out by the Party resolution of June, 1953, and by the Party Congress in the spring of 1954.

The Central Committee listened enthralled to the "old man." These men who, for the last ten years, had grown used to approving without argument anything that was submitted to them were carried away with enthusiasm because now, for the first time, they had a say in the country's affairs. Moreover, everything Imre Nagy had said was not only clear and convincing; it was also popular. They knew that it would be much easier to win supporters for this program than for Gero's starvation program. A Communist Party official, keeping his eye on "higher interests," is always ready to enforce even the most hateful measures; yet, when given the opportunity, he would still prefer to present more agreeable measures to the masses.

The members of the Central Committee—Istvan Kovacs, Andor Berei, Marton Horvath, and Zoltan Vas—who had all once been the faithful servants of Gero and Rakosi, rose from their seats and assured Imre Nagy of their full support. Some of them harbored certain grievances toward the bald little Party leader who had, in the past, frequently offended them despite their loyalty; some—the spineless Muscovite, Andor Berei, for example—drew their enthusiasm from the thought that Imre Nagy was, after all, Moscow's trusted man. Still, it seemed certain that the "old man" had succeeded in arousing this indifferent congregation. Only one man stood up openly and honestly for the program submitted by the runaway Gero: he was Gero's First Deputy, Istvan Friss, also a Muscovite. The members of the Political Committee (including Rakosi), who had participated in the development of the Gero program, promised Imre Nagy their complete backing in his program.

The "old man" had won. It was evident that his victory had weakened not only Gero's position but also Rakosi's: the members of the Central Committee were openly saying how pitiful

Rakosi's address to the Central Committee had been and suggesting that it was high time "collective leadership" was introduced in the Party. They were saying that the Central Committee had now proved that it was a mature and responsible group, and that from now on it would participate actively in the management of the country's affairs.

Rakosi was well aware of his defeat. Reverting to a good old Muscovite habit, he, too, declared he was ill and went to the Soviet Union for treatment.

Imre Nagy was at the head of the Government and Mihaly Farkas was at the head of the Party. There seemed to be no obstacle to an all-out drive to put the "old man's" ideas into practice.

Following the approval by the members of the Central Committee, Imre Nagy received further strong and unexpected support from the highly intelligent members of the editorial board of *Szabad Nep*. Simultaneously with the meeting of the Party's Central Committee, this staff, which consisted of the best known of Communist journalists, held a three-day conference; and this conference was equivalent to a rebellion.

The mental agonizing that had taken place among the majority of the Communist journalists was substantially the same as that of the young Communist writers. They had belonged to the same generation, for most of the *Szabad Nep* editors were between twenty-five and thirty. They had run the same course, for the journalists, too, had joined the Party in their early youth. They, too, had had the same problems: the conflicts between truth and falsehood, between the interests of the Party and those of the people, and between reality as they saw it and reality as they were ordered to see it. The writers were perhaps more sensitive, but the journalists were better informed: they had known more details of the crimes committed, and they had known every detail of the plan directed against Imre Nagy by Gero, Rakosi, and their supporters.

There was, however, an apparently technical yet essential difference that now caused the journalists to raise their problems with even greater vigor and passion. The writer, being shocked, disappointed, and depressed, could easily permit himself the luxury of retiring, for a while, to fight his inner battles and to think through and assimilate everything he had experienced; and, even more important, he could permit himself never again to write so much as a line or a word of which he did not fully approve.

The work of a journalist was, however, different: he had to write. He had to produce. And, as long as he believed what he wrote, everything would run smoothly. Most of the *Szabad Nep* journalists had always worked fourteen to sixteen hours a day. They had put their hearts and souls into the work, and some had not been on vacation for years because they were serving a cause they held sacred. They had believed the "big lies" that every Communist had to believe—the Rajk trial, the Tito case, the Stalin glorification, and the Rakosi legend—and this was natural. But they had also propagated deliberate falsehoods that they had considered necessary "in the interest of the cause." For instance, it had been a custom for years that, when the Meteorological Institute announced rainy weather for May 1 (a day of demonstration throughout the country), the weather forecast had had to be changed. The science of meteorology could be treated as a science only when its predictions pleased the Party.

Now that their eyes were opened, now that the journalists no longer believed either the large or the small lies, their work became like a battle fought anew every day, and the principal battleground was the life of the working class. *Szabad Nep* devoted a great deal of space to the problems, tasks, and achievements of industry, and to the production and cultural problems of the workers. This had been easy as long as the journalists had believed their own reports—reports of ceaseless victories, dotted here and there with a courageous criticism of some local Party secretary or of a deputy manager who had not fully recognized the importance of the advanced Soviet methods. The photographs and life histories of exemplary workers—the so-called "Stakhanovites"—had appeared day after day, seasoned with news of champion laborers who had exceeded production norms by 200 to 500 per cent, and with interviews and declarations pointing out that work in our country was no longer work but a "matter of honor and glory." And working-class mothers had written letters to the editors, saying that at last the Party had brought them and their families a security and prosperity never dreamed of in the past.

But now, just as Peter Kuczka, Imre Sarkadi, Erno Urban, and their fellow writers had discovered a year earlier in the sand of the Nyirseg and in the Transdanubian hills the real face of the Hungarian village, the editors of *Szabad Nep* discovered during these weeks the real face of the working class in the plants and factories. Now the astute reporters, sent out to write an enthusiastic report on some Stakhanovite or other, discovered by talking to the workers (who spoke more openly since the Imre Nagy program) that the entire Stakhanovite movement was pure humbug. In the overwhelming majority of cases, it was simply not true that the worker had achieved the results reported by overzealous managers; and, where it had been true, it had been made possible only because a man or a "brigade" had been assured of special labor conditions. While their fellow workers had stood idle for half-days because of raw-material shortages, or of useless tools, or of contradictory orders, these showcase workers had been given every advantage in order to increase the prestige of the factory and in order to win bonuses for the Party secretary and the manager.

Now the reporters discovered again and again that the alleged letters of gratitude had been written either at the express order of the Party secretary or else that they had been fabricated in the correspondence department of *Szabad Nep*. The working-class mothers who actually did write letters to *Szabad Nep* demonstrated to the amazed journalists more reliably than the Institute of Statistics that the price of bread, fat, flour, meat, and fruit was now higher (and the living standard lower) than in Horthy times. The reporters could not reassure themselves

by assuming that they were listening to the "class enemy," for
it was the working class itself that spoke, and they knew that
these workers had no desire to bring back the capitalist past,
with its rule of bankers and industrialists. These workers valued
the achievements in education, the summer-holiday scheme, and
the advances in public health. But they also measured the real
trends of the living standard by their purses and trouser belts.

During these weeks, another "peace loan" was floated throughout the country. One of the many ingenious devices of the
Communist state, this loan deprived the workers of one month's
salary each year. Had it been called simply a "tax," the people
would perhaps not have minded. But what they did mind was
that it was described as a "voluntary offering" of workers
enthusiastically vying with each other to give more and more
because they knew that, with their money, they were "defending the cause of peace." Now the reporters who were sent out
into the factories to report on this enthusiasm observed with
amazement the various methods used to blackmail the workers
into signing the loan: threats of dismissal or prison and relentless
torment by the Party "agitators"—all of which were met by
clenched fists and loud oaths on the part of the workers.

The reporters returned to the editorial offices and wanted to
write what they had seen. Having been raised in the schools
of the regime and educated in Party dialectic, they were much
too politically astute to describe their experiences without a suitable veneer. They were careful not to leave out the "positive
aspects" (i.e., the promising factors), in order that there would
be no distortion of proportions between good and bad. That is,
they portrayed reality in a correct and loyal Party manner.

It should be noted here that, in these anxious and excited
days, there did seem to be some relaxation of the severe control
that had nipped all initiative in the bud for years: a few articles
that were no longer far from the truth saw the light of day.
These articles—if for no other reason than because they formed

an island in the sea of unreadable, official, empty propaganda—achieved an almost unbelievable success. The whole country discussed them, and the reporters received hundreds of encouraging, congratulatory letters.

Thus, the journalists were spurred on to new efforts. They came to the conclusion that truth is the best instrument of propaganda, and that a mendacious press has neither prestige nor power of persuasion. This was the argument they advanced when their efforts began to meet more and more obstacles.

And these obstacles multiplied. *Szabad Nep* had had its own large control department, which checked every item of information contained in its articles before they went to press. If a reporter wrote that the Obuda shipyards had fulfilled their plan to 104.6 per cent, the staff of the control department would telephone the shipyard as well as the Ministry of Heavy Industry in order to check this information. If they found that the plan fulfillment was not 104.6 but 104.7 per cent, they would either make the correction or, if the paper was already being printed, stop the presses. In the case of a more serious mistake, the reporter would pay a fine, receive a Party punishment, or be dismissed. *Szabad Nep* had been the most exact, the most carefully checked, and the most detailed newspaper in the history of Hungary. Only truth had been entirely absent from it.

But now the journalist appointed by the editorial board to write an inspiring article on the Stakhanovite movement wrote, on the basis of his experiences, *not* that the entire movement was a slave-driving and disgusting swindle, but the following: "Though the life of the workers has changed and improved a great deal in the last ten years, many of them still have serious problems. Many are still living in overcrowded and shabby apartments. Many have to think twice before buying their children a new pair of shoes or going to an occasional movie!" (Though he did add that, despite these everyday worries, the workers participated with festive enthusiasm in the labor competitions organized by the Party, his attempt at "objective" reporting was in vain. The telephone on his desk began to ring the next morning, and Mihaly Farkas, entrusted with the supreme Party control of *Szabad Nep*, screamed at him with rage: "What do you mean by that article? Do you think we will tolerate this agitation?")

At this time, however, preparations had been made everywhere for council elections. One of the most gifted reporters for the paper, Tibor Tardos, had visited a working-class district, Bihari Avenue, to observe and report on the election of a candidate for council member. At the meeting, five of the electors had voted for the Party's candidate, and eleven against him. After the votes had been counted, the representative of the District Party Committee and the representative of the District Council had declared that the candidate had received a majority of votes. Tardos could scarcely believe his ears. He had no illusions about the 98.8 per cent national election results, but he was still shocked to find that even the election of candidates was an out-and-out swindle. His written report of the election concluded with these comments:

> After the meeting, I went up to the little dark-haired chairwoman and asked her why she had agreed to this transparent falsification.
> "I am sorry, Comrade," she said, "these were my instructions."
> So these were her instructions.
> "And, well . . . who gave you these instructions, Comrade Chairwoman?"
> . . . I immediately felt that the question had been entirely superfluous, and I stopped asking questions because I knew it made no difference whatsoever what organ, what committee, what person she named. Never send to know for whom the bell tolls; it tolls for thee. . . . I gave her her instructions, and you gave her her instructions. We gave her instructions. We shall never again give such instructions. The shoots of the people's will are tender, its flowers sacred. They need watering and a great, protective love. The residents of Bihari Avenue are adult,

intelligent people. We must leave the affairs of Bihari in the hands of those who live there. . . .

Marton Horvath, head of the editorial board, had not allowed the article to appear.

"This writing," he had said, "tolls the bell for the system!"

Perhaps he had not known what he was saying, though he was a very alert and clever man. But the clear implication had been that, once the workers took their fate into their own hands, the system was finished.

Now the *Szabad Nep* journalists remained unconvinced by such an argument. They still had more confidence than this in the strength of the Party and of the system. At the three-day conference of the staff members, the cub reporters and the members of the editorial board rose one after the other. Now, the things that were said had never before been said in the editorial office of a Party paper.

They said that in every area of life throughout the entire country there were to be found troubles, difficulties, faults, abscesses. They reported that big and little dictators were everywhere trampling on the will of the people. They complained of being unable to write truly about this situation because Party censorship made factual reporting impossible.

"We can no longer work in this way!" the Communist journalists shouted furiously. "We cannot face our readers squarely with further evasions of the truth."

Here was one of the mainsprings of the rebellion: the increasing pressure exerted by the ordinary Party members as well as by non-Party people—i.e., the readers.

A member of the paper's directing body, Lajos Feher—a tall, thin young man who was known to be a very close friend of Imre Nagy—spoke:

"I fully agree that we should not show only the seamy side of life. But I do not agree that this should be an excuse to keep silent about the troubles, about the most delicate, the most tormenting problems which touch the masses most deeply. . . .

We can no longer tolerate a situation in which the majority of our readers think we do not speak openly, that we gild our information, and that we don't discuss the real problem."

Then the paper's economic reporter rose and proved by serious, calm, and thorough analysis that not only was the work of certain factories, plants, and ministries bad and altogether misdirected, but that the entire structure of the Hungarian economy was rotten. The workers had not the least confidence that the factory was, as they were told, theirs. They had no right to voice an opinion as to how production should be organized (for that was done by a central—indeed, an over-centralized—bureaucracy), and, what was even more serious from an economic point of view, there was absolutely no incentive in either the production mechanism or in the wage scale, although the two essentials of development are profit and personal incentive.

This quiet, almost scientific analysis was followed by several fervent addresses. The journalists now discussed the fate of the innocently imprisoned and executed people. Who had been responsible for these crimes? Who guaranteed that such things would never happen again? Why did the Party give no satisfactory answers to these grave questions?

A tousle-headed, dark-eyed, slow-speaking young man—the head of the paper's ideological column, Pal Locsei*—delivered a moving and impassioned statement, castigating himself, as well as the Party, for the complete degeneration of Communist morality.

"The old, sectarian political morality," he said, "was based on the infallibility of certain individuals. It demanded blind faith and blind discipline. It tolerated no outspoken criticism, no determined struggle against bootlicking, flattery, and careerism. Persuasion was often replaced by violence and intolerance. And [Locsei raised his voice] this old, sectarian morality often

---

* Locsei, who was the first in Hungary to raise openly the question of Kadar's illegal imprisonment, is now serving an eight-year sentence in one of Kadar's prisons.

silenced us with the catch-phrase of 'Party discipline' when what was really called for was courage. It prevented me, for instance, from demanding that the Party should account for the fate of a talented, promising man like Comrade Janos Kadar. It prevented me and others from exercising the rights granted us by Party democracy, by Party rules, and by the Constitution to raise our voices against the various villainies which trampled on even the appearance of legality. It is obvious that not only this sectarian moral education but also my personal cowardice is to blame. We must all learn our lesson from the past. We must learn that fear is the most dangerous enemy of the search for truth and of the enforcement of justice."

At this point, Marton Horvath, who had been a member of the Political Committee when Kadar was tried, nervously interrupted Locsei.

"Did you perhaps know that Kadar was innocent?" Horvath asked.

"I did not know that he was innocent," Locsei replied. "But I did know it was intolerable that someone should be imprisoned for years without having had a trial according to the requirements of the Constitution and legality."

"In the Constitution," Horvath argued, "there is no mention of a need for public trial."

Now Peter Kende, the young and enthusiastic Party secretary of *Szabad Nep*, interrupted the argument.

"The sentence was not even made public!" Kende said.

Locsei turned to Horvath.

"So, it is your opinion that we are not responsible for these violations of legality?" Locsei asked.

Marton Horvath lowered his eyes, remained silent for a few seconds, and then, in an entirely different voice, said very quietly: "Yes. We are responsible . . ."

There was no argument that could have silenced the members of the *Szabad Nep* editorial staff. The pink-faced Lajos Szilvasi, and Endre Kovesi, and many others were simply intoxicated with the pleasure of speaking their minds at last. Burning with

idealism and conscious of their own guilt, they revealed their
innermost feelings. They told of the disgust with which they
had read the latest speech of Erno Gero—a speech in which he
had suddenly pretended to be an enthusiastic partisan of the
Imre Nagy program.* They asked why they were being encouraged to criticize boldly, uncompromisingly, and without regard
to the prominence of the one criticized, when, in reality, they
were permitted to criticize only insignificant Party officials and
never those responsible for the greatest crimes.

"What we need in this country," said one of the speakers,
"is a purifying storm which would cleanse the country from
top to bottom of all dirt, all filth, all resistance to the new
program, all that is bad. The storm not only destroys. It also
fertilizes. Let this storm destroy all that is rotten and bring new
life to all that is good. . . . And this storm must not be dissipated into random breezes."

Szabad Nep's three-day meeting represented an overwhelming
victory for Imre Nagy's program.

In the end, nobody dared to oppose the rebellious journalists,
though Marton Horvath tried to calm those passionate youths
who demanded Erno Gero's immediate dismissal, asking them
to be a little more patient. "The wheels of a cart should not
be changed en route," Horvath said.

The triumph of the partisans of the new trend was obvious,
and it was just as obvious that this rebellion went much further
than the editorial offices of *Szabad Nep*. For a few days, the
entire Party talked of nothing else. The mimeographed minutes
of the meeting were read in the Writers' Association, and the
members of the Party Academy studied this semi-legal, semi-
illegal, incendiary document.

---

* When he returned from the Soviet Union, Gero behaved as if the
program rejected by the Central Committee had not been his at all. He
delivered a speech in Szolnok, one of the large provincial towns, demanding that all those who opposed the Imre Nagy program "be swept away
with an iron hand." This hypocrisy, this shifting of responsibility, created
great indignation among the overwhelming majority of the Party membership.

The entire structure was creaking and shaking: it was obvious that, unless the flood were dammed in time, nothing could stop it.

Erno Gero's position was severely endangered. Imre Nagy had made the mistake of not taking advantage of the enthusiastic mood of the Central Committee meeting to demand Gero's immediate removal. But now it turned out that the Party membership insisted on the economic dictator's removal, though the Communist journalists did attack other members of the Political Committee as well as Gero: Andras Hegedus, the Minister of Agriculture, who was one of the propagators of collectivization by force; Bela Szalai, the Chairman of the National Planning Bureau,* who was sabotaging the conversion of heavy industry and the stepping up of light industrial production; and many others.

And the journalists attacked—not once, but many times— the man appointed by the Party to control *Szabad Nep*: Mihaly Farkas, the Secretary of the Central Committee. This vest-pocket Napoleon, protégé of Soviet Ambassador Kisselev and enthusiastic supporter of Imre Nagy, had begun to revert to the old line—that is, to side with Rakosi. His devotion to the new trend had lasted less than a year. But, that he should have broken his promise was not surprising. It was not the attacks upon Gero and his economic policies that caused Farkas' change of heart; nor was it the rebellion of the writers and journalists. These he could have tolerated. What he feared was that the next issue to be raised would be that of the violations of legality. This man, who was personally responsible for the arrests, the tortures, and the hangings, saw clearly that he would not be permitted to play the innovator within the Party much longer. So he had decided to gamble for the highest stakes: life or death.

More and more details of the murders were coming to light.

---

*After the October meeting of the Central Committee, Szalai was relieved of his post, and Andor Berei, the strongest supporter of Imre Nagy's economic plan, was appointed in his place. It was, however, characteristic of the equivocal situation that Szalai remained a member of the Political Committee, the supreme directing body of the country.

It was revealed that, together with Kadar, Farkas had persuaded Rajk to admit his uncommitted crimes. Then, on the
day of Rajk's execution, Farkas had thrown a wild party and
distributed gold watches among the AVO officers who had
"worked" with him on the case. When they were all quite
drunk, he had had Cardinal Mindszenty brought up to him
from his cell. Farkas had offered the Cardinal a glass of champagne and, when the Cardinal had refused, he had thrown the
contents of the glass in his face.

Now, in the present rebellious time, Farkas felt that the Imre
Nagy line did not offer him sufficient protection—not even if
he preached it loudly day and night. The only protection he
could hope for was the continued role of his accomplices and
superiors in crime, Rakosi and his gang. He began to speak less
and less about the dangers of "sectarianism" and "leftism," and
more and more about the dangers of "rightist deviationism."
He no longer encouraged the writers—as he had done a year
earlier—to reveal the truth with courage; on the contrary, he
constantly warned them of radicalism and of petty-bourgeois
panic.* When the journalists demanded their right to criticize,
he thundered: "We are not a debating Party. We are not Social
Democrats. Here, the Party leadership decides what should be
done!"

Scarcely three weeks after the October meeting of the Central
Committee and the overwhelming victory won by Imre Nagy,
it looked as though the Communist Party were divided into two
equally strong, equally determined camps.

One of these camps was headed by Imre Nagy. The constitu-
ent Congress of the Patriotic Popular Front, which was to be
completely reorganized, was held at the Municipal Theater of
Budapest at the end of October. Imre Nagy had far-reaching
plans for this mass organization, which had hitherto been com-

---

* Farkas ordered the seizure of an issue of *Uj Hang,* the literary
periodical of the Hungarian youth movement, because it contained a
highly "subversive" poem by the very gifted young poet Gyula Sipos.

pletely impotent. He believed that, through it, he would be able to draw into active support of his political line all those who had been outside the Party's sphere or had been repelled rather than attracted by it—all the honest and democratic forces that had been silenced, put aside, or driven into passivity by the violent and dictatorial line introduced in 1948.

This Congress of the Patriotic Popular Front was like a triumphal march. Though there were still signs of over-organization and of artificiality, many of the speakers were outspoken as they had never before been, and it was quite evident that, with his successful struggle in the Central Committee, Imre Nagy had again consolidated the country's confidence behind his own person and his political line. His address to the Congress, with its human warmth and its beautiful language, was an unprecedented success. After giving a detailed account of his program, he asked: "Does this Congress grant me its confidence for the carrying out of this program?" The answer was evident. The entire audience rose from its seats and shouted: "We do!"

Perhaps there was something theatrical in this scene. But it was, at least, theatrical according to the best Hungarian traditions. The behavior of those participating in the Congress recalled to mind the glorious Hungarian fight for freedom of 1848-1849, when Lajos Kossuth had asked the National Assembly the same question and had received the same answer. Everyone felt that Imre Nagy's political line—though it was still led by the Communist Party—was more sincere and more *national* than the one hitherto followed. It was at this time that Nagy was at the very peak of his first Prime Ministership.

Mihaly Farkas sat at Imre Nagy's side at the Congress, and he, too, enthusiastically gave him his support. Even Matyas Rakosi sent the Congress a telegram of good wishes from the Soviet Union in which he called the Congress the "most important event" of the last ten years. Yet, even then, these treacherous political adventurers were busy preparing the rope with which to hang Imre Nagy, for, in the shadow of the October resolution, the camp opposing Nagy was diligently working to undermine the Prime Minister.

Taking advantage of Imre Nagy's trusting nature and, to a certain extent, of his weakness, this opposing camp prevented Nagy from carrying out important personnel changes in the leadership. Thus, the supporters of the Rakosi line sat everywhere, firmly in their places. Party officials were given orders to collect the documents of "reactionary" and "rightist" manifestations. True, in that atmosphere of greater freedom, there were indeed such manifestations, but even if they had not existed, the imagination of the Party officials would have ascribed every mild sigh or wistful look to proof of such manifestations.

It was the editorial staff of *Szabad Nep* which, however, stood in the center of the attack. It was the mimeographed minutes of these journalists which were supplied to the Party officials and which circulated "undeniable evidence" on the basis of which the journalists could be accused of "irresponsible demagogy," of "undermining the authority of the leadership," of "lack of confidence in the Party," and of many other terrible crimes against Party unity, discipline, and obligatory devotion.

The "counter-attack" by the opposing camp was launched with an article, published in *Szabad Nep*, entitled "Those Who Bid Higher"—an article written, under the supervision of Mihaly Farkas, by Jozsef Darvas, Minister of Culture. Six months previously, Darvas had been one of Imre Nagy's most fervent supporters, as well as the author, together with Marton Horvath, of the famous memorandum on the aims of Hungarian literature. Now, however, together with Horvath, Darvas had followed Farkas back into Rakosi's fold—for, though both Darvas and Horvath hated Rakosi and Farkas, their fear of the latter two men was stronger than their hatred, and, although their hands were not as bloody as were Rakosi's or Farkas', they trembled lest the purifying storm might sweep them, too, from their luxurious villas and their automobiles and their velvet chairs. The article entitled "Those Who Bid Higher" set forth

Darvas' conception of the writers and the journalists who, not being content with the Party's self-criticism, wanted to go even further. In his own particularly unctuous style, Darvas explained that the principal task was to work against these high bidders, for, so he said, they prevented the introduction of proper criticism and self-criticism.

It was clear that the publication of the article would nip in the bud all more liberal trends throughout the country. In the first place, the article would put an end to the hopes which Imre Nagy had entertained for the reborn Patriotic Popular Front. Thus, the Nagy disciples on the editorial board protested against the publication of the article, and, when it came to the vote, the editorial board voted four to two to reject the Darvas article.*

Yet, the article still appeared, for Mihaly Farkas and Marton Horvath decided that the editorial board was merely an "advisory body" and that the last word belonged to the Political Committee and to its appointed secretary, Mihaly Farkas. The reason: the vote, following upon the three-day meeting, had shown beyond a doubt that the partisans of Imre Nagy were in a majority in the paper's leadership, and this fact had induced Farkas and the other Rakosi followers to "arrange" the affairs of this important Party organ.

After many an ignored instruction and threat, the entire editorial board of *Szabad Nep* was called before the "council of gods." Since Rakosi was absent, Farkas was the chairman.† The four members of the editorial board who had voted against the publication of the Darvas article were called upon to employ self-criticism and to revoke their statements. All four refused.

---

* Those who voted against publication were: Lajos Feher, Sandor Fekete, Sandor Novobaczky, and Tibor Meray. Those in favor were Marton Horvath and a Muscovite journalist named Imre Komor.

† Unfortunately, Imre Nagy was also absent from the meeting. He had excused himself, saying that he had an important address to prepare. In reality, however, he did not participate because, in order to maintain the appearance of Party unity, he could not have openly defended his followers; and yet he did not want to repudiate them.

Thus, the "council of gods" faced a new experience: four young Communist journalists were refusing to obey the Party's highest body! After several hours of argument, during which all four men stuck to their guns, the Political Committee was "generous enough" to allow the four black sheep two or three weeks' time to change their minds.

But a second meeting was never convened, for, a few days after the first, Matyas Rakosi returned from the Soviet Union.

The telephone began to ring on the desks of the district and the county Party secretaries, the members of the Central Committee, the ministers and the generals. A well-known voice inquired about their state of health. Then, without waiting for a reply, the voice declared that, contrary to the October resolution of the Party, not "leftism" but "rightism" was the principal danger. The voice said that harmful and intolerable nationalist, reactionary, petty-bourgeois manifestations had taken place in the country in the last few weeks—and that these had taken place not only within the country, but even within the Party itself.

Said the voice: "The time has come to put a stop to such things."

The same voice informed the editors of the various papers and the leading Communist writers that, since a new day was dawning, the time had come for them to return to their senses. If someone tried to protest, if someone referred to a Party resolution which was still valid and which pointed to sectarianism and leftism as the greatest dangers, the calm voice called the "comrade's" attention to dialectics and to Stalin's famous theory —a theory according to which the main danger is that danger which is not being attacked.

The writers and journalists had every reason to ponder dialectics—and even more to ponder what would happen next. It seemed certain that Rakosi had achieved something in Moscow. It seemed certain that he had used his holidays in the Soviet Union not so much to improve his health as to improve his position. If this were not so, he would hardly now dare to act with such self-assurance.

At this time, nobody knew what had really happened in Moscow, for the struggle between Malenkov and Khrushchev was still unknown in Hungary. What the leading Communist writers and journalists knew was that Imre Nagy was fighting a desperate battle with the Political Committee—entirely alone— and that all the others were on Rakosi's side. The writers also knew—for the Party had made no secret of it—that Farkas had ordered the editorial staff of *Szabad Nep* to appear at his office at ten o'clock on the morning of December 16.

On the occasion of this meeting, on December 16, 1954, the rubber-faced general announced that, as a result of the events that had taken place at *Szabad Nep*, the Political Committee had decided to transfer Peter Kende, Endre Kovesi, and Lajos Szilvasi to provincial newspapers, to dismiss Tibor Meray and to send him abroad, and to give a Party punishment to Marton Horvath because he had not sufficiently opposed the rebellion.*

The punishments were not very severe, particularly if compared to the punishments meted out in the Stalinist era, for Imre Nagy was still Prime Minister and the Number Two man in the Political Committee. Yet, it required no great political ingenuity to discover that the rebellion at *Szabad Nep* had been defeated, that the counter-attack of the Rakosi gang was in full swing, and that Imre Nagy apparently lacked the force to protect his own people.

The struggle was not quite over, of course, for the "old man" still walked the corridors of Parliament, calm and collected, and he smiled his friendly smile at receptions, and there was still a hope that his retreat was merely temporary. Yet, the

---

* At the same time, in order to strengthen the "proletarian spine" of the paper, the general appointed Tivadar Matusek and Janos Kukucska (two men who, though they had never worked in journalism, were honest and reliable comrades) to the editorial board. These two names, which have an amusing ring in Hungarian, later became veritable symbols in Hungarian literary life of ignorant illiteracy and of very loyal officialdom, and of "appointed" writers and journalists.

partisans of Imre Nagy, the writers and the journalists, had heard the bell toll, and they no longer asked for whom it tolled. They were, in fact, very, very anxious lest it tolled for them.

The Reception at the Golden Bull

On the rainy winter morning of December 21, 1954, four special trains carried a festive group to Debrecen, the hometown of Hungarian enlightenment, of Calvinist rationalism, and of stubborn Kumanians, to pay respectful homage on the tenth anniversary of the formation of the Provisional Government to the people's power, to the new Hungarian freedom, to the building of socialism, and to the fortress of peace and happiness— in short, to the Hungarian People's Democracy. The members of the festive group numbered those privileged few whom the protocol department of Party headquarters had weighed and had not found wanting.

The town of Debrecen, built in the blowsand of the lowlands on the outskirts of the Hortobagy, had for centuries kept noble national traditions alive throughout hot, dusty summers and freezing, windy winters. The town itself was not much more than a large village, lying at a distance of 230 kilometers in a northeasterly direction from the capital city, with low peasant houses and broad and dusty acacia-bordered streets and a square that had two characteristic features: a hotel and a church. The giant hotel, which was named the Golden Bull, had been built in the cheap secessionist style of the nineteenth century, with cold corridors, pseudo-baroque woodcarvings and badly furnished rooms. Years ago, in the ugly, barnlike dining rooms, the rich landowners of the lowlands had drunk until daylight to the accompaniment of gypsies playing melancholy Hungarian melodies.

The church of Debrecen was one of the most beautiful examples of classic Hungarian architecture, and behind it stood the centuries-old college which had raised many a famous poet and which had always been the center of the town's most progressive traditions—traditions embodying reformation and enlightenment that had had a lasting influence on the development of the nation. In this church, Lajos Kossuth, legendary leader of the 1848-1849 Revolution, had declared Hungary's independence from Austria. And it was here that the first Hungarian Republic had been proclaimed.

The town had also seen the formation of the Provisional Hungarian Government in 1944; and the Provisional National Assembly had held its first session in the church.

Now, ten years later, the whole town was bedecked in flags to welcome the festive group which was arriving. Diligent hands had swept all the streets clean. The Golden Bull had been completely redecorated in preparation for the great day, and, when the guests walked through the hotel's open gate in the early afternoon hours, the smell of whitewash filled the air.

The festivities of the next morning were routine and monotonous. These included the placing of wreaths at the heroes' monument and at the Soviet monument. But the afternoon promised some excitement in the grey and insignificant succession of festivities, for two speeches were to be delivered in the church that afternoon. One of these speeches was to be delivered by the people's wise father and beloved leader, Matyas Rakosi, who was Secretary of the Party. The other was to be delivered by Imre Nagy, Chairman of the Council of Ministers.

Never had that church seen such a crowd, for it had become generally known that the conflict between Rakosi and Nagy was reaching its peak. Everybody in this cool, fragrant church knew that, in October, Imre Nagy had been stronger. They also knew that, in recent weeks, a certain change had taken place, and that the partisans of the bald Party leader—who were in the majority here in this church and who had, for months, followed events with growing anxiety—hoped that Rakosi would show his claws and hit back at the "rightist deviationists" lined up behind Nagy, taking the reins into his own hand and making some sign to them which would indicate that the time had come to counter-attack.

Never had the walls of this old church experienced such a storm of applause as that which exploded when the neckless little dictator mounted the platform with a sheaf of papers in his pudgy hand. Suddenly the church was no longer a church. It was, instead, an arena. The duel had begun.

Who would come out victorious?

Rakosi began. He was self-assured, loud, and superior. His words were clear and to the point: he spoke about the problems of building up socialism and he spoke about the outstanding achievements of the past ten years, stressing the importance of a strengthened army and of a strengthened state security organization.

The audience was well-versed in reading between the lines. They knew that if past mistakes were not even mentioned, if unmistakable threats were voiced, and if the strength of the Party were emphasized, this meant that Rakosi had the upper hand.

Thus, the faithful cheered the leader ecstatically. But, in the background, the writers and journalists listened to the speech with clenched teeth and with faces crimson with fury.

A year and a half previously, perhaps they, too, would have applauded furiously. But now they clapped their hands only for form's sake. Now they hated intensely this old murderer, this henchman of the innocent, this torturer of their friends who stood there on the platform.

Yet, except for their formal applause, they kept silent.

They were waiting for Imre Nagy. They were waiting—though, indeed, after Rakosi's speech, there was not much hope left to them—for the Prime Minister to hit back at Rakosi with courage and determination. They were waiting for Nagy to dispel, at last, that growing tension of the past few months which they, the writers, felt more acutely than did anyone else.

They knew that Rakosi's return to absolute power would smother the budding popular movement, that it would kill the healthy young shoots of a reviving literature, and that it would bring the accelerating pulse of the entire country to a standstill. They knew that, instead of bringing an era of atonement for past crimes, Rakosi's return to power would introduce a new era of crime. They knew that the country would, under these circumstances, continue to slide down the slope on which its fast descent had been halted temporarily.

They waited.

And they were disappointed.

Imre Nagy's speech was weak and faltering. It was seasoned with historical phrases. But it lacked stability, and it lacked the straightforwardness which was needed in the new situation. One could not have deduced from one word of Nagy's speech that the Prime Minister had noticed the conspiracy against him—even though his calm tone, his appearance, his voice, and his beautiful delivery harmonized so completely with the atmosphere of the lovely old Hungarian church and made so striking a contrast with the Party jargon of the dumpy little man who had spoken before him that his friends almost forgave him the lack of content and energy—and the shadow of defeat looming ahead of him.

There was also something else that the writers could not ignore, though they would have liked nothing better than to do so. They knew the mechanism of Party leadership far too well to believe that the duel could be decided here in the church of Debrecen. Clearly, it had already been decided elsewhere—in the meetings of the Political Committee, or, rather, in Moscow.

How silly it was of them, then, to hope for the miracle of his taking a determined stand here in front of a large audience! It was not that the "old man" didn't know what was happening behind the scenes in the conspiracy against him and his political line. It was, instead, that the speech he was making here was far removed from his personal opinions. It was a speech prepared in advance and censored by the Political Committee. The only thing he could do—and that, too, was a form of resistance—was to make his speech finer and nobler than Rakosi's speech.

The writers knew all this. And, yet, they were filled with bitterness, not only because the political situation was deteriorating but also because they had hoped against hope to witness the miracle of an open break with the Rakosi gang.

To drown their bitterness, their hatred, and their disappointment the writers returned to the wine tables of the Golden Bull. Here, the long white tables in all the dining rooms were laden with excellent foods and with the noblest and the best of Hungarian wines which, since they were intended for export only, were never seen in Hungary by the ordinary mortal. Here, a gypsy band played in the corner, and the warm air was saturated with the fragrant smoke of good cigarettes.

The writers sat down around one of the tables and watched the happy revelry. It was with deep disgust that they heard the loud laughter and the intimate whispers of these revelers.

It was the new elite of a new society which was assembled here amid the warmth and the smoke and the heavy smell of food and wine. These were the top men who held the fate of the nation in their hands. These were the privileged, who were *more* equal than the equal. They were the destined representatives of the people—representatives who had no other task than to keep a vigilant eye on the people's wealth and to create with their work and their devotion and their selfless revolutionary militancy the rich and happy socialist future of the country. This was a severe and demanding task. But it had to be shouldered in the interest of the community and of the Revolution and of world freedom.

Well, they were shouldering the task, for here sat the captains, the colonels, and the generals of the People's Army, all of them gathered around the tables in new and uncreased uniforms which were, both in color and cut, identical with the uniforms of their great mentor, the Soviet Union. Here sat the members of Parliament in black or in navy-blue double-breasted suits (suits which were now, too, almost a uniform) and in white shirts and silver ties, a glass of wine in their hands and a gay twinkle in their eyes. Here were the ministers, the Party secretaries of large industrial plants, the town and county council chairmen, the high-ranking economic experts and political commissars, the directors of the Party schools, the "professional revolutionaries" of the Party apparatus, the department heads, the instructors and advisers, and, last, but not least, the members of the Political Committee and of the Central Committee.

For these men, this atmosphere—the food, the wines, the cigars, the smells—was nothing new, nothing unusual. In the past ten years, they had participated in innumerable similar receptions and had never grown tired of them, always experiencing a thrill at the constant reminder of the wonderful and exalted status they enjoyed in the life of the country. It is easy to get used to the good things in life, and these men had also found it easy not to grow blasé about these good things. Most of them had spent their childhood in dark and damp proletarian homes, under the grey sky of constant financial worries, on the outskirts of large towns or in the poorer quarters of villages. Their parents had been broken by hard work, and they themselves had grown up in the streets or on the dusty mudtracks of the villages, lonely and neglected. They themselves had been made to work while still children, for the families were large, and there was never enough to eat. And, thus, they had become adults before they had ever been really young. The majority of the generals and ministers, the deputies and the Party officials, and the members of the various Party committees were indeed of peasant or working-class origin, raised by the new regime from squalor. This new regime had given them respect and position. It had given them villas, automobiles, and, what was even more important, power. They had never forgot whence they came, and they were proud of their origins. If, formerly, it had been an insult to call someone a peasant, it was today a compliment. In place of the nine-branched crown, the heraldists engraved the names of working-class districts on the escutcheons of the new nobility.

True, they had left those districts long ago, and they were living far from squalor. Today, when they visited the factories or fields as respected guests, exchanging a few condescending words with former schoolmates who still led *their* former life, these former schoolmates felt a little jealous of these possessors of unlimited privileges, the leaders of the country.

For, the new nobility occupied a position of envy and respect. And they enjoyed that position. They felt like living models who symbolized the infinite democracy of the new system. In their country, as in Napoleon's army, every peasant and working-class kid carried a marshal's staff in his pocket! They became accustomed to brilliance. The rarefied air of the peaks was now the very stuff of their lives.

Naturally, not everybody in the dining room was of peasant or working-class origin. At least half of the glorious assemblage could not boast of being sons of the "people." These were the sons of petty-bourgeois parents or, at best, of intellectual parents, and, because of their unforgivable backgrounds, their whole lives were rendered miserable, or, at least, uncertain. Though their rights and their duties were identical with those of the fortunate ones who had been born, by chance, in proletarian homes, they could not conceal from themselves the fact that the system did divide the others from them. A father who was a shopkeeper or a clerk, or, worst of all, a lawyer (the lawyer was the characteristic servant of the bourgeoisie) became a very uncomfortable burden to his son who, fearing that one could conceal nothing from the thousand-eyed Party, preferred to forget him altogether. No, it was not advisable to conceal anything from the Party. They knew the fate of those who, in a moment of weakness, had falsified their backgrounds and had declared that their fathers, who had in reality been artisans working with four assistants, were simple workers. To lie to the Party was an unforgivable sin. It was a blunder which revealed one's lowest character; and so, willy-nilly, they admitted the truth and faced the consequences. Their loyalty to the Party, their disciplined proletarian attitude should be enough to make them—despite this blot on their official record —equivalent in the Party's eyes to those of the real aristocracy, the workers and peasants.

Thus, they made every effort to live and talk and behave in such a way that the superficial observer—who had no access to the official files—would never suspect the smallest blot. They spoke the idiom of a certain region better than did the comrades living there. They sprinkled their speech with typical working-class expressions. They never wore a hat, but always a cap; and sometimes they said, as if it were the most natural thing in the world: "At my plant, it was usual in those days . . ." All this was calculated to make their listeners believe that they were authentic, one hundred per cent workers.

Slowly, then, the differences disappeared and the similarities prevailed. For, in a strange way, all these people began to resemble one another. They resembled each other in their behavior and in their manner of speaking (a manner learned at the Party schools) ; and even their expressions, their articulation, and their phrasing became stereotyped. "Let me tell you frankly," they always began, whether they were proletarians or petty bourgeois. "We workers expect our writer comrades to portray our life, our problems." They always spoke in the first-person plural: it was "*our* life," "*our* literature," "*our* opinion," because that is what they had learned from their idol, Matyas Rakosi, and because it emphasized their identity with the community and the Party. As a matter of fact, they rarely had an opinion of their own. They said only what they had heard or learned, though they said it as if the idea had just been born in the complicated convolutions of their brain. "What is the situation?" they asked expertly, because this was how Comrade Stalin was wont to put his questions. Or they said: "The imperialists allege that our system is not the system of workers, peasants, and intellectuals. Is that true, comrades? No. It is not true." They loved this turn of phrase. It suited their temperament and their limited ability to think. "True, a plain working man like myself knows little about litera- ture . . . ," they liked to begin, first because this stressed their being working men, and, second, because it stressed their being ordinary. They said this a little ironically and boastingly, because they knew only too well they were not ordinary at all. On the contrary, they alone were, due to their origin and position, quali- fied to judge the order and the development of all things. Yet, good manners and the unwritten social code prescribed that they should talk in this way, especially since the second part of the sentence continued: ". . . yet, I must tell you frankly that what our writer comrades produce nowadays may be described as any- thing but socialist realism. The comrades are forgetting the Party . . . the Party!" This formula made it entirely clear that the ordinary worker knew much more about literature than did the erudite author—that he knew much better what the writer might be able to express more beautifully, and that the writer's heart was still tormented with petty-bourgeois ideas and that he was still not sufficiently at one with the Party. "And is that as it should be, comrades?" he would continue. "No, it isn't. . . ."

This attitude was common to workers and petty bourgeois alike. Gradually, they forgot the trade they had learned. They forgot their childhood and their youth and the hard work in the factories or the fields. They were filled with the same new dreams, the same new fears. They had all grown used to pros- perity and, at the bottom of their hearts, they were constantly afraid that, should they make a mistake in word or deed, they would be driven back to lathe or plow to toil with those who, today, existed for them only in a hazy distance. And, although they repeated frequently and easily their banalities ("We have it easy," they said. "We can always return to the shop and make a decent living like thousands of others!"), they feared nothing more than to live again as one of the toiling thousands.

It would indeed have been strange to return from this way of life to that other. In the morning, an automobile took them to their offices. It was a comfortable, curtained automobile. The driver—though they called him "comrade" and, on trips to the country, invited him to their table—opened the car door wide. They climbed in with *Szabad Nep* in their hands in order to read the editorial of the day, before they got to their office. It was obligatory for them to know what the official paper said. Besides, one could never know beforehand whether there was not something interesting in it—some attack against their person, against their place of work, against their Party organization, or, perhaps, even some praise. "Well, what's new, Comrade Kis?" they asked the driver, not because they expected an answer but rather out of habit or a sense of obligation, because they knew that they were expected to treat the driver as a human being and because he was in the same Party and had the same rights as they themselves had at Party meetings.

Then they burrowed into the paper.

The automobile glided away from the modest four- or five-room villa requisitioned—or rather allotted to them—by that department at Party headquarters which dealt with the housing difficulties of the leading Party officials. The villa had formerly belonged to a deported or absconded "alien-class" bourgeois "element" and was usually richly and tastefully furnished. The villa gave them little cause to worry. They paid no rent, or practically no rent. The Party wanted its best officials to enjoy their very limited leisure after a hard day's work in beautiful and ideal surroundings. Their wives usually worked in the Party machinery or some mass organization, too, and these wives were loyal partners of their husbands and devoted servants of the Party, and thus the wives had no time to look after their homes or to worry much about their children. They hired domestic servants whose life histories were carefully and thoroughly studied by the State Security Organization so as to make sure that no unsuitable person or foreign agent should penetrate into that repository of important secrets, the house of the master.

The young peasant girl who had been approved by the AVO soon learned her way around the house. In the morning, when the comrade and his wife departed to their offices, she waited for the car to return for the children. The older children were taken to that exclusive school organized for the sons and daughters of Party officials, the Gorki School, where the teachers were all Soviet citizens and where the children learned Russian before they learned Hungarian and knew more about Russian history than about Hungarian history. Their fathers and mothers were inordinately proud of this fact, and, when Soviet guests arrived, the children were brought from the nursery to converse with such exalted guests. It was practically impossible for anyone, except the children of the highest officials, to attend the Gorki School. And, of course, it seemed natural to the children to vie with each other, not in their lessons but in the size of their parents' car.

When the older children had left in the car, the young servant took the small child to the corner of Pasaret Avenue and Aron Gabor Allee where, at exactly 8:45 a.m., the special autobus, which took them to the Rakosi Nursery, stopped. When the bus with the twittering children departed, the young servant climbed into her master's car, for it had in the meantime returned for her. Then she took her place beside the driver and drove to the food warehouse on Fo Street. While housewives all over town queued up for hours for a little meat or butter (and often went home without getting any), everything was available in this warehouse at 30 or 40 per cent below the market prices. Here, there were oranges and dates and bananas—goods that the town had not seen in decades.

The servant finished her shopping and climbed back into the car that took her back to the villa. After flirting for a minute with the state security guard standing at the gate, she continued with her daily routine. She had no reason to be jealous. The guard was there permanently. The Party kept solicitous watch over its loyal officials. For the officials themselves, the trouble was only that very frequently they could not be quite sure whether the guard was there to protect them or to spy on them.

Whenever a higher Party official left his house, he was followed by a morose state security officer who had no other task than to watch over the physical and spiritual safety of his ward and to submit a daily report to his superiors concerning the activities of the official.* They were like spiders caught in their own nets. They could never talk to their friends in private, and they could never go for a walk unguarded. Even the driver who drove them to the office and home again was an AVO employee, and they had to account to the Party for every second of their lives.†

Naturally, the Party was very anxious that its leading officials should spend their summer holidays quietly and very comfortably. The country's most beautiful holiday resort was simply expropriated for the high-ranking Party and state officials so that they and their families might spend the summer entirely free of charge. During the summer season, the beautiful highway leading to Lake Balaton, the "Hungarian sea," was always crowded with automobiles bearing official license plates and carrying these important people back and forth.

As in every other field, "socialist hierarchy" manifested itself here, too. The Party was strongly opposed to "equalitarianism" —a petty-bourgeois remnant. Only inveterate bourgeois dreamers imagined that Mihaly Farkas, let us say, bathed in the same waters of the Balaton that washed over the bodies of simple county council chairmen, not to speak of the ordinary mortals. For, the feared and honored "foursome" who controlled the country's fate—Rakosi, Gero, Revai, Farkas—stood at the top of the privilege list. Their four villas, built in the most beautiful part of the capital, the slope of Szabadsaghegy (i.e., "Freedom

---

* Even in their private lives, the leading officials could never rid themselves of their watchdogs. Istvan Kristof, secretary of the Presidium, liked to swim. The guests at the swimming pool were greatly amused to observe that, while the boss had his daily swim, his watchdog, naturally fully dressed, walked backwards and forwards along the edge of the pool to keep pace with the swimmer.

† Janos Csergo, who was then, as now, Minister of Smelting and Machine Industry and who was a nice, jovial, very fat, and stupid young man and one of Rakosi's pets, often complained to me that he could never go anywhere alone and that he was constantly watched and controlled. One evening, my friend Miklos Vasarhelyi and I practically "kidnapped" him from the ministry, evading the AVO driver and taking Csergo on a binge to give him a few hours of freedom.—T.A.

Hill"), and with a view of the city down below, cost more than twenty-six million *forints* ($650,000).*

Then came the members of the Political Committee.

Then came the members of the Central Committee.

Then the Ministers.

And the Deputy Ministers.

And so on, down the list.

It was quite obvious that the members of the Political Committee enjoyed greater privileges than did the members of the Central Committee. Thus, they obtained their daily supplies in the secret larders of other warehouses, and paid nothing for them. In 1950, at Gero's initiative, the so-called "open current account" for Political Committee members was introduced. As a result, these leading statesmen could withdraw from the accounts deposited in their names whatever they wanted whenever they wanted it—and without having to account for any of it to the Party. A member of the Political Committee paid no rent. His clothes were paid for by the Party. His coal was ordered and delivered to his villa by the Party. His domestic servant, his gardener, and his drivers (each had two, working alternate shifts) were paid by the Party. So were all the expenses of his family. It was not a socialist system in which they lived. It was, instead, an already perfected commune, where, as Marx, Engels, Lenin, and Stalin teach us, money loses its purpose and everybody shares in the available goods according to his needs and desires.

It was only natural that they should have a special holiday resort of their own where they were not compelled to mix with those beneath them in the social and the Party hierarchy. Their holiday resort at Balatonaliga was surrounded by barbed wire,

---

* This amazing figure was dug out of the files during Imre Nagy's first premiership by the then Chairman of the Central Control Commission (today one of the Party secretaries and Minister of State) Karoly Kiss, in order that he might submit it, as proof of his own moral indignation, to the Central Committee. This was how Kiss, who hated and feared Rakosi, tried to take revenge but almost burned his fingers. Imre Nagy saved him from jail. Later, to prove his loyalty to the Party, Kiss expelled Imre Nagy from the Party.

and it was "protected" by armed state security guards. Those who
came too near the barbed wire fence were stopped. Their identity
papers were checked, and, in some cases, they were taken away
for questioning.

The place itself was not extraordinary. It was not much better
than the holiday home of a Western millionaire. At the resort
stood a number of comfortable villas which had, naturally, been
built at state expense; and in these lived the members of the
Political Committee. Each villa had its own servants to do the
cleaning and to serve the food. The servants were, of course,
addressed as "comrade." The specially-built beach was provided
with a jetty for small yachts, sailing boats, and row boats. A
reinforced barbed wire fence ran along the entire length of the
beach and deep into the water around it; and vigilant state
security guards watched constantly for suspicious phenomena.

The members of the Central Committee frequented Bala-
tonoszod.

The workers of the Party apparatus frequented Balatonlelle.

There were also Party rest homes in the mountains, on the
Dobogoko, in the Matra mountains, and at Parad.

The high-ranking Party and state officials had also, naturally,
other means of amusement at their disposal. One of the most
popular of these was hunting. This eminently aristocratic pastime
was, in aristocratic Hungary, outside the sphere of poor people.
In the People's Democracy, this was, naturally, changed. Ministers and generals, sons of the working class and the peasantry,
hunted in the forbidden hunting grounds where, apart from the
august few, only the beaters were allowed inside the grounds—
very often the same beaters who had in the past assisted the
counts and barons, since the socialist system greatly valued the
experts.

It was only fair that these hard-working, very busy people
should have their leisure made as relaxed and as comfortable as
possible. Who would have grumbled? Only their wives sometimes
grew discontented and complained to their husbands that the
inhabitant of the neighboring villa had a brand new Mercedes,

while they were still using that shabby little Pobeda. At such times, the husbands did their best to calm down their spouses— spouses who had been raised, as had they themselves, in the streets of working-class districts. But sooner or later they, too, became infected with their women's impatience and would not rest until they, too, had their brand new Mercedes.*

There were many such family quarrels. It was rumored, for instance, that the wife of Imre Dogei,† a Transdanubian peasant woman, nagged her husband unceasingly because there was no aquarium filled with sea water in their villa, although Sandor Czottner,‡ a former miner, had one. (These quarrels were, however, child's play compared to the rumpus raised by Comrade Mihaly Farkas, Commander of the Hungarian Army, when, in looking over his new villa, he had noticed that the swimming pool in its garden could not be *illuminated from below*. He had refused to move in until this severe omission was corrected.)

There was a special section of seats at the People's Stadium which was used exclusively by members of the Political Committee, of the Central Committee, and of the Council of Ministers. From these seats, these officials could, whenever they were in the

---

* The Party's hierarchy was evident in the official cars. The district secretaries and the department heads at the ministries had Skodas, small Czech cars which used very little gasoline. The county secretaries, the municipal secretaries, and the deputy ministers drove in strong but clumsy Soviet Pobeda (meaning "Victory") cars. (Later this stratum in the hierarchy received Mercedes 180's.) The ministers had Soviet-manufactured ZIS's (meaning *Zavoda Imjni Stalina*, the automobile factory named after Stalin) but these used up so much gasoline (30 liters per 100 kilometers) that they were later exchanged for the somewhat smaller ZIM (for *Zavoda Imjni Molotova*, the automobile factory named after Molotov). The members of the Political Committee, however, used American Chevrolets with built-in radios and air conditioners, and strongly armored. The same protocol was observed as far as license plates were concerned. Usually the Hungarian license plates consisted of two letters and three figures (for instance, CA-900), but the ministers and Party heads travelled in cars bearing one-letter-one-figure numberplates (for instance, A-5). The police had orders never to stop these cars, even when their drivers had committed some traffic offense.

† Imre Dogei is Minister of Agriculture in the Kadar Government.

‡ Sandor Czottner is Minister of Mines and Power in the Kadar Government.

mood, watch sports events of international significance, and it was a section which, contrary to all others, was covered to protect its august audience from rain or sunshine. Its entrance could be reached only by car, which stopped not in front of it, but underneath it. Unsparing of time and money, the architects had designed a special auto tunnel under this section of seats so that two cars could advance side by side. To make certain that the poisonous gases escaping from the motor caused no harm to the precious comrades, a suction and ventilation mechanism was built into the tunnel at a cost of three million *forints*. (At that time, the average earnings of a Hungarian worker amounted to 1,000 *forints* a month.) And the directors of the People's Stadium offered sandwiches and drinks to the exalted guests in two large, specially installed reception rooms furnished with comfortable armchairs and delicate little coffee tables.

All this goes to show how tenderly and solicitously the People's Democracy watched over the comfort of its beloved leaders. These leaders grew fat and pink. The deep lines which had been furrowed into their faces by the struggles of their early years now filled in and disappeared. They were no longer the same men. Having left their old working-class environs behind, they had also left behind their old friends and acquaintances. They shaved every morning and put on fresh shirts every day (shirts of the finest silk poplin because nylon was regarded as an imperialist extravagance). They forgot that one could get from one place to another in any other way than by automobile,* or that one

---

* To mention but one example: Imre Komor, an old Muscovite journalist and one of the editors of *Szabad Nep,* decided one day that he would show a group of "renegade" writers how to write a short story on the beautiful and happy life of the working classes in order to stop them from continually writing complaints about mistakes and shortcomings.

He called in his secretary and began to dictate: "Peter Szabo, a worker of the Hungarian Screw Factory, left his factory at six in the afternoon. Before leaving for home, he looked back once more at the large building. His heart swelled with happiness and pride, for this factory belonged to him—to him and his fellow workers—and the work accomplished that day benefited not the capitalist but him and the others. . . . Smiling to himself, he walked down to the bus station. . . ."

Komor stopped, thought for a moment, then turned to his secretary.

could spend his holidays anywhere except in a private villa at Oszod.

In this way, the courageous and ambitious revolutionaries of the past turned into wise, well balanced, precocious, and circumspect petty bourgeois, more petty than even the pettiest. They had no passions because they were dried up inwardly. They had no feelings because they despised such things—particularly love, which they considered an anti-Party sentiment. If it occurred that one or another of their married collaborators had the misfortune to fall in love, they called him into their beautifully furnished offices and there, calmly and kindly, annihilated him. They explained to him that what he was doing was immoral and petty-bourgeois, and that it was utterly unworthy of a revolutionary, whose first duty was to his Party, whose second duty was to the people, and whose third duty was to his family. What would the Party or the people say if he abandoned his family? "Think it over, Comrade," they would explain. "We don't want to interfere in your private life, but a good Communist has no private life. So, perhaps, you should give it some thought. . . ."

And the comrade usually did give it some thought.

If—although he was just as much in love as before—he returned to his family, the incident was forgotten. Or, if it was not forgotten, it was at least shelved. But if he persisted in his love affair, he had to face such consequences as humiliation at Party meetings, or, frequently, expulsion from the Party, or loss of his job. Even if he were lucky enough to escape all this, he became a suspicious character, and it was marked down in his official file that he was an unreliable man with family troubles.

For, the august leaders never had any family troubles. They deceived their wives in secret, usually with their pretty secretaries

---

"Comrade," he said, "I should like to ask you something. But give me your word that you will never speak of it to anyone."

The pretty, blonde woman, who was the wife of a well-known poet and who had never in her life kept a secret, nodded.

"Tell me," said the editor, his face serious and thoughtful. "How does a bus look from the inside?"

whom they took to the "sanctuaries" which were reserved at the most beautiful Budapest hotel, the Gellert, for ministers and high Party officials. Everything was permitted to the leaders. There was but one moral law: that they should not be found out. The Party itself knew there were no secrets from the Party, but it paid little attention to such insignificant blunders, for, after all, even Communists are human—and particularly if they are ministers or Party officials. The storm broke forth only when people began to whisper that this or that Political Committee member or minister had a mistress and that they had been seen together.

These Party officials turned into hypocritical conservatives who were no longer interested in anything new, who were content to maintain the status quo. They preached against misconduct because it harmed the Party's prestige. They condemned infidelity and corruption. And they fought with fire and sword against favoritism (though this did not keep them from granting their cousins, their fathers-in-law, or their close friends the greatest privileges, nor did it prevent them from creating for them new, unnecessary, and miraculously well-paid positions).*

This large family of top Party officials lived as an exclusive and isolated caste: they intermarried; they had no social life except among themselves; and they completely ignored the

---

* In the early fifties, Hungarian public life resounded with battle cries against favoritism and corruption. Officials were relieved of their posts because they had helped their relatives to good jobs. All over the country a campaign of "purification" was being carried on to unmask family connections. At the same time, Rakosi's brother, under the assumed name of Zoltan Biro, was made director of the Party Academy, his younger brother Ferenc was managing director of the Csepel (Matyas Rakosi) Iron Works (later, he was Deputy Minister of Medium [i.e., "Armament"] Industry), and Ferenc's wife, a Russian woman, was managing director of the new Csepel Automobile Works. In addition, the husband of Rakosi's niece, Maria, was Istvan Dekany, Lieutenant General of the State Security Organization; Mihaly Farkas' son, Vladimir, was, at the age of twenty-eight, Colonel of the State Security Organization (the AVO); Vladimir's wife, Vera, was the daughter of Andor Berei, Chairman of the National Planning Office, and of Erzsebet Andics, notorious Muscovite historian (and Vera, too, filled an important economic position); and Jozsef Revai's brother, Dezso Revai, an absolutely useless, unintelligent fellow, was managing director of the only Hungarian Film Studio.

masses, toiling and suffering below them—the masses in whose name they planned and replanned, cursed or blessed, and appointed or executed each other.

All these officials had come far in the decade they were now celebrating in Debrecen. The once ordinary—and, for the most part, honest—men had turned into vain, haughty leaders 'who despised anyone outside their own circle, but who were supremely powerful, so that a smile or frown from them could decide the fate of tens of thousands. Their lives, their souls, their innermost sentiments had been crushed by the devilish mill that had now ground into nothing the men they once had been. They no longer thought. They only obeyed. They obeyed and carried out orders.

They lived in an air-tight, isolated world, in a glittering glass sphere into which no sound from the outside could penetrate. They lived according to their own rules, and they answered their own questions in the way they wanted to answer them. Life was an endless succession of victories, and they were the conquerors. True, for a while after June, 1953, the machine had not functioned properly. But now everything was in order, and balance had been restored.

Therefore, they were even gayer and more carefree than usual now in the dining room of the hotel—except for a few writers, who sat around their own table morosely, with clenched teeth, exchanging meaningful glances when one or another of the "powerful ones" passed by.

For the writers knew these men. They knew them far too well by now. They knew who they were, whence they came, and how they lived. They knew why, among the millions of workers and peasants, *these* had been selected by the invisible, caressing but threatening, rewarding but punishing, hand of the Party.

Such selection was not left to chance. It was the result of years of careful and thorough study. The mechanism which had made them its servants wanted men who would obey the orders and instructions of a central brain without thought, without doubt, without argument, and without anxiety or conflict of conscience.

For this task, no sharp-eyed, cultured, courageous, or gifted men, alert with doubts, were needed. The men needed were those who could, without resistance, be turned into the wheels of a machine, into robots without heart or brain. The machine needed servile souls who, in their youth, had been rebels. It needed revolutionaries who had devoted their lives to the cause and, in that service, had slipped into servility. The truly revolutionary ones and the really talented ones broke away from the herd after a while. But, whether they did or not, the herd trampled them underfoot. There was no choice. One had to break or perish. The Party was the triumph of slave mentality and of mediocrity. It was the greatest counter-selection of history, invariably destroying the best, the most gifted. The work of these really talented ones was needed, and so they were used and exploited. Sometimes —when it seemed necessary—they were even praised and rewarded. But it was always in a way that made the really gifted one ashamed, because he was made to feel that the reward came from above and that the hierarchy was doing *him* a favor by even accepting the fruit of his talent and application. In reality, the officials were afraid of talent. Subconsciously, they hated everyone who was gifted, and they concealed their fear and their hatred behind a show of contempt and haughtiness and superiority. Gradually, the officials actually came to believe that those of them who had graduated from a six-month or one-year Party school and who were familiar with the magic passwords and who enjoyed the confidence of the Party, really knew more and were of more value than anyone else.

Therefore, of course, the officials also knew more than did anyone else about literature. They had learned in the seminars that a good Communist must be well-read and cultured, that it is shameful not to be familiar to at least some extent with Soviet and Hungarian literature. Therefore, they read. At Party meetings, they pledged that in their spare time and on Sundays they would thoroughly study the latest issue of the Cominform publication (*For a Lasting Peace and a People's Democracy*), that they would make notes on Matyas Rakosi's latest speech, and that they would, within two weeks, finish Zsigmond Moricz's novel *The Relatives,* in which the great Hungarian writer unmasked—though, naturally, within his own bourgeois limits—the Hungarian upper classes under Horthy, revealing the network of family connections and the community of interests separating this stratum from the toiling masses. ("How different," they could then say, "from our new, healthy society!") They pledged to finish within the month Sholokhov's *The Plow Cuts New Furrows,* which—as Comrade Revai pointed out—was worth ten pamphlets dealing with the collectivization of agriculture. To them, obligatory reading was indeed obligatory. They treated it as homework which—whether the book was good or not—had to be done, because the Party had need for well-read members. Thus, they never chose their own books. They were always told what to read. They were always told what fitted the momentary political situation or what supplemented Party instruction. And, therefore, instead of learning how to read, instead of finding pleasure in literature, they lost even the last trace of the interest they had brought with them from their youthful "pre-official" years. To them, reading was one of the forms of building socialism, of Party work. It was another difficulty to be overcome. To it, they sacrificed themselves, because the building up of socialism required many sacrifices.

Now, here in the dining room, the writers watched them. They watched part or, perhaps, the bulk of their reading public, because, so they had been led to believe, these leaders indeed read their books, these people *enjoyed* their novels and poems even at a time when the ordinary people, the real readers, had long ago given up the products of new Hungarian literature and were reading Dickens and Balzac (they had, of course, no access to more modern Western literature). These selective people did not consider their descriptions of the workers' happy life or the peasants' passionate yearning for the cooperatives a pack of lies, because these literary works were the exact replica of those reports of victorious progress which these men themselves sent to headquarters from their factories and counties week after week.

These were the people who praised the writers. They slapped them on the back saying: "Well, well, comrade writer, that was a wonderful description of how the kulak tormented that unfortunate farmhand. . . . I forgot his name . . . but let me tell you frankly and openly that your portrayal of the heroes of the new life is not affectionate enough. Yes, that's the important thing. It's the positive heroes you must have, if you want to become a true socialist realist!"

The writers watched them now and felt sick at heart in remembering that, for ten years, they had written primarily for these people and had served their literary tastes and interests. Yet it was not the mediocrity nor the dullness of these people that filled them with the greatest horror and disgust. After all, no machinery of state consists of geniuses alone. No, it was not this steaming, greasy, drunken crowd which repelled them. It was, instead, that which lay concealed behind it all. Who would have grudged them their good life, their villas, and their automobiles, if they had really accomplished something, if they had really brought prosperity to the country? But they had not. Behind the distinctions and the orders, behind the memoranda which reported success upon success, behind the holiday resorts and the special warehouses stood a ruined country, a defrauded people, and the shadow of the internment camp and the gallows. This self-satisfied and haughty gang had spoiled and squandered everything in those ten years which they now so cheerfully celebrated. They were a cloud of locusts. They were birds of prey, thriving on what they had stolen, and continuing to rob the people.

Even more unbearable was the hypocrisy with which they committed all their unspeakable crimes in the name of the people. Was this the rule of the working class, of the working people? These former workers and peasants had nothing in common with the class of their origin. They were using their humble births as shields to protect themselves against any attack. The trouble was not that they lived the way they lived. The writers knew well enough that, in the Western capitalist countries, there were even more glaring social differences. An American automobile manu-

facturer or a British oil magnate had considerably more than did
Matyas Rakosi or Erno Gero. But there, at least, nobody pretended that everything belonged to the people. There, the millionaire and the oil magnate never warned the factory or the oil
field worker to keep a watchful eye on every tool or every drop
of oil because these were the people's property!

Why was it that the automobiles had become hated symbols of
the rule of Party officials? It was not only because there were
very few automobiles in Hungary. It was not only because the
leaders were using cars, for this is always so in every country.
But when a working mother, trying to climb into an already overcrowded bus in the morning to take her children to nursery
school before going to work, saw a huge ZIM swishing by with
one child in it (the child of a Party official), or when a football
fan walked all the way to the stadium to save the bus fare and,
arriving there, saw hundreds and hundreds of cars belonging to
Party officials standing in front of the entrance, or when, to
make things worse, they were told again and again in the press,
the radio, and the newsreels that these cars were the *people's
property*—then it was small wonder that their hands clenched
into fists and that their lips formulated the most extravagant
curses. This transparent "Tartuffe-hood," combined as it was
with the most atrocious crimes, was one of the most poisonous
and revolting features of the Communist system.

So the writers asked themselves this question: Was all this as
"necessary" to the building up of socialism as were the accelerated plans for industrialization and the plans for the forced
collectivization of agriculture? They knew that in every country
the leaders lived better than did the followers and that, even in
a People's Democracy, skilled labor deserved greater moral and
material reward than unskilled labor. But was *this* skilled labor?
And, even supposing that it was, were private swimming pools
lighted from beneath, were holiday resorts surrounded by barbed
wire fences, were hypocrisy and lies—were all these absolutely
necessary in a regime that had set out on a road to power under
the banner of social justice and of prosperity for all? Yes, the

writers at last understood that these things were necessary. It was absolutely necessary to have this kind of leaders, because only such men would exploit the workers as they were exploited, or would impose the graveyard silence that reigned over the country, or would do such violence to the economy and the culture of the nation. And, in order to keep these leaders in line, they had to be granted the privileges they now enjoyed. They had to be granted the benefits they now received from the regime. The writers were beginning to realize that all this, together with the crimes of which they had only recently learned, were essential and indispensable elements of the system. But this system had nothing, absolutely nothing to do with the people, nor with the working class, nor with socialism.

What hurt the writers most as participants in the Debrecen celebrations was that—had anyone asked them—they would have had to admit that they, too, belonged to this privileged stratum. True, they did not get their supplies from the special warehouses, nor did the system put automobiles at their disposal, nor did they spend their holidays free of charge on Lake Balaton, nor did their children attend classes at the Gorki School. But they, too, enjoyed numerous privileges for supporting and glorifying the regime with their writings—i.e., with their lies! The Hungarian Writers' Association owned a beautiful rest home at Visegrad, on the Danube, and another one at Szigliget, near Lake Balaton. And the leading Communist writers lived in villa apartments, travelled abroad, and enjoyed absolute material security. Yes, even the invitation to participate in the Debrecen festivities and to travel down in the special train showed clearly where they belonged—not to speak of the Kossuth Prizes and the other distinctions, nor of such generous gestures as a seat of honor at a gala performance at the opera house, nor of membership in Parliament. The fact that these privileges were rewards for their services or, more cruelly, for their servility to the regime, manifested itself clearly in the difference between their fate and that of their fellow writers, who refused to submit to the regime and who, with the exception of a few good tacticians, struggled hard to make ends

meet and eked out a meager existence by making literary trans-
lations. Yes, they, too, were products of the country-wide counter-
selection which was based on Party loyalty and on unconditional
service and on yesmanship rather than on talent. They, too, were
a part of the all-pervading mediocrity: either their talent was
mediocre or they had successfully brought it down to the required
level.

No, they could not go on with it. Now that the truth had at
last become clear to them (now that they could no longer
delude themselves that all that was going on around them served
the interests of the people and of socialism) they were filled with
disgust at what they saw—disgust with themselves—and they
resolved to renounce their privileges rather than to share in the
crimes. Neither material security nor position could tempt them
to keep silent and to suppress the truth as they now saw it. If
they were filled with horror at the sight of this self-satisfied,
happy, victorious gathering of Party and state officials—if they
made up their minds to break with their world and their way of
life—it was, in the first place, because they were filled with horror
at their own unconscious share in the crimes and at their own
past activities.

Exactly opposite, at the other end of the room, a cheerful,
laughing company had assembled. At the head of the table, as
always, sat Matyas Rakosi with a glass of wine in his hand. On
his left sat his faithful and reliable disciple, the notorious fighter
for peace and Muscovite historian and filler of various Party and
Government functions—the once beautiful Erzsebet Andics. Next
to her sat her husband, Andor Berei, just then head of the Party's
Agitation-Propaganda Department; and next to him sat his
deputy, Eva Lakatos, a Muscovite old maid who was the very
symbol of bitter rigidity and of Party loyalty. Next came Lajos
Acs, member of the Political Committee, and the others, each
listening with wide-open eyes and unflagging attention to the
great leader and wise father who, as usual, was holding forth
without surcease. The writers kept their eyes averted. Lately, they

had been very careful always to avoid their former idol so as not to speak or shake hands with him.

Three steps led from the other dining room to the one in which they sat.

A short, portly man with a mustache and a pince-nez was now walking down these steps, looking about him with interest. He was not followed by a suite or by a circle of courtiers. He came alone, apparently enjoying the cheerful atmosphere as if he were someone who was at home in the town and in the hotel.

The writers immediately noticed him.

It was Imre Nagy.

Erno Urban, author of *The Cucumber Tree,* rose. He was a close friend of Nagy.

"I'll call him over," Urban said.

The others nodded approvingly.

They had much to tell Imre Nagy concerning the events of the last few weeks and concerning his own speech today. They knew that they had to tell him what they thought, that they could no longer remain silent. Besides, the "old man" always listened to their opinions with interest.

Nagy immediately accepted the invitation. As soon as he was seated, the waiter appeared with a fresh bottle of Badacsony wine, the old man's favorite drink. Soon, new guests arrived at the table: Jozsef Bognar, a young and very intelligent non-Party (formerly a Smallholder) politician who was now Minister of Commerce and whose preference for the new political line was notorious—and who (although he gave his support to the Communist Party) had always behaved with moderation. Bognar was a man who knew his job and did it well. The writers liked him because of his directness and because he was much more cultured than was any other high-ranking official, and at the same time he was modest and had good manners—something that could not be said about his colleagues, not even with the maximum of good will.

Bognar poured himself a glass of wine.

Then came a small, skinny, and exhausted-looking man with a haunted look in his eyes. This was Erik Molnar, former Minister of Justice, an old underground Communist, and a well-known Marxist historian. Molnar was a tired and disillusioned man who, as Minister of Justice and a member of the Central Committee, had had every opportunity to observe what was going on behind the "Potemkin" walls of socialist construction, and who hated the entire leadership passionately, but who still never opposed it nor resigned his post, because he lacked the courage to do so. After Imre Nagy had become Premier, Molnar had made no secret of his adherence to the new political line, and, as a member of the Rehabilitation Committee, he had done everything in his power to unearth every detail of the villainies committed. He had never said so, but everyone knew that, in all matters at stake, he agreed with the writers. Thus, nobody was surprised when he found a chair for himself and brought it over to Imre Nagy's table.

Others also came. There was Kalman Kovacs, the Deputy Minister of Justice who had spent four years in jail, and there were writers and journalists, and Communists and non-Communists.

The writers did not keep silent. They told Imre Nagy that they had been disappointed in his speech.

The old man was not offended by their criticism; it was evident that there was much he would have liked to say, but could not say. Therefore, he only said:

"All right. Don't be so severe and impatient. . . . Everything will turn out well."

The writers were not in the least convinced that he was right. But why should they badger the man who, they knew, would have made an entirely different speech if it had been up to him?

So they began to tell him what was going on in the country.

Erno Urban was the loudest. This young man, who liked to talk like a peasant in a play, had only recently returned from Tokay, one of the foremost wine regions of Hungary. He related almost unbelievable, yet accurate, details of how the economic policies of Rakosi and Gero had destroyed this prize product of the Hungarian soil.

The old man nodded.

"I know of it," he said. "It is terrible. . . . But don't worry. We shall put everything right. Experts are already working on the plans. Let us have another glass of that excellent wine. . . ."

He calmed them down. He reassured them. It was just as if Rakosi had made no threats in the church. It was just as if this cloud of locusts in the Golden Bull were not waiting impatiently for—nor preparing for—his downfall.

The writers told him about Mihaly Farkas. Farkas was then the highest authority on literary matters. The writers said that they would no longer cooperate with Farkas. This ardent supporter of the "new phase" was, they said, in the process of reverting to the old line, and he was stupid, ignorant, and violent in trying to dictate to them. He was voicing the same demands by which he had already once put an end to anything that could be described as literature—demands which he had passionately denounced only a few months ago. The writers told Nagy that, when they disobeyed (for, now, they did disobey) or when they answered back (for, now, they did answer back), Comrade Farkas banged the table with his fist.

The old man's face clouded over.

"If anyone bangs his fist on the table in front of you," he said, slowly, "you bang your fists on it too." Then, musingly, almost dreamily, he added: "If you think that I don't have to bang my fist on the table—"

That was all he said on that subject. It was enough. It was easy to imagine what was going on among the leaders of the Party. But, more important to the writers than the balance of power, was the fact that the old man, whom they so completely trusted, had not thrown in his hand and was still defending the principles that he proclaimed. He, too, was in the process of turning away, or rather, of turning against that mob of parasites, of power-intoxicated rabble, of big and little dictators who had seized the Hungarian people and who were now living on the people's blood and toil.

Imre Nagy took off his pince-nez and wiped it. His face, like that of a child, was innocent, kindly, and serene. He was a man, not a god. He was one with the others, and not above them. The writers felt that even if his cause—even if their common cause— were to be defeated, they would rather share in this man's defeat than in the victory of that other man at the table opposite.

Soon the gypsy violinist came up to the table. New bottles of wine were brought, and Imre Nagy drank his wine and sat peacefully among his friends and supporters, humming Hungarian songs. At the opposite table, Rakosi sat with his back to them. They could not see Rakosi's face. But the faces of those around him were flushed with hatred and fury. Erzsebet Andics whispered something in Rakosi's ear. They could not hear her, but it was not difficult to guess what she must have said.

The writers were drinking a little too much to remain pessimistic. The gypsies played their favorite melodies, and the old man was even more kindly and more friendly than usual (for, he could be very formal and stiff if he wanted to be so). Thus, though they could clearly discern the storm clouds gathering on the political sky, the writers deluded themselves, at least for a few hours, that everything would turn out well. The wine and the music drew a tender veil over their anxious hearts. Time flew. When Imre Nagy rose to go, one of the non-Communist writers put his arm about the shoulders of a Communist colleague and said in a half-whisper, his eyes soft either with wine or emotion: "Friend, if they would only let him, this man would lead the Hungarian people straight to socialism!"

BOOK IV

ISOLATION

Comrade Non at Work

During the early winter months of 1955, tension was constantly rising, and those who still had hopes for Imre Nagy's ultimate victory were beginning to lose heart. Rakosi, who remembered all the lessons he had now learned, had decided that the time was ripe for a counter-attack and for a punitive expedition to revenge himself for all the injuries suffered during the past year and a half. There was a great disparity of forces. Rakosi was backed by the entire Party machinery, by a good part of the Army, and by the entire force of the state security police. Imre Nagy was backed "only" by a few writers and by the entire Hungarian people.

The decision, however, lay elsewhere. It lay in the Soviet Union. Parallel with developments in Hungary (and in explanation of them), significant changes were taking place in the Soviet Union. Indicative of these changes was the fact that Prime Minister Malenkov, like Imre Nagy in Hungary, was relieved of his job. The accusations against Malenkov were, in fact, approximately the same as those brought against Imre Nagy, the first among them being that Malenkov had underestimated the importance of heavy industry—though it was obvious that such charges were only a pretext, that the underlying motive lay in personal rivalry, and, even more obvious, that events in Hungary were merely a projection of the Kremlin's race for power (a race which was made more deadly by the Hungarian leaders' own race for power).

There was, however, one important difference between the events in Hungary and those in the Soviet Union. This difference lay in the fact that, though Malenkov had broken into orgies of self-criticism upon his dismissal, admitting that the accusations against him were well-founded, Imre Nagy had refused to admit his "errors." At the last conference in Moscow, which was held early in 1955, the Soviet Party leaders had invited Imre Nagy to confess to his "rightist" mistakes. Had the "old man" agreed, he would clearly have remained in the leadership, though perhaps not as Prime Minister. But the heads of the Kremlin had been in for a surprise unprecedented in the practice of the Communist Party. Imre Nagy had not been ready to obey. On the contrary, he had stuck stubbornly to his views and had declared that, in his opinion, another sudden change of policy would lead to catastrophic consequences in Hungary.

Where did this old Bolshevik, this experienced Comintern worker, find the courage to resist the leaders? True, he had a stubborn streak in his nature. But there was more to it than that. During his career in the Party he had repeatedly been faced with similar problems, and, in such times, he had always been ready to "confess his errors" without visible resistance. The fact was that now, however, both the situation and, even more, the man had changed. In all his career, it was only during the years of Nagy's Premiership that he had met with mass sympathy. And Imre Nagy, who had always yearned for such sympathy, would (unlike other leaders) not forget his strong ties with the people who had given him such sympathy. His faith had become stronger than his fear. His confidence in his calling had become stronger than his Party discipline.

At that point at which Party discipline stops, the break with the Party begins. The ruthlessly enforced and meekly accepted discipline of the Communist Party is like a barbed wire fence around freedom. But it is a discipline which functions only as long as men continue to delude themselves. Free thought is a step away from the strict line of dogma, and the decisive impulse which flings the adventurers out of their usual course with such force into the opposite direction (sometimes with such force that they themselves hardly know where they have landed) is usually a moral impulse. Imre Nagy's sense of ethics—and this was extremely unusual under Communism—had remained unimpaired, or at least soberly balanced, even after he had spent years in the Soviet Union. He had been deeply moved by the series of unspeakable crimes that had at last come to light, and he, if anyone, knew who was responsible for these crimes. As a result, he was morally indignant, not only because he was asked to "confess his errors" when he knew he was right, but because he was asked to humiliate himself in front of murderers.

Nagy's moral indignation was strengthened by a certain moral obligation: his obligation to his friends, the Hungarian writers. His influence upon them was no greater than their influence upon him. He had seen how passionately and with what determination his writer friends stuck to their convictions, and it was their moral consistency which determined also his own.

Very characteristically, Rakosi had tried to get the Hungarian writers (i.e., those who would be most opposed to doing so) to condemn Imre Nagy before the meeting of the Central Committee in early March. As early as February, at the plenary session of the Writers' Association, he had attempted to pass a resolution in which the "principal danger of rightist deviationism" (the Party appellation for the Imre Nagy line) would be openly condemned. Before and during the meeting, Rakosi had repeatedly telephoned to find out whether this important sentence had or had not been included in the resolution. One of the present writers, Tamas Aczel, had talked with him at least twice, and Sandor Erdei, First Secretary of the Writers' Association, had talked with him three times. But the attack was successfully repulsed. The writers had refused to be made a part of the campaign against Imre Nagy.

It was the Central Committee meeting held a month later, in early March, that brought complete victory for the Rakosi line.

The resolution passed at that meeting condemned Comrade Imre Nagy's rightist deviationism (although he *was* still called "Comrade") and pointed to the various symptoms of rightist deviationism in political, economic, and cultural life. In addition to accusing Imre Nagy of having neglected the development of socialist heavy industry and of having favored a disproportionate development of light industry, the meeting also reproached him for his "nationalism." The resolution quoted from a sentence of one of his speeches. In that speech, he had said: "Nine and a half million Hungarian hearts beat for the fulfillment of the Government program." This—so the resolution said—had been an anti-Marxist, anti-Leninist, petty-bourgeois, nationalist statement because it had ignored class differences and had implied that all Hungarians were equal, when in fact, so the resolution said, it was obvious that there were insoluble antagonistic differences between fellow Hungarians—between workers and capitalists, and between poor peasants and kulaks. The man who forgot that, so the resolution said, had deviated from the road of Communist ideology.*

The resolution also branded Imre Nagy's agrarian policies as rightist because—so it said—these policies neglected the socialist sector of agriculture by dissolving the producer cooperatives and thus fundamentally deviating from the practices of socialism in the Soviet Union.

The resolution also reproached Imre Nagy for his connection with "rightist, petty-bourgeois writers without any perspective," as if to say that this offender against the basic principles of Marxism-Leninism was making strange friends.

There was, however, much about which the resolution kept silent. It did not mention the condition in which the country had

---

* Of course, the resolution omitted mentioning the fact that, at the "free elections" held in the Rakosi era, the program of the Communist Party always won 99.7 or 99.8 per cent of the votes and the fact that this could have been used as an argument against the "antagonistic" differences between Hungarians and Hungarians—at least as far as the support of the Party was concerned.

been when Imre Nagy had taken over, and it drew a heavy veil of silence over the fact that, whatever Imre Nagy had said or done had been said or done not only with the unanimous approval of the Central Committee but by the direct order of the Soviet Communist Party.

The fact was that the Soviet leaders attacked him today for the very "deviationism" that had prompted them a year and a half ago to appoint him Prime Minister.

It was not in the least surprising that Rakosi and his gang should have thirsted for revenge. The bald little Party leader had been impatient to pay Imre Nagy back for that day when he had been compelled to sit in the second row. It was the revelation of the utter baseness of the members of the Central Committee that was surprising. The same men who in June, 1953, and in October, 1954, had unanimously and enthusiastically accepted Imre Nagy's proposals, now unanimously accepted the opposite of their own resolutions. Istvan Kovacs, Andor Berei, and Marton Horvath, who had been Nagy's principal supporters in October, now became his principal accusers. This corrupt clique of "professional revolutionaries," seeking to protect their positions and their velvet chairs and their automobiles and villas, now condemned without batting an eyelid all the measures of which they had formerly approved, because power politics demanded it and because Moscow had given new orders.

In this action was to be observed the Communist dialectic governing "changed situations and changed conditions," and, as a result, the writers as well as the people of the entire country had no doubts left as to what the Party was—that Party which many of them had so deeply loved and revered, and which had embodied in their eyes infallibility and consistency and wisdom and superior morality. Neither, too, had they now any doubts left as to the value of Hungarian independence.

In those days, Imre Nagy had been gravely ill. He had been bedfast with a thrombosis of the heart, and he had not been able to participate in the meeting of the Central Committee. So he had sent a message to the meeting, asking the Party's leading body not to pass a resolution without first giving him a hearing.

To demonstrate his own generosity and his own Communist loyalty, Rakosi had agreed that, although the meeting would decide political questions, Imre Nagy's actual fate would be decided only when he, Nagy, was well and could express his own point of view. Thus, in the famous March resolution, they had not even deprived Imre Nagy of his Premiership. It was only in early April that the impatience of the little dictator to deprive his rival (whose popularity he envied) of all power made it impossible for him to keep his promise and, barely three weeks after the March resolution, prompted him to convoke another session of the Central Committee at which he crushed his enemy, as he believed, once and for all. At this meeting, Imre Nagy was relieved of his post, expelled from the Central Committee, made to resign his Parliamentary seat, and dismissed from his chair at the University of Agriculture.

In order to make his victory complete and to kill two birds with one stone, the old Comintern fox also chose (with a refined instinct for Party intrigue) this auspicious moment to rid himself of his accomplice and helper, the former Supreme Army Commander and outstanding expert on questions of literature, Mihaly Farkas—a man who had, in all events, been too deeply involved in the Rakosi tortures and illegalities. The old fox accomplished this extraordinary feat by means of a very ingenious trick: he accused Farkas of rightist deviationism and of having been a too enthusiastic supporter of Imre Nagy! Being lumped together with the murderer was the price that Imre Nagy now had to pay for having believed Kisselev's promises and for having cooperated with Farkas for a time.

The Party officials threw themselves with enormous zeal into the "work" of popularizing and of translating into practice the new resolutions of the Party. In June, 1953, and in October, 1954, everyone had been aware of the wrangling that had pre-

ceded the putting into practice of the Nagy resolutions because
of the reluctance of the Party apparatus to execute measures
opposed to its own interests. Now there was no such reluctance.
Speed was important. Even while the Central Committee was
still in session, Rakosi, being certain of victory, had the text of
the resolution already printed and had it already distributed
among the lower (municipal, county, and district) Party locals.
Membership meetings were immediately convoked, and, at these,
the members were obliged to cheer the resolution, to condemn
Imre Nagy and rightist deviationism, and to pledge to support
the new, the infallible, and the unquestionably correct political
line. The Party press published hundreds of pledges of loyalty
and hundreds of congratulatory telegrams which were sent by
factories and villages. There was only one Party organization in
the whole country that listened to the resolutions in silence and
that declined to cheer the new developments: the Party organization of the Communist writers. It was still too early for them
to be able to *reject* a Party resolution, but it was not too early
for them to be able to *demonstrate* against such a resolution by
silence.

It was during those days that the majority of the Communist
writers also completely lost every illusion concerning the role of
the Soviet Union—if, indeed, they still had any left. It was far
too obvious that this latest harmful—and even tragic—turn of
events was the work of those same Soviet leaders, who had, a
year and a half earlier, prompted the discontent. The writers lost
every hope that the Soviet leaders might prevent a return to the
Rakosi dictatorship. It became evident that, to the Soviet leaders,
the whole problem was secondary, and that the only thing that
mattered to them was to have a man in Hungary who would
obey their every order with absolute servility and without
condition.

Naturally, the Party leadership did not resign itself to the
writers' silence. What these leaders wanted was loud approval
and self-imposed discipline and unconditional surrender; and,

early in May, Rakosi invited the Communist faction of the presidium of the Writers' Association to meet with him for a little chat.

This "little chat" lasted from 4 p.m. until 11 p.m. Apart from Rakosi, there were present Erno Gero; the new Premier Andras Hegedus (a short, pink-cheeked, very young man who had once been Gero's—then Rakosi's—secretary); Istvan Kovacs (the stupid and spineless Party secretary of Budapest); Marton Horvath, Erzsebet Andics, and the writers.

The conversation was fruitless. In vain did Rakosi try to win them over with humor. In vain did Gero rant, beside himself with rage. Nothing helped. These one-time geniuses, the wise father and great leader of the Hungarian people, and the dictator of economic life, and the loud and loquacious people's judges sat there impotent, playing their old, worn-out records, until the writers looked at each other in amazement. Were these the men they had once believed and revered? Had it been these bloated idiots, these insignificant Soviet agents intoxicated with power? Had it been these clowns, whose mediocrity was surpassed only by their self-adoration and whose self-adoration was surpassed only by their thirst for power? Had it been these criminals, whose only ambition was to mask the fact that they were unmasked?

Erno Gero called every writer by name and faced him with this question:

"Do you or do you not agree with the Party resolution?"

In the tense silence in the sanctuary of the "council of the gods," the answers rang forth loudly and determinedly:

"As a member of the Party, I am obliged to obey. But I cannot agree with the resolution."

It became evident that the writers were determined to stick to their guns, that they would never again keep their opinions to themselves out of loyalty to the Party, and that they would never again allow crimes to be committed behind their backs and in their names. The break between them and the Party was now open and complete.

When the meeting ended, Rakosi whispered to Tamas Aczel

to come to his room, since he wanted to talk to him. Aczel entered the room. Rakosi did not ask him to sit down, but, exhausted, old, confused, and almost demented with the novelty of an unsuccessful meeting, he began to shout at Aczel:

"What do you want? Tell me, what do you want? Haven't we given you everything? Kossuth Prize, Stalin Prize? . . . You have a nice car, a beautiful flat. . . . What else do you want? Tell me!"

Aczel made no reply.

Rakosi looked at him for a while, reproachfully and incomprehendingly. Rakosi was like a tired old man.

Why was it that during this period the writers resisted Rakosi's political line more consistently and more determinedly than did any other stratum or class of the country? Certainly not because, say, the ironworkers of Csepel or the miners of Salgotarjan loved the squat little dictator more than did they, or because these were more enthusiastic about Imre Nagy's downfall than were the Communist writers! Still, the workers unanimously approved the March resolution at their factory or plant meetings and they unanimously condemned the "dangerous trend" which Imre Nagy had tried to impose on the Party.

There was a good deal of apathy in these workers' attitudes. They had so often been made to send telegrams in the past ten years. They had so often been either praised or condemned that they hardly paid attention to such things. They merely did whatever their Party secretary told them to do. They knew only too well that their wishes or opinions were a matter of utter indifference to the Party leadership, that they had no influence whatsoever on the affairs of the country, and that, if the leaders so badly wanted their meaningless and empty "approval," they could have it, and to hell with them!

It was the writers who, partly because they were too conscious of their responsibilities and partly because their consciences demanded action to make up for their former passivity, could not pass over matters so lightly. At the same time, too—and this facilitated their task—the writers enjoyed greater freedom and greater possibilities than did, for instance, the Csepel workers or the Salgotarjan miners. It was much easier to imprison or intern a nameless worker than it was to do so to a well-known Kossuth Prize poet. As had happened so often before, the Party had defeated its own ends. For years it had praised and celebrated and distinguished—and often created—writers and artists. It had pointed to them as examples to be followed. It had glorified their loyalty to the Party, and, now, when the same writers refused obedience, it found it highly uncomfortable to admit that perhaps these very writers were not so gifted after all and that their loyalty to the Party was not quite so exemplary as the Party had insisted.

This privileged situation of the writers was also evident in the difference between the treatment meted out to them and the treatment meted out to the rebellious journalists. The editor in charge at *Irodalmi Ujsag*, Miklos Molnar, who had also joined the opposition, was expelled from his job from one day to the next, before the showdown with Imre Nagy.*

When Imre Nagy was at last thrown from the saddle, the Party settled its accounts with the rebellious editors and staff writers of *Szabad Nep*. Seven journalists were relieved of their jobs without delay. These were: Lajos Feher, Sandor Novobaczky, and Tibor Meray, who were members of the editorial board; Janos Kornai,

---

* Together with other works inspired by the same spirit of rebellion, Miklos Molnar published in his paper a poem by Laszlo Benjamin entitled "The Magic of Everyday." The poem was a moving indictment of the last few years. It was a passionate and sorrowful condemnation of Benjamin's own life and work, of his barren years, and of the successes he had won as the "reward" of complicity. The poem was a tremendous success. Party leadership singled out this poem and harped on it for weeks, analyzing it and picking it to pieces as the foremost example of petty-bourgeois lack of perspective, of panic at the sight of difficulties, and of "rightist" underestimation of the achievements of the last few years. At a reception on the "Day of the Hungarian Press," Mihaly Farkas, who was then still in office, came upon the editor and criticized him in abusive terms. Molnar made a brief reply, but two days later he published an article by Tibor Dery in which the novelist acclaimed Benjamin's poem as the most beautiful creation of the new Hungarian literature. This was too much: Molnar was immediately dismissed.

editorial secretary; Imre Patko, Party secretary of the editorial offices; Gabor Lenart, editor of the agrarian column; and Terez Laky, of the domestic politics column. But it was not quite so easy to dismiss the writers of Hungary in general. Though the Party could—and did—introduce punitive measures (for instance, by forbidding the publication of a novel, a short story, or a poem, etc.), it could not "relieve" Tibor Dery of his job as a writer and appoint a reliable Party official in his place.

There was, at that time, something new in the situation. It was something which could not be ignored and which detracted a little from the seeming boldness of the writers. It lay in the fact that the condemning Party resolutions and dismissals and accusations were not, as previously, followed by arrests. Those relieved of a higher function were simply given more humble posts. Miklos Molnar, for instance, received a scholarship (which corresponded to his salary at *Irodalmi Ujsag*) to the Party academy, the Lenin Institute; and the other journalists were offered other positions with provincial newspapers, with scientific institutes, etc. It was clear to all that Rakosi, if it were up to him, would have dealt with the opponents in a highly different manner and that this mildness was due to the fact that—at least for the present—the Soviet leaders tolerated no return to the methods which had been applied in Stalin's day.

Thus, the writers did not run the risk of being arrested. They could, at most, be silenced—with only the resultant reduction in their material well-being. And yet, they could not feel entirely secure. The measures taken against Imre Nagy demonstrated again that, in this system, nothing was impossible, that nothing was ever permanent, and that nothing could be taken for granted. There was no guarantee that the Soviet leaders—who had been both the patrons and the persecutors of Imre Nagy—would not themselves return to Stalinist methods. They might at any time have given Rakosi the "all clear" signal to resume arrests and hangings. Therefore, the writers, though they took advantage of greater opportunities while they lasted, were fully aware of the danger threatening them.

The early summer, however, brought new changes and, it seemed, favorable ones. A Soviet airplane landed on the airfield of Belgrade, and its Number One passenger, Nikita Sergeyevich Khrushchev, alighted, hat in hand, to ask Marshal Tito's most humble forgiveness for the insolence of the Soviet Party, the Soviet Government, and the Soviet propaganda that had for years called Tito a lap dog and a vile agent of British-American imperialism.

The next day, when Khrushchev's speech was published in full in the Budapest press, a short, squat young man rose at the Party meeting in the editorial offices of *Magyar Nemzet* ("Hungarian Nation") and asked, very simply, this question: If Tito were innocent and if the accusations against him (those first contained in the indictments of the Rajk trial) were false, then why were not Rajk and his companions, who had been accused of having been "Titoist agents," rehabilitated without delay?

This young man's name was Miklos Gimes. He had, for years, been a staff member of *Szabad Nep,* and he had constantly devoted his inexhaustible energy and extraordinary erudition to the cause which—so he believed—would save the world. He had for years been the Number One assistant to Jozsef Revai. He had, in 1950, also been entrusted with the working out of the theses in the Dery debate. But those who knew him well had noticed even then that a violent inner conflict had been raging beneath his outward, self-imposed calm. This very sensitive, kind-hearted young man, a former Yugoslav partisan, had even then had certain doubts about the methods used by the Party, though he had never doubted the dogma; and, though he could not help noticing the inhumanity about him, his faith in the Party had never wavered, and he had simply tried, in cases of obvious injustice, to help the people concerned. In fact, Revai and Horvath, who exploited his energies to the full, had constantly reproached him angrily for "playing the lawyer again."

The grey and oppressive years had not, however, killed Gimes' love of humanity nor his faith in the people. He was one of the most cultured men in the country. He spoke four languages fluently, and his memory was sometimes frightening. He could quote—and always correctly—whole pages from *Don Quixote* or *Candide,* and he never had to think twice when he needed a few lines from a poem for one of his articles. Yet, his thinking was by no means mechanical. Even at the time of his complete ideological blindness, he had had original ideas and he had deeply despised those second-rate dogmatists who had had nothing to support their arguments except paragraphs and chapters from the works of Stalin and Lenin. If there can be such a thing as a man of standards in a world without standards—or originality in a world of dogma and catechisms—this was what Miklos Gimes tried to be.

Yet, why had he believed in the Party? The answer: his faith had evolved from a life of torment, from the yearning of a lonely man for a real community, from the persecution that had turned him into a persecutor, from a quasi-religious devotion to a worldwide outlook that held all the answers, from a self-imposed discipline (a delightful self-torture to a man born to freedom), and from a fear enclosed in an armor of fearlessness. Nevertheless, as soon as Gimes realized that he had been lied to and that he had been betrayed, he was among the first to declare war on his own past and to go into battle for the future.

Did Gimes, when he raised his voice at the Party meeting of the editorial offices, have a high opinion of Khrushchev, or did he nourish unwarranted hopes about the politics of the Soviet Union? Not at all. He was far too intelligent to shut his eyes again once they had been opened, and—like the majority of the Communist writers—he had no illusions left after Imre Nagy's dismissal. Still, after the trip to Belgrade and on the threshold of the Geneva Conference, it was obvious that there were many contradictions in Moscow's political line and that nobody knew exactly what was happening: nobody knew whether it was only a fight for power between Khrushchev and the Stalinists (who were led by Molotov) or whether it was Khrushchev himself who was muddled and inconsistent. Thus, the actions of Gimes and of most of the rebellious Communists were not motivated by admiration for Khrushchev. They were, instead, motivated by shrewd intention to take advantage of the Moscow and Belgrade developments in order to get rid of Rakosi and his gang as soon as possible. Though the writers were constantly referring to Soviet politics, they were, in reality, beginning to engage in independent, or rather Hungarian politics, taking account of the Soviet Party line as an important factor, but developing individual ideas and keeping national interests in mind. Theirs was a realistic political line, or at least they hoped it was realistic insofar as that is possible in a small country under foreign occupation.

As a result of his question concerning Rajk's rehabilitation, Gimes was summoned before a Party jury and, since he consistently refused to exercise self-criticism, he was expelled from the Party. Simultaneously, Gyorgy Fazekas, a journalist and a former partisan in Slovakia, was also expelled, and Miklos Vasarhelyi, a former underground Communist and the head of the Office of Information in the Imre Nagy Government, was given a final warning. The crime of these two men was that they had supported Gimes' sacrilegious speech in which he had asked his question.

Yet, in those days, the writers could no longer be restrained. No threat or punishment could prevent them from fighting openly for the truth they had at last discovered. The Party punishments and expulsions and dismissals were only fuel to the already inflamed passions. The question raised by Gimes was not his individual problem. It was in the air. More and more, people were openly discussing how much longer the Party would maintain that the execution of Rajk and his companions as Titoist agents had been just and justified—at the same time that the Moscow leaders were humiliating themselves before Tito?

Rakosi was far too shrewd not to realize that Gimes' question could, sooner or later, cost him his head, for, after all, he had been the stage manager of the Rajk trial—that trial which had provided the most important evidence to the Cominform parties, enabling them to call Tito's Yugoslavia a bridgehead of imperialists and the Yugoslav Party a gang of agents and hired assassins. Thus, Rakosi was ready to negotiate about anything except the accusations against Rajk.

Once, Rakosi invited Zoltan Zelk, one of the outstanding Communist poets, for a little chat and asked him what it was that had so incensed the rebellious Communist writers. Zelk enumerated all the questions which were still unanswered and all the injuries and complaints. Then, Zelk could not refrain from telling the stiffly listening dictator to his face that the writers would never rest until the entire country was told the whole truth about the Rajk affair.

Rakosi's face turned a furious red. He jumped from his chair and began to shout. He was beside himself with rage.

"You can rest assured, all of you, that we shall never, never rehabilitate Rajk!" he cried.

But, Rakosi's screams were no longer frightening. In fact, they rather reassured the writers. They were no longer a sign of strength, but of weakness. They were a sign of nervousness instead of self-assurance. It was quite clear that Rajk's rehabilitation or non-rehabilitation did not depend on Rakosi. It was quite clear that larger interests were at stake—that the Rajk affair had become the central issue of the Khrushchev-Tito relations as it had once become the central issue of the Stalin-Tito relations. At that former time, Rakosi's zeal had served to accelerate events. Now he could, at most, delay them. But he had no power to change their course, and this fact gave the writers a new assurance. They felt—and after Khrushchev's trip to Belgrade, they were certain of—the drama. Sooner or later, new developments would follow.

During that summer of 1955, the Communist writers concentrated less on politics and more on their work. This was the period when the awakenings and the discoveries and the painful inner struggles and the loss of illusions began to ripen and assume form. New poems and short stories were born. Plays and novels were written with more or less similar basic themes. The ruthless struggle between humanity reawakened, and inhumanity in power expressed itself in a multitude of ways. This was the summer when Tibor Dery began to work on his short novel *Niki*, which dealt in a beautiful and poetic and symbolic way with the tragedy of the innocently imprisoned, and when Gyula Hay, the foremost Communist playwright, wrote a drama entitled *Justice for Gaspar Varro*, a moving portrayal of the persecution suffered by the ordinary Hungarian people.

Even the Hungarian film set out on new roads. Felix and Judit Mariassy's film, entitled *A Glass of Beer*, and Zoltan Fabri's *Merry-Go-Round* treated the problems of youth in towns and villages. But the most powerful voices in the chorus were those of the Hungarian poets. That young generation of poets which had supported Party literature with all its might—Benjamin, Zelk, Konya, Kuczka, Sipos, Devecseri, and Somlyo—came to grips with its own past, and the new poems, like a fresh breeze, blew away the stagnant, fetid air that had for so long poisoned the literary atmosphere. *Irodalmi Ujsag*, the colorless and odorless literary bulletin edited on the Soviet pattern, turned suddenly into an alive and exciting publication. It was filled with excellent writings which reflected reality in truthful terms. Only now did it become evident that the writers, who had voluntarily accepted the senseless discipline of socialist realism, had hitherto lived under the direst intellectual slavery. From behind the rapidly crumbling prison walls where they had, for years, held their talents in check and had written below their own level, the writers emerged, renewed, to throw themselves headlong into the fresh and purifying stream and to swim in it side by side with those non-Communist writers who had for a decade been condemned to silence. It was as if a new Golden Age were dawning.

The storm broke on a warm September day in 1955. Early in the morning Gyorgy Hamos (who had been appointed to replace Miklos Molnar at *Irodalmi Ujsag*) learned that the latest issue of the journal, which was to appear on that day, had been confiscated "on orders from above." Without informing the editor of the paper, the "authorities" had given the order directly to that administrative department of the paper which handled distribution. This was obviously because the "authorities" feared that Hamos would protest violently.

It was very difficult to find an answer to two questions concerning this affair: 1.) What was the reason for the confiscation? and 2.) Who had given the order? As usual, the responsible person could not be found. Party headquarters, being urgently and repeatedly called on the telephone replied that it knew nothing about the confiscation. The Ministry of Culture knew about it, but it had no idea where the order had come from. The fact was that every department, being aware of the situation and of the ugly mood of the writers, attempted to shift responsibility onto another department. Thus, for a while, what lay behind this measure—a measure rather unusual in a People's Democracy, for it had never before been necessary to confiscate a newspaper since the newspapers never printed anything that would have called for such a measure—remained a secret. Then, since the "orders from above" prescribed that, after deleting any "critical" parts, the paper should be reprinted and distributed, it turned out that the confiscation had been caused by two rather insignificant poems. One of these poems had been written by Lajos Konya. It had contained one line about the regrouping of allotments—a regrouping in which the peasants had been given plots of land much inferior to those which had been taken from them and which had been incorporated into a cooperative. The other poem was a six-line limerick about the writer-minister Jozsef Darvas. Its gist: You have preached enough about literature. / You have instructed us how to write. / Now the time has come / for you to show / what you can do. / *Hic Rhodus. Hic salta!*

After that it was easy to find the man responsible for the confiscation order. He was an overzealous young Party creation named Gyorgy Non, who was Deputy Minister of Culture.

What had happened was that Comrade Non had read an issue of the paper early in the morning at his office and had been deeply shocked at the temerity with which an insignificant writer had criticized the all-powerful minister. Since Jozsef Darvas was on vacation, Non had telephoned Party headquarters, where everybody was on vacation except Lajos Acs, who was one of the pillars of the Political Committee and who, when informed by Non about the unprecedented attack in *Irodalmi Ujsag,* had given his blessing to the confiscation.

Gyorgy Non was enthroned, happy and triumphant, in his velvet chair. He was a tall, good-looking young man with a deep voice and silver streaks in his dark hair. He was one of the most reliable and most loyal of Rakosi's officials, and like many other politicians, he had acted as the wise father's secretary for a time. This one-time youth leader and member of the underground Communist Party and alternate member of the Central Committee, was the personification of Party loyalty and Party discipline. He was as persevering as a camel, as changeable as a chameleon and, to keep pace with the "flexibly changing" Party line, as agile as a kangaroo. He was never surprised when, from one day to the next, his bosses and teachers changed opinions which had been stated with such conviction on the previous day, for he, too, shared the conviction of the ancestor of dialectics, Heraclitus— or, at least, he would have shared it had he ever heard about the great G····². philosopher.

The most basic trait of Non's character lay in his inability to think or to waver or to doubt. He could only believe, and the source of his faith was his unequalled stupidity. He was by far the stupidest of all the stupid officials selected by the Communist Party for Hungarian public life, and, thus, it was only natural that he should have been appointed Deputy Minister of Culture. To give him his due, he had protested a little against this appointment. But when Rakosi had reassured him that the Party would help him overcome any initial difficulties, he had set to work without delay to make himself worthy of the task entrusted to him. On his first day in office, he had summoned the official in charge of literature to his private office and had, with determined kindness, ordered him to get together a list of the books with which he, the new chief of literature and the arts, must become acquainted. He had immediately added, however, that it did not make much difference what the official "prescribed" for him, since, to tell the truth, he had never in his life read a Hungarian literary work.

His face shining with innocent idiocy, he had walked the corridors of the Ministry of Culture as the very embodiment of smugness. The bursts of laughter which constantly accompanied his public speeches did not disturb him in the least.* Comrade Non was untouched by "petty-bourgeois" public opinion. He was calm and self-assured for he was supported in whatever he did by the strong hand of his master, Matyas Rakosi.† Thus, he had no qualms about ordering the confiscation of *Irodalmi Ujsag*. He also had no idea of the storm he was unleashing and of its unpredictable consequences. He sat, calm and stiff, in his office while telephones rang and while violent protests were voiced and while Hungarian literary life resembled a disturbed ant hill. It did not even occur to him that the confiscation had been entirely senseless, nor that the two incriminating poems would have gone unnoticed (for, many much more passionately critical writings had already been published) and that, by his stupid and superfluous measure, he himself had called attention to these very poems and had given them added importance. He felt that he had protected the Party's interests and he was duly proud of himself.

Indignation rose from hour to hour. The issue at stake was no longer Non's stupid measure. This mistake—it appeared— now furnished the writers with an excellent opportunity to launch

---

* At a conference on fine arts, Comrade Non said, word for word, the following: "I know that you despise me, but even I am not idiotic enough not to know how great a painter Torricelli was!" He probably meant Botticelli, but who knows?

† Once Non summoned Gabor Devecseri, the best Hungarian translator of Catullus, Horace, and Homer to his office. Devecseri arrived at 3 p.m., as he had been requested to do, but the secretary told him that Comrade Non was in conference. Devecseri waited. He waited fifteen minutes— then thirty, then forty-five minutes. Finally, having grown tired of waiting, he said to the secretary: "Look, tell Comrade Non that I was here and that I waited for him, but that I could wait no longer. My message to him is that I shall still be a Hungarian poet when he will be nothing but a Latin negative particle."

a frontal attack against Rakosi's cultural policies and, through them, against the entire Rakosi line. At a quickly convened conference, the Writers' Association condemned the confiscation. The mood of rebellion was so strong that even the most sectarian out-and-out Stalinist (and generally-hated old Muscovite), Sandor Gergely, began to waver. For, even he disapproved of the confiscation.

Party headquarters naturally supported its favorite child. The officials there probably knew that Non had made a grave mistake, but they could not tolerate—in this very critical situation—the possibility that the writers could be right in *anything*. Comrade Non symbolized the Party, and thus the Party could not retreat before the renegade writers. So, while the writers were determinedly and uncompromisingly demanding that Non be made to face the consequences of his action, the Party leaders were not only defending their fair-haired boy. They were, instead, dismissing Gyorgy Hamos, an editor of *Irodalmi Ujsag,* for having published—so they said—anti-Party writings.

This dismissal only added fuel to the fire of the writers' indignation. The Communist faction of the presidium of the Writers' Association demanded that Erzsebet Andics, supreme commander of literature at Party headquarters, immediately call a conference. But that lady took fright. In agreement with the Party leadership, she put off the conference from day to day, then from week to week.

When, after four weeks, it became evident that Comrade Andics' promises were worthless and that she was only playing for time, the Communist faction of the presidium of the Writers' Association decided to act. As a protest, every Communist member of the presidium resigned from office and so informed the Chairman of the Writers' Association, Peter Veres, in writing.*

----

* The six Communist members of the presidium now resigning were: Tibor Dery, Lajos Konya, Zoltan Zelk, Laszlo Benjamin, Peter Kuczka, and Tamas Aczel. Three members of the newly-appointed secretariat also resigned. These were Sandor Erdei (also a member of the presidium), Ferenc Karinthy, and Endre Veszi.

This was an entirely new phenomenon in the Party. It was a well-known fact that, in this Party, one could not resign. Everybody was appointed by the Party, and, consequently, nobody could be dismissed except by the Party. The bold step taken by these nine writers aroused the entire country, and the Party almost choked with fury, for public protest was unheard of and utterly intolerable. Then, the Party began to exert pressure. It brought compulsion, threats, and persuasion to bear on the situation. But nothing helped. The writers declared that they would revoke their resignation, but that they would do so only after certain conditions had been fulfilled. The conditions: 1.) the punishment of Comrade Non; 2.) an official declaration condemning the confiscation of *Irodalmi Ujsag*; and 3.) an immediate and open discussion of all the pressing problems. The wrangling went on for several weeks. Rakosi summoned the writers before the Political Committee and promised to fulfill all their demands if they would first revoke their resignations. But the writers told Lajos Tamasi, the Party secretary of the Writers' Association who was wavering desperately, that they would revoke their resignations only if their conversation with Rakosi had the desired results. There could, they said, be no question of revocation beforehand.

This was too much for Rakosi: the Political Committee went into session without the resigning members of the presidium, and Rakosi appointed other members from among his followers. Yet, the situation remained unchanged, and the tension was almost unbearable, for everyone—Party leaders as well as writers—knew that the matter was not ended, and everyone was preparing for the next act of the drama. Half-forgotten now were such minor issues as Gyorgy Non and the confiscation of *Irodalmi Ujsag*. What was at stake was the throwing off of Party fetters—i.e., the freedom of literature.

At this stage, a young and well-known journalist who was known for his "rightist" political ideas and for his close connection with the rebellious writers paid a visit to the old, non-Party peasant writer and Chairman of the Writers' Association, Peter

Veres. The journalist did not want simply to talk about the situation. In reality, he wanted to learn what the silent, cunning old peasant, smiling calmly under his mustache, thought about the conflict and what he thought about the passionate change of face of the young Communist writers. Playing innocent, he asked the old man:

"Tell me, Uncle Peter, for heaven's sake, why can't these writers be brought to their senses?"

The old peasant waited for a while, his attentive eyes on the journalist's face. He knew what he knew, and that was not a little. All he said, however, was:

"Because, son, they don't want to be duped again."

The Memorandum

Early in November, the Communist Party organization of the Hungarian Writers' Association held a membership meeting.

Before the agenda, a greying man of about fifty with protruding eyes and with several broken teeth, rose and asked permission to speak. Erzsebet Andics and Marton Horvath, both presiding over the meeting behind a table covered in red cloth, raised their brows. The man wanted to speak before the agenda? Why? But finally Zoltan Zelk, twice a Kossuth Prize poet, was given permission.

In a voice husky with emotion, yet very articulate and clear, Zelk read the following text to the meeting:

MEMORANDUM

Together with all members of the Communist Party, we cultural workers, writers, artists, and journalists received with pleasure the resolutions of the June, 1953, session of the Central Committee and of the Third Congress which, once and for all, ban from the political-ideological work of our Party those anti-democratic methods of violence, administrative interference, and despotism that demoralize sincere Communist Party life. The March resolution of the Central

Committee supported and confirmed those parts of the June, 1953, and Congressional resolutions dealing with this question.

We notice, however, with deep anxiety that certain organs and officials of the Party apply more and more frequently the harmful and forceful methods repeatedly condemned by the Central Committee and by the Congress. This practice violates the valid resolutions of our Party and sharply contradicts the true and broad-minded cultural policy, if one takes into consideration the specific features of the enlightened cultural work which is carried on in the Soviet Union.

Although we are certain that the Central Committee knows about these instances of forceful interference, it may not be superfluous to point out a few particularly striking examples:

1.) In the past six months, two responsible editors of *Irodalmi Ujsag* have been removed from their jobs.

2.) The publication of Lajos Konya's *Notes*, as well as the publication of volumes of poetry by Laszlo Benjamin and Laszlo Nagy has been prevented.

3.) Attempts have been made to introduce preliminary censorship in the case of certain writers.

4.) The autonomy of the Writers' Association has been constantly infringed upon and ignored.

5.) All this has been crowned by the recent confiscation of *Irodalmi Ujsag*, and it is certain that nothing like this— the confiscation of a paper edited in a Communist spirit by Communists—has ever occurred in a People's Democracy.

To this series of events belongs the case of *The Tragedy of Man*—a case which has severely harmed our Party. To it also belong the banning from the stage of the National Theater of Laszlo Nemeth's *Galileo* and the unworthy wrangling about the performance of *The Miraculous Mandarin*, etc. Not only the actors but also the Communist composers consider the despotic, anti-democratic methods of our cultural leadership more and more unbearable.

In the last ten days, a considerable number of the best-known Communist journalists have been removed from the editorial offices of *Szabad Nep*. Other Communist journalists have been excluded from the press, expelled from the Party, or given other severe punishment for having expressed their opinions in a way loyal to the Party. A member of the editorial board of *Szabad Nep* was removed from that board because of a speech made at the Communist activists' meeting at the Writers' Association.

The Central Committee certainly knows that if there is a field where anti-democratic administrative measures and the suppression of all criticism are particularly harmful, that field is the field of cultural enlightenment. We, too, see clearly that unhealthy phenomena and incorrect, anti-Marxist views are raising their heads in our cultural life. But the methods used prior to June, 1953, are by no means suited to combat these phenomena. These methods can only increase and deepen the difficulties. It is our opinion that, in a People's Democracy, the only basis for eliminating difficulties and wrong opinions, for stimulating creative cultural work, and for producing a sincere and effective enlightenment serving the cause of the building of socialism, is a free and sincere and healthy and democratic atmosphere imbued with the spirit of popular rule. The evolution of such an atmosphere has been made impossible by aggressive and bureaucratic interference. It is our firm conviction that if the Central Committee does not put a stop to these harmful practices, not only will the progress of our cultural life be prevented, but also those new, fresh shoots which owe their lives to the creative force of our people since the liberation will perish.

Therefore, we take the liberty of requesting the Central Committee to enforce energetically the resolutions of the Central Committee and of the Congress against those department officials who are distorting the cultural policy of the Party and who are applying anti-democratic methods which cripple our cultural life and which destroy the prestige and the influence of our Party. We request the Central Committee to correct the wrong administrative measures hitherto taken and to ensure to the workers for culture and to the press an atmosphere of pure and sincere Party life—and to ensure that which is the equivalent: an opportunity for undisturbed creative work serving the people and the cause of socialism.

For a second, the listeners thought that Zelk was stating his own personal opinions—*in pluralis majestatis*. But this was only for a second. For, after a brief pause, the poet began to read names—the names (and the positions) of those who had participated in this statement.

This letter to the Central Committee of the Hungarian Workers' Party—which became known as the "Memorandum"—was signed by the following:

Tibor Dery, novelist and Kossuth Prize-winner.
Gyula Hay, playwright and Kossuth Prize-winner.
Laszlo Benjamin, poet and twice Kossuth Prize-winner.
Zoltan Zelk, poet and twice Kossuth Prize-winner.
Lajos Konya, poet and twice Kossuth Prize-winner.
Gabor Devecseri, poet and Kossuth Prize-winner.
Peter Kuczka, poet and Kossuth Prize-winner.
Istvan Simon, poet, Kossuth Prize-winner, and chief editor of *Uj Hang* ("New Voice").
Ferenc Juhasz, poet and Kossuth Prize-winner.
Ferenc Karinthy, author and Kossuth Prize-winner.
Imre Sarkadi, writer and Kossuth Prize-winner.
Gyorgy Hamos, writer and Kossuth Prize-winner.
Tamas Aczel, writer and Kossuth and Stalin Prize-winner.
Tibor Meray, journalist, writer, and Kossuth Prize-winner.
Tamas Major, actor, twice Kossuth Prize-winner, Outstanding Artist of the People's Democracy, and Director of the National Theater.
Agi Meszaros, actress, twice Kossuth Prize-winner, Outstanding Artist of the People's Democracy, and member of the National Theater.
Ferenc Bessenyei, actor, Kossuth Prize-winner, and member of the National Theater.
Magda Olthy, actress, Kossuth Prize-winner, and member of the National Theater.

Zoltan Varkonyi, stage manager, twice Kossuth Prize-winner, and member of the National Theater.

Istvan Horvai, stage manager, Kossuth Prize-winner, and Director of the Madach Theater.

Miklos Gabor, actor, Kossuth Prize-winner, and member of the National Theater.

Zoltan Fabri, film director and twice Kossuth Prize-winner.

Marton Keleti, film director, three times Kossuth Prize-winner, and a Worthy Artist of the People's Democracy.

Felix Mariassy, film director and Kossuth Prize-winner.

Endre Szervanszky, composer and Kossuth Prize-winner.

Andras Mihaly, composer and Kossuth Prize-winner.

Istvan Antal, pianist and Kossuth Prize-winner.

Zoltan Vasarhelyi, conductor and Kossuth Prize-winner.

Istvan Orkeny, writer.

Gyorgy Somlyo, poet.

Sandor Erdei, First Secretary of the Hungarian Writers' Association.

Lajos Tamasi, poet and Secretary of the Writers' Association's Party organization.

Endre Enczi, writer and editor of *Irodalmi Ujsag*.

Tibor Tardos, writer.

Lehel Szeberenyi, writer.

Endre Veszi, writer.

Gyula Sipos, poet.

Miklos Gyarfas, chief editor of the periodical *Theatre and Film*.

Emil Kolozsvari Grandpierre, writer.

Boris Palotai, writer.

Miklos Molnar, critic and editor.

Peter Nagy, literary historian and editor of the Belles Lettres Publishing House.

Laszlo Nagy, poet.

Sandor Lukacsy, literary historian and critic.

Sandor Csoori, poet.

Sarolta Lanyi, poet.

Geza Kepes, poet.

Sandor Haraszti, journalist.

Geza Losonczy, journalist.

Miklos Vasarhelyi, journalist.

Sandor Novobaczky, journalist.

Imre Demeter, journalist.

Gyorgy Gal, journalist.

Szilard Ujhelyi, journalist and head of the film department
of the Ministry of Culture.

Endre Marton, stage manager and member of the National
Theater.

Eva Ruttkay, actress and member of the Army Theater.

Peter Bacso, film script writer.

Geza Partos, stage manager and Director of the State Village
Theater.

Judit Mariassy, journalist.

Zoltan Zelk finished reading, and a storm of applause broke
forth. Not only the text of the Memorandum, but also the names
of the signers, showed beyond a doubt that here was an event of
national significance. The Memorandum was signed by the elite
of Hungarian Communist intellectual life, by the favorites of the
regime, by the "stars" whose pictures were constantly in the
papers and whose appearance was a great event in the social life
of the country. This list of names expressed the determination of
the Communist writers and artists to fight against the cultural
policies of the Party and the discontent of these writers and artists
with the existing situation.

Because of its careful and circumspect wording, the Memorandum was rather a mild document. But this did not detract
from its strength and its boldness. In fact, its moderation and
respectfulness in wording was perhaps more disagreeable and
annoying to the Rakosi clique than was its content. It was a
Communist text—and, therefore, it was all the more damaging
to Party leadership. This Memorandum, which referred to the
Soviet example and to the March resolution condemning Imre
Nagy, could in no way be branded either as a hostile document
or as the work of the enemy. In protesting against the confiscation of books and of newspapers and against the dismissals and
the persecutions, the document stressed the fact that, under such

conditions, even *Communist* writers and journalists and artists found it difficult to work.

However—and this increased the importance of the document —the signers defended not only the rights and interests of the Communist group. They also demanded the right of non-Communists to speak and to publish, too. The leading clique had banned not only the plays of the Communist playwright Gyula Hay, but also those of Laszlo Nemeth, and thus, willy-nilly, Rakosi and his followers had strengthened the united national front which had just then begun to evolve. The fact that the Communists fought for the non-Communists and for those who had been silenced for years was due not only to a sense of justice regained. It was also due to a desire to make good their own past mistakes. The writers and artists who had themselves enjoyed privileges from the Party now felt conscience-stricken and guilt-ridden about their innocently imprisoned comrades and about their non-Communist colleagues who had eked out a meager existence while being excluded from the cultural life of the country. Among these non-Communists were national writers and poets who were in many cases more gifted and more significant than were those who had received official recognition. If this literature, driven underground by the regime, had not perished, it had not been due to the Kossuth Prize-winners. It had been due to a few good friends and to a few honest bureaucrats who had given these men jobs as rewrite men and as translators.

A distinguished group of writers had been thus deprived of their right to publish their works. The group had included the greatest poet-philosopher of the nation, Lorinc Szabo. It had also included Sandor Weoreos, a gifted young poet in whose hands the Hungarian language attained the perfection and beauty of music. And it had included such masters of the novel as Aron Tamasi and Janos Kodolanyi, as well as one of the most brilliant minds of Hungarian literature, the novelist, playwright, and essayist Laszlo Nemeth. It could not be denied that some of these men had committed mistakes in the past. Some of them—though they had not been fascists, as the Rakosi clique had labelled them

—had indeed had certain rightist leanings before and during World War II. Yet, this had not been the real reason for muzzling them, for others who had been much more involved in right-wing politics had been received with open arms by the regime because of their willingness to submit to the Party's autocracy and to serve it in their works. These writers had been condemned to silence only because they opposed Party dictatorship, not so much in the political as in the literary field, and because they had declined to subordinate their art to the requirements of Zhdanovism. They had preferred to follow the dictates of their heart and to write for themselves or for a few good friends instead of submitting to Revai's dictates.

The Communist writers now felt an admiration mingled with envy for these writers who had remained unsullied while they themselves had done so much to be ashamed of. To fight for Lorinc Szabo's or Laszlo Nemeth's right to publish was, for the rebellious Communist writers, a moral obligation. It was, in effect, a "self-criticism which manifested itself in deeds," and thus it was a real pleasure.

Of great importance in the Memorandum was that paragraph which protested against the banning from the stage of the greatest work of Hungarian dramatic literature, Imre Madach's *The Tragedy of Man*. For years the cultural policy of the regime had banned the performance of this nineteenth-century masterpiece which was known as "the Hungarian *Faust*" because it was alleged to be pessimistic in its conclusions. During Imre Nagy's premiership, it had been revived and performed before crowded houses at the leading theater of the country, the National Theater. But after Imre Nagy's dismissal, Rakosi had again banned it,*

---

* For ten years, the Party had demanded that literature and art should be politically conscious. Now that its orders had been obeyed, it discerned between the lines its own death sentence: Gyula Hay's play, *Justice for Gaspar Varro*, portrayed the fate of the innocently imprisoned; Laszlo Nemeth's drama *Galileo* concerned itself with the burning problems of the conflicts between justice and power and between dogma and truth. The latter play raised the question (and it answered it by Galileo's example) as to who furthers human progress more—a man who blindly accepts dogma or a man who battles for truth. The scene in the play in for it contained a series of truths that the bald little dictator felt to be insulting both to himself personally and to the system.

The fact that the Memorandum demanded the performance of *The Tragedy of Man* made it clear that the rebellious Communist writers were representatives of a national culture and of national traditions in contrast to the narrow-minded and anti-national clique who ruled the country and the Party.

Of similar significance was the fact that the signers of the Memorandum demanded the revival of Bela Bartok's *chef d'oeuvre, The Miraculous Mandarin.* This modern ballet had by then been performed on all the important European and American stages and had brought fame to its creator as well as to the Hungarian people. Only the Budapest opera house was forbidden to put it on. The reason: this work of Bartok's was branded as "formalist" and "decadent," since it contradicted all of Zhdanov's theses on music. During the first premiership of Imre Nagy, the ballet chorus of the opera house had begun rehearsals of *The Miraculous Mandarin*, but the Stalinists had forbidden its performance when they returned to power.

This paragraph of the Memorandum broadened its scope: through it, the writers became spokesmen not only for literature but for all the arts, and this fact was manifested in the signatures to the Memorandum. The most progressive Communists in the other branches of the fine arts—in the theater, in music, and in

---

which Galileo was tortured called to mind the torture chambers of the prisons of the People's Democracy. Concerning the former play, it was not surprising that, when in the first scene of *The Tragedy of Man,* Lucifer attacked the Lord (as the spirit of negation of the omniscient) and the Lord replied, *"I am to be revered, not criticized,"* a storm of applause broke loose in the audience, for this reply revealed the very character of the regime. It was typical that, after *The Tragedy of Man* had again been banned by Rakosi, an article appeared in *Pravda* which was written by the paper's Budapest correspondent, a certain Krushinski, who reported that the Budapest workers had approved of the ban because they considered the play damaging to them. The truth was that, while the drama was still playing, the Budapest industrial plants had ordered 100 to 500 tickets for every performance. But, of course, *Pravda* always knew better than did the workers themselves what they wanted.

film—had also been persuaded to sign the Memorandum, and, by rallying around the writers, they lent not only greater weight but also greater breadth to the resistance movement.

The real significance of the Memorandum lay not so much in its text as in the very fact of its existence. Its content was only a protest against the anomalies of cultural life and against the sectarian cultural policies of the Party. Yet everyone, the signers as well as all others, knew that much more was at stake. They knew that the condemnation of the entire Party line and of the present leadership of the country was implicit in the writing of the Memorandum. The text was not important. It was the deed that counted. The very gesture, entirely unprecedented in Communist Party practice, was an open challenge to the clique dominating the country and the Party. It was, in fact, a slap in their faces.

The blow was all the more resounding since it fell during a breathless silence which, at that time, reigned over the entire country. In those days, not a word, not even a breath of protest was heard against the policies of the Rakosi clique, once it had returned to power. The Party organizations carried out orders from above without argument, and the people had bitterly resigned themselves to the fact that Imre Nagy's program was irrevocably defeated and that the regime was again revealing its true character. There was nothing surprising, nothing extraordinary in this. It was the program that Imre Nagy had tried to impose that had been surprising and extraordinary. People went about their work silently, convinced that, under this system, anyone who tried to create something different, something better, was doomed to failure.

In this atmosphere of oppression and hopelessness, the Memorandum had exploded like a bomb.

Preparations had had to be made in the shortest possible time in order that the clique in power should not have got wind of them and have thus been able to prevent the action. The first plan had been that the writers and artists and representatives of Hungarian culture should address a document to the Government of the Soviet Union and to the United Nations which would reflect a broad national unity. This plan had, however, soon been discarded, for Imre Nagy and his closest collaborators had violently protested against giving the affair international publicity. They had insisted that it should remain not even a national, but an internal Party affair; and thus it had been decided that the Memorandum would be signed exclusively by Party members and that it would be addressed to the Party's Central Committee.

It had taken approximately a week before the writers, after numerous meetings and discussions, had drawn up a text acceptable to the majority—a text mild in tone, yet incorporating all the essential points. It had been very important that the Memorandum be short and exact and to the point. Such a document would be difficult for the Rakosi clique to attack.

Very soon there had been a long column of signatures under the one-and-a-half-page text. Its authors had got in touch with their friends and their close acquaintances. Telephones had rung. Appointments had been made. Excited conversations had taken place in little cafes, because it was important that nothing suspicious should occur in the chief haunt of Hungarian literary and art life, the Cafe Hungaria, where, as all of them knew, the majority of the waiters were in the service of the AVO.

The typewritten document had become dirty and wrinkled.

Then it had been signed by Tamas Major, the Kossuth Prize-winning Director of the National Theater, and by the leading actors and stage managers of the theater. Major's signature had proved a very important one, since it carried a great deal of influence among other people who would probably have refused, but who, seeing the name of the highly respected Communist artist, had resisted no longer.

There had been those who, when they had heard about the Memorandum, had come forward voluntarily, not wanting to be left out.

There had been those who had refused to sign because the Memorandum was against Party discipline, and there had been those who had admitted frankly that they were afraid of the consequences of signing—consequences that had indeed been un-predictable. Among those who had refused was Gyorgy Lukacs, not because he did not agree with the text, but because his long career within the Party had taught him to be careful.

The Party leadership had remained passive. Nobody had known whether or not news of the Memorandum had reached that leadership, or whether its members were waiting for develop-ments or were preparing to strike a blow at the critical moment.

The Memorandum had then been signed by Lajos Tamasi, the wavering, uncertain Party secretary of the Writers' Association. He could not refuse, since the names under the document placed him under the moral obligation to join.

Immediately after his name came the signature of Endre Enczi, the most recently appointed editor of *Irodalmi Ujsag*. He had been appointed six months after the last editor had been appointed, and it was expected of him that, after the "rightist deviationism" of his predecessors, he would restore the official Party line. He had signed the Memorandum on the very day of his appointment.

By that time, there had been fifty-nine names on the docu-ment, and the collecting of signatures had been going on for almost a week. Then the writers had not quite known what to do. Should they continue to collect signatures? After all, almost everyone who played an important role in Party and/or in artistic life had already joined the movement. It was decided that fifty-nine names were sufficient and that the Memorandum should be forwarded that same day to Party headquarters.

The day had been November 2, 1955.

There was something intoxicatingly exciting, terribly danger-ous, and triumphantly satisfactory in this action. The writers felt that they had at last done something. Their eyes shone when the Memorandum was mentioned.

But they had no illusions.

They realized that the changes discernible in the Soviet Union would reach their small country very slowly—if ever. True, dur-ing the last year in the Soviet Union, there had been no execu-tions and no arrests of innocent men, but that state of affairs might change from one minute to the next, and nobody knew how long the period of the "thaw" would last, nor when the Soviet Union would decide to return to the old line. In Hungary, as a matter of fact, everything had remained unchanged: at the helm stood the same men who had once hanged and then forgiven the innocents whom they had branded as criminals. Imre Nagy was no longer at the helm to protect the writers, and the Twentieth Congress had not yet taken place.

At that moment, the writers had been, in fact, alone.

Those who investigate the history of the Hungarian Revolution usually describe and analyze the events of the spring and the summer of 1956. True, that spring and that summer were like a succession of fiestas, complete with fireworks and with sensational events and heroic struggles. But the autumn and the winter of 1955, with their quasi-hopeless efforts and churning passions and feats of real courage, had already inflicted deep wounds upon the clay-footed giant.

This was the heroic age of the Hungarian writers' resistance movement.

The men who had at last broken out of the Party corral had rediscovered not only their souls and their real character, but also the world which, for so many years, they had observed through dark and distorting glasses. Their rediscovery was a pure joy, a source of constant happiness. At last, they could breathe freely and swim in the sweet sea of freedom.

They were, of course, afraid. But being afraid was natural and human, and, at last, they could be afraid because of something they themselves had done and not because of something that others had done behind their backs. Such a fear was entirely different from the unacknowledged anxiety and terror of the past. It was entirely different from the painful and exhausting concentration to make sure that every word they pronounced, that every action they undertook should run parallel with the Party line—a fear that had once marred every day of their lives and that had now lifted and disappeared like fog.

Perhaps there is no such thing as "freedom from fear," for

one is always afraid of something. But if there is a difference among degrees of heroism (as exemplified by the different medals for bravery), then there are also differences among the various degrees and shades of fear. And the writers found that the fear of arrest for deeds *undertaken consciously* was much superior to the watching with blind faith and adoration while Rakosi was having others arrested—and to the trembling at the scolding telephone calls of the great leader.

In those days, more and more people approached the writers on the buses and in cafes and on the streets, pressing their hands and congratulating them on their courage, and this sincere and increasing affection was very pleasant. But the writers knew that they were far from being such great heroes. They were simply nauseated by the pleasures and the fears of the past, and they were yearning for new pleasures and, yes, for new fears.

And, stronger than any other feeling, the writers did not want to be dishonorable. This was a feeling most clearly and strikingly expressed by the poet Zoltan Zelk:

> I am not worthy of your praise.
> Believe me, friend, it burns me deeply
> When you praise me for my courage.
>
> I live like a man and not like a tiger.
> My tortured heart houses only fears.
> I am afraid, believe me!
>
> I am a man and live like a man.
> How could I be heroic?
> But I fear more to lose my honor,
> More, I tell you, than I fear death!

After the pressure of a self-imposed censorship the writers now rediscovered their talent—a talent that had almost been smothered in the grip of socialist realism. There was no more careful measuring of words. There was no more suppression of sentiments. There was no more simulated delight nor forced en-

thusiasm, the artificiality of which they had often felt. Suddenly
they had become receptive to love and to loneliness, to sorrow
and to happiness, and they were torn by feelings as a tree by a
storm. A deep gratitude rose in them because these grey and lying
years had not been able to kill the man nor the poet within them
and because they could still—or, rather, once more—respond to
the blue skies and to the fresh fields. They delighted with a not
hitherto experienced intensity in a glass of wine, a kiss, a chat
with a friend. The idols and taboos had fallen to dust in their
souls as well as in the world outside, and no other idols, no other
taboos took their places. They experienced chaotic—sometimes
accusing, sometimes conciliatory but always human, always independent—thoughts which, contrary to the confining Marxist-
Leninist system of thought that knew the answer to every question, gave no universal and final answer. These thoughts came
and went, illuminating a corner of life, or of society, or of the
human heart, but leaving the rest in darkness. The fact was that
these thoughts were more human and deeper and richer than had
been their previous thought patterns.

This is how the writers, though already adults, became adults
once more. They felt that only now had they really become human
beings.

For three days after the Memorandum was read before the
plenary meeting of the Party organization of the Writers' Association, these Communist writers attacked with growing passion
the ideology that had kept them in its power and under its spell
for so many years.

In 1945, the Hungarian Writers' Association had been founded
on the Soviet pattern at Communist initiative, in order to make
it, like the other mass organizations, a "transmission belt" between the Party and the writers—a "transmission belt" by which
the central engine might give momentum to and manipulate the
delicate machinery of literature according to its own interests.
And the task of the Writers' Association's Party organization had
been to receive and to "popularize among the masses" (i.e., in

this case the non-Party writers) the instructions and intentions of the Party.

And now the "transmission belt" had turned into an independent engine that moved or stopped moving without requesting permission. The Writers' Association, with its five hundred members (three hundred of whom were Party members) had become an independent engine functioning parallel with Party headquarters and with the "council of the gods." But it was going parallel in the opposite direction. It was the only honest and progressive and Hungarian engine visible in the whole of Hungary.

One after the other, the best-known Communist writers rose at the meeting of the Association at which the Memorandum had been read and condemned the cultural policies of the Party in biting words. They proved that literature was constrained under the present conditions, because it was not free to reflect the truth. They attacked those literary policies of the last ten years which, as Tibor Dery expressed it, "made a clown out of a writer, placing a jester's cap on his head and ordering him to dance to the tunes whistled by uncultured and amateurish Party clerks."

The most effective feature of the meeting was that there was always a spirited response ready for the Central Committee members' really pathetic attempts at argument. These committee members represented the Party at the meeting.

"What is the miracle that you all expect from the performance of *The Miraculous Mandarin?*" Marton Horvath asked, complainingly.

The reply was:

"The miracle of seeing the masterwork of the greatest Hungarian composer on the *Hungarian* stage!"

Marton Horvath tried again. He said:

"Tibor Dery's present attitude is not in the least surprising. After all, he was the Hungarian translator of André Gide's anti-Soviet book."

The writers replied:

"When we agreed with everything you said and did, nobody

ever brought up André Gide's book, nor its Hungarian translation. Now, when we no longer agree with you, and when we express our own opinion, you continue to refer to 'mistakes' of the past. These are not literary methods. They are police methods."

After that, it was the writers who asked the questions.

"We were informed," said one of the writers, "that Gyorgy Non, that uneducated, narrow-minded Party clerk and member of the Central Committee, declared at a public meeting that the writers are in the service of a foreign power. Non added that the writers' Bible was a pamphlet by Edward Kardelj.* Does the Party consider it permissible that Communist writers should be accused of espionage because they read the writings of the leader of a friendly country? How long does the Central Committee intend to maintain an antagonistic attitude toward Yugoslavia, when Comrade Khrushchev has declared that it is a socialist country?"

Beside herself with rage, Erzsebet Andics jumped from her chair.

"And you are spreading this nonsense around? You are discussing it publicly?" she cried.

The writers answered calmly:

You see, Comrade Andics, they said, herein lies the trouble. You do not object to Comrade Non talking nonsense, but you object to our discussion of his idiocy. The trouble is not that Non confiscated *Irodalmi Ujsag*. The trouble is that we protested against it. Do you call that justice? Why does the Party favor Gyorgy Non over the writers? How many kinds of justice are there, and where is the proof that, in this case, the Party is right? It was the opinion of the writers, said the writers now, that the Party was once again mistaken and that it would, sooner or later, have to admit its mistake.

Toward the end of the third day, the presidium of the Party

---

* The pamphlet in question was a transcript of a speech delivered by Kardelj at the Oslo Congress of the Social Democratic Party and published under the title of *Some Problems of Yugoslav Socialism.*

meeting suspended the actual meeting. Andics, Zoltan Vas, Marton Horvath, and Lajos Tamasi retired to the "Party office" to draw up a draft of a resolution. After a long interval, they returned with a draft resolution condemning the Memorandum, condemning the stubborn "rightist deviationism" of the writers, condemning the breach of Party discipline, and condemning the factionalism which had been manifested in the collection of signatures.

The draft resolution was submitted to the membership.

By an overwhelming majority, the membership rejected it.

The majority of the Communist writers voted for the Memorandum, for truth, and for loud protests—against confiscations and against the Party leadership.

After the voting, Zoltan Vas, a member of the Central Committee and an old Muscovite who had spent sixteen years in the Horthy regime's prisons (and who, in his secret heart, as was clear from his private conversations, was strongly attracted to the Imre Nagy line), jumped up. He was excited and frightened.

"But this is impossible, comrades," he cried. "Impossible! You don't know what you are doing! Vote again!"

The membership, however, knew very well what they were doing.

"We have already voted," they replied, "and once is enough."

Nothing like this had ever before happened. The majority of the Communist writers had turned against the official Party line in an open vote. Now a Party organization existed, a *Communist* Party organization, where the will of the Party, where the official Party line—had been defeated.

This was no longer an ordinary Party meeting with its formalities and its polite smiles and its obligatory nods. It was the new parliament of the people which was sitting here, debating and arguing with conviction and passion. The writers knew as well as did the Party officials that everything that was said here expressed the thoughts and feelings and complaints of those who had not as yet raised their voices.

"I am accused of being bitter," Laszlo Benjamin said. "And

they are right. I am bitter. But behind my bitterness lies the bitterness of the peasants, who have been robbed of their grain and deprived of their bread for years. Behind my bitterness lies the bitterness of those workers who subsist with their large families on 600 or 800 *forints* a month. Behind my bitterness is the bitterness of the doctors, the engineers, the scientists, and the artists who know the truth but who are not allowed to express it."

Walking home from the meeting late on that autumn night, the writers felt that something significant, something great had taken place in that narrow room in Gorki Street. Some remembered the night when, after the Dery debate, they had come out into the street with Revai's harangue resounding in their heads.

Then everything that the Party proclaimed and promised had been so clear—and yet, at the same time, so chaotic, so incomprehensible, and so dark.

Today, all their expectations from the Party were dark and threatening—and yet everything was clear and pure. It was worthwhile and rational.

Crucify Them!

Two thousand Communist Party officials do not equal two thousand men. Nor do two thousand Communist Party officials equal four thousand ordinary men. For, not only the mental attitude of the ordinary mortal, but also that of the Party official, changes when he becomes one of the mass. Mass psychology offers a more or less clear explanation of the hysterical, the uncontrollable, the over-emotional, and the uninhibitedly passionate strength that takes possession of the individual when he becomes part of a mass group and thus turns from spectator into participant. At the mass meeting of Communist Party officials in the building of the Free Trade Union of Steel and Ironworkers on December 6, 1955, it became evident to the writers of Hungary that two thousand Party officials were possessed by mass psychology.

Or was the former child of the working class, the barely thirty-two-year-old Bela Biszku, Party secretary of the Thirteenth District, really himself when he rose at this meeting and demanded the writers' blood?* Biszku had for a year and a half fully agreed with everything the writers had said and done. Furthermore, he hated Matyas Rakosi passionately and he was

---

* Biszku, who is today Minister of the Interior, was ordered by the Central Committee to speak at the meeting. He visited Kadar and explained to him that he was unable to obey the order because he was unreservedly on the side of the writers and therefore thought that the best course for him would be to go on a trip or to report sick. Kadar,

the closest friend of Janos Kadar, who had recently been released from prison.

Or was the small, skinny, delicate little female Party secretary from one of the largest Budapest textile factories (where day after day she witnessed the desperate struggle of the working-class women for another slice of bread) really herself when she stepped on the platform and corrected the writers, saying that there was not a word of truth in what they had written about the appalling misery of the workers and that every figure of Party statistics was true?

Or was Bela Illes, who had first-hand knowledge of all the Party's crimes and villainies and falsifications, really himself when he faced that hysterical crowd jumping up and down in their seats and cheering the Party at the top of their voices and working themselves up to a lynching mood, while Illes told them that the writers were lying?

Or was the cowardly and spineless Secretary of the Budapest Party Committee, Istvan Kovacs, really himself? For years, this man had lived in abject terror lest Rakosi, who had sent Kovacs' brother and his best friends either to jail or to the gallows, should "liquidate" him as well. Yet, now, it was Kovacs who shouted to the writers, already anxious about their fate, that the fist of the working class would deal them a mighty blow.†

---

who also agreed with the writers, remained true to his former—and subsequent—self. "True," he told Biszku, "the writers are right. Yet you cannot disobey the Party." After a long argument, he persuaded Biszku to speak at the meeting and, out of "Party discipline," to make one of the most inciting addresses.

† It was an interesting fact that the speakers at the meeting were constantly referring to the Budapest working class as if "it" (an etymological impossibility) were present, and as if the workers themselves were there to punish the writers for their "anarchistic, nihilistic, cynical, petty-bourgeois, revolutionary, and anti-Party factionalism." Anyone who walked past the headquarters of the Trade Union, must have wondered at the prosperity of this "working class," which was obviously richer than the working classes of the Soviet Union and even of the United States. From early afternoon on, a cordon of police diverted traffic from streets close to the building. The 2,000 Party officials (among whom there was not a single manual laborer) arrived in approximately 500 luxurious automobiles which were parked around the building and filled all the side streets. Nobody except the forty invited writers arrived on foot or by bus or by streetcar.

The writers sat in their places, increasingly anxious and nervous and pale. They had never been in America and had never witnessed a lynching, but it could not be very different from this hysterical, mystical, almost animalistic ritual. True, there were no white-clad Ku Klux Klan members here, and there were no burning crosses of tar. But there was something even more frightening, even more hair-raising: the speakers of the meeting, spitting forth accusations and lies and filth at the writers, acted in the name of the supreme cause of the people, the nation, humanity: they acted in the name of socialism and of the Revolution.

The cheerful, laughing, drinking generals and Party secretaries, high-ranking state and Party officials of the reception at the Golden Bull were now *at work*. It was as if they were trying to prove to the boss, who was sitting in the presidium,* that they deserved their salaries. The bald dictator (whom, by then—sarcastically, because of his baldness—everyone called the "shaggy one") could be proud of his army of followers, who were always ready to obey his wishes however contradictory these might be. But it is not surprising that the dictator treated them like mere tools, or like a circus of trained animals. A flick of his eyes was sufficient to drive them into an ecstatic frenzy.

The Party still retained its talent in stage managing and in using symbols, even though it was itself becoming more and more afraid of the disguised or undisguised symbolism of literature. It was, for example, evident that both the Party officials and the

---

* Formalities, as always, were duly respected. The carefully selected board of presidents represented the unity of the Party. In the middle sat Rakosi. To his right and left sat the usual crowd: Stakhanovites, Kossuth Prize-winning blacksmiths, and textile workers mingled with the Party officials and the "loyal" intellectuals who hastened to condemn the writers' attitude. Naturally, it was almost impossible to refuse an invitation to be seated among the "great ones," and those invited, whatever they thought, considered it safer to accept. Nobody paid any attention to the writers, who were deeply wounded that Gyorgy Lukacs sat among the notables. Lukacs could have stayed away, the writers thought, and they were much relieved when he disappeared at intermission time and did not return for the second "act" of the meeting.

anxious writers understood the "shaggy one's" intentions when
he decided to hold this threatening meeting in the very room
where, five years before, Laszlo Rajk and his companions had
been condemned to death. On that day a "blood council,"
headed by Judge Peter Janko,* had been sitting on the platform.
On the spot where, five years ago, the "people's prosecutor,"
Gyula Alapi, had read his terrible indictment against the innocent victims (an indictment which, it was now known, had been
written by Jozsef Revai), Istvan Kovacs was now reading his
accusations against the writers (accusations written, this time, by
Marton Horvath).†

But, contrary to the "legal" and well-organized process at the
Rajk trial, the verdict—and fortunately a less deadly one—was
now distributed among the audience before the reading of the
indictment.

Everyone who entered the room was given a copy of this
verdict.

In December, 1955, the verdict was called a Party resolution
or, an official "Resolution of the Hungarian Workers' Party's
Central Committee Concerning the Rightist Phenomena Which
Had Manifested Themselves in Hungarian Literary Life."

---

* Janko became the only man at the Rajk trial to face the consequences
of his deeds: In the summer of 1956, after Rajk's full rehabilitation, he
committed suicide.

† Most of the "workers' " speeches had been organized in the same way.
One of the most characteristic—and most enthusiastically applauded—
addresses was delivered by Lajos Balogh, the Party secretary of the
Georghiu-Dej Shipyards and a former shipyard worker and one of the
stupid, narrow-minded and incapable Party clerks who had completely
forgotten his origin. Approximately one month after the meeting, a few
writers, among them those Balogh had so violently attacked, paid a visit
to the shipyard and talked to Balogh. It turned out that he had never in
his life heard anything about the Memorandum he had so passionately
denounced, had never read one word by the writers he condemned, and,
finally, that his address had been written by one of the staff members of
Szabad Nep. When the writers asked him why he had condemned things
he was ignorant of, he shrugged his shoulders and replied: "Well, if the
Party says so, it must be true!"

In the upper righthand corner of the elegant four-page leaflet appeared some mysterious figures surmounted by a warning. The figures read "H/95/1955," and the warning read "*Confidential!*," stressing the importance of the matter. The leaflet had been printed at the Party's own printing shop, maintained for the very purpose of printing confidential Party resolutions, statistics, circulars, and other internal information, and the secretaries and typists who distributed these copies warned the recipients in a low voice that the document was not to be taken out of the building. After the meeting, it would be collected at the exit. There was no doubt: the writers were holding in their hands the Party's reply to the resignation of the Writers' Association's presidium, to the Memorandum, and to the passionate three-day Party meeting.

As was to be expected, the document was full of falsifications reminiscent of Rakosi's best efforts. It was also very strongly worded in order to indicate that the "shaggy one" had come to the end of his patience and was now determined to crush the writers' rebellion, by violence if necessary.

The introduction was threatening enough:

> Certain writers, among them Party members, have forgotten that literature must serve the people and that only by supporting the efforts of the Party can writers contribute to the people's advancement and that only thus can they create works of abiding value. These writers have lost the perspective of socialism. They have lost their confidence in the working class. And they have become pessimistic and faint-hearted. These qualities now, of course, manifest themselves in their work.
>
> This kind of literature, which has been printed in *Irodalmi Ujsag*, and also elsewhere, does not serve the people. On the contrary, it has turned against the people and serves as a shield for the forces of reaction. These literary tendencies are a direct consequence of the fact that there were writers (Tibor Dery, Zoltan Zelk, Tamas Aczel, and others)

who rejected or only simulated their acceptance of the
March resolution of the Central Committee.*

Those who still did not quite understand what the "Party
Resolution" was all about were soon to discover its meaning from
the following paragraphs:

According to the natural law of things, this antagonistic
attitude toward the Party and the people soon reached a
point where it has discarded the disguise in which it first
appeared and has revealed its true face. This happened at
the November 10 meeting of the Party organization of the
Writers' Association, when certain writers attacked the Party
and the People's Democracy. These writers were repeating,
parrot-like, false reports spread by the bourgeoisie concerning the conditions and the living standard of the peasantry
and the working class. Under the guise of criticism, these
writers used a hostile tone toward leading state and Party
organizations and officials. They denied the necessity of
Party guidance in literature. Through moral pressure and
threats, they tried to exert terror over the Communist writers
who disapproved of these attacks upon the Party.

All this was rendered even more serious by the organized
character of the action. Certain members of the presidium
of the Writers' Association, appointed to their posts by the
Party, violated Party discipline by ostentatiously resigning
from their positions. Dery, Zelk, and others prepared a
memorandum and organized protests against political and
cultural steps taken by the Central Committee in connection
with the execution of the March resolution. This memorandum is an open attack on Party and state leadership. . . .
This memorandum is, as a matter of fact, an anti-Party
platform addressed to the Central Committtee only for the
purpose of enabling its preparers to publicize it at Party and
other meetings, and so use it against the Party. . . . The
majority of the writers and artists condemned this attempt,

---

* The March resolution condemned Imre Nagy and "rightist deviationism."

and the majority of the signers revoked their signatures when the true character of the memorandum became evident.*

Naturally, these openly anti-Party views have received no support from the majority of Communist and non-Communist writers and artists, who are loyal to the Party and who approve its policies. Therefore, certain people (Gyula Hay, Tibor Meray, etc.) have attempted to create an anti-Party atmosphere by using the slogan "freedom of literature." . . .†

The writers, after they had been handed the document and had begun to read it, felt the perspiration break out on their foreheads. They wondered whether they should speak at all. The

---

* For three whole weeks the most important work of the entire mobilized Party machinery, including the leaders Rakosi, Gero, Nogradi, and Marton Horvath, was to compel the writers and artists to revoke their signatures. In their first astonishment at the number and importance of the signers, they decided that, since the whole thing could not be undone, it could be made less effective by forcing writers and artists to revoke their signatures. Then came a period of threats, persuasions, and promises. The leaders made every effort to see that the most important names should be erased from the list. After a week, this concentrated effort began to show some results. At the personal intervention of Erno Gero and Istvan Kovacs, Tamas Major, Director of the National Theater, at last agreed to revoke his signature, and his example was followed by the actors. By December 6, the date of the meeting described, the majority of the film directors, the musicians, the journalists, and the actors had indeed yielded to pressure and revoked their signatures. Only the writers' signatures remained. But after the resolution, a number of these signers also retreated: though they maintained that every word of the Memorandum was just and true, they revoked their signatures under coercion. In the end, only four writers, three journalists, and one composer remained who, in spite of the almost unbearable pressure, refused to revoke their signatures. These were Tibor Dery, Zoltan Zelk, Laszlo Benjamin, Tamas Aczel, Sandor Haraszti, Geza Losonczy, Miklos Vasarhelyi, and Endre Szervanszky. The important point is, however, that once a man had signed the Memorandum, it was absolutely irrelevant whether his signature was revoked or not.

† After having been discharged from the editorial board of *Szabad Nep,* I was, as a punishment, sent to Berlin, supposedly so that I might be helped "to come to my senses," but in reality in order to isolate me from the staff of the Party organ. After Imre Nagy's fall, I was recalled with the excuse that "they wanted to inform me of the new situation." They did not let me return to Berlin, but, together with six of my fellow journalists, I was discharged altogether from the paper. A member of the Politburo summoned me to his office and offered me another job. I refused. From then on, I wrote film scripts and took an active part in the movement within the Writers' Association.—T.M.

truth was that, although they were prepared for a counter-attack, they had not been prepared for a counter-attack of this proportion and violence. The carefully written speeches in their pockets lost their significance. If they were to speak at all, their speeches would have to be improvised. They knew exactly what to say and how to tear apart the resolution, for they had sufficient arguments and much to say. But, as time went on and as one speech followed another, they gave up their plan to argue with this crowd of yelling dervishes. There was no point in trying. They would have been silenced anyway. As they sat there among the horde of officials (officials intoxicated with their own importance and with the omnipotence of their Party, and who had probably been told by Rakosi that it was their positions and their good life which the writers were after), they lost every desire to make themselves heard. And, at the same time, they were overtaken by a strange pity for their bloodthirsty judges, the Party officials.

This pity, mixed with contempt, was founded on joy and, in fact, on an ecstatic happiness, for they were no longer part of this deaf and blind mass of robots, but were, instead, persecuted by them. They had to admit to themselves that, though they were afraid and though they could hardly breathe (and this was not only because the room was unbearably hot and stuffy), they were proud that their former comrades and approving readers had expelled them from their circles. To tell the truth, they were proud of being the target of the Party resolution, and they felt pity for the human wrecks who considered hatred their most human emotion; and, with the Marxist-Leninist ideology of socialist humanism in their hearts, they would have attacked their accusers bodily if they had been permitted to do so. Once upon a time, these writers had had dreams and desires. They had had courage and revolutionary passions—the courage to look reality in the face, which is the greatest courage on earth. But when they had signed their contract with this bald Mephistopheles, they had had to give away their most valuable possession, their human emotions, in exchange for automobiles and villas and special food stores and holiday resorts. To the writers, the loss of the ideological ballast meant that, at last, they could really live. To the army of officials, such a loss would have meant the loss of everything for which they now lived.

In spite of their fears, the writers felt that the tragicomedy which was taking place in the meeting room was utterly ridiculous.

"Our comrades, the writers," thundered Istvan Kovacs, "believe that they know more about literature than anyone else. True, literature is their trade, and they are experts in it. But there is someone who knows more about mining than the miners, who knows more about turning than the turners, and who knows more about literature than the writers. That somebody is the Party!"

Two thousand officials rose in their seats and shouted in chorus: "Long live the Party! Long live the Party!"

This cheap comedy—the "shaggy one's" *commedia dell'arte*— turned into tragedy a few seconds later. Gyula Hay, who had been attacked by name in the resolution and who had grown tired of the stream of curses repeated by the speakers, asked permission to speak. Once on the platform, his face pale and his voice low, he began:

"I have been a member of the Communist Party for thirty years—"

But the "shaggy one" had no intention of permitting Hay to continue. He wrinkled his brows and winked at the crowd, and they understood. Hay was pelted with shouts as with rotten tomatoes.

"That's the trouble!" roared someone in the audience.

"Don't speak of the past. Speak of the present!"

"Do you or don't you agree with the resolution? Tell us that!"

After a few sentences, Hay gave up. It was useless and hopeless. Accompanied by ironical comments from the crowd, he returned to his seat.

They knew very well, of course, that there was but one method by which to make people listen and even applaud. The method: self-criticism. All they would have had to do would be to climb to the platform and begin their speeches with the following sentence: "Comrades! I thank the Party from the bottom of my heart for its just criticism. I fully and unreservedly approve of the resolution!" It would, perhaps, even have been enough to say: "I approve of the resolution. Even if not fully, I agree with it in principle." It was not too late. It was still not too late. The Party would have received them, like straying sheep, with open arms, and they would have been better off and more appreciated and more spoiled than those who had never "rebelled."

This was, indeed, the only scene missing from the drama: the writer who, after being criticized, followed the old Communist custom by repenting publicly and begging the Party for forgiveness. Would it not have been wonderful? Rakosi and his gang would have given much to achieve this end.

But there was not a single writer ready to follow the old custom. They had gone a long way. It made them almost dizzy to look back. Two or three years ago, a mild warning from the Party had sent the majority of them into orgies of "self-analysis," and then it had never taken them long to admit their crimes in public. And then it had not been out of careerism, but because they were convinced that the Party was wise, that the Party knew more than they did, and that it was invariably right.

It was not because they had become haughty that they were now silent. It was only because they knew that, if they had risen from the mire, it was only because the Party had sunk deeper into it. They knew they were in debt and that they owed a "self-criticism"—and that they would owe it perhaps to the end of their days. But it was not to this heinous assembly that they owed it. They owed it to the people, the Hungarian people, because they, the writers, had once, too, been the members of just such assemblies. Now, they had begun to act upon that larger self-criticism, and they would continue to act upon it. But to humiliate themselves before these raving maniacs, these crazy clowns? Never! Never, never again!

The meeting ended after ten o'clock at night, after the participants, who had never read the Memorandum, voted unanimously to accept a resolution that had already been passed.

That night the writers—and particularly those mentioned by name in the resolution—slept very little. They were waiting for the AVO to come to arrest them.

"The competent organs of the Party," the resolution had read, "are called upon to investigate the case of the writers who opposed the March resolution of the Central Committee and who tried to organize an opposition within the Party."

This was an open and undisguised threat. And, as it was impossible to know what was meant by the "competent organs of the Party" (for the Central Control Committee as well as the AVO, and the Budapest District Court as well as the Beer Brewers Association, were Party organs in a country where everything belonged to the Party), all the nights to come were wrought with danger for the writers who had now been branded the enemies of the people.

For days, nothing happened. There was silence. Absolute, incomprehensible silence. Then, ten days later, the telephones began to ring. The members of the Central Control Committee, which was the disciplinary organ of the Party, were inviting the writers to have friendly conversations with them.

The purpose of these conversations was to persuade the writers to exercise self-criticism and to confess their errors and to accept the resolution of the Central Committee.*

Not one writer was prepared to do so.

They were told, then, that their case would come before the Party court (i.e., the Central Control Committee) before Christmas.

The first cases were "tried" between December 21 and 24.

The writers appeared before fifteen members of the Central Control Committee, over whom Karoly Kiss, the most loyal of all, presided. Kiss enumerated the accusations. The writers replied to them, calmly. They cared little whether the Party would expel them or not. To tell the truth, they hoped they would be

---

* These requests for self-criticism are the most characteristic features of Communist Party mechanism. The Party was utterly indifferent as to whether the writers were sincere or not. What the Party wanted was a *statement*.

expelled. They had no wish to remain in the same Party nor to breathe the same air with Rakosi and Farkas and their followers.

The writers made no secret of their opinions.

They pointed to Gyula Alapi, who had been the prosecutor in the Rajk trial and who was now one of the members of the Control Committee sitting before them; and they declared that, as long as this man sat in judgment over them, they were in no mood to argue.

The members of the Committee listened attentively and without interruption to the well-founded and just verdicts that the accused pronounced upon them.

Then Karoly Kiss sent the writers from the room. The Control Committee wanted time to make up its mind.

Outside, the writers laughed at the comedy. They knew that the verdict had, as usual, been handed to Karoly Kiss well in advance. It had been drawn up by the Political Committee, and the men here were merely the executors.

However, formalities had to be respected. Appearances were all-important.

After about forty-five minutes, the Control Committee announced its verdict:

For Sandor Haraszti and Miklos Vasarhelyi: expulsion from the Party.

For Tibor Dery, Laszlo Benjamin, Geza Losonczy, Endre Szervanszky,* and Tamas Aczel: a severe reprimand and final warning. (This was the severest punishment before expulsion.)

---

* When Szervanszky's case came up, Karoly Kiss asked him who had submitted the Memorandum to him for his signature. Szervanszky shrugged his shoulders and said he could not remember. But Kiss insisted.

"Comrade Szervanszky," said Kiss, "this is very important. You must try to remember."

"Yes," said the composer, "now I remember."

"Well?" Kiss asked, excitedly. "Who was it?"

"What?" shouted Szervanszky, beside himself with rage. "Do you expect me to denounce someone? Do you expect me to tell you anything? Me, the son of a Hungarian army officer?"

Szervanszky was the son of a Hungarian army officer, but he had also been a member of the underground Communist Party. The members of the Control Committee bowed their heads.

For Sandor Erdei, Peter Kuczka, Tibor Meray, Gyula Hay, and Lajos Konya: a severe reprimand.

For Ferenc Karinthy and Endre Veszi: a reprimand.

Rakosi and his clique were not, however, content to let things go at that. Confidential instructions were given to the publishing houses, the editorial offices, the radio and the film studios: publication, royalties, and all income were to be stopped. For months, these writers did not get a line published. Their films were banned; their radio programs, though already recorded, were taken off the air. The royalties were simply withheld. The purpose behind these measures was clear: the gang was trying to starve the writers into submission.

Now, it seemed that the hope which had, for months, given heart to the Communist writers and spurred them on, was at last taken away from them. The fact that Rakosi dared to act with such determination and such ruthlessness showed that he was once again in the saddle, that he enjoyed Moscow's full confidence, and that he—and not the writers—knew what was going on in the Kremlin. Under such conditions, it seemed at that moment that the struggle must end. True, nobody submitted and nobody exercised self-criticism either publicly or privately. But neither was there any offensive on the part of the writers. There was only silence. Yet, though the writers had neither the desire nor the courage to attack, their silence indicated their disapproval.

In order to present a complete picture of the situation as it then stood, however, it must be added that, in spite of the difficulties, there were certain new occurrences that gave the writers some comfort. Rakosi decided that the previously confidential Party resolution should be published in *Irodalmi Ujsag,* and it soon turned out that he had made an irreparable mistake. In his mood of triumph, he had wanted to humiliate the writers before the entire country. But he thus achieved just the opposite. At last, the country learned something about the writers' struggle. Now, for the first time, the great masses of the people found out that the Communist writers, whom they believed to be fair-haired boys of the regime (i.e., the "official" writers), had turned against their masters. One did not have to be well-versed in reading between the lines of the text of the resolution—and particularly not when reading that part which referred to the living standard of the workers and peasants—in order to realize what it was that these writers were fighting for.

No less important was the fact that, by publishing the resolution, Rakosi informed not only the country but the world-at-large of the writers' rebellion. Long articles appeared in the Western press about the writers' rebellion against Rakosi, most of them analyzing the text of the resolution. Since there were not many facts to go on, most of these articles contained guesses and deductions, but, even so, the affair had reached the London *Times* and the *Neue Zuercher Zeitung* and numerous important Western newspapers.

At first, the Rakosi clique was astonished at the Western reaction. They had not thought that the West would pay attention to this "unimportant literary quarrel." Then, however, they tried to take advantage of the situation by making their accusations against the writers even more threatening and by declaring that, since the "imperialists" were capitalizing on the writers' attitude, here was the proof that, willy-nilly, the writers were strengthening the forces of reaction and that, therefore, it was high time for these writers to exercise self-criticism.

Two weeks after the announcement of Tibor Meray's Party punishment, in the first days of January, 1956, Marton Horvath sent Meray an urgent message to come to see him. After a few polite phrases, Horvath came to the point. He showed Meray a pile of newspapers lying before him on the table.

"These are Western papers," he said, "and they are making a big issue of our literary debates. 'Rebellion against Rakosi,' 'Party writers against the Party,' and such trash. . . . I presume this is no news to you."

"I have heard rumors," Meray replied. "But only rumors.

Since you had me removed from the editorial offices of *Szabad Nep,* I cannot lay my hands on Western newspapers."

"Here they are," Horvath said. "You can read them all. Let me tell you what we want you to do. Write an article in *Szabad Nep* in which you rebuff this Western interference. After all, this literary debate is our own affair. It does not concern the imperialists."

"You are quite right," Meray replied. "Our debates do not concern the imperialists, and neither have they anything to do with us—the accused—personally."

"The Party has a right to publish its resolution."

"Certainly. And every newspaper in the world has the right to quote from the resolution the Party has seen fit to publish."

"This is not what I wanted to talk about." Horvath was now nervous. "I wanted to talk to you about the article we want you to write, in which you will deny that you are being accused of rebellion against the Party."

"Forgive me," said Meray. "I have not read these papers and so I don't know what they accuse me of. But I have read the Party resolution, and there, together with four other writers, I am accused of activities against the Party and the people. In order to reject the accusations of the Western papers, I should first have to refute the accusations of the Party resolution. After all, it is from this resolution that the Western press has its information."

"What do you mean?" Horvath frowned. "You want to argue with the imperialists and the Central Committee at the same time?"

"Look," Meray said. "It would be much more practical if an editorial in *Szabad Nep,* rather than I, explained to the imperialists that I am neither an enemy of the Party nor an enemy of the people."

"That would be futile," Horvath said. "The article must be written by someone mentioned by name in the resolution. You must write it. What we need is one of those good 'Korean' articles signed by Meray."

"But I've told the Central Control Committee frankly that I

do not agree with the Party resolution. That is what concerns me. That is my opinion, and I don't care what the Western press does or does not write."

The two could not come to terms. They agreed only that Meray would come back in the afternoon and that he would think it over in the meantime, while Horvath discussed with the "comrades" (i.e., with Rakosi) to what extent Meray could argue in any article with the Central Committee.

When Meray left, Horvath wanted to give him the Western papers to read. "When you have read this collection," he said, "you will be so angry that you will write that article immediately."

Meray did not accept the papers, though he was curious about them. But he knew that if he took them along, it would be indeed more difficult for him to refuse to write the article. He felt extremely bad. To him, this was the most hellish moment of the entire literary struggle. It was a "trap" in the best Rakosi tradition. If he agreed to write the article, it would be a blow which would lose much prestige for the writers' movement, and it would also lose prestige for Meray himself at home and abroad. If, on the other hand, he persisted in his refusal, they would use that as a weapon against him and against the whole movement. "These people," they would say, "have sunk so low that they are making common cause with the imperialists." And, in a People's Democracy, there can be no more serious accusation.

Still, when afternoon came, Meray had decided to refuse to write the article, no matter what the consequences. He would write no more "Korean" articles!

The afternoon meeting was brief.

"Well, have you decided?" Horvath asked.

Instead of answering him directly, Meray asked, "What did the comrades say? Can I say what I think about the resolution?"

"You can say that there are disagreements between us, but that these are our own internal affair. No more."

Meray said that he was sorry, but that, under such a condition, he could not write the article.

But Horvath could not believe his ears.

"Here is the material," he said, pointing to the collection of newspapers on his table. "Think it over."

"I have already thought it over," Meray replied.

"Please yourself," he said in a voice of icicles. "Naturally, I must inform the comrades . . ."

"Naturally," Meray said. "Go ahead and inform them."

"The comrades will be surprised . . . very surprised . . ."

Meray left the room and felt worse than ever. He could clearly see Rakosi's face when Horvath informed him about his decision not to write the article. To dispel all Meray's doubts on that score, Horvath called after him before Meray had closed the door.

"You don't know what you are doing," he said. "And you seem not to realize where this will land you."

Indeed, Meray did not know. But it was easy to guess what was meant. Within twenty-four hours, all his writings, radio scripts, and film scenarios were banned. But that things did not go even further and that he did not land where Horvath had predicted he would was not due to himself—and even less to Matyas Rakosi.

The writers did not know whether to be glad or frightened at this turn of events. They did not know whether it was better to be praised by the Western press—or to be forgotten. If the world's public opinion should pay no attention to their fight, it was easier to get rid of them. It seemed as though everything were bad for them, including even that which was good.

In the meantime, a good many Western journalists and radio commentators were declaring that, though the writers' rebellion was interesting, it should not be taken too seriously. The whole rebellion was, so they conjectured, probably a put-up job—a put-up job not only tolerated but inspired "from above."

BOOK V

UNTIL THE STATUE FALLS

Khrushchev Helps

For almost three months, there was quiet. The works of the punished writers were banned, but, for the time being, no more radical steps were taken. The atmosphere was oppressive and unbearably sultry. It was as if both camps were waiting for the other to make the first move.

And then, on February 13, 1956, Peter Erdos, a young journalist whose sympathies for the writers' movement and whose close friendship with some of its members was generally known, was suddenly arrested. This was not his first sojourn in Rakosi's prisons. In 1951, Erdos had been arrested and condemned to three years behind bars because he had spent the years of World War II in Switzerland and, according to the indictment, had been in contact with Tibor Szonyi there.*

At the time of the great rehabilitations, Erdos had been released from prison. Since then, he had worked as a journalist. This passionate, red-haired young man was known for his straightforward and often heedless defense of the truth; in bistros, coffeehouses, and editorial offices, he had abused the "shaggy one"

---

* Szonyi was a Communist official who had fled to Switzerland before the Nazis. He was tried during the Rajk trial and later executed because he had allegedly become a member of Allen Dulles' spy ring during his emigration.

and his clique with biting irony and unbridled emotion, although everyone knew that all his words were reported to the ruthless leader who sat behind his desk sharpening his axe for the next act of revenge.

It is characteristic of the utter cynicism of the regime that the AVO officer who came to arrest Erdos was the very same man who had arrested him four years earlier. He knew his man and did not have to be coached for the job. The only difference was that, while he had been rude and offensive four years ago, he was now (having once admitted the young journalist's innocence and asked his pardon) smooth, polite, and almost kind.

He assured Erdos that he had no cause for anxiety, that nothing would happen to him. Erdos' wife and little daughter were also given the same assurances.

Then he searched the house. He was looking primarily for Yugoslav material.

He took away a few official Yugoslav pamphlets, Kardelj's well-known speech on the problems of socialism, and Vladimir Dedijer's biography of Tito, which in those days passed from hand to hand in Hungary.

Then he put his old acquaintance in an automobile and went off with him.

The next day, the news of Erdos' arrest spread through the city like wildfire.*

---

* I remember that I learned about it the next day. The wife of a writer friend of mine came to my flat, pale and terribly anxious. I looked around quickly to make sure there was nothing "dangerous" in my flat. The Dedijer book was out; I had lent it to Janos Kadar, who had wanted to read it for a long time. On the other hand, there was a manuscript of Imre Nagy's Memorandum, later to become world-famous, that the "old man" had given me a few days before to read. The Memorandum was addressed to—and sent to—the Party's Central Committee, but before sending it off, Nagy had had several copies typed to show to his friends.
Since it seemed certain that I and my friends would be arrested next, I did my best to get rid of all incriminating documents, among them Nagy's manuscript, which I burned in the stove.
About a week later, I went to see Imre Nagy and told him what had happened to the manuscript. He grew very angry and gave me a good lecture.
"That manuscript should have been defended," he said, "not burned."
I admit that I was deeply ashamed.—T.A.

The arrest indicated that, after the Party's December resolution reprimanding the writers, Rakosi and his clique had made up their minds to go one step further and to begin with the "administrative" liquidation of the writer and the journalist groups. Their choice of Erdos as the first victim indicated that they found it easier to begin on the peripheries of the movement and arrest someone less well known who had, by publicly denouncing the Party leaders, furnished an excellent excuse for punitive action.

However, everybody agreed that Erdos' arrest was only the beginning. The rest would inevitably follow. The question was not *why* they had arrested Erdos, but *who would come next.*

The atmosphere was heavy with fear and anxiety. The next night seemed filled with danger. But nothing happened.

The next morning, still exhausted from the long and sleepless night, the writers opened their copies of *Szabad Nep*. Suddenly, in the space of a second, they were more wide-awake than they had ever been in their lives. There, in large, black letters, stood the explanation!

The paper quoted the full text of the official Tass announcement concerning the opening in Moscow of the Twentieth Congress of the Soviet Communist Party. This dry and rather laconic announcement was the most amazing, the most anomalous, and almost the most grotesque statement that those who had survived the last few years in Hungary had ever seen.

On the first page of the paper, they came face to face with the following words, printed in italics: *"The participants of the Twentieth Congress rendered homage to the memory of J. V. Stalin . . . and the great fallen of the working class with one minute's silence."*

Was that all that remained of Stalin's glory—of the "leader of mankind," the "shining torch of the Party," the "teacher of all peoples," the "wise builder of Communism," at whose grave the "worthy successors to his life's work" had pledged eternal allegiance? Not even a minute of homage to Stalin alone? Only that? Only so little?

There had already been rumors of the battles waged around

the dead lion and of the trimming of his abundant and still growing mane. It was obvious: all was not well with Stalin! There
had been no celebrations in Hungary on Stalin's birthday, December 21. *Pravda* had neglected to mention the great day,
though, in the past, it had devoted pages and pages to the glorification of Stalin, the unique earthly repository of heavenly grace
and wisdom, the possessor of omnipotent goodness and of super-
human knowledge. At the same time, much had been said of
"collective leadership" and of the absolute error of "one-man
leadership." Even the self-abasement in Belgrade had been nothing but a blow in the teeth to Stalin, with a somewhat cynical
wink. All this was abundantly supported by ideological thesis—
basic truths which Lenin had long ago expressed but which
Stalin appeared to have forgotten, and mainly about the role of
the masses in history. Still, no name was mentioned, and when
long articles appeared denouncing the "cult of personality," it
was never indicated who that "personality" was: Julius Caesar,
Napoleon, or Joseph Vissarionovich Stalin.

This "divided" homage to Stalin's memory was now a much
more open and, it might be added, a much more revolting act of
contempt than any of the previous manifestations. This was particularly so because the delegates of the Twentieth Congress were
the very same men who, at the Nineteenth Congress, had cheered
themselves hoarse and had applauded steadily for twenty to
thirty minutes every time Stalin's name had been mentioned by
one of the speakers. And this "one-minute homage" was only a
prelude to things to come.

In a speech which had lasted several hours, Nikita Khrushchev
—First Secretary of the Party, Stalin's one-time disciple, and the
principal speaker of the Congress—had refuted, one after another, all the principles Stalin had proclaimed and to which, only
two days before, people, parties, and governments had sworn
allegiance. The speech was the very catechism of a new heresy.
A number of basic principles that had hitherto been more bind-
ing than the law had suddenly become harmful and dangerous
ideological aberrations. Things that, had they even been insinu-

ated a few days before, would have cost the bold offender his life, were now enthusiastically approved by every delegate to the Twentieth Congress and became first resolutions, then law. Khrushchev had refuted Stalin's thesis which declared that in the dictatorship of the proletariat the class struggle increases after the consolidation of power. This, Khrushchev had declared, was nothing but the ideological justification of terror. Stalin was also absolutely wrong when he had stated that the proletariat could seize power only by armed uprising. Khrushchev admitted that there was also a parliamentary way, something that had hitherto been considered the "Social Democratic betrayal of socialism." The third important point of Khrushchev's speech had been that he had admitted that socialism could be built in ways other than the *Soviet* way—that is, by taking into account the specific features and character of each country. If such things as "rightist deviationism," "revisionism," and "reformism" were possible within the Communist Party, then Khrushchev's speech was the *very essence* of these.

As the days went by, the measure, the significance, and the character of the change became even more clearly defined. *Szabad Nep* published the speeches of Suslov, Mikoyan, Kaganovich, and Malenkov.* The fall of Stalin and of Stalinism and the launching of a new course became obvious to even the most ignorant reader.

Doubtless, many of the old elements were still present in these speeches: self-adulation and the dull repetition of principles not yet refuted. Yet, the people—and among them the Communist writers—noted with excitement all that was new and of an innovational character. To the writers, who in those days lived in constant danger of arrest, this Congress, with all its nauseating slogans, was like a liberating army of a besieged fortress. To them, the most decisive feature of the Congress was its unequivocal attack upon dogmatism within the Party—i.e., leftist deviation-

---

* Molotov was the only one who refused to malign the memory of his dead friend and master. His speech dealt strictly with the old schemes, and he omitted any mention of Stalin.

ism (in the language of everyday politics) or the Rakosi line
(in Hungarian political language).

As a matter of fact, the new Soviet attitude fully justified Imre
Nagy and the movement of the Hungarian writers. After six
weeks of deep silence and inactivity, these now felt that they were
backed by a tremendous force—by Khrushchev and the Twentieth
Congress—and this backing encouraged them to continue their
fight. In those exciting days, it became clear that Rakosi and
his clique had known nothing of these new developments in the
Kremlin, or of the preparations for the Twentieth Congress and
the declaration of "socialist legality." Clearly, the Hungarian
dictator had been just as uninformed as the Communist writers
whom he had expelled and reprimanded. There could be no
more striking evidence of this than the fact that Peter Erdos had
been arrested *one day* before the opening of the Congress. Rakosi's lack of knowledge indicated that the "shaggy one" was no
longer in the confidence of the Kremlin and that he perhaps
had as much to fear from the Kremlin as those he so passionately persecuted had to fear from him.

Beyond a doubt, the balance of forces had changed, and
"Stalin's foremost Hungarian disciple" must have felt much more
uncertain about his fate after the Twentieth Congress. Hungarian
literature received a new impetus in this hope that perhaps now
Hungary could rid itself forever of the little dictator.

This is not to say that, after their first joyful surprise, the
Hungarian writers had looked with awe and admiration on
Khrushchev, nor on the other speakers of the Twentieth Party
Congress; they were no longer capable of such feelings. But there
was a good deal of truth in what Nikita Sergeyevich and his
companions had said, and the militants of literature made good
use of these truths.

There was, however, a fundamental difference between the
masters of the Kremlin and the writers. The latter had arrived
at an understanding of the cruelty, the falseness, and the basic
dishonesty of Stalin's teachings through years of suffering, conflicts, disappointment, and guilt feelings; they had tried to tell

the story of their struggles and awakening, frankly and unreservedly, in public speeches, articles, and literary works. The Kremlin leaders, on the other hand, spoke as if their revelations were self-evident and required no further elucidation, neglecting to mention, however, that they themselves had also been responsible for all the atrocities committed under Stalin's rule.

There was, of course, a certain courage in Khrushchev's aboutface—this the writers had to concede—and in the way he overthrew the idol he had helped to build. Perhaps his actions were prompted not only by imperative political necessities, but also by an inner urge that had been present before Stalin's death and had grown more insistent afterward. The psychological motive which manifested itself, for example, in Mikoyan's passionate attack on the dead tyrant was clearly that Stalin's death and the lifting of the Stalinist terror was a. source of joy and relief even to those who had actively participated in maintaining it. It seemed obvious that the men who were now tearing down the idol had often trembled in the shadow of that idol; their power had been secure only so long as their services and idolatry were required. Thus, they served and worshipped—and they seized the first opportunity to give free vent to their accumulated hatred and fear.

The Communist writers, understanding the motives behind the revelations, did not expect any agonizing soul-searching on the part of the Soviet politicians. That was the fate of writers, not of those who governed empires and ruled millions. However, they not only expected but *demanded* that the Soviet leaders should draw the inevitable conclusions from that bloody and cruel era: they should realize and publicly admit their responsibility. The fact that these words were never pronounced discredited the Soviet leaders' attitude in the eyes of the writers. Thus, it seemed a merely tactical maneuver, deprived of any merit; and it stressed the absence of any assurance that the Stalinist crimes would never again be repeated.

This, naturally, did not prevent the writers from reaching the moral as well as political conclusion that the time was ripe for a concentrated and decisive attack. Certain details of Khrushchev's confidential speech in a closed conference of the Congress began to leak out, although Rakosi made every effort to keep the speech from the Hungarian public. The Western radios were already broadcasting the full text of the Khrushchev speech, though no one except the highest officials had seen the authentic material. It was no longer possible to keep it secret. Rakosi excerpted portions of the speech, and these excerpts were read at Party meetings. But the full text was never published in Hungary. Budapest slang, which lashed out furiously at the "shaggy one" (who grew increasingly confused and uncertain), called this abbreviated and emasculated form of insouciance a "children's version" and laughed at Rakosi for still trying to protect the "Stalinist humanism" which had been unmasked to the last horrible detail by Khrushchev.*

Things reached the point where the Hungarian press omitted not only comments from the London *Times* and the *Manchester Guardian,* but also from *Pravda.* The Polish press was a source of even more trouble to Rakosi. Day after day, the Warsaw papers published articles reflecting the passionate desire for truth on the part of Polish writers and journalists who were intent, as

---

* In those days, the following joke about "Stalinist humanism" went the rounds in Budapest:

At a Party meeting in the Soviet Union, Stalin delivered an important speech. The audience listened in deep silence, rigid with attention. Suddenly somebody sneezed, and Stalin interrupted his speech. As the icy hand of fear gripped the assembly, Stalin raised his eyes from the papers in front of him.

"Who sneezed?" he asked.

There was no answer.

"Who sneezed?" Stalin asked, irritably.

There was silence.

As Stalin gave a signal, the doors opened and a detachment of GPU men entered the theater. Their machine guns swept the first row, killing all the occupants of the seats.

"Who sneezed?" Stalin asked again.

In the silence, the GPU men shot down the people in the second row.

"Who sneezed?" Stalin asked. "Who sneezed, comrades?"

Somewhere in the back of the audience an old *muzhik* rose, trembling. "It was me, Comrade Stalin," he said in a shaky voice.

Stalin's broad face lit up with a kindly smile.

"God bless you, Ivan Ivanovich," he said.

were the Hungarian writers and journalists, on admitting and so ridding themselves, once and for all, of the crimes and errors of the past. Suddenly, the publications of the hitherto "fraternal" Polish Party became forbidden in Hungary, just as were those of the "imperialist" press.

Not long after the Twentieth Party Congress, the Italian Party press published an article by Palmiro Togliatti, head of the Italian Communist Party, in which he very pertinently posed the question of whether the crimes, the reigns of terror, the executions of innocent men, the concentration camps, and the genocide could be ascribed *solely and exclusively* to Stalin and explained away by the so-called "cult of personality." Wrote Togliatti in reply to his own question: "The roots are deeper, for even the 'cult of personality' is only the product of something else. If one were looking for the true Marxist explanation, one could not escape the logical conclusion that these crimes grow from the soil of the system itself."

Togliatti's speech was banned in Hungary by the "shaggy one," and the country learned about the Italian leader's opinions only when *Pravda* criticized his "exaggerations" and when Togliatti was thus obliged to exercise self-criticism.

The Communist writers were deeply impressed by Togliatti's arguments—even those who had long ago come to the conclusion themselves that the source of the trouble lay in the system, in the "structure" itself. Even from a Marxist viewpoint, Togliatti's explanation was more correct than—and far superior to—the official attitude.

The fact is that, from then on, the writers' task became easier. At Party meetings, they no longer had to rely on their own arguments alone. There were the latest publications of the Polish Party press or certain paragraphs from Togliatti's article, one or the other dealing a blow to the Rakosi clique.

By then, practically every printed word could be used as an argument against Rakosi. An article about the corrupt practices of a colonial governor in Africa, another about the prisons of a South American dictator—in fact, every line in world literature which dealt with tyranny tied Rakosi to the stake. In those days, the Hungarian National Theater revived Shakespeare's *Richard III*, and it became evident that that bloody murderer of the Middle Ages, who had "determined to prove a villain," was an exact replica—that is to say, an exact forerunner—of this modern mass murderer. The drama had been last performed in 1945, and then everyone had compared Richard III to Hitler. Ten years later, the comparison with Rakosi was just as evident. The most horrible moments were those when, after the execution of Lord Hastings, the actor who played the part of the scrivener came out before the curtain to recite his brief monologue:

> Here is the indictment of the good Lord Hastings;
> Which in a set hand fairly is engross'd,
> That it may be to-day read o'er in Paul's.
> And mark how well the sequel hangs together:
> Eleven hours I have spent to write it over,
> For yesternight by Catesby was it sent me;
> The precedent was full as long a-doing:
> And yet within these five hours Hastings liv'd,
> Untainted, unexamin'd, free, at liberty.
> Here's a good world the while! Who is so gross
> That cannot see this palpable device?
> But who so bold but says he sees it not?
> Bad is the world; and all will come to naught
> When such ill dealing must be seen in thought.

The audience indicated by prolonged applause that it well understood the allusion: Hastings, executed without an indictment, became identical with the innocently executed Laszlo Rajk, and the "bad world" with the world in which the audience lived —a world which must necessarily come to nought because truth was forbidden in it.*

Gyorgy Non, Deputy Minister of Culture, attended the third or fourth performance following the premiere. When, after the

---

* Tamas Major, Director of the National Theater, played a joke for his own enjoyment: he gave the role of the scrivener to an old, narrow-minded, incorrigibly sectarian Communist actor.

monologue, the applause almost took the form of a demonstration, he jumped up from his seat, flushed with anger, and hurried into Tamas Major's dressing room to harangue the director, who sat before him in the costume of Richard III.

"I know," he panted. "I know very well, Comrade Major, that this play was put on with the sole purpose of making fun of Comrade Rakosi."

Major rose calmly and donned his sword belt.

"Comrade Non," he said, coldly. "No one but you would say such an idiotic thing."

Non raised his arm to hit the director. So Major raised his. Only the intervention of the deathly pale Gyula Kallai, Deputy Minister of Culture, prevented a scandal. Yet that same night everybody in the capital knew about the incident.

There was no escape. There was no pardon. Everything argued and agitated and incited against Rakosi and his clique.

That was when Gyula Illyes wrote his short but biting and barely disguised poem about the sunflowers:

Images of the sun, sun's sons,
Large, golden-winged sunflowers,
Finished with curtsies and bows all around,
You are beheaded.

You are beheaded. The sun still shines.
In the autumn radiance, your heads
Are now set down to dry
At the feet of the father.

No more curtsies, or bowing, or scraping,
Each of you is but a large, gaping eye.
Look upward now. There is no solace.
Neither is there any answer.

Indeed, there was no solace, and neither was there any answer. There were only questions, urgent, open questions—questions that answered themselves and were nevertheless unanswerable.

In the first place, stubbornly and unavoidably, there was the question about the Rajk affair.

In November, 1955, the "shaggy one" made a last desperate attempt to save himself. He forced a resolution on the Central Committee which, due to pressure from the Yugoslav side, admitted that Rajk was not a Titoist agent, but which simultaneously justified his death sentence by declaring that, though Rajk had not been an agent of Belgrade, he had, in the days of the underground Party, been a spy for the Horthy police.

Even in 1949, nobody had believed this lie. And, after the revelations of the Stalinist crimes, the accusation sounded even more offensive, and pressure exerted by the Party membership, in which the writers naturally played a prominent part, compelled Rakosi to clarify the Rajk affair for the second time. Since he would not—or perhaps he dared not—speak in Budapest, he traveled to one of the most beautiful provincial towns of Hungary, the beautiful baroque town of Eger, and there, in an unexpected masterpiece of eloquence, he began calling Rajk "comrade." At the same time, he shifted the entire responsibility for Rajk's execution onto the shoulders of Beria and Gabor Peter.

But in those days it was no longer possible to gloss over matters so easily. There was an increasing number of impatient and curious and hard-headed men in the country.

A black-haired and bushy-browed man, nearly six feet tall and rather bent, the son of Debrecen peasants, rose at one of the Communist Party meetings. In his deep, booming voice he began to speak:

"I had a friend," he said. "He was a truck driver, and an honest man who neither drank nor played cards, but who loved his profession and took care of his truck as if it were his own. Yet, an accident happened: one day he landed in a ditch. He was unhurt, but his load was ruined. He was arrested and, although the court found that he was not responsible for the accident, he was condemned to five years in prison. What is more, he was deprived of his driver's license and thus of his livelihood.

I now have only one question to ask: What should happen to those who turned the whole country's load into the ditch?"

The next day, he was summoned to Party headquarters and warned to stop this "irresponsible demagogy."

The black-haired man nodded and returned to his office. However, he rose again at the next opportunity and, holding Matyas Rakosi's collected articles in his hands, read aloud in a booming voice that paragraph in which the wise leader and father of the people boasted of the sleepless nights he had spent unmasking the cursed Rajk gang.

"I have only one question to ask," he said. "What was Matyas Rakosi doing during these sleepless nights?"

He was expelled from the Party, but he could not be silenced. He was Jozsef Szilagyi, former police captain and one of Imre Nagy's closest friends.

Early in April, at the membership meeting of the Hungarian Writers' Association, a young literary critic, Sandor Lukacsy, called Rakosi a "Judas." The membership meeting was suspended and Lukacsy was expelled from the Party, but a week later, when the meeting resumed, the questions and accusations continued for three whole days.

Then the moment came when, at the meeting of the Thirteenth District Party activists, a young secondary school teacher, Gyorgy Litvan, rose and, turning to Rakosi who sat on the platform, said: "I must tell you, Comrade Matyas Rakosi, that the Hungarian people no longer trust you!"

Then he sat down.

The next day, he was summoned to Party headquarters and asked to word his speeches more carefully and less rudely.

The end of the world had arrived. If, in Hungary, an unknown, nameless nobody, a young teacher, could throw the people's verdict in Rakosi's face and get away with it, it was surely the end of the world. Yet, he was not arrested. He was not imprisoned. He was not hanged.

Only four months earlier, the writers had been surrounded by the glass walls of silence which surrounded the entire country. Alone and isolated from the rest of the world, they had gone into battle against Rakosi and his clique, against a catastrophic, anti-national political line. And now—thanks to the Twentieth Congress and Nikita Khrushchev—they were no longer alone.

In the spring of 1956, an elderly gentleman wearing a sports suit, a green hat, and yellow kid gloves appeared more and more frequently in the elegant streets of the Budapest shopping center, looking into the shop windows and throwing covert glances from behind his pince-nez at the pretty women whispering excitedly behind his back. He was greeted by the male passers-by with a raising of hats, and whether he knew them personally or not, people stopped him to inquire about his health and ask what he thought of the political situation.

The gentleman smiled delightedly, although it was obvious that he was a little ashamed of his contentment. Modestly, he replied to the inquiries about his health and brushed away the political questions. He behaved not at all like a fallen Communist prime minister who had been slandered and persecuted for years by the entire Party press. He seemed more like a handsome, middle-aged cavalier who did not despise the pleasures of life, but had been taught by experience to be circumspect and moderate in his behavior.

He often had his grandchildren with him—a five-year-old boy and a four-year-old girl, whom he took to Budapest's best confectioner's, Gerbeaud's, for an ice cream, looking after them with grandfatherly tenderness. By then, his popularity was so great that bus drivers stopped between stations to pick him up, and young girls rose to give him their seats.

When Matyas Rakosi heard about these cheerful promenades in town, he was beside himself with rage.

"We'll show that Imre Nagy," Rakosi screamed. "He won't be walking along Vaci Street for long!"

An Unexpected Guest

The telephone rang in the tiny editorial office of the weekly *Beke es Szabadsag* ("Peace and Liberty"). The editor lifted the receiver, gave his name, and waited.

"Party headquarters here," he heard from the other end of the wire. "We should like to know whether the paper has already gone to press."

"Not yet," the editor replied. "They'll start printing in an hour."

"Then hold it until we telephone again. It's Party orders."

"Why? What is it all about?"

"The Central Committee is issuing an important statement."

"What about? Can't you tell me?"

"You will find out when it gets there."

It was July 18, 1956, and the time was eleven a.m. In the tiny room which, under normal circumstances, could hold no more than three persons (its furniture consisted of a desk, two armchairs, and a file cabinet) ten people awaited further developments.

Circumstances in those days were not "normal" in Budapest. An atmosphere of terror again pervaded the capital. Less than five months had gone by since the Twentieth Party Congress—the time of great revelations and of growing hopes—and once again they were afraid. During these few months, it had become obvious that the reputations of both Stalin and Rakosi were morally bankrupt in Hungary. But while Moscow trampled on the dead (Stalin), it would not touch the living (Rakosi). On April 4, the anniversary of Hungary's liberation, Khrushchev and Bulganin sent Rakosi a telegram of congratulation. Those in the know believed that Rakosi had had to beg for it several times; in analyzing the text, they noted that the telegram called Rakosi a "veteran of the working-class movement," which could easily mean that he was soon to be pensioned off. Actually, though, the sending of the telegram was a political act which strengthened Rakosi's position, and the "shaggy one" took ample advantage of it. All over the country, tens and thousands of Party meetings were assembled to hear the telegram. Shortly afterward, one of the secretaries of the Soviet Party, Suslov, arrived in Budapest—allegedly vacationing as a private citizen. But, being a good Bolshevik, he visited factories and producer cooperatives, mostly in Rakosi's company, and the newspapers gave conspicuous space to their photographs. The intention was transparent: instead of relieving him of his post, Moscow was doing its best to strengthen Rakosi's unstable position. The writers, artists, and journalists who had—from the time of Peter Erdos' arrest—drawn the conclusion that Rakosi knew nothing about the Kremlin's plans now came to the conclusion that the Russian text of the Twentieth Congress simply could not be applied in Hungary, as they had thought. Yet, because their minds and hearts rebelled and they could no longer tolerate the rule of "Stalin's best Hungarian disciple," they continued to attack him. As the tension grew, the situation became more and more equivocal: relying on Moscow's support, Rakosi tried to repress the writers; and the writers, relying on the Twentieth Congress, tried to unseat Rakosi.

The struggle reached its peak in the Petofi Circle. This Circle, whose exact function could not be determined, began its activity in March, not only legally but under the patronage of the Communist youth organization, the DISZ (Federation of Democratic Youth). Its original aim was to organize debates about the application of the Twentieth Party Congress teachings to the various fields of Hungarian intellectual life. At first, the Party leadership encouraged it as a good opportunity for youth to let off steam. It was considered wise to create some kind of forum—neither too large nor too important—where the intellectual youth could discuss their anxieties, complaints, and troubles. In this way, the disagreeable points of view of the Twentieth Congress would gradually be assimilated on a juvenile level and disappear from public consciousness.

Quite possibly, this was the original idea of the DISZ and of the Party headquarters bureaucrats. However, the leaders of the Petofi Circle—Gabor Tanczos, Balazs Nagy, and Pal Jonas— had entirely different ideas about the matter. These enthusiastic, gifted, and idealistic young men—most of whom had begun their careers in the so-called People's Colleges Movement and were later accused of nationalism or Titoism and imprisoned by Rakosi—took the conclusions of the Twentieth Congress very seriously, particularly the unmasking of Stalin and Khrushchev's statement that every country had the right to attain socialism in its own way. And they took everything that could be applied to the work of the Petofi Circle seriously. Every field of Hungarian intellectual life was to be cleansed of the mud which clung to it; they intended to discuss openly the specific forms and methods best suited to spread the real ideals of socialism in their country. They did not envisage the Circle as a valve through which accumulated steam could escape from the furnace; rather, it was to be a generator of steam to provide greater speed for the engine. They were enthusiastic disciples of Imre Nagy. They established contact with the "old man" and with the rebellious writers, and they asked them for help, support, and guidance.

The series of debates was opened with an economists' discussion of the Five-Year Plan. The opinions voiced by the country's foremost economic experts, among them many Party men, were simply astounding. It became evident that the new Five-Year Plan was just as unrealistic, as foolish, and as neglectful of the country's interests and resources as its predecessor had been.

The economists declared: "We pointed out all the shortcomings of the previous plan, only to be called 'petty bourgeois,' 'fainthearted,' and so on. Later on, those who had not believed us were compelled to exercise self-criticism. Now we can only repeat: the plan is bad from beginning to end. We would like to convince those in authority in time, before millions and millions of *forints* are squandered in vain."

Another debate, among historians, was attended by Erzsebet Andics. The young historians took her to task for all the falsifications in official historiography that she herself had committed, in both Party history and Hungarian history. They did not have to look far for examples. Only recently, *Pravda* had rehabilitated Bela Kun, the leader of the 1919 dictatorship of the proletariat in Hungary and the man whom Stalin had ordered executed as a Trotskyite agent and of whom the history of the Hungarian Communist Party spoke as a depraved enemy of the working class. Until now, the young historians said, it had been forbidden even to mention Bela Kun's name in Hungary. Everyone knew that he was the leader in 1919, and yet—regardless of whether he was good or bad—the historians had been compelled to learn and teach that the greatest figure of the Hungarian Revolution was Matyas Rakosi, who was known by everyone to have held only the very modest post of Deputy Commissar of Trade.

Erzsebet Andics stammered and blushed: "Yes, there have been mistakes and shortcomings . . ."

"What were those mistakes? What were the shortcomings? Who was responsible for them?" the young historians shouted, constantly interrupting her.

The next meeting was held by the members of the defunct People's Colleges Movement, which had helped hundreds of working-class and peasant boys and girls to receive the university educations that had been more or less closed to them in the past. In 1949, the movement had been dissolved and branded as Titoist. Its members had been persecuted ever since, for wherever they went the omniscient official file followed them—a People's College graduate, hence unreliable. Now free and happy, they sang their beloved songs and demanded that the Party resolution of 1949 be revoked and that a popular and really useful movement be reorganized.

Four or five days later, the philosophers met at the Petofi Circle. The main theme of their debate was the rehabilitation of Gyorgy Lukacs. The philosophers refuted, one by one, all the arguments used by Revai as the basis for silencing the outstanding Marxist philosopher. One of Lukacs' former students, a certain Jozsef Szigeti, rose and declared that he was deeply ashamed of himself for having betrayed his master and supported Revai's criticism of Lukacs' work. He admitted that Lukacs had been right on every point. Old Professor Lukacs—who, in the course of his Party career, had grown used to being constantly criticized and forced to exercise self-criticism, and who had remained aloof from the writers' struggle during the past few years—watched sympathetically in the background. He listened to this passionate defense of his life's work and this quasi-glorification of his person with a broad smile. He would never have believed it possible that his views would triumph during his lifetime.

The most dramatic meeting was that of the old Party activists and the young intellectuals. It was planned that, at this meeting, the old militants of the Party would tell the young people about their struggles and experiences. The only trouble was that the majority of these veterans of the underground Communist Party had, at best, been excluded from public life during the last ten years and, at worst, had spent years in Rakosi's jails. The climax of the meeting was the address delivered by Laszlo Rajk's widow, Julia, a tall, bony woman who had herself been imprisoned for five years.

"Comrades," Julia Rajk began, "I stand before you deeply moved after five years of prison and humiliation. Let me tell you this: so far as prisons are concerned, in Horthy's prisons conditions were far better even for Communists than in Rakosi's prisons. Not only was my husband killed, but my little baby was torn from me; for years, I received no letters and no information about the fate of my little son. These criminals have not only murdered Laszlo Rajk. They have trampled underfoot all sentiment and honesty in this country. Murderers should not be criticized—they should be punished. I shall never rest until those who have ruined the country, corrupted the Party, destroyed thousands, and driven millions into despair receive their just punishment. Comrades, help me in this struggle!"

There is no doubt that, had this speech been made by anyone else, that person would have been arrested immediately by the Rakosi clique. But it would have been far too embarrassing to put the widow of the rehabilitated Laszlo Rajk, only recently renamed a "comrade," back behind prison bars. Not even the bald dictator could permit himself such utter villainy.

The Petofi Circle arranged one open forum after another. Then came the greatest of events, and undoubtedly a historical one: the so-called "press debate" of June 27, 1956. By that time, the entire country knew of the Petofi Circle, and the audiences had been increasing by leaps and bounds—from 300 at the economists' debate to 1,000 at the philosophers' debate to 1,500 at the Party activists' debate.

The press debate was attended by 6,000 people. It was held in the Officers' House of the People's Army, a large, two-story building in the center of town. The meeting was scheduled to begin at 7 p.m., but by 4 p.m. it was already impossible to enter the building. Not only the large meeting hall, but all the small rooms, offices, and corridors were crowded to capacity. Finally, a microphone was fixed over the street entrance to calm the discontented crowd outside. The audience consisted mainly of university students, laborers, white-collar workers, intellectuals of the free professions, and Army officers. A great number of Party officials also appeared, as well as a few Yugoslav, Swiss, and British journalists.

The debate went on for nine full hours. It was raining, but no one left the courtyard; nor did a single member of the audience inside leave the crowded premises. For eleven years, people had been compelled to attend innumerable conferences, "blitz meetings," debates, membership meetings, seminars, discussions, activists' small or mass meetings, and "peace meetings"—where they had heard the same old trivialities, the same stale, empty slogans *ad nauseam*. Now, at last, they were able to listen to the things they wanted to hear.

Writers, poets, journalists, and scientists rose to speak. In fact, the debate was simply a continuation of the *Szabad Nep* and Writers' Association membership meetings. The real significance of the Petofi Circle was that everything which had, for two years, been confined to small rooms and discussed, at the most, in front of 200 or 300 people now reached the masses at last. One of the accusations later made was that here, in disloyalty to the Party, the Party's internal problem had been shouted from the housetops. Though it may seem strange that the Communist Party should be afraid of the people, the accusation was entirely true: thoughts that had long perturbed the people and been expressed only at small Party meetings were now openly discussed before the man in the street.

They were at last put into words. And how much was put into words!

Tibor Dery mounted the platform—as usual, without a tie and with his shirt collar turned down over his jacket collar. At last, the day had come when he was no longer sitting in the dock in that small room of Party headquarters. Instead, he stood before 6,000 people—one can safely say, before the entire country—and Jozsef Revai's cultural policy, which had once so ruthlessly persecuted him, was being judged.

First, Dery spoke about Jozsef Revai and his two assistants, Marton Horvath and Jozsef Darvas. But he did not speak in the tone they had used against him for he was a writer and not an ideological slave-driver. And his skill as a writer enabled him to present masterly portraits of these three men that were

more humiliating than any political accusations could have been.
Here are some of the things he said (taken from the shorthand
minutes of the meeting):

> From 1948 until recently, the trend has been to obscure
> the truth in this country. The process is still going on in
> some ways, but I hope not for long. I am not particularly
> fond of using political terms, but for the sake of clarity I
> shall say: this has been the Stalinist age of our literature. . . .
> As long as we direct our criticism against individuals
> instead of investigating whether the mistakes spring from
> the very system—from the very ideology—we can achieve
> nothing more than to exchange evil for a lesser evil. I trust
> we will get rid of our present leaders. All I fear is that
> the limping race horses will be followed by limping don-
> keys. . . . Whenever the Party alters its attitude—and this
> may happen several times in succession—it is the duty of
> the members of the Central Committee, the other Party
> clerks, and the ordinary Party members to represent and
> defend the Party's current political line. Even though they
> may not agree with it! What follows from this, comrades?
> Dear friends, don't you notice that I have here laid my
> hands on a structural mistake, on something independent of
> people? . . . We must seek in our socialist system the mis-
> takes which not only permit our leaders to misuse their
> power, but which also render us incapable of dealing with
> each other with the humanity we deserve. The mistakes in
> question are structural mistakes that curtail, to an entirely
> unnecessary degree, the individual's rights and that, again
> unnecessarily, increase his burdens. . . .
> Some 1,500 to 2,000 men—almost always the same men—
> go from one debate to another. . . . We shout and rant,
> we use up a lot of big words and enjoy them as children
> enjoy the cardboard trumpets bought at fairs. But we do
> not notice that our words remain empty words, that our
> hopes remain vain, and that things around us hardly change.
> What will the outcome be? Must we sell our right to act
> merely for the opportunity to spout words freely?
> I don't like oratorical tricks, and I am not striving for

theatrical effects when I say that I trust in our youth. Let me ask the young people, the Hungarian youth, not to forget their predecessors, the youth of March. We may call them also the youth of 1948. It is my desire, comrades, that we may have a youth of 1956 that will help the nation conquer the future.

Tibor Tardos, a young journalist and one of the *Szabad Nep* rebels, said:

How easily the freedom of the Hungarian press was won 108 years ago! Vasvari* and Petofi were standing in front of the Heckenast printing shop,† and old Uncle Heckenast said very loudly, "No, I cannot do it, I cannot print it! There is censorship." However, he whispered to his young besiegers, "Seize one of the presses!" Petofi and his friends smiled broadly and cried, "In the name of the people, we seize this press!" And they put their hands on the very old, black, oily printing press. And a mere touch of the hand brought about freedom of the press in Hungary.

For years, the Petofi statues have been looking down upon us questioningly, severely, with loathing. It seems to me that they want us to account for the freedom of the press. . . . We know from experience that there aren't many peasants, workers, and intellectuals in this "satellite" Hungary who wish to restore Horthyite Hungary—at least, I haven't met many. . . . But there are many who consider this dogmatic leadership, this bureaucratism, this lack of information, this obscurantism alien to our people and to our ideals. They are right, and it is up to the leadership to draw its own conclusions, to change its line, to analyze its theories and alter its practices—not gradually and imperceptibly, but unequivocally, immediately, and structurally.

---

* Pal Vasvari, like Petofi, was one of the most brilliant young heroes of the 1848 Revolution, and, again like Petofi, he met his death on the battle field.

† The Landerer and Heckenast printing shop was one of the oldest book printers in the country. In the 1848 Revolution, old Heckenast, though of German descent, behaved like a real Hungarian patriot.

Professor Lajos Janossy, who had taught at Trinity College
in Dublin during the war and was now Chairman of the Hungarian Atomic Energy Commission, had this to say:

> Recently, when we went to Moscow to confer with our
> Soviet colleagues, it turned out that they knew considerably
> more about the Hungarian uranium fields than we did. We
> knew next to nothing about them, but our Soviet colleagues
> were kind enough to put some of the data at our disposal.

Sandor Fekete, a young journalist and staff member of *Szabad
Nep*, came to the meeting directly from the airfield. He had
just returned from Moscow, where he had reported to his paper
on the Khrushchev-Tito encounter. He said:

> My experience is that we must expect neither Moscow nor
> Belgrade to solve our problems for us. We must solve our
> problems ourselves, right here in Budapest.

Tibor Meray said, among other things, the following:

> The last decade has distorted our way of thinking, and
> therefore, necessarily, it has also distorted truth. This harm-
> ful and distorted outlook that has cast us under a spell has
> prevailed in our assessment of not only Hungarian but also
> international events. Whenever something could not be fitted
> into our aprioristic opinions, our mechanized thought proc-
> esses pressed it forcibly into the scheme. . . . This judgment
> pronounced upon ourselves, this self-criticism, is not imposed
> upon us from the outside, at orders from above. . . . On
> the contrary, from above they are trying to talk us out of
> it. But we can no longer remain silent. The telling of truth
> is our most imperative inner necessity. Without it, we can
> no longer face ourselves or our people. . . . It is not the
> state-owned automobiles, the alternating drivers, the special
> stores, the extra-high salaries, the protocol list, etc., that
> make the journalist. It is whether or not he is a militant
> of truth. And let me add: even now, after the Twentieth

Congress, we must fight to be able to tell the truth. They are still trying to smother the writers and journalists by stressing Party loyalty. But what Party loyalty is that which opposes truth? What kind of a situation is it when truth is disloyal to the Party? Two half-truths do not make one full truth. We want the full truth. Only the full truth will satisfy us. But you can have truth only where there is freedom. And therefore, first and foremost, we demand freedom! Not the freedom of the oppressors, but the freedom of the people.

Participating in the debate were three members of the Central Committee: Sandor Nogradi, head of the Agitation-Propaganda Department, Marton Horvath, and Zoltan Vas, who had spent sixteen years in jail with Rakosi and was now Deputy Minister of Foreign Trade. All spoke at great length, but without success. These people hated Rakosi from the bottom of their hearts, and yet, in the name of Party unity and discipline, they rushed to his defense. Though their addresses contained traces of self-criticism, they were trying hard to find excuses for the bankrupt mechanism and its dictator. But the crowd was impatient and interruption upon interruption smothered their voices, calling them and the entire leadership to account for their deeds.

To give an impression of the atmosphere of the meeting, we quote part of Sandor Nogradi's speech (from the shorthand minutes of the meeting):

I . . . if the comrades will permit, take exception to the radical views voiced by Comrade Dery and, in many respects, by Comrade Tardos . . . [Loud interruption.] Patience, comrades! If you please, I am very glad of the applause, very glad of the abuses [Hear, hear!], because they show that a new March is needed, a new revolution . . . [Yes, yes!] Patience, comrades! My opinion is that our Party, our Communist Party—together with the membership, together with the people and because we are together with

them—has recognized the tragic errors and grave mistakes
the Party has committed and will know how to correct
them. [Loud interruption.] . . . It is our tragedy, but if
you will permit me, I shall speak also in your name . . .
[No, no!] Our tragedy is that we thought in the way we
thought. . . .

When Zoltan Vas said that Rakosi's dismissal would be a
tragedy for this old militant of the working-class movement, he
was answered:

"We prefer the tragedy of one man to the tragedy of a
nation!"

It must have been 2:30 a.m. when a bespectacled, dark-
haired, fortyish man rose to speak—the last speaker of the meeting. His name was Geza Losonczy, and he was one of the most
gifted, most unusual, and most tragic figures of the regime.
Losonczy had studied to become a secondary-school teacher of
French and Hungarian, and he had attended the Sorbonne in
Paris during the thirties. This son of a Protestant minister had
then, though barely twenty, been a member of the underground
Hungarian Communist Party and had performed a brave Party
task—that of smuggling Jozsef Revai's book *Marxism, Populism,
and Hungarianism* (written in Moscow) into Hungary.* In
1945, when the book had received legal publication in Hungary,
Jozsef Revai had expressed his gratitude to the brave and loyal
ex-student, and Losonczy had risen rapidly until he had become
one of the best-known leaders of the country. He was the Party
favorite, or rather Revai's favorite. The Party could make good
use of this Debrecen Calvinist who had been one of the founders of the anti-fascist organization called the "Front of March."
He was an intelligent, cultured, and handsome young man, a

---

* Not much later the book was published in Budapest under the name
of a young journalist, Gyula Kallai, who then worked, together with
Losonczy, in the editorial offices of the Social Democratic daily *Nepszava*,
having been sent there by the Party. Revai, as a Muscovite, could not use
his own name in Hungary.

gifted publicist, and an excellent speaker. He was a member of the Central Committee, the editor of the Party's weekly *Tovabb* ("Forward"), a member of the Hungarian delegation to the Paris Peace Conference, the principal speaker at the World Peace Meeting of intellectuals at Wroclaw, and the youngest member of the Hungarian Government delegation that visited Stalin in 1948. Later, he became Deputy Minister of State and subsequently, when Revai was Minister of Culture, he became Deputy Minister of Culture.

Where was the modest and shy Paris student of the past? Losonczy's manner had become supercilious, his articles longer and emptier, his speeches full of slogans and devoid of truth. He had become a man of importance. He had never pretended to be an expert on music, yet a full-page article now appeared in *Szabad Nep* under his name—an article about Bela Bartok. This was a Hungarian variation on Zhdanov's Party criticism of Shostakovich and Prokofiev which sought to prove that, though Bartok was indeed a gifted musician, he was not "our example" because his music was full of "decadent and formalistic elements." The Budapest opera house, Losonczy wrote, had committed an error in performing Bartok's works so frequently. Thereafter, the Budapest opera house played Bartok's music less frequently. And the inhabitant of the elegant villa in Buda believed that he was infallible.

Then, suddenly, the atmosphere around him had grown dense. The AVO arrested his father-in-law, Sandor Haraszti. And rumors spread that Losonczy was not quite so blameless, either. There was no concrete accusation against him, but he had been very friendly with Laszlo Rajk and some of the others who were arrested. First, he was relieved of his post as Deputy Minister, and then—together with Janos Kadar, Ferenc Donath, Gyula Kallai, Szilard Ujhelyi, and other non-Muscovite leaders—he had been arrested early in 1951. This had been the second act of the Rajk case—an act much less sensational than the first because the accused simply disappeared. There had been no indictment and no public trial. It happened that, six

months later, one or the other of the people who had disap-
peared was telephoned at his office by some uninformed person.
All the secretary had said was, "The comrade is on sick leave.
It is uncertain when he will return."

Geza Losonczy had returned after four years. Neither his
former fellow students nor the companions of the "glorious
years" had then recognized him. The tortures, the solitary cells,
and the endless questionings had ravaged him more than many
of his fellow prisoners, though he had spent the last months of
his prison life in the infirmary with a hemorrhage of the lung,
his mind deranged.*

He was, however, cured. He spent long months in a sana-
torium and had a lung operation; his mental illness disappeared
as though it had never existed. When he returned to public life
in the summer of 1955, he was a new man, modest and quiet,
understanding and calm, uninhibited and gay—a man who
knew that no one in whom human sentiments and impulses
had died could live and act worthily. He had accepted no high

---

* In August, 1954, Marton Horvath summoned me to his room. "I
should like to inform you," he said, "that Losonczy has been released from
prison, and he and many others have received amnesty."

[In those days, it was only "amnesty," not "rehabilitation."]

"Look," he continued uncomfortably, "I also want to tell you that poor
Losonczy is badly deranged by these years in prison. As a matter of fact,
he is not quite normal. Now, the doctors say that it might do him good
if he were taken to some of the places where he formerly worked."

I was deeply shocked by what he said and waited for him to continue.

"Listen," Horvath went on, "his wife and brother are to bring him up
here in about half an hour to talk to me. Do you think it would be a
good idea to send down one of our collaborators to meet him at the
door?"

"Certainly," I said.

We discussed who, among the old members of the paper, that person
should be.

"I won't ask you to be present at the conversation," Horvath said.
"Perhaps it is better for him to meet only one person. But, I wanted you,
an old friend of his and a member of the editorial board, to know about
it."

I don't know what went on at the meeting, but Losonczy's wife later
told me that, when they left, Losonczy stopped in the street and said:

"I knew it was all a comedy. Now they tried this to wring an admission
out of me."—T.M.

position from the hands of those in power, but had become one of Imre Nagy's closest friends.

When Losonczy rose to speak at the meeting of the Petofi Circle, the audience was almost dead with exhaustion, and he spoke in a voice so low that even in the first rows it was difficult to catch what he said. He was nervous and shy, for this was his first public appearance in six years. At first, the audience fidgeted as it listened to him reading uninteresting statistical data which compared the conditions of the press during the Horthy and the Rakosi regimes. He unmasked the latter without, however, praising the former. Some people felt that it was time to go home, but others encouraged him with cries of "Louder!" and "Faster!" Gradually, he warmed to his subject, and his voice became louder. As if his five years in prison had not been enough, he politely apologized to Hungarian intellectuals, and particularly to the Hungarian musicians, for the article in which he had offended Bartok's memory. Then he spoke of the state of the country. He did not mention details—others had done that before him—but he pointed out the moral anomaly that the very same men who had thrown innocent people into prison were now "rehabilitating" them, and that the very same men who had murdered innocent people were now talking of "socialist legality." And he said it was an untenable situation that, day after day, the press should attack and falsely accuse Imre Nagy, that good Hungarian and loyal Communist, without even giving Nagy an opportunity to defend himself.

When he mentioned Imre Nagy's name, thousands of people rose in their seats, and thousands of voices shouted repeatedly:

"Long live Imre Nagy! Long live Imre Nagy!"

And then again, for minutes on end:

"Take him back into the Party! Take him back into the Party!"

For, strange as it may seem, the audience of the Petofi Circle did not demand the dissolution of the Party. They did not demand that it should disappear from Hungarian public life. All they demanded was that Imre Nagy should be one of its

leaders and that the renascent Party should make good what
the former leadership had spoiled. Whether their demands were
realistic, whether the Communist Party could ever change its
colors—that was another question. Those who were branded
by the Central Committee three days later as an "anti-Party,
counterrevolutionary, and reactionary" assembly perhaps believed in such a possibility.

Dawn was breaking when the participants of the meeting
left the building. It was 3:30 a.m. on June 28.

A few hours later, several hundred kilometers away, the
Polish workers revolted in Poznan.

To Rakosi, the Poznan uprising was a godsend. This master
of improvised trials was immediately ready with his latest im-
provisation: Poznan and the Petofi Circle were parts of a great
international movement fostered by the imperialists.

It seemed certain that the "shaggy one," fighting to retain
power, would not be satisfied with the immediate expulsion of
Dery and Tardos from the Party by the Central Control Committee, but that he was planning other, unforeseeable steps. That
is why the writers and journalists who were assembled in the
little editorial office of *Beke es Szabadsag* had felt a cold hand
on their necks when the mysterious announcement had come
that the Central Committee was about to make an important
statement. They were intellectuals—branded "rightists"—and
active participants of the Petofi Circle's debates. The most "com-
promised" among them thought, for the thousandth time in
the last two years, that they would surely be arrested.

An hour went by, then two. They lit one cigarette after
another, drank innumerable cups of strong black coffee. Some
leafed through their notebooks, tearing out a page here and a
page there. Someone telephoned Imre Nagy's apartment to find
out whether the "old man" was home. He was. They warned
him that something was in the offing. He thanked them, but
said nothing more. To him, waiting for arrest was hardly a
new experience. He had lived with that expectation for more
than a year.

Toward noon, the telephone on the editor's desk rang. It was Party headquarters. The same cool, unconcerned voice dictated a communiqué which, it said, must be published in the next issue of the paper. The communiqué read as follows:

> Recognizing Comrade Matyas Rakosi's merits in the Hungarian and international working-class movement and in the fight for the Hungarian people's future happiness and for a socialist Hungary, the Central Committee relieves him, at his own request, of his membership in the Political Committee and of his post as First Secretary of the Central Committee.

For a few moments, the little room was absolutely silent. The journalists simply could not believe their ears. It was too good— far too good to be true. The "shaggy one" was defeated. Rakosi was no more!

Then laughter rang out loud and unafraid, and joy welled up like a geyser—powerful, almost tearful joy. Glasses appeared on the table, and, from some hidden drawer, a bottle of apricot brandy. They drank. They laughed and drank. Was it true? Had they really won?

The truth is that their joy was unmarred even after they found out that Gero had been appointed Rakosi's successor. They knew that Gero was no better than Rakosi, but they also knew that Rakosi was the worst of all. And he was gone. The strongest pillar had crumbled. It would be much easier to smash the second pillar.

However, they still did not know how it had all happened— so rapidly and unexpectedly. Twentieth Congress or no Twentieth Congress, that old rascal had withstood so many storms, had pulled himself up so many slopes after having slithered halfway down (and these last weeks it had seemed as if his position had again been reinforced) that something of importance must have happened to make him slide all the way down.

Twenty-four hours later, they knew. Imre Nagy's circle had a constant informant in the Central Committee. This was Kalman Pongracz, the Mayor of Budapest, and it was he who, smiling broadly and with great gusto, now told them the authentic story of Rakosi's fall.

The "shaggy one" had indeed devised a plan to continue and to bring to a spectacular end his persecution of Imre Nagy and the Petofi Circle—a plan that was fully worthy of him. He had prepared a list of writers, journalists, student leaders, and Army officers whom he intended to have arrested in one night. There were four hundred names on his list.

Since those were the days of "collective leadership," he had submitted his plan to the Political Committee. The committee members were perturbed—not by the arrests, for they had accomplished bigger things in their days, but by the problem of how they might incorporate this action with the new political line, with the slogan of "socialist legality," and with the "noble ideals" of the Twentieth Congress. They had suggested that a decision be postponed until they had discussed the matter more thoroughly.

An hour later, Istvan Kovacs, Party Secretary of Budapest and a member of the Political Committee (and a calculating, sinister careerist) had telephoned the Soviet ambassador and told him what Rakosi was planning to do. The Soviet ambassador had immediately telephoned Moscow and informed the Kremlin.

While the Political Committee met in a second session to discuss the plan, a Soviet airplane landed on one of the Soviet military airfields near Budapest, and the plane's single passenger climbed into a waiting automobile and sped toward the Academy Street Party headquarters without previously informing anyone of his arrival. The passenger was none other than Anastas I. Mikoyan, First Deputy Chairman of the Soviet Council of Ministers. The AVO guard at the entrance, surprised and impressed by the visitor, probably forgot to ask him for identification papers and did not dare to ask him whether he was armed.

Mikoyan went straight to the "council of the gods." (In his

presence, of course, the gods remained at best demigods.) When Mikoyan entered, Rakosi was telling his colleagues that the arrest of the four hundred must be carried out without fail.

At the sight of the unexpected guest, the words stuck in Rakosi's throat. But Mikoyan kindly asked him to continue and to act exactly as if he were not present. To stress his insignificance, he placed himself modestly at the end of the table.

And Rakosi continued. He was not too pleased with this unscheduled arrival, but there was nothing he could do about it. He explained that the Party could no longer tolerate this anti-Party agitation, that it had to use force—or else the enemy would become even more impertinent.

He sat down. There was a painful and protracted pause. Nobody dared speak, nobody dared voice an opinion because nobody knew why the long-nosed Armenian had come. To arrest, or not to arrest?

At last, Mikoyan had had to break the silence. As modestly as he had come, he posed but one single question: What did Comrade Rakosi think of the Petofi Circle?

Perspiration broke out on Rakosi's forehead while he explained once more that the Petofi Circle was an organized and hostile anti-Party movement.

"Interesting," Mikoyan said in a low voice. "We in Moscow have received information that at the meeting of the Petofi Circle, the Party was loudly and rhythmically cheered for minutes on end. Is that true?"

"It is true," Rakosi said, "but I must add . . ."

"A strange anti-Party movement," Mikoyan interrupted him, "that cheers the Party."

This was all he said, and nothing more was needed.

Gero took the cue. This old Comintern fox knew immediately that Rakosi was lost. And after eleven years of staunch and loyal support of Rakosi on every issue, this man—who would have had no qualms about executing the mass arrests himself—turned on Rakosi. In fact, it had always been his desire to be leader of the Party, and now he felt that the great

moment had arrived at last. Ruthlessly and "courageously," he
opposed Rakosi's plan. With "Bolshevik straightforwardness,"
he criticized his hitherto religiously obeyed boss for not having
applied the glorious directives of the Twentieth Congress to
the Hungarian situation.

One after the other, all rose to speak. And with the exception of the quite stupid Jozsef Mekis, they all agreed—miraculously—with Gero. Rakosi, the wise father of the people, the
beloved leader of the Party and the country, remained alone.
Even his most loyal disciples, the followers who had been no-
bodies until he had promoted them, deserted him as soon as
they sensed that the Russians were no longer backing him.

Mikoyan's task was then easy: all he had to do was to sum
up the discussion. It was not his intention, he said, to interfere
in the internal affairs of another Party—far from it. Still, his
fraternal opinion was that, since the majority of the Political
Committee appeared not to agree with Comrade Rakosi, it
would perhaps be advisable for Comrade Rakosi to draw his
own conclusions and resign his post as First Secretary of the
Hungarian Party.

Rakosi was livid. He could not bring himself to realize that
such a thing as this could happen to him. That he—HE—should
be dismissed and requested to give up his power. His lips trembling, he warned Mikoyan that he did not understand what he
was doing, that this decision would have unforeseeable consequences within the Party and, indeed, throughout the country.

Mikoyan replied calmly, "Comrade Rakosi may rest assured
that the Party will remain in good hands."

Rakosi continued to protest. His only remaining hope was
that Mikoyan spoke merely in his own name. So he went into
the other room and telephoned Khrushchev.

"The Party needs me," he said. "If I leave, everything will
collapse . . ."

"Have no fear," Nikita Sergeyevich reassured him, kindly.
"But the Moscow Politburo thinks that it would be advisable
for you to resign."

His fate was thus sealed. There was no one left to whom he could appeal. And to make his lot even more bitter, at the Central Committee meeting held the next day in Mikoyan's presence, he was compelled—according to time-honored Bolshevik traditions—to exercise self-criticism:

> Honorable Central Committee!
> I request the Central Committee to relieve me of the post of First Secretary of the Central Committee and of my membership in the Politburo. One of the reasons for my request is that I am in my sixty-fifth year and my illness, with which I have now been suffering for two years with increasingly aggravated effects, hinders me from discharging the work devolving upon the First Secretary of the Central Committee. . . .
> As regards my condition of health, I have been suffering hypertension for the past two years. My blood pressure is rising, and a few days ago the physician sent to the Politburo a report from which I would like to quote one sentence: "We do not in any way consider Comrade Rakosi's present condition satisfactory, and consequently we ask for the most urgent intervention in order to prevent a deterioration of his condition."
> My comrades have frequently mentioned in the past two years that I do not visit the factories as often as I did in the past. They are right; the only thing they did not know is that this was due to the deterioration of my health. My state of health began to tell on the quality and amount of work I was able to perform—a fact that is bound to cause harm to the Party in such an important post. So much about the state of my health.
> As regards the mistakes that I committed in the field of the "cult of personality" and the violation of socialist legality, I admitted them at the meetings of the Central Committee in June, 1953, and I have made the same admission repeatedly ever since. I have also exercised self-criticism publicly.
> After the Twentieth Congress of the CPSU and Comrade

Khrushchev's speech, it became clear to me that the weight
and effect of these mistakes were greater than I had thought
and that the harm done to our Party through these mistakes was much more serious than I had previously believed.

These mistakes have made our Party's work more difficult; they have diminished the strength of attraction of the
Party and of the People's Democracy; they have hindered
the development of the Leninist norms of Party life, collective leadership, constructive criticism and self-criticism,
democracy in Party and state life, and the initiative and
creative power of the wide masses of the working class.

Finally, these mistakes have offered the enemy an excellent opportunity for attack. In their totality, the mistakes
that I have committed in the most important post of the
Party work have caused serious harm to our socialist development as a whole.

It was up to me to take the lead in repairing these mistakes. If rehabilitation has at times proceeded sluggishly
and with intermittent breaks, if a certain relapse was noticed
last year in the liquidation of the cult of personality, if
criticism and self-criticism together with collective leadership have developed at a slow pace, if sectarian and dogmatic views have not been combatted resolutely enough—
then, for all this, undoubtedly, serious responsibility weighs
upon me, since I have occupied the post of the First Secretary of the Party. . . .

He did not believe a single word of his "self-criticism." He
was firmly convinced that, although he was indeed ailing, he
could have gone on leading the Party for years. And he believed
even more firmly that all his actions had been correct and that
Khrushchev was making a fatal mistake in dismissing him. What
he said was the exact opposite of his firm convictions. This is
what is called "loyalty to the Party."

The Central Committee unanimously accepted Rakosi's resignation, as well as Gero's appointment. It elected as members of
the Political Committee Karoly Kiss, the Chairman of the Central Control Committee, and the gravely ill Jozsef Revai, who

(although he furiously denounced the writers and Imre Nagy) had lately turned against Rakosi because the "shaggy one" was holding up the "rehabilitation" of the released prisoners— among them Gyorgy Marosan, a "leftist Social Democrat" who had always cooperated with the Communists, and Janos Kadar, both of whom he personally liked. All this was intended as a guarantee that, though the members of the old guard were still in power, the old times and, particularly, the illegal practices would never return again.

On the same day, Mikoyan left Budapest for Yugoslavia to confer with Marshal Tito on the island of Brioni. He took as a gift to the Yugoslav people the news that Matyas Rakosi, the planner of the Rajk case and one of the principal organizers of the anti-Tito campaign, had fallen. This made it obvious that the dominant cause of Rakosi's fall was not the Petofi Circle, not the writers' rebellion and the list of four hundred, but the Soviet Party's efforts to win back Tito's favor at any price. Tito had been demanding Rakosi's removal, but the Soviet leaders had wavered and bargained. Now they sold him down the river. The list of four hundred names came in handy as an excuse. This realization was rather humiliating to Hungarians, but nobody really minded. They were too happy to worry about the political background of the maneuver.

Matyas Rakosi—father and leader of the Hungarian people, first and foremost Hungarian patriot, teacher of the Party— boarded a plane and departed for Moscow. He was not even given time to pack his belongings. For eleven years, he had been a ruler over life and death. Now he left the country like a dismissed domestic servant.

A few weeks later, his wife returned to Budapest to collect a few valuable carpets, pictures, and the table silver.

The Ordeal of the Bier*

The summer of 1956 was rather unsettled, with sudden heat waves, unexpected showers, blinding lightning, and ominous thunder. After Rakosi's fall, the country began to breathe more freely: the leech that had so long been sucking its blood had dropped from the body of the nation. In the first ecstatic moments, the people almost forgot that other leeches remained. In the glow of a happier future suddenly revealed, they almost forgot the unhappiness of the past. This was partly because the remaining parasites, warned by the not too enviable fate of the Party leaders, had thought it prudent to withdraw from the public scene for a while and to lurk in the background, watching events from their office windows. The "professional revolutionaries" sniffed cautiously to find out which way the wind was blowing.

With the easing of international tension, phrases like "rotten imperialism" and "American fascist reinforcements" disappeared from the pages of the newspapers. Suddenly, everything became more objective and sober.

---

* The ordeal of the bier is an ancient Hungarian folk custom. When someone was murdered and the murderer could not be found, the entire population of the village or town had to pass in single file before the bier. It was believed that when the murderer passed by, the dead victim's wound would reopen and begin to bleed.

Gradually, against much resistance, negotiations with Imre Nagy were set in motion from not only the Hungarian but also the Soviet side. The Soviet ambassador in Budapest had frequent meetings with Nagy to discuss the problems of a final solution. The new First Secretary of the Party, Erno Gero—well aware that his advancement had not been greeted with exaggerated enthusiasm throughout the country—made himself almost invisible. This tactical retreat resulted, however, in the disintegration of the Party machinery. The majority of the Party officials in the Rakosi clique were more or less paralyzed. They hardly dared to raise their voices in the new atmosphere, and, when they did, they were very careful and circumspect, trying hard to master the new language that, willy-nilly, they had to learn. They were forced into the realization that their sun was setting. Now that the AVO could no longer be used as a supreme weapon in an argument—i.e., as the dominant answer to any question—the system was necessarily and inescapably doomed to failure. In the present atmosphere, the terrorist organization was nothing more than an assembly of roaring but toothless lions. In addition, symptoms of crisis and disintegration were beginning to manifest themselves within the AVO as well. A wave of indignation and protest swept among the officers who had not participated in the political trials, who had not committed crimes, and who had refused to be made responsible for the bloodshed of others. They demanded that those responsible for the trials, arrests, and "purifications" be called to account.

The process of dissolution in the Party, the state machinery, and the political police brought a number of features to the surface. It became evident that the loyal Party members—the Communists of such deep convictions!—were badly disillusioned, cynical men filled with hatred and contempt for the omnipotent Party. The best example was perhaps Gyorgy Mate, Party Secretary of the Writers' Association and an old member of the underground Communist Party. Mate had been one of the most disciplined Party members for two decades. Without the slightest protest, he had executed every resolution, following every twist of the Party line. He had some merit as a journalist, but was best known for his entertaining and ironical little writings published in *Szabad Nep* during the first years of the regime, in which he had exposed the anomalies to be detected in the life of the Party. After a while, the Party had grown tired of these jibes, the series had been stopped, and Mate had been informed that it would be much better if he paid more attention to the positive features of Party life. Mate had understood the hint: henceforth, his sense of satire had manifested itself only in private conversations, and even there only with great moderation. In public, he had always been quite careful, hyperloyal, circumspect, and dignified. As a member of the underground Party, he had, for years, been earmarked for eventual arrest.

In the summer of 1956, however, Mate threw circumspection to the winds. The withered roots of his humor, suppressed for years, suddenly broke through with renewed life. His attacks were the sharpest—and the wittiest. Nothing was sacred to him—not even the Party. He was the father of the bitterest and the most sarcastic jokes of that period, and more often than not, they revealed his utter disillusionment. As presiding officer at the meetings of the Writers' Association, he vigilantly watched over the "prestige of the Party"—and this prestige had no more zealous and successful saboteur than the Party Secretary himself.

During the course of the summer, the barbed wire fences were taken down and the land mines lifted out of the western and southern frontier belts. It seemed as though—slowly but ever more certainly—the Iron Curtain was being raised.

A few journalists visited Yugoslavia, the country whose leaders had for years been branded as "murderous hirelings of imperialism," "imperialist lap dogs," and the like*—the coun-

---

* At the Army's target-shooting practices, for instance, heads of Tito had been used as targets. Now these were replaced with the usual circular targets.

try that had bravely opposed Stalin and Stalinism for years. When these journalists returned, they wrote with sympathy about the neighboring country, but they also said that it was only a more moderate form of one-man dictatorship, with different slogans and a few really novel institutions but with the same terrorist organizations and "personality cult" that had now been condemned in the Soviet Union. The journalists reported that Tito's portrait hung on the walls of every restaurant and coffeehouse; though they knew and admitted the difference between the two men, it displeased them after having had to face Rakosi's portraits practically every minute of their lives. They reported that the living conditions not only of peasants and workers but also of the intellectuals were worse (though for partly understandable reasons) than those in bankrupt Hungary. They discovered that there was much less freedom of the press and of opinion in Yugoslavia than in Hungary *that summer*, that the writers could deal much less openly with their country's problems—in other words that, as a result of the struggles of the last few months, Hungary had surpassed Yugoslavia in democratic progress. These findings confirmed the journalists and writers in their conviction that, as far as freedom was concerned, it would be bad for both them and the Hungarian people to cling fast to the Yugoslav stage of development—formerly used as a prop and an argument, and as a model for Hungary's future. If they wanted to progress, the *only valid method*, they said, was to find a way to promote socialist development by democratic means, taking into account the conditions, the stage of development, the traditions, the resources, and the mood of the country.

Simultaneously with the removal of the land mines, individual and collective trips were permitted to the nearest Western capital, Vienna. Austrian neutrality had given new life to this city which had been nearly dead for years. Its atmosphere of freedom, its beautiful shop windows, its busy traffic could not help but deeply impress the groups (consisting mainly of writers, journalists, and artists) who streamed toward the Austrian capital by train, bus, and ship. Vienna and Budapest had always been rivals; the Austro-Hungarian monarchy had linked historically these two capitals which had so much in common structurally. The visitors now noted bitterly how far Vienna was ahead of Budapest. The bustling streets, the sleek automobiles, the lovely products that had disappeared from the Hungarian markets years ago, the amazing variety of nylon goods that were in Hungary considered the very symbols of elegance—all these spoke of a richness that rendered the superiority of the Soviet type of socialism very doubtful.*

The Hungarian visitors discovered that, in Vienna, the orange juice was made of oranges (not of tar, as in Hungary), that shoe polish shined the shoes (instead of ruining the shoe leather), that the traffic cop here directed the traffic (instead of concentrating on the political reliability of the individual). But above all, they discovered that not only the capitalists but also the workers lived better and more freely than in Hungary, where the proletariat was allegedly in power. The comparison between the two systems gave rise to passionate emotions—and often to unjust remarks. After all, the Austrian workers had *always* lived better than their Hungarian fellow workers; the Hungarian system could be reproached only for having *increased*, instead of lessening, that difference. It was, however, a fact that could no longer be obscured by propaganda that Hungary had become a "poor relation" in the last decade and that its overnationalized economic system had failed the test at the first opportunity for comparison.

---

* The following joke, fashionable at that time in Budapest, is illustrative:

Two Hungarians meet on the Kahlenberg, near Vienna. One sniffs the air, his face twisted in a strange grimace. The other asks him what he is doing.

"Can't you smell?" the first man asks. "Don't you smell how it stinks here?"

"No. What kind of smell is it?"

"A smell of rotting capitalism!"

The Marxist expression "rotting capitalism" appeared in the Hungarian press so frequently that everyone understood the joke.

When the ships returned to Hungary, they brought angry and determined people who looked around with distaste at the badly lighted Budapest streets, at the coffeehouses which served execrable coffee, at the dirty railway stations where every train was late. The returning travelers took a gloomy view of the whole situation. Yet, in many respects they were wrong. If, for instance, one observed Hungarian theatrical life, Hungarian films, or Hungarian publishing that made the classics available to all—then the country had nothing to be ashamed of in comparison with its Western neighbor. Still, who could blame the travelers? One could hardly expect the inhabitants of a ruined country to be objective. Hungary's backwardness pained them not only because one could buy oranges, bananas, and excellent coffee in Vienna, but because they thought of the almost infinite possibilities inherent in a neutral Hungary—should the country be given the opportunities Austria had!

The summer of 1956 belonged to the writers of Hungary. Rakosi's fall had fully justified them and had defeated the swaggering Party officials, the "lynch gang" of the Ironworkers Headquarters, and the threatening terrorists. In August and September, the writers and journalists who had received the most severe Party punishments less than six months previously were called to Party headquarters, where they were solemnly told that, although they had indeed committed formal mistakes, they had been in the right. The Party admitted having been wrong, and revoked the reprimands.* Even those who had been expelled from the Party were now reinstated, and their little

---

* In the corridors of Party headquarters, immediately after the Central Control Committee's self-criticism, I ran into Karoly Kiss, Chairman of the Committee and "distributor" of the punishments. He was very kind and polite.

"Believe me," he said, "we knew *even then* that you were right. You must remember that we did not even argue with you."

"Then, why did you do it?"

He looked dreamily into the air and sighed deeply. "Rakosi," he said. "It was his fault. You must understand that we could not do otherwise. The main thing is that now we are rid of him. No such thing will ever happen again."—T.A.

red membership books were returned. A Rehabilitation Committee was formed in the Journalists' Association to investigate not only the case of the offended Communists but also that of the so-called "bourgeois" journalists who had been silenced for years. They did not receive moral and financial compensation.

What surprised the *apparatchiks* most was that the writers were not in the least delighted with the beautiful apologies. These writers were still dissatisfied not only because Imre Nagy's case (and the cases of Tibor Dery and Tibor Tardos) had not been settled as yet—facts that rendered their "rehabilitation" meaningless. It was also because they felt that more was at stake than just the rectification of individual injustices. The affairs of the entire country had to be put in order. So it was that none of the *Szabad Nep* rebels accepted his old post at the paper when it was offered and that each refused to go back unless all confirmed Stalinists were removed from the editorial board. The writers declared, one after the other, that they were completely uninterested in a "rehabilitation" until Dery and Tardos were given satisfaction. In the end, the repeal of the Party punishments was carried out in exactly the same way as their distribution—without asking the interested parties or, rather, against their wills.

As far as the writers were concerned, gestures meant nothing: they demanded action. They cared little about the various commentaries in their official files. What they really cared about was free and open talk. They wanted to publish at last the writings hidden in their desk drawers. They wanted to tell the things they had for years been prevented from telling. The "rehabilitation" of thought and work was more important than that of the people.

But much happened in that field also. The demands of the writers, contained in the incriminated Memorandum, were now fulfilled almost without exception. The opera house performed Bartok's *The Miraculous Mandarin* with tremendous success. Volumes of poems were published by Laszlo Nagy and Laszlo Benjamin. The National Theater resumed the performances of

The Tragedy of Man, put on Laszlo Nemeth's *Galileo*; and rehearsals of Gyula Hay's *Justice for Gaspar Varro* were also in full swing. A new atmosphere of freedom reigned in the publishing houses, editorial offices, theaters, and film studios.

Bookshops displayed Tibor Dery's wonderful short novel *Niki*, which depicted the tragedy of the innocently imprisoned through the fate of a dog. The Attila Jozsef Theater performed a play by the gifted young playwright Jozsef Gali. It was *Szabadsaghegy*,* a moving exposure of the life of the high Party officials. At the film studios on Gyarmat Street, sharply satirical films were being made at a speed unequaled in the last decade.

Bold, uncompromising writings appeared in the various newspapers. The circulation of *Irodalmi Ujsag* jumped from eight or ten thousand to 30,000—and stopped at 30,000 only because the Party bureaucracy, complaining of a shortage, would allow no more paper. Thus, it came about that the paper, whose official price was one *forint*, sold for twenty to thirty *forints* throughout the country, and fights for the last copy of the paper were frequent occurrences at the newsstands. A number of news dealers took advantage of the situation and would sell *Irodalmi Ujsag* only if the customer also bought *Szabad Nep* or some other dull publication as well. The paper's articles and poems were often typed out and circulated. Gradually, the tone of *Irodalmi Ujsag* permeated other quarters. The Peace Council's weekly, *Peace and Freedom*, adopted it; so did *Cultured People*, the journal of the Ministry of Culture (now rid of Gyorgy Non).† A new weekly, *Monday News*, also took the same tone; in it, Miklos Gimes—expelled from the Party a year before because of his inquiries into the Rajk affair—publicly demanded for the first time that Matyas Rakosi and Mihaly Farkas be called to account.

---

* The Szabadsaghegy is one of the most beautiful residential districts of Budapest, the favorite district of the past and present ruling classes.

† Non was at last relieved of his position as Deputy Minister and given a high position—that of leading public prosecutor in Hungary. His qualifications for this job were that he knew as little about law as he did about culture.

This was the summer of thought freely expressed. Troubles
and desires, accusations and hopes were at last openly articu-
lated. A poet who had spent years in prison, Gyorgy Faludy,
now told of his experiences. A young journalist, Domokos Varga,
declared that "the Stalinist program of industrialization, which
was hitherto the basis of our conception, has become fully useless, however hard we may try to adapt it to Hungarian conditions." An outstanding publicist, Gyorgy Paloczi-Horvath, wrote:
"Let us look back with the eyes of a child upon all the measures
taken in these last years. This era was unsuitable for children."
A young critic, Sandor Lukacsy, addressed the Hungarian Minister of Culture, Jozsef Darvas: "Tell us at last how many trials,
how much blood, what mourning, how many sobbing peasants, how many disturbed minds, blinded eyes, base acts, loud
hypocrisy, sorrow, madness, how much gall mounting to the
height of your mouth, you would have needed to taste, at last,
the bitterness and retch up words of 'purification?'" A young
writer, Tibor Tardos, described how the people had been cheated
and betrayed: they had been promised a "sea full of lemonade,"
by the loudspeakers screaming lies at them, but "at home people
had looked into the jug. A few drops of salt water clung to its
bottom, a few seaweeds and nothing more. They looked at each
other apathetically. They washed out the jug and drank water
from the well as before. But they were not happy."

The writers expressed their conviction that there were no
two truths—a "socialist" and a "bourgeois" truth—and that
there were only truth and lies, and that the whole theory served
only to cover up illegal deeds and violence. And they declared
that, hereafter, they would demand the full truth and absolute
freedom. Their spokesman was Gyula Hay:

> Well, let us get it over quickly. We are talking about the
> *full freedom* of literature. We understand by this the most
> absolute, the most unlimited freedom possible among people
> living in a society. In other words, nothing should be for-
> bidden to literature that is not forbidden in the laws of the
> country. Thus, literature should not be permitted to incite

to murder, arson, robbery, theft, the overthrow of the
People's Democracy, atrocities against certain strata or professions, racial discrimination, bureaucratic autocracy, etc.
Literature should not be permitted to slander or offend certain laws that, though unwritten, are accepted by the majority as ethical norms. . . .

However, the writer, like anybody else, should be allowed
to tell the truth without restrictions; to criticize everybody
and everything; to be sad, to be in love, to think of death;
not to wonder whether his work contains "positive" and
"negative" elements in the prescribed proportion; to believe
or disbelieve in the omnipotence of God; to doubt the
accuracy of certain statistics of plans; to think in a non-
Marxist way; or to think in a Marxist way even if his
thought has not as yet figured among the officially proclaimed and obligatory truths; to consider the living standard of people low; to consider as unjust something which
is officially described as just; to dislike certain leaders; to
suggest honest solutions to problems, even if our political
and economic leaders consider these suggestions unrealistic
and even if it turns out later that they were, indeed, unrealistic; to portray difficulties without presenting a solution;
to consider the New York building ugly, though it is proclaimed a monument and many millions were spent on it;
to notice how the town deteriorates because there is no
money to repair the houses; to condemn the way of life,
tone, and style of work of certain leading personalities; to
fight for humane conduct, even where less sensitive souls
notice no inhumanity; to admire Stalintown, or not to admire Stalintown; to write in an unusual style; to oppose
Aristotelian dramaturgy, or to insist on Aristotelian dramaturgy; to despise certain writings that persons of authority
have found exemplary, and vice versa; to respect certain
literary values, and to ignore certain literary values; etc.,
etc., etc. Who could deny that of all this, much was forbidden only a short while ago—forbidden, at least in practice, under the threat of sanctions—and that even today it
is only tolerated instead of declared free. This is the freedom we writers have to demand, come fire or sword.

One week later, on September 17, at the plenary meeting of the Hungarian Writers' Association, all that Gyula Hay had demanded became a practical reality. The meeting, imbued with the spirit of national unity and democratic freedom, revealed to the whole country the results of the writers' struggles. This plenary meeting swept away all obstacles from the path of literary progress. The election of the officials was carried out democratically and by secret ballot (the country had probably never seen such elections), and the election results showed it.

Excluded from the new leadership were all who had remained loyal to the last to Stalinist-Rakosi dogmatism, and who had supported Rakosi's attempts to hinder the free development of literature, and who—through their names and activities—had helped to cover up the series of crimes committed in the course of the last ten years. Among those dropped were the despised Jozsef Darvas, Bela Illes, Sandor Gergely, Kalman Sandor, and Erno Urban.* Elected in their places were writers who had been shelved for a decade by official cultural policies: Pal Ignotus, Aron Tamasi, Laszlo Nemeth, Jozsef Fodor, Lajos Kassak, and others. The meeting also elected those members of the older and younger generation of Communist writers who had, in the struggles of the last few years, turned against their own past and proved that they had the will and the talent to hold their own in a renewed literature: Gyula Hay, Tibor Dery, Zoltan Zelk, Laszlo Benjamin, Peter Kuczka, Imre Sarkadi, and others.

The elections threw some light on the development of the three groups of Communist writers—the Muscovites, the old Communists, and the new Communists. With the exception of Hay and Lukacs, the Muscovites retained their former views. It was too

---

* The author of *The Cucumber Tree* had turned against Imre Nagy when the latter was dismissed and expelled from the Party, and had protested against the "accusation" that he had ever been on terms of friendship with him. Nobody was particularly surprised. When Revai had persecuted Dery, Urban had turned against Dery. When Imre Nagy was in power, Urban had boasted of their friendship and that he was the *first* among the writers to describe the conditions in the country. When Imre Nagy was defeated, Urban took his hat and went to the other side: Rakosi seemed the better bet.

late for them to change. The problem was even more complex in the case of the older Communist writers. Several of them were unable to make a clean break with their past; they wavered and hesitated. Although they were attracted to the *new,* their exaggerated fear of a return to the old methods of the system and their almost grotesque attachment to Party discipline prevented them from taking an unequivocal stand in the literary movement. However, the overwhelming majority declared themselves partisans of a national unity in literature and of the freedom of literature.

The elite of this group—Tibor Dery, Zoltan Zelk, and others— had, in the course of time, become the leaders and philosophers of the writers' movement. Their names were a guarantee of the high standards, the political strivings, the honesty, and the moral value of the movement. Although it was never stated in so many words, the young writers considered Dery the most outstanding figure of the movement—a movement to which, they gave the impetus, the optimism, and the energy, for the fact that their representatives were now elected to leading positions in the Writers' Association was a recognition of their role in the struggle.

The second surprise of the plenary meeting—if one can talk about surprises at all—was that socialist realism as the only possible and only permissible literary trend was defeated in open vote. The writers had had enough of this stupid and anti-literary method which sought to force the richness and variety of life into a lifeless scheme. They had had enough of a reality that was constantly being changed to fit the current Party line. They refused to be tied down any longer to empty forms.

This passionate and strange movement—whose inspirers and militants had been the wardens of a literary prison for years— reached its peak during those days. By attacks and temporary retreats, stubbornly and without fear, it had achieved—if only for a while—the aims it had set itself: freedom of thought and freedom of speech. It must be admitted, however, that this new, fresh, and popular movement did not lack errors and weaknesses. Its leaders and participants were not only writers but also human beings—and, being human, they made mistakes and had certain shortcomings and weak spots and were in some ways politically naïve. The source of their weaknesses as well as of their virtues was perhaps the very circumstance that they were *writers,* and not politicians. Fortunately—or, perhaps, unfortunately—they did not realize that the moral compulsion which provided the impetus for their movement could provide neither the basis nor the material for political action—a realm which is, more often than not, immoral. While fighting for absolute truth, they often forgot the requirements of political realism; and by looking neither to the right nor to the left, they committed mistakes in the eyes of both. In the purifying storm which they had invoked, they paid no attention to the intrigues and etiquette of daily politics; they wanted to manage the affairs of the country and its people in the name of the absolute. But they were right in everything they said—and also in the way they said it. If they erred, their error sprang from their yearning for truth and from their enthusiasm. They remained aloof from considerations of power politics and of military strategy in Hungary and on the international scene.

There were certain other understandable human weaknesses. Some of these people, who, for many years, had been spokesmen for falsehoods and lies (whether they knew it or not), felt that now they were in the right at last. This would not have mattered much had not certain exaggerated, though human, personal ambitions come to the fore. For the first time in a decade, the writers were truly popular. After the false popularity that had surrounded them for so long, they enjoyed bathing in the love and unity which pervaded the country. It was wonderful for them to feel that there was real response to their writings, that people pronounced the word "writer" with respect and admiration, and that they were in the front lines of a national movement for liberty and reform. And it was indeed so: the people truly respected the writer who dared to put into words what, for years, they had hardly dared to think. The ties between writer and reader had, in fact, never been so strong. The editorial offices received stacks of letters applauding this new courage and raising other, hitherto untouched problems which they asked the writers to deal with also. Visitors came, one after the other, because now they were no longer afraid to tell the writers about their personal problems. They trusted them. They believed in them.

It is also true that the writers were never before so deeply respected by the Party: whenever they pointed out in the press some error in public life, these errors were usually corrected within forty-eight hours. It seemed as though no one dared to oppose those who held the power of the increasingly free pen in their hands. Small wonder, if the writers felt a little proprietary toward the country and, after drinking deep draughts from the miraculous and healing source of popularity, drove themselves ever forward to new achievements. This was particularly true of those who had not participated in the movement at all, or who had participated with a certain amount of reserve. These now suddenly became the boldest of all. They were in a hurry. They had to make up for lost months or, rather, years.

There was, for instance, Pal Szabo, who had once belonged to the group of peasant writers, but who had served Rakosi during the last decade just as rigorously as had the Communist writers. His little waverings had strengthened rather than weakened his position. Now, at last, he made up his mind which side he was on. He had to come forward with something sensational, for too much time had been lost. It was no longer sufficient to unmask conditions prevailing in the country. Something more was needed —a challenge which would prove to all concerned that he was braver and dared more than the others. He wrote a long article on the Hungarian prisoners-of-war still retained in the Soviet Union. No one knew for certain whether there were any Hungarians in the Soviet Union, but it was probable that, if there were, they numbered far fewer than the Germans and Japanese. To give Szabo his due, it was indeed inhuman to prevent these men from going home to their families eleven years after the war. But it was obvious that his raising of this question in the current situation and his emphasizing of it so strongly was hardly more

THE REVOLT OF THE MIND

than a personal bid for popularity. There were more urgent and more agonizing unsolved problems of Hungarian-Soviet relations.

The most regrettable characteristic of the writers' movement was its almost entirely negative objectives—i.e., it was *anti-Stalinist, anti-Rakosist*. The positive program that should have inspired the whole movement was still lacking. The formulation of a comprehensive program required time and reflection; but as long as obstructing forces lay in the path of progress, the central problem was the removal of these forces, and it absorbed all their energies. The movement was ready to fight the past, but not yet ready to fight for the future.

The situation was much more complex than it seemed. The cause of liberty had not yet triumphed, although the articles published in *Irodalmi Ujsag* sometimes created that impression. The summer and the autumn passed in the shadow of a great variety of contradictions.

On the surface, everything seemed quite calm. Despite the numerous problems still remaining to be settled, it seemed as though the greatest obstacles had already been removed. An atmosphere of terror was replaced by a sense of freedom and of happiness and of the excitement of *action*. Peter Erdos, who had been arrested on the eve of the Twentieth Party Congress, was released from prison; Mihaly Farkas, Vladimir Farkas, and a number of high-ranking AVO officers were arrested in his place. No longer did one have to tremble at a chance meeting with Sandor Haraszti* in the street or on a streetcar or bus, and the

---

* Haraszti, Geza Losonczy's father-in-law, spent four years in jail in connection with the Rajk affair. Two of these years were spent in the condemned cell, in the shadow of death. After his release from prison— he was then almost sixty—he made no attempt to suppress his hatred and contempt, and asked everyone he met to spit in Rakosi's face for him, should he ever come across him. He was an old Communist and knew more about the villainies Rakosi had committed during the Horthy era than did anyone else. He had an inexhaustible fund of stories and anecdotes aimed at a single target: the "shaggy one." He did not mind the fact that everything he said went back to Rakosi; on the contrary, this knowledge inspired him. When he was summoned to Party headquarters and politely asked to express his opinions less loudly and less publicly (if he could not keep them to himself), he shrugged his shoulders and an-

old journalist began to shout gaily to his friends and acquaintances, "How is your 'friend'—that bald old murderer? Hasn't he been hanged yet?" At that time, it did not seem improbable that Rakosi would also have to face trial.

Thus, superficially, things progressed smoothly. But those who were in a position to penetrate beneath the surface and to judge the situation by something more than these conspicuous and highly interesting phenomena knew that things were not quite so promising as they seemed. The fact was that the reactionaries, who had to clench their teeth and cede to the pressure from below, continued to be active in the background. Compelled to retreat before the continuous attacks of the writers and the increasingly firmly expressed will of the people, the Party—including its highest organ, the Political Committee—took every opportunity to hinder or at least to slow down developments.

The writers now worked in a relatively free atmosphere, but they continually ran up against this sabotage in the political field —such tactics as the refusal to settle Imre Nagy's case† and the months-long delay in the rehabilitation of Tibor Dery, Tibor Tardos, and the Petofi Circle.‡ The Party was unrelentingly and desperately defending its positions.

The conference held at Party headquarters in August was characteristic of the attitude of Party officials. The conference was called by Janos Kadar, who had been elected to the Political Committee. It was attended by editors, chief editors, and staff writers of the large newspapers and periodicals. Kadar launched a sharp attack on the "anti-Party" views voiced in the press and added: "The writers believe that they were responsible for the changes which took place in July [Rakosi's dismissal]. Let them

---

swered that, if they didn't like it, they should dismiss Rakosi, because every word he said was true. He was expelled from the Party, but that did not keep him quiet. The summer of 1956 fulfilled his desires. Apart from this *idée fixe* about Rakosi, he was a good and clever tactician, and a close friend and adviser of Imre Nagy.

† Nagy was taken back into the Party on October 13, 1956, ten days before the outbreak of the Revolution.

‡ In fact, Dery's and Tardos' rehabilitation never came about.

finally understand that this change was initiated by the Central Committee of the Party, by the ordinary members, the workers and peasants. The writers remind me of the fly that settles on the shaft bar and believes that he pulls the cart." This sarcastic remark characterized the Party's fear of anything not accomplished by itself and of anything the writers might do. To Kadar and his kind, the change was not important in itself. What really mattered was that the prestige should not go to anyone except themselves.*

The writers were deeply irritated by the deliberate procrastination in the political life of the country. When writers had to be condemned, when Imre Nagy was excommunicated, when the task was to crush "rightist deviationism"—at such times, the machinery worked quickly, smoothly, cheerfully. But now, when the time had come to call to account those who had ruined the country, it turned out that "it was difficult to draw the line" between the good and bad officials, that the writers were demanding a "public witch-hunt," that they wanted to persecute the entire guard of Party officials. Those who had not feared for the "unity of the Party" when they expelled Imre Nagy now used this slogan to protect the men chiefly responsible for all the crimes committed. Nothing can throw a more glaring light on the hypocrisy and actual falseness of the workings of the Party than the fact that one day the Party officials humiliated themselves by asking pardon of the slandered writers, while the next day they published an article in *Szabad Nep* saying that the Party punishments had been lifted because the writers had exercised self-

---

* This was particularly characteristic of Kadar. After his release from jail, he behaved as if he sympathized and fully agreed with the movement of the writers; he encouraged them by secret signals and messages. But as soon as the movement was in trouble—at the time of the Memorandum—he incited Bela Biszku to attack the writers at the "lynch meeting." And, as soon as he was within the battlements of power and had become a secretary of the Party, he began to abuse those to whom, in the last analysis, he owed his advancement. He always retreated behind the slogan of "the Party first." But in practice, the Party meant to him his own position!

criticism. The writers had no fear for their prestige (for, it stood high in these days), and, at any rate, no one believed a word of what was printed in *Szabad Nep*. What they and everybody else minded was the fact that leadership was still in the hands of the basest villains, and there was absolutely no guarantee that the mistakes and crimes of the past would not be repeated again.

This was what worried the writers and every honest man in the country when the stage was set for the most tragic and anomalous act of the regime—the second burial of Laszlo Rajk and of his three executed companions.

The idea for the funeral was conceived during the summer, but neither Gero nor the current Prime Minister, Andras Hegedus, would hear of it. Rajk's widow, however, did not give up. She wanted her innocent, murdered husband to receive his due: official rehabilitation and an official funeral. She wanted the body of her husband, which had been drenched in lime, dug up from the hole into which it had been thrown. She wanted him to lie in state in the Parliament Building and to be then buried with fitting ceremony in the Pantheon of Great Hungarians in the cemetery of Kerepes.

Gero and his followers protested. Finally, after months of negotiations, they came to terms: Laszlo Rajk and his companions would be buried by the Government in the cemetery of Kerepes.

October 6, the anniversary of the execution of thirteen generals of the 1848-1849 War of Independence, is an official day of mourning in Hungary. The Rajk funeral was held on October 6, 1956, as if to symbolize the national martyrdom of the executed innocent men.

It was a cold, windy, rainy autumn day. The flames of the large silver candelabra darted about in a wild *danse macabre*. Mountains of wreaths lay at the foot of the biers.

From early in the morning, Julia Rajk and her little son, Laszlo, stood in deep black by Rajk's bier.

The guard of honor was changed every five minutes.

Old friends, released fellow prisoners, former collaborators, writers, and artists stood guard, wearing ribbons of the national colors on their sleeves.

There was silence—a cold, hard, threatening silence.

The people of Budapest came in quiet, orderly, endless columns: workers from the factories, workers from the offices, students, a few peasants, the tormented, the offended, the long-suffering.

There, with a black ribbon on his sleeve, stood Imre Nagy.

But—and this was the most revolting part of the tragicomedy —there, too, were the henchmen burying and paying official tribute to the very men they had murdered.

Rain poured down in torrents.

And then a bald, old, bespectacled man mounted the platform set up for the funeral orators. He was Ferenc Munnich, a veteran Communist who had been by-passed for years by the Rakosi clique.

"He was not allowed to die a great death, a death worthy of heroes," Munnich said of Rajk. "He was killed by sadistic criminals who had crawled into the sun from the stinking swamp of a 'cult of personality.' This swamp was a breeding ground for the falsification of history, for careerism, for contempt for tradition and law. . . . Those in whose name I now say farewell to Laszlo Rajk will fight for a strong and inviolable socialist democracy in our country, for socialist humanism and legality. . . . There shall never again be Rajk trials in Hungary."

The masses remained silent. Behind the Kossuth Mausoleum, the AVO stood alert for action.

After Munnich, a short, dark man mounted the platform: Antal Apro, one of Rakosi's loyal men and a "permanent" member of the Political Committee who had voted for Rajk's execution and had later sworn allegiance to Imre Nagy and then betrayed him.

"The Party and the Government," he said, "condemn these occurrences. At the grave of our comrades, we pledge, in the name of all Hungarian Communists, that—learning from the mistakes of the past—we shall do our utmost to prevent such acts of terror as those which caused the death of our dear comrades from ever occurring again. . . . Many will ask, 'What is the guarantee that similar infringements of the law will not be repeated?' The question is justified. . . . The guarantee is the Party. We are the guarantee, because we are determined and we can learn from the mistakes of the past."

Nobody believed him. Nobody believed either of them—neither their pledges nor their guarantees. This complete lack of confidence was thrown in their faces by the writer Bela Szasz, who took leave of Laszlo Rajk in the name of his fellow prisoners and friends:

"When hundreds of thousands march past the coffins," Szasz said, "they are not only paying the last honors to the victims, but it is their passionate desire, their unshakable determination to bury a *whole era*."

It was indeed the funeral of an era. It was a Shakespearean drama comparable to *Richard III*.

Late in the afternoon, there were minor demonstrations in town. The police intervened, and the demonstrators dispersed.

But the flame would not be quenched. The solemn formalities of the funeral had reminded the people, instead of making them forget, that, *fundamentally*, nothing had changed and nothing would ever change until the troubles were uprooted—until the contradictions of the whole structure were resolved.

Everyone knew, however, that the roots lay not in the Hungarian soil but in the Soviet swamp, and that the contradictions could never be resolved as long as there was Soviet occupation— as long as Hungary was only a *colony*, a politically and militarily controlled colony of a great imperialist power, the Soviet Union. Everybody knew it, yet this was the very thing that could not be brought into the open, despite the growing atmosphere of freedom.

And this was the very thing the Hungarian people wanted to express, so that acts of terror like the Rajk trial should never again occur, so that the country might be rid of its spineless

Come, Liberty!

On the morning of October 23, university students stuck posters on the walls of houses and on trees along the boulevards in Budapest, proclaiming their demands. Among their fourteen points, the most important were: The establishment of a new Government headed by Imre Nagy; the withdrawal from Hungary of all Soviet troops; the bringing to trail of Matyas Rakosi and Mihaly Farkas; the reorganization of Hungarian economic life and the revision of Hungarian-Soviet economic contracts; absolute freedom of opinion, of speech, and of the press; the revival of the old Hungarian Kossuth emblem in place of the Soviet imitation now in use.

At 3 p.m., the young people marched to the Petofi statue on the bank of the Danube. Here, Imre Sinkovics, a young actor of the National Theater, recited the national anthem—the poem that had been read from the steps of the National Museum in Budapest at the outbreak of the Revolution of 1848. In the name of the Writers' Association, Tibor Dery addressed the people.

Then the demonstrating crowd marched to the statue of General Bem (a Polish general in the 1848-1849 Hungarian War of Independence), where they expressed solidarity with the uprising of the students and workers in Poland, who were bringing

Gomulka back to power. Peter Veres addressed the people in the name of the Writers' Association.

Neither Dery's nor Peter Veres' speech affected the rebellious masses. They had no microphone, and it was difficult to hear their words, and—even more important—leadership had slipped from the hands of the writers and had been taken over by students, workers, and soldiers.

A little after 8 p.m., hundreds of thousands crowded the square in front of Parliament to listen to Imre Nagy's speech.

At approximately the same time, at the Radio Building, the first shots were fired at the demonstrating masses.

The crowd took the first victim to the *Szabad Nep* building and besieged the editorial offices of the Party paper. Jozsef Revai was in the building. Beside himself with rage, Revai screamed, "Shoot . . . shoot . . ."

Two young journalists, Miklos Gimes and Pal Locsei, saved Revai from the ire of the incensed people by smuggling him out by the back door.

Long before midnight, several thousands of demonstrators marched to the Stalin statue in the City Park. They threw a wire rope around the metal giant's neck and, when they found they could not overturn it by hand, severed the statue at the knee with welding torches. Two giant bronze boots remained on the red marble pedestal.

DRAMATIS PERSONAE

The Hungarian Revolution lasted from October 23, 1956 to November 4, 1956. On November 4, Soviet military intervention crushed the Hungarian people's fight for liberty. Since then, a counter-revolutionary clique, supported by Russian tanks, has been in power in Hungary.

The authors of this book consider it their duty to inform the reader of the fate of the most important personalities in this book:

ERZSEBET ANDICS and her husband, ANDOR BEREI, declared themselves Soviet citizens during the Revolution. They returned from the Soviet Union in 1958 and now have union Party jobs in Budapest.

ANTAL APRO is now Minister of State.

ISTVAN BATA became Minister of Defense in the Nagy Government during the Revolution, then fled to the Soviet Union. He returned to Hungary in 1958.

LASZLO BENJAMIN still lives in Hungary.

BELA BISZKU is now Minister of the Interior.

JOZSEF DARVAS is now Director of the Hungarian Film Studios, Chairman of the National Peace Council, Chairman of the recently reorganized Hungarian Writers' Association, and one of the exponents of the Party press.

TIBOR DERY remained in Hungary after the Revolution was crushed. He was arrested in April, 1957, and, in November, 1957, was condemned to nine years in prison.

GABOR DEVECSERI still lives in Hungary.

ENDRE ENCZI lives in London, where he is on the staff of
Irodalmi Ujsag, now published in exile.

ISTVAN EORSI was arrested after the Revolution and sentenced
to eight years in prison.

SANDOR ERDEI still lives in Hungary.

PETER ERDOS was arrested in 1957. He was released in July,
1958.

GYORGY FALUDY has lived in London since the Revolution and
is now literary editor of *Irodalmi Ujsag.*

MIHALY FARKAS was sentenced to sixteen years in jail after
the Revolution. He is said to be in the Soviet Union.

VLADIMIR FARKAS, son of AVO Colonel Mihaly Farkas, was
sentenced to sixteen years in jail. According to rumor, he is now
in the Soviet Union.

LAJOS FEHER supported the Nagy Government. He is now a
member of the Political Committee of the Communist Party.

JOZSEF GALI worked as a journalist during the Revolution. He
was arrested and condemned to death, together with journalist
Gyula Obershovszky, but his sentence was commuted to fifteen
years, while Obershovszky's sentence was commuted to life imprisonment.

ERNO GERO fled to the Soviet Union during the Revolution.
His fate is unknown.

MIKLOS GIMES became one of the editors of the underground
publication *October 23* during the Revolution. He was arrested
on December 5, 1956, and executed with Imre Nagy.

SANDOR HARASZTI was kidnapped after the Revolution from
the Yugoslav Embassy, together with Imre Nagy. He was later
sentenced to eight years' imprisonment.

GYULA HAY remained in Hungary after the Revolution. He
was arrested in February, 1957, and was condemned to six years
in prison at the same trial as was Dery.

ANDRAS HEGEDUS fled to the Soviet Union during the Revolution. He returned to Hungary in 1958.

MARTON HORVATH is now Director of the Budapest Petofi
Museum.

BELA ILLES is a permanent contributor to the Party press. According to unconfirmed rumors, he behaved with honesty at Dery's trial, where he was a witness. He supports the present regime wholeheartedly.

GYULA ILLYES still lives in Hungary.

JANOS KADAR, Minister of State in the Nagy Government during the Revolution deserted to the Russians on the night of November 1. The Soviet Army, crushing the Hungarian Revolution, made him Prime Minister. At present, he is First Secretary of the Communist Party.

BELA KELEN is now Party Secretary of Budapest.

LAJOS KONYA still lives in Hungary, but was forced to resign his seat in Parliament.

ISTVAN KOVACS fled to the Soviet Union during the Revolution. His fate is unknown.

PETER KUCZKA still lives in Hungary.

PAL LOCSEI worked as a journalist during the Revolution. He was arrested and condemned to eight years in prison.

GEZA LOSONCZY, Minister of State in the Nagy Government during the Revolution, was kidnapped along with Nagy when they left the Yugoslav Embassy. According to the official communiqué announcing Imre Nagy's execution, Losonczy died of an illness in prison. The place, time, circumstances, and cause of his death are unknown.

GYORGY LUKACS, Minister of Culture in the Nagy Government during the Revolution, asked for political asylum at the Yugoslav Embassy, but left the Embassy two days before Imre Nagy was kidnapped. He was deported for six months to an unknown destination and returned to Hungary in the spring of 1957. He is now retired, but he is still under constant attack in the Hungarian, the Soviet, and the other People's Democracy's presses.

TAMAS MAJOR is a member of the present Central Committee.

GYORGY MAROSAN is now Minister of State.

MIKLOS MOLNAR has lived in Switzerland since the Revolution.

ZOLTAN MOLNAR was arrested early in 1957 and sentenced to two years in prison.

FERENC MUNNICH, Minister of the Interior in the Nagy Government, deserted to the Russians, together with Kadar. He is now Prime Minister of the Hungarian People's Democracy.

IMRE NAGY went to the Yugoslav Embassy in Budapest on November 4 for political asylum. On November 22, having been granted a *salvus conductus,* he was enticed to leave the Yugoslav Embassy and was then kidnapped by armed Soviet forces. On June 16, 1958, at 12:20 a.m., Radio Moscow announced that Imre Nagy and three other Hungarian patriots had been executed. The place, time, and method of execution are still unknown.

LASZLO NEMETH still lives in Hungary.

SANDOR NOGRADI is now Hungarian Minister to Peking.

GYORGY NON was dismissed from his post as Public Prosecutor during the Revolution. He still lives in Hungary.

GYORGY PALOCZY-HORVATH has lived in London since the Revolution.

GABOR PETER was released from prison in 1959. According to rumors from Hungary, he has returned to his original trade—that of a tailor.

KALMAN PONGRACZ is a member of the present Central Committee.

JULIA RAJK, widow of Laszlo Rajk, took refuge with her little son at the Yugoslav Embassy. She was kidnapped along with Imre Nagy, but was released at the end of 1958.

MATYAS RAKOSI went to the Soviet Union after his dismissal. According to unconfirmed reports, he is now managing director of a paper factory in Outer Mongolia.

JOZSEF REVAI remained in Budapest after the Revolution. Though ill, he continued to represent the Stalinist line whenever he was able to work. He died in July, 1959.

IMRE SARKADI still lives in Hungary.

PAL SZABO still lives in Hungary. He is a member of Parliament and Vice-Chairman of the Patriotic Popular Front.

BELA SZASZ has lived in London since the Revolution.

JOZSEF SZIGETI, a former Lukacs student who exercised self-criticism in the Petofi Circle for having abandoned his master, has now exercised self-criticism for this previous self-criticism and is again first voice in the chorus attacking Lukacs. He is Deputy Minister of Culture.

JOZSEF SZILAGYI, head of Imre Nagy's Secretariat during the Revolution, was executed with Nagy.

ARON TAMASI still lives in Hungary.

LAJOS TAMASI still lives in Hungary.

TIBOR TARDOS remained in Hungary after the Revolution. He was arrested in 1957 and condemned to eighteen months in prison, but was released after fourteen months.

ERNO URBAN is a member of Parliament and a contributor to the official Party press.

DOMOKOS VARGA was arrested in February, 1957, and sentenced to three years in prison. He was released in 1958.

ZOLTAN VAS, Minister of Supply in the Nagy Government during the Revolution, took refuge at the Yugoslav Embassy and was kidnapped along with Nagy. He is living as a pensioner in Budapest.

MIKLOS VASARHELYI, head of Imre Nagy's Office of Information during the Revolution, was condemned to five years in prison.

PETER VERES is a member of the present Parliament.

ZOLTAN ZELK remained in Hungary after the Revolution. He was arrested in February, 1957, and was condemned to three years in prison. He was released in September, 1958.

THE AUTHORS fled Hungary via Yugoslavia at the end of November, 1956, after Nagy's kidnapping. They left because they were certain of being arrested, and, even had they not been arrested, they could not have lived and written in Hungary any longer. They left—last but not least—in order to tell the story of the events in this book.